lonely planet

Discover
Great Britain

Contents

Throughout this book, we use these icons to highlight special recommendations:

The Best...
Lists for everything from bars to wildlife – to make sure you don't miss out

Don't Miss
A must-see – don't go home until you've been there

Local Knowledge Local experts reveal their top picks and secret highlights

Detour
Special places a little off the beaten track

If you like...
Lesser-known alternatives to world-famous attractions

These icons help you quickly identify reviews in the text and on the map:

Sights

Eating

Drinking

Sleeping

Information

This edition written and researched by

Oliver Berry,
Fionn Davenport, Marc Di Duca, Belinda Dixon,
Peter Dragicevich, David Else, Damian Harper,
Anna Kaminski, Catherine Le Nevez, Fran Parnell,
Andy Symington, Neil Wilson

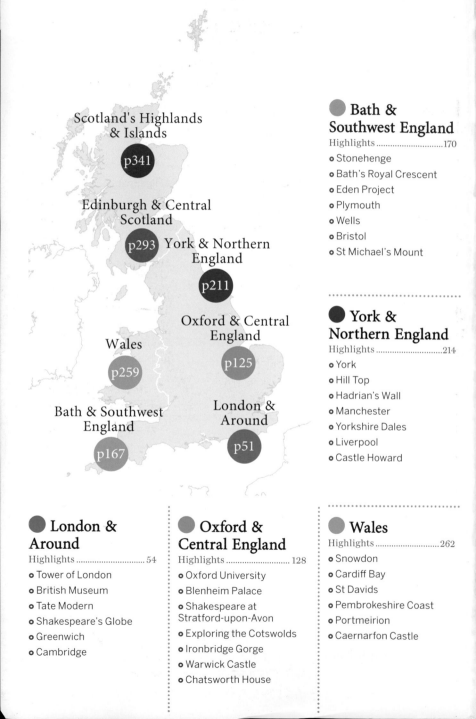

Contents

Contents

On the Road

This Is Great Britain

Few places pack so much into such a tiny space as Britain. It's barely 600 miles from England's south coast to Scotland's northern tip so you can cross the island in a day, but you could spend a lifetime exploring and only scratch the surface. This proportionally challenged island manages to cram more sights into each square mile than a country 10 times its size.

History is undoubtedly one of the major highlights of a visit here. From clifftop castles and medieval cathedrals to stone circles and Roman ruins, the British landscape recounts a story that stretches back 5000 years. On your journey, you'll encounter a collection of kings and courtiers, heroes and villains, engineers and inventors, not to mention a host of writers, poets, painters, architects and artistic visionaries.

The landscape is another jewel in the nation's crown. Encompassing everything from green fields to isolated islands, rolling plains to wild hills, and sandy beaches to snowcapped mountains, the British landscape is astonishingly varied. Iconic cities such as London, Manchester, York, Bath and Edinburgh are stuffed with amazing architecture, captivating culture and hundreds of historic sights. And beyond the metropolises are 15 stunning national parks which now cover over 10% of the landscape, as well as countless quaint villages, hamlets and market towns – all of which make exploring this green and pleasant land an unbridled pleasure.

Of course, Britain isn't actually one country at all – it's three rolled into one. Some of the differences between the nations of England, Wales and Scotland are obvious (particularly the accents of the people), but others are more subtle, and getting to grips with their individual quirks is a fundamental part of what makes travel here so fascinating. It's called Great Britain for a reason, you know – and you're about to find out why.

> " *Few places pack so much into such a tiny space as Britain* "

St Paul's Cathedral (p69), London
CHRIS HEPBURN/GETTY IMAGES ©

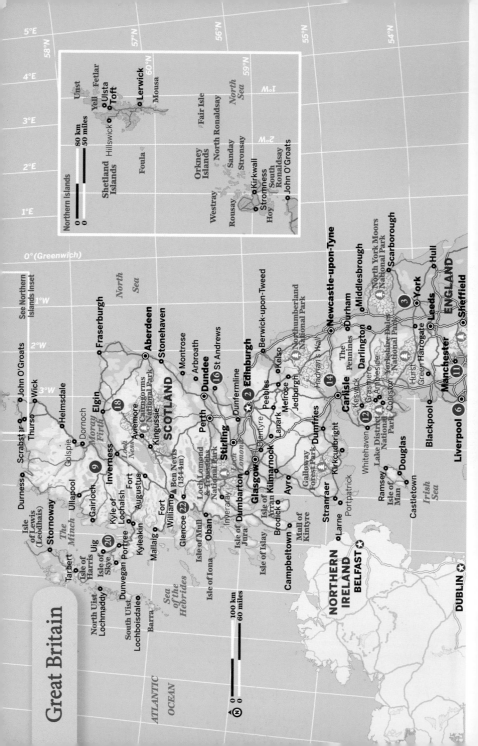

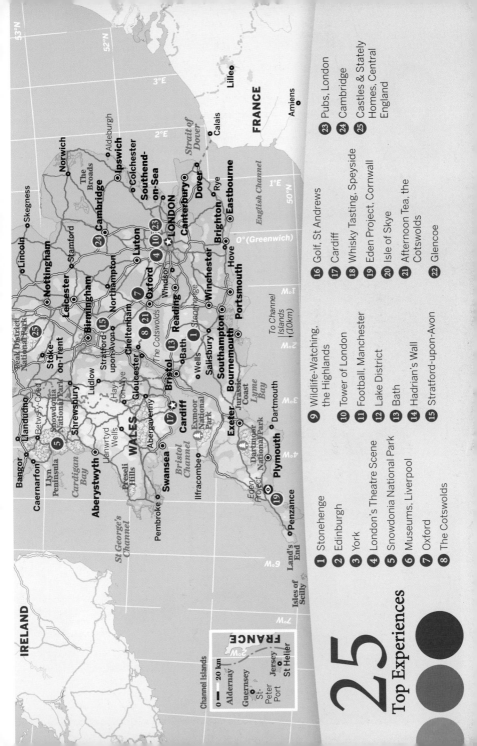

25 Great Britain's Top Experiences

Stonehenge

Mysterious and compelling, Stonehenge (p184) is Britain's most iconic ancient site. People have been drawn to this myth-rich ring of bluestones for the last 5000 years, and we're still not sure why it was built. Most visitors get to gaze at the 50-ton megaliths from behind the perimeter fence, but with enough planning you can book an early-morning or evening tour and walk around the inner ring. In the slanting sunlight, away from the crowds, it's an ethereal place – an experience that certainly stays with you.

1

PETER ADAMS/GETTY IMAGES ©

M. TURNER PHOTOGRAPHY/GETTY IMAGES ©

2

Edinburgh

Scotland's capital city is famous for its summer festivals, but even outside festival time, this is a fascinating city to explore – full of winding lanes, hidden courtyards and architectural sights. The top draws are the city's clifftop castle and the palace of Holyroodhouse, but Edinburgh (p306) is a city of subtle pleasures, whether that means a picnic in the grounds of Holyrood Palace, a pint in an Old Town pub or a stroll along the Royal Mile. Edinburgh Castle

GREAT BRITAIN'S TOP 25 EXPERIENCES

York

With its Viking heritage and maze of medieval streets, York (p224) is a showcase for English history. For a great introduction, join one of the city's many walking tours through the snickelways (narrow alleys), then admire the intricacies of York Minster, the biggest medieval cathedral in northern Europe, or explore the history of another age at the National Railway Museum. York Minster

The Best...
Historic Towns

CHESTER
Walk round Chester's medieval walls, the finest in England. (p241)

CANTERBURY
Stately town with an even statelier cathedral. (p105)

WINDSOR & ETON
Home to the Queen's second home and England's poshest public school. (p114)

BUXTON
Spa-town splendour in the middle of the Peak District. (p161)

BRISTOL
This southwest harbour city has a salty sea-faring past. (p185)

The Best...
Landmark
Buildings

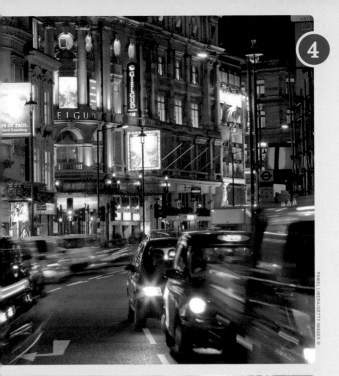

London's Theatre Scene

4

London has been famous for its shows ever since the days of William Shakespeare, and nothing much has changed. Theatre (p97) is still a major part of the capital's cultural life, and you should definitely find time to catch a show while you're in town – whether it's a musical in the West End, a bit of Shakespeare at the restored Globe Theatre, or a cutting-edge play at the National Theatre or Royal Court. Shaftesbury Ave, West End

Snowdonia National Park

5

Wales' best-known national park (p281) has the most breathtaking scenery this side of the Scottish Highlands. The busiest part is around Snowdon itself, Wales' highest mountain, where hardy visitors hike to the summit, and everyone else lets the train take the strain by climbing aboard the historic Victorian railway. On a clear day, you can see clear to the Irish Sea.

Liverpool's Museums

Liverpool (p242) will forever be associated with The Beatles, but this city now has even more to offer. After a redevelopment, the old Albert Dock has become a World Heritage Site, and has museums exploring the city's maritime past and murky slave-trading history. And fans of the Fab Four will find places to indulge, from the Cavern Club to the Beatles Story. Museum of Liverpool

MARK AVELLINO/GETTY IMAGES ©

THEBIGGLES/GETTY IMAGES ©

Oxford

For centuries the brilliant minds and august institutions of Oxford University (p138) have made this city famous across the globe. You'll get a glimpse of this revered world as you stroll hushed college quads and cobbled lanes roamed by cycling students and dusty academics. The beautiful buildings and archaic traditions have changed little over the years, leaving Oxford much as alumni such as Einstein or Tolkien would have found it. Christ Church College

The Cotswolds

The most wonderful thing about the Cotswolds (p144) is that no matter how lost you get, you'll still end up in an impossibly picturesque village complete with rose-clad cottages, a honey-coloured stone church and a cosy local pub serving a choice of real ales. It's easy to leave the crowds behind and find your very own slice of medieval England – and some of the best boutique hotels in the country.

ADAM BURTON/GETTY IMAGES ©

8

The Best...
Viewpoints

WHITE CLIFFS OF DOVER
Stroll along these celebrated chalk cliffs on England's south coast. (p109)

LAND'S END
The very end of Cornwall – and Britain. (p208)

SNOWDON
Stand on the roof of Wales. (p281)

BEN NEVIS
Enjoy glorious views over the Highland glens. (p356)

GLASTONBURY TOR
Enjoy 360-degree views over Somerset from this mythical hill. (p196)

Wildlife-Watching in the Highlands

It might not be an untouched wilderness, but Britain still has a wealth of wildlife. From spotting red deer on Exmoor to spying ospreys in the Lake District, there are numerous opportunities to get acquainted with the island's animal inhabitants. The best place to discover this wild side is in the Highlands (p352), where you can take a boat trip in search of dolphins and whales, or spy eagles above snowy peaks.

The Best...
Castles

WINDSOR CASTLE
The largest and oldest occupied fortress in the world, and the Queen's country retreat. (p114)

WARWICK CASTLE
Perhaps the classic British castle, and still impressively intact. (p151)

CAERNARFON CASTLE
Moody castle and military stronghold on the Welsh coast. (p286)

EDINBURGH CASTLE
Edinburgh's fortress has enough to fill several visits. (p306)

STIRLING CASTLE
Perched on a volcanic crag, and quieter than Edinburgh. (p328)

MARK HAMBLIN/GETTY IMAGES ©

10 Tower of London

With its battlements and turrets overlooking the Thames, the Tower of London (p68) is an icon of the capital. The walls are nearly 1000 years old, established by William the Conqueror in the 1070s. Since then, the Tower has been a fortress, royal residence, treasury, mint, arsenal and prison. Today it's home to the Crown Jewels, the famous red-coated Yeoman Warders (known as Beefeaters) and a flock of ravens which – legend says – must never leave. White Tower

Football

In some parts of the world it's called soccer, but here it's definitely football (p391). The English Premier League has some of the world's finest teams, including Arsenal, Liverpool and Chelsea, plus *the* most famous club on the planet: Manchester United. North of the border, Scotland's best-known teams are Glasgow Rangers and Glasgow Celtic, and their rivalry is legend. In Wales the national sport is most definitely rugby. Football at Old Trafford, Manchester

12

Lake District

William Wordsworth and his Romantic chums were the first to champion the charms of the Lake District (p250), and it's not hard to see what stirred them. With soaring mountains, whaleback fells, razor-edge valleys and – of course – glistening lakes (as well as England's highest hill), this craggy corner of northwest England has some of the country's finest vistas. Come for the comfortable lakeside hotels, or come for hardy hiking – whatever you choose, inspiration is sure to follow.

13 ## Bath

Britain boasts many great cities, but Bath (p188) is the belle of the ball. The Romans founded a huge bathhouse here to take advantage of the area's natural hot springs, which you can still visit to this day; but it's Bath's stunning Georgian architecture that really makes a visit here special. The city was redeveloped on a grand scale during the 18th century and its streets are lined with fabulous buildings. Georgian terraces

Hadrian's Wall

Hadrian's Wall (p255) is Britain's most dramatic Roman ruin. Built almost 2000 years ago, this great barrier marked the division between the civilised lands of Roman Britain and the unruly territory of the Celts and Picts to the north. Though much has disappeared, you can still see many surviving sections of wall and several original forts.

ALAN CRAWFORD/GETTY IMAGES ©

14

The Best...
Wild Spots

YORKSHIRE DALES
Green and grand, made famous by James Herriot's novels. (p233)

GOWER PENINSULA
Beautiful coastal scenery within easy reach of Cardiff. (p275)

DARTMOOR NATIONAL PARK
These wild southwest moors stir the imagination. (p199)

ISLE OF MULL
Whale-watching trips run from this craggy Scottish island. (p358)

EXMOOR
Spot deer on a wildlife safari. (p197)

The Best...
Nightlife

LONDON
With its many clubs, pubs and theatres, you'll never be bored in the capital. (p97)

BRIGHTON
South-coast town with lively nightlife and the biggest gay scene outside London. (p113)

MANCHESTER
Catch a band in music-mad Manchester. (p241)

GLASGOW
Pubs and bars aplenty ensure Scotland's second city never sleeps. (p327)

15

Stratford-upon-Avon

The pretty town of Stratford-upon-Avon (p152) is famed around the world as the birthplace of the nation's best-known dramatist, William Shakespeare. Today the town's tight knot of Tudor streets forms a map of Shakespeare's life and times, while crowds of fans enjoy a play at the theatre or visit the five historic houses owned by Shakespeare and his relatives, with a respectful detour to the old stone church where the Bard was laid to rest.

Left: Shakespeare's Birthplace;
Above: Prince Hal statue

Golf at St Andrews

It may be a 'good walk spoilt' but golf is one of the most popular sports in Britain, both with participants of all levels and thousands of spectators too (especially during major tournaments). With courses across the country, visitors to Britain with a penchant for the little white ball will surely want to try their skill. A highlight for aficionados is a round on the Old Course at St Andrews (p334), the venerable home of golf.

16

ANDREA PISTOLESI/GETTY IMAGES ©

CHRIS HEPBURN/GETTY IMAGES ©

Cardiff

17

The exuberant capital of Wales, Cardiff (p270) has recently emerged as one of Britain's leading urban centres. After a mid-20th-century decline, the city has entered the new millennium with vigour and confidence, flexing architectural muscles and revelling in a sense of style. From the historic castle to the ultramodern waterfront, lively street cafes to infectious nightlife, and Victorian shopping arcades to the gigantic rugby stadium, Cardiff is definitely cool.
Cardiff Bay

Whisky Tasting in Speyside

If you fancy trying a wee dram or two, then Speyside (p339) in Scotland is the place to head. Some of the country's most prestigious whisky distilleries are dotted around this remote valley, many of which offer guided tours and tasting sessions. Before enjoying your tipple, remember a couple of tips: in Scotland, whisky is never spelled with an 'e' (that's the Irish variety); and when ordering at the bar, asking for 'Scotch' is something of a faux pas (ask for whisky). Whisky distillery, Speyside

The Best...
Museums

BRITISH MUSEUM
Delve into the vast collections at the nation's foremost museum. (p82)

NATURAL HISTORY MUSEUM
Giant dinosaurs and geological treasures in a Victorian landmark. (p79)

IMPERIAL WAR MUSEUM NORTH
The Manchester outpost of London's moving war museum. (p237)

NATIONAL MUSEUM OF SCOTLAND
Scottish treasures by the sporran-load. (p310)

KELVINGROVE ART GALLERY & MUSEUM
Quirky Glasgow museum full of Victorian curiosities. (p326)

ANDY STOTHERT/GETTY IMAGES ©

Eden Project

Cornwall's coastline is well worthy of a trip in its own right, but the county's top attractions are the three space-age biomes of the Eden Project (p206), which re-create diverse habitats from around the world such as the humid Mediterranean and the tropical rainforest, and shed light on some of the environmental challenges facing the world in the 21st century. It's educational and inspirational, and is definitely one of the southwest's must-sees.

IMAGES ETC LTD/GETTY IMAGES ©

The Best...
Stately Homes

CASTLE HOWARD
Baroque masterpiece that featured in *Brideshead Revisited*. (p231)

CHATSWORTH HOUSE
Known as the Palace of the Peaks, and stuffed with priceless treasures. (p164)

BLENHEIM PALACE
Winston Churchill's birthplace and the seat of the dukes of Marlborough. (p142)

STOURHEAD
Glorious southwest mansion, best known for its landscaped parkland. (p181)

CULZEAN CASTLE
The most impressive Scottish stately home, with antiques and artworks galore. (p328)

20 Isle of Skye

Of all Scotland's islands, Skye (p361) is the best loved. Ringed by cliffs and beaches, cloaked with fields and moors, and framed by the rugged Cuillin Hills, Skye is a paradise for lovers of the Scottish landscape, and a popular getaway for thousands of people every year. The island is easily reached from the mainland by boat or bridge, which makes it a great add-on to any Scottish road trip. Make sure you pack the camera.

Afternoon Tea

No one does tea quite like the British – it's not just a tradition here, it's a religion. To appreciate it at its best, head to a cafe, such as Huffkins (p146), or a country hotel that serves proper afternoon tea – a gourmet spread that includes cakes, sandwiches and a pot of loose-leaf tea, sipped (of course) from china tea cups. Even better, every region serves its own slightly different version. Traditional Devonshire tea

KARL BLACKWELL/GETTY IMAGES ©

21

22

KATHY COLLINS/GETTY IMAGES ©

Glencoe

In the Highlands of Scotland you're never far from a knock-out view, but the area around Glencoe (p354) still raises a gasp. This wild valley has perhaps the most iconic view of any Scottish glen, hemmed in by mountains, which tower above the snaking road. In summer it looks beautiful and benign, but in the depths of winter it's another story. Nearby lurks Ben Nevis, Britain's loftiest mountain, and the lively town of Fort William, dubbed the 'Outdoors Capital of the UK'.

● ● ● **GREAT BRITAIN'S TOP 25 EXPERIENCES**

Britain's Pubs

It's no secret that the Brits like a good drink, and the pub's still the place where most people do it. The classic pub has been the centre of British social life for centuries, and wherever you travel there'll be a local to discover: from ornate Victorian boozers in London (p95) to country pubs, hunkering under timber beams and warmed by a crackling hearth. The traditional drink is a pint of real ale – served warm and flat, and an acquired taste.

23

The Best...
Ruins

FOUNTAINS ABBEY
The remains of Britain's greatest abbey, torn down during Henry VIII's Dissolution of the Monasteries. (p232)

HOUSESTEADS
Wander among the ruins of this evocative fort on Hadrian's Wall. (p255)

TINTAGEL CASTLE
Dramatic clifftop ruins on the Cornish coast, with legendary connections to King Arthur. (p195)

GLASTONBURY ABBEY
Another mighty medieval abbey reduced to rubble. (p197)

Cambridge

Abounding with exquisite architecture and steeped in tradition, Cambridge (p117) is a university town extraordinaire. The tightly packed core of ancient colleges, the picturesque riverside 'Backs' (college gardens) and the surrounding green meadows give Cambridge a more tranquil appeal than its historic rival Oxford. Highlights include the intricate vaulting of King's College Chapel, and no visit is complete without an attempt to steer a punt (flat-bottomed boat) along the river and under the quirky Mathematical Bridge. Bridge of Sighs

The Best...
Cathedrals

ST PAUL'S CATHEDRAL
London's most beautiful cathedral, and Christopher Wren's masterwork. (p69)

YORK MINSTER
York's mighty minster is known for its ornate towers and medieval stained glass. (p226)

CANTERBURY CATHEDRAL
The mothership of the Anglican Church has centuries' worth of history. (p105)

SALISBURY CATHEDRAL
Has the tallest spire of any English cathedral, so you'll need a head for heights. (p182)

WINCHESTER CATHEDRAL
Gothic wonder with one of the longest medieval naves in Europe. (p180)

VISITBRITAIN/BRITAIN ON VIEW/GETTY IMAGES ©

JEREMY SAGE/GETTY IMAGES ©

25

Castles & Stately Homes

Britain's turbulent history is nowhere more apparent than in the mighty castles that dot the landscape, from romantic clifftop ruins such as Corfe or sturdy fortresses such as Caernarfon, to formidable Stirling and still-inhabited Windsor. And when the aristocracy no longer needed castles, they built vast mansions known as 'stately homes' at the heart of their country estates – Chatsworth House (p164) and Castle Howard (p231) are among the finest.

Corfe Castle, Dorset

Great Britain's
Top Itineraries

London to Bath
The Bare Essentials

5 DAYS

Five days is barely enough to get started, so we've picked out only the key stops for this whistle-stop itinerary.

LONDON
WINDSOR
BATH
STONEHENGE
English Channel
(La Manche)

❶ London (p62)

London simply has to be the start of any tour of England, but with only two days in the capital you'll need to work fast. On day one tick off **Trafalgar Square** plus **Buckingham Palace** and **Westminster Abbey,** followed by the **Houses of Parliament** and the tower of **Big Ben**. You'll just about have time for an afternoon at the **Tower of London**, and an evening ride on the **London Eye**. On day two, visit **St Paul's Cathedral** in the morning, spend the afternoon at the **British Museum**, and catch an evening show in the **West End** or at **Shakespeare's Globe**.

LONDON ❍ WINDSOR

🚃 **One hour** Direct trains run from London Waterloo to Windsor Riverside; trains from London Paddington require a change at Slough.
🚗 **45 minutes** 25 miles via the M4.

❷ Windsor (p114)

The Queen's country getaway at **Windsor Castle** makes an ideal day trip from London, and is packed with priceless portraits and fascinating architecture.

Tower Bridge (p68), London

WINDSOR ❍ SALISBURY (FOR STONEHENGE)

🚃 **2½ hours** Take the train from Windsor Riverside and change at Clapham Junction
🚗 **90 minutes** Via the M3 and A303

❸ Stonehenge (p184)

Salisbury is ideal for an afternoon excursion to **Stonehenge**, which lies about 10 miles to the north across Salisbury Plain. Back in Salisbury itself, the needlelike spire of **Salisbury Cathedral** is the tallest such tower in England, and affords glorious views across the medieval Cathedral Close and beyond.

SALISBURY ❍ BATH

🚃 **One hour** Frequent trains to Bath Spa train station. 🚗 **One hour** Follow the main road (A36), detouring via Stonehenge.

❹ Bath (p188)

West from Salisbury is the stunning city of **Bath**, a must-see for its incredible Georgian architecture and beautifully preserved **Roman Baths**. If time allows, relax in the naturally hot waters of the futuristic **Thermae Bath Spa**.

5 DAYS

London to Stratford-upon-Avon
English Idylls

This trip through the English countryside features the dreaming spires of Oxford and the quaint villages of the Cotswolds, and finishes in Shakespeare-central, Stratford-upon-Avon.

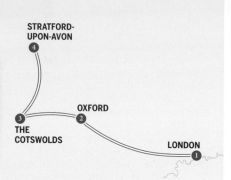

STRATFORD-UPON-AVON ④

OXFORD ②

THE COTSWOLDS ③

LONDON ①

① London (p62)

You could devote your two days in London to its top-ticket sights, or you could delve a little deeper and take in a few of the more out-of-the-way attractions: perhaps a river trip down the Thames to maritime **Greenwich**, a visit to one of London's bustling markets such as the ones on **Camden Lock** or **Portobello Road**, or a scenic stroll through **Hyde Park** or **Hampstead Heath**. On day two focus your time on the capital's countless museums: the art-oriented **Victoria & Albert Museum** and **Tate Britain**, or the scientifically inclined **Science Museum** and **Natural History Museum**.

LONDON ➲ OXFORD

🚃 **One hour** From London's Paddington Station direct to Oxford. 🚗 **90 minutes** (traffic permitting) From central London to Oxford on the M40.

② Oxford (p138)

The city of Oxford is one of England's most famous university towns. Take your pick from the many colleges, but make sure to visit **Christ Church College** and **Magdalen College**. With a bit more time you could also take in a tour of the **Radcliffe Camera** and the **Ashmolean Museum**, and perhaps factor in a visit to the fabulous mansion of **Blenheim Palace**.

OXFORD ➲ THE COTSWOLDS

🚗 **30 minutes** Buses are limited, so you'll need your own wheels to explore. The quickest route from Oxford is the A40, which heads 20 miles west to Burford, one of the gateway villages.

③ The Cotswolds (p144)

With their country pubs and thatched cottages, the villages of the Cotswolds paint an idyllic vision of olde-worlde England. There are many to discover, but **Stow-on-the-Wold** and **Chipping Campden** are particularly photogenic. Many, such as **Broadway** and **Minster Lovell**, date back to the days of the Domesday Book. The surrounding countryside is littered with walks and bike rides, and there are lots of gorgeous boutique hotels and B&Bs to choose from.

THE COTSWOLDS ➲ STRATFORD-UPON-AVON

🚃 **One hour** Buses run regularly from Chipping Campden to Stratford-upon-Avon.
🚗 **30 minutes** From the northern edge of the Cotswolds to Stratford-upon-Avon.

④ Stratford-upon-Avon (p152)

Arguably England's most important literary town, Stratford-upon-Avon is awash with Shakespeare sights, including **Shakespeare's Birthplace**, his wife **Anne Hathaway's Cottage** and his grave at **Holy Trinity Church**. The town gets very busy in summer, so try to visit in spring or autumn to see it at its best. Whatever time of year you come, you'll need to book ahead if you want to catch a play courtesy of the renowned **Royal Shakespeare Company**.

Anne Hathaway's Cottage (p153)
PETER SCHOLEY/GETTY IMAGES ©

10 DAYS

Brighton to St Ives
Go West

A tour along England's scenic southern coastline, veering via the cities of Brighton, Bristol, Bath and Plymouth, before finishing in style on the Cornish seaside.

Cardigan Bay

BRISTOL
③ ④ BATH
Bristol Channel

WINCHESTER
② ①
BRIGHTON

ST IVES
⑥ ⑤
LAND'S END
PLYMOUTH

*English Channel
(La Manche)*

❶ Brighton (p109)

The buzzy seaside town of Brighton is only an hour from London and is known for its nightlife, eccentric shopping and excellent restaurants. One sight you definitely shouldn't miss is the bizarre **Brighton Pavilion**, designed in extravagant Oriental style by Queen Victoria's husband, Prince Albert.

BRIGHTON ➡ WINCHESTER

🚃 **2¼ hours** You'll need to change at Southampton. 🚗 **1¾ hours** Take the A27, then turn onto the M3.

❷ Winchester (p180)

The former capital of England, Winchester has an enticing mix of history and architecture. The town's main landmark is its immense **cathedral**, which looks plain on the outside, but conceals a wonderland of soaring pillars and dazzling stained glass inside.

WINCHESTER ➡ BRISTOL

🚃 **Two hours** Change again at Southampton. 🚗 **1¾ hours** On the A34 and M4.

❸ Bristol (p185)

Once Britain's third-largest harbour, Bristol has reinvented itself as a creative city with a distinctly quirky side. It has some great galleries and museums – make time for the impressive **M-Shed** and the decks of the SS *Great Britain*, one of the greatest steamships of its day. Spend the afternoon exploring the genteel suburb of Clifton and its famous suspension bridge.

BRISTOL ➡ BATH

🚃 **15 minutes** Two or three direct per hour. 🚗 **30 minutes** On the A4.

❹ Bath (p188)

It's a half-hour drive from Bristol to Bath, but for fans of English architecture it's an essential detour. At **No 1 Royal Crescent**, you can step inside one of Bath's finest townhouses, restored using 18th-century techniques and materials. Another famous terrace, the **Circus**, is a short walk away.

BATH ➡ PLYMOUTH

🚃 **2¾ hours** Change at Bristol or Westbury for Plymouth. 🚗 **Three hours** Direct via the M4 and M5, or cross-country via Wells.

❺ Plymouth (p200)

Plymouth has a rich maritime history: the Pilgrim Fathers' *Mayflower* set sail for America from here in 1620, followed 150 years later by Captain Cook. Today the **Mayflower Steps** mark the point of departure. The wild national park of **Dartmoor** is also nearby.

PLYMOUTH ➡ ST IVES

🚃 **2¼ hours** Change at St Erth for the scenic branch line. 🚗 **1¾ hours** Via the A38 and A30.

❻ St Ives (p206)

Seaside St Ives makes a gorgeous base for exploring Cornwall. Galleries abound, including **Tate St Ives** and the **Barbara Hepworth Museum**. Further afield are the eco-domes of the **Eden Project**, the island abbey of **St Michael's Mount** and the sea-smashed cliffs at **Land's End**.

St Ives (p206), Cornwall

10 DAYS

London to Peak District
Palaces & Peaks

Head west from London to take in Wales' top sights, before turning north for a day in medieval Chester, lively Liverpool and the picturesque Peak District.

IRISH SEA

SNOWDONIA NATIONAL PARK ③
LIVERPOOL ⑤
⑥ PEAK DISTRICT
④ CHESTER
BUXTON
CHATSWORTH HOUSE

GOWER PENINSULA
② CARDIFF
① LONDON

1 London (p62)

Kick off this trip with a couple of the capital's outer attractions: the incredible botanical gardens of **Kew** and then **Hampton Court Palace**, perhaps the most glorious Tudor structure in England.

LONDON ➡ CARDIFF

🚃 **Two hours** Direct from London Paddington, or with a change at Bath. 🚗 **2½ hours** On the M4.

2 Cardiff (p270)

Then it's on from one capital to another. Seaside Cardiff has completely reinvented itself in recent years, and the waterfront is now awash with interest, including the **National Assembly Building** and the **Wales Millennium Stadium**. **Cardiff Castle** is another essential stop, as are the nearby **Gower Peninsula** and the moody ruins of **Tintern Abbey**.

CARDIFF ➡ BETWS-Y-COED

🚃 **Four hours** Cross-country to Llandudno, then change for the Conwy Valley line. 🚗 **3½ hours** Along the A470.

3 Snowdonia National Park (p281)

Wales is known for its knock-out scenery, but few places can top Snowdonia in terms of sheer spectacle. It's home to the country's highest mountain: dedicated hikers will want to walk to the top, but if you're short on time you could just take the **Snowdon Mountain Railway**.

BETWS-Y-COED ➡ CHESTER

🚃 **1½ hours** Change at Llandudno. 🚗 **1½ hours** A470 north towards Llandudno, then the A55.

4 Chester (p241)

For medieval atmosphere, Chester is definitely a must-see. Its rust red city walls and cobbled streets are full of charm, especially along the **Rows** – a photogenic tangle of galleried arcades that have hardly changed since the Middle Ages.

CHESTER ➡ LIVERPOOL

🚃 **45 minutes** Several trains per hour.
🚗 **45 minutes** Via the M53, A41 and Mersey Tunnel.

5 Liverpool (p242)

There are plenty of reasons to visit Liverpool, but there's no getting away from the fact that the Fab Four are still the major draw. Fans will find plenty to satisfy their fascination, especially among the memorabilia on show at the **Beatles Story**. Other highlights include the renowned **Walker Art Gallery**, the historic waterfront of **Albert Dock** and the moving **International Slavery Museum**.

LIVERPOOL ➡ BUXTON

🚃 **Two hours** Change in Manchester.
🚗 **1½ hours** Take the M62 and M60.

6 Peak District (p161)

This rugged range of valleys, hills and villages is one of northern England's most popular countryside getaways, and offers a wealth of opportunity for hiking and biking. Afterwards you can relax in the elegant spa town of **Buxton** or take a trip to **Chatsworth House**, a classic example of country-house extravagance.

Formal gardens, Hampton Court Palace (p86)
SIMON GREENWOOD/GETTY IMAGES ©

2 WEEKS

London to Edinburgh
The Full Monty

This long-distance adventure links Old London Town with Scotland's capital, taking in the historic towns of Cambridge and York and two of England's finest national parks en route.

① London (p62)

There's not much time to spare on this long-distance tour, so you'll probably have to limit yourself to just a day in London. Spend the morning browsing around the **British Museum**, head down to **Buckingham Palace** for the Changing of the Guard at 11.30am, whizz over to **St Paul's Cathedral**, cross the river to the **South Bank** and the **Tate Modern**, and finish in the West End via the **Palace of Westminster** and **Trafalgar Square**.

LONDON ⟶ CAMBRIDGE

🚌 **1¼ hours** From London Kings Cross or Liverpool St. 🚗 **1½ hours** Once you're clear of the London traffic, head to Cambridge on the M11.

② Cambridge (p117)

Arch rival to Oxford and England's second celebrated seat of academia, Cambridge is equally famous for its history and architecture. Key colleges to visit include **Trinity College**, the largest and arguably most impressive, as well as **King's College**, with its wonderfully ornate chapel. It's also well worth strolling along the **Backs** for their picturesque riverside scenery; look out for the wonderful **Mathematical Bridge**.

CAMBRIDGE ⟶ YORK

🚌 **2½ hours** Change trains at Peterborough.
🚗 **Three hours** It's a long drive to York of around 160 miles via the A1.

③ York (p224)

It's easy to while away a full day in the graceful city of York. All streets in the centre lead to the mammoth **Minster**, but don't overlook the medieval street known as the **Shambles** and the smells-and-all re-creation of a Viking settlement at **Jorvik**. Northwest of York lie the **Yorkshire Dales**, a rugged landscape of peaks and valleys that are guaranteed to have you reaching for your camera.

YORK ⟶ MANCHESTER

🚌 **One hour, 20 minutes** Direct to Manchester Piccadilly. 🚗 **1½ hours** Straight across via the A64 and M62; expect traffic around Leeds.

Grasmere (p252)
PETER ADAMS/GETTY IMAGES ©

Wordsworth all lived here – but it's best known as one of England's best places for a hike. Trails wind out over the park's jagged hills, while vintage cruise boats chug out across the surface of **Windermere** and other nearby lakes.

WINDERMERE ⇒ EDINBURGH

🚌 **2½ hours** Change at Oxenholme for main-line services north. 🚗 **Three hours** You'll cover at least 150 miles along the M6, A74 and A702.

⑥ Edinburgh (p306)

You'll need at least a day in Edinburgh to cover all the must-sees, such as **Edinburgh Castle** and the **Palace of Holyroodhouse**, as well as the scenery of the **Royal Mile** and the shopping on **Prince's St**. If you have time, detours to the **Royal Yacht Britannia** and **Rosslyn Chapel** will reward the effort.

EDINBURGH ⇒ STIRLING

🚌 **One hour** Direct from Edinburgh's Waverley train station. 🚗 **One hour** Along the M9.

⑦ Stirling (p328)

From Edinburgh it is relatively straightforward to reach the historic **Stirling Castle** and the nearby **Wallace Monument**. With a bit of extra time, you could head onwards to visit scenic **Glencoe** and legendary **Loch Ness**.

④ Manchester (p237)

Manchester is a lively metropolis with a wealth of cultural institutions and a cracking music scene. Make time for the **Imperial War Museum North**, the **Lowry** and the revitalised area around **Salford Quays**. Meanwhile football fans will want to make a pilgrimage to **Old Trafford**, Manchester United's home stadium, and the brand-new **National Football Museum**.

MANCHESTER ⇒ WINDERMERE

🚌 **1½ hours** From Manchester Piccadilly, you'll usually need to change at Oxenholme.
🚗 **1½ hours** Along the M6.

⑤ Lake District (p250)

Britain's favourite national park has numerous literary connections – Beatrix Potter, Arthur Ransome and William

Great Britain Month by Month

Top Events

 Edinburgh Festivals, August

 **Glastonbury**, late June

Notting Hill Carnival, August

Braemar Gathering, September

Hay Festival, May

January

😺 London Parade

A ray of light in the gloom, the New Year's Day Parade in London (to use its official title; www.londonparade.co.uk) is one of the biggest events of its kind in the world, featuring marching bands, street performers, classic cars, floats and displays winding their way through the streets, watched by over half a million people.

😺 Up Helly Aa

Half of Shetland dresses up with horned helmets and battle axes in this spectacular re-enactment of a Viking fire festival (www.uphellyaa.org), with a torchlit procession leading the burning of a full-size Viking longship.

March

☆ Six Nations Rugby Championship

Highlight of the rugby calendar (www.rbs6nations.com), with the home nations playing at London's Twickenham, Edinburgh's Murrayfield and Cardiff's Millennium Stadium.

☆ University Boat Race

Annual race down the River Thames in London between the rowing teams from Cambridge and Oxford Universities (www.theboatrace.org), an institution since 1856 that still enthrals the country.

April

☆ Grand National

Half the country has a flutter on the highlight of the three-day horse race meeting at Aintree

Left: Notting Hill Carnival (p44)
PHOTOGRAPHER: SIMON GREENWOOD/GETTY IMAGES ©

(www.aintree.co.uk) on the first Saturday of the month – a steeplechase with a testing course and notoriously high jumps.

London Marathon

Superfit athletes cover 26.22 miles in just over two hours, while others dress up in daft costumes and take considerably longer. (www.london-marathon.co.uk)

Spirit of Speyside

Based in Dufftown, this is a Scottish festival of whisky, food and music (www.spiritof-speyside.com), with five days of art, cooking, distillery tours and outdoor activities.

May

FA Cup Final

Grand finale of the football (soccer) season for over a century. Teams from across England battle it out over the winter months, culminating in this heady spectacle at Wembley Stadium.

Brighton Festival

Lively three-week arts fest (www.brightonfestival.org) taking over the streets of buzzy south-coast resort Brighton. Alongside the mainstream performances there's a festival fringe as well.

Chelsea Flower Show

The Royal Horticultural Society flower show at Chelsea (www.rhs.org.uk/chelsea) is the highlight of the gardener's year.

Hay Festival

The ever-expanding 'Woodstock of the mind' (www.hayfestival.com) brings an intellectual influx to book-town Hay-on-Wye.

Glyndebourne

Famous festival (www.glyndebourne.com) of world-class opera in the pastoral surroundings of East Sussex, running until the end of summer.

June

Derby Week

Horse-racing, people-watching and clothes-spotting are on the agenda at this week-long meeting in Epsom, Surrey (www.epsomderby.co.uk).

Cotswold Olimpicks

Welly-wanging, pole-climbing and shin-kicking are the key disciplines at this traditional Gloucestershire sports day (www.olimpickgames.co.uk), held every year since 1612.

Trooping the Colour

Military bands and bear-skinned grenadiers march down London's Whitehall in this martial pageant to mark the monarch's birthday.

Royal Ascot

It's hard to tell which matters more, the fashion or the fillies, at this highlight of the horse-racing year in Berkshire (www.ascot.co.uk).

Wimbledon Tennis

The world's best-known grass-court tennis tournament (www.wimbledon.org) attracts all the big names, while crowds cheer or eat tons of strawberries and cream.

Glastonbury Festival

One of Britain's favourite pop and rock gatherings (www.glastonburyfestivals.co.uk), invariably muddy and still a rite of passage for every self-respecting British teenager.

Royal Regatta

Boats of every description take to the water for Henley's upper-crust river jamboree (www.hrr.co.uk).

August

⭐ **Edinburgh Festivals**

Edinburgh's most famous August happening is the International Festival and Fringe, but this month the city also has an event for anything you care to name – books, art, theatre, music, comedy, marching bands... (www.edinburghfestivals.co.uk)

⭐ **Notting Hill Carnival**

London's famous multicultural Caribbean-style street carnival in the district of Notting Hill (www.nottinghillcarnival.biz). Steel drums, dancers, outrageous costumes.

⭐ **Reading Festival**

Venerable rock and pop festival (www.readingfestival.com), always a good bet for big-name bands.

⭐ **National Eisteddfod of Wales**

The largest celebration of native Welsh culture, steeped in history, pageantry and pomp (www.eisteddfod.org.uk); held at various venues around the country.

⭐ **Pride**

Highlight of the gay and lesbian calendar (www.pridelondon.org), a technicolour street parade heads through London's West End.

July

⭐ **T in the Park**

World-class acts since 1994 ensure this major music festival (www.tinthepark.com) is Scotland's answer to Glastonbury.

◎ **Royal Welsh Show**

Prize bullocks and local produce at this national farm and livestock event (www.rwas.co.uk) in Builth Wells.

⭐ **Cowes Week**

Britain's biggest yachting spectacular (www.skandiacowesweek.co.uk) on the choppy seas around the Isle of Wight.

September

⭐ **Bestival**

Quirky music festival (www.bestival.net) on the Isle of Wight with a different fancy-dress theme every year.

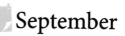 **Great North Run**

Tyneside plays host to the one of the biggest half marathons in the world (www.greatrun.org), with the greatest number of runners in any race at this distance.

Abergavenny Food Festival

The mother of all epicurean festivals (www.abergavennyfoodfestival.co.uk) and the champion of Wales' burgeoning food scene.

Braemar Gathering

The biggest and most famous Highland Games (www.braemargathering.org) in the Scottish calendar, traditionally attended by members of the royal family. Highland dancing, caber-tossing and bagpipe-playing.

October

Dylan Thomas Festival

A celebration of the Welsh laureate's work with readings, events and talks in Swansea (www.dylanthomas.com).

November

Guy Fawkes Night

Also called Bonfire Night (www.bonfire night.net), 5 November sees fireworks fill Britain's skies in commemoration of a failed attempt to blow up parliament way back in 1605.

Remembrance Day

Red poppies are worn and wreaths are laid in towns and cities around the country on 11 November in commemoration of fallen military personnel (www.poppy.org.uk).

December

New Year's Eve

Fireworks and street parties in town squares across the country. In London, crowds line the Thames for a massive midnight fireworks display.

Far left: Highland dancing, Braemar Gathering **Left:** Reading Festival

What's New

For this new edition of Discover Great Britain, our authors have hunted down the fresh, the transformed, the hot and the happening. These are some of our favourites. For up-to-the-minute recommendations, see lonelyplanet.com/great-britain.

1 QUEEN ELIZABETH OLYMPIC PARK, LONDON

In 2012 a huge swath of East London was transformed into the Queen Elizabeth Olympic Park, creating a landscaped legacy to the 2012 London Olympics. (p84)

2 EMIRATES AIR LINE CABLE CAR, LONDON

Initially a public-transport solution linking Olympic venues, the spectacular cnable car across the Thames has become an attraction in its own right. (p82)

3 THE SHARD

This soaring spike of steel and glass is now officially London's tallest skyscraper, and the newly opened viewing deck provides a truly sky-high panorama of the city. (p75)

4 RIVERSIDE MUSEUM, GLASGOW

Glasgow's rapidly developing waterfront has been graced with an extraordinary new museum focusing on the history of transport. (p324)

5 DOCTOR WHO UP CLOSE, CARDIFF

The huge success of reinvented TV classic *Doctor Who,* made in Cardiff, is celebrated with this new attraction – complete with Tardis and Daleks, of course. (p271)

6 NATIONAL FOOTBALL MUSEUM, MANCHESTER

This celebration of football (soccer) recently moved to a new home in Manchester, and is a must-see for fans of the beautiful game. (p237)

7 HOLBURNE MUSEUM, BATH

After a multi-million-pound refit, Bath's grandest art gallery has reopened its doors, allowing visitors to revisit works by Turner, Gainsborough, Stubbs and many more. (p191)

8 M SHED, BRISTOL

Lodged in a massive old dockside warehouse, Bristol's new museum is a treasure trove of memorabilia – from slave-trade reminders to Massive Attack record decks. (p186)

9 MUSEUM OF LIVERPOOL

Liverpool's multilayered past is celebrated at this interactive exploration of cultural and historical milestones: poverty, wealth, football, plus – of course – The Beatles. (p245)

Get Inspired

📖 Books

o **Oliver Twist** (1838) Tear-jerking social commentary from Charles Dickens.

o **Pride and Prejudice** (1813) Jane Austen's quintessential English love story.

o **White Teeth** (2000) Zadie Smith's literary debut explores life in multicultural London.

o **London: The Biography** (2001) Peter Ackroyd's fascinating account of the life of Britain's capital.

o **An Utterly Impartial History of Britain** (2007) Comic jaunt through Britain's past by humourist John O'Farrell.

🎬 Films

o **Brief Encounter** (1945) David Lean's classic portrayal of typically British buttoned-up passion.

o **The Ladykillers** (1955) Classic Ealing crime caper set on the grimy streets of London.

o **Chariots of Fire** (1981) Oscar-winning story of Olympic endeavour.

o **Four Weddings and a Funeral** (1994) Classic British rom-com starring Hugh Grant.

o **The King's Speech** (2010) Story of George VI's struggle to overcome his stammer.

🎵 Music

o **Sergeant Pepper's Lonely Hearts Club Band** (The Beatles) The Fab Four's finest moment.

o **Exile on Main Street** (The Rolling Stones) Classic album from Britain's other iconic band.

o **Village Green Preservation Society** (The Kinks) Poppy melodies and wry English observations.

o **London Calling** (The Clash) Seminal punk with a point.

o **Different Class** (Pulp) Brit-pop tales of English eccentricity.

🖱 Websites

o **BBC** (www.bbc.com) News and entertainment.

o **British Council** (www. britishcouncil.org) Arts and culture.

o **Traveline** (www. traveline.org) Invaluable public-transport planning.

o **Lonely Planet** (www. lonelyplanet.com) Destination information, traveller forums, hotels and more.

⏰ Short on time?

This list will give you an instant insight into the country.

o **Read** *Notes from a Small Island*, a hilarious travelogue from US-born Anglophile Bill Bryson.

o **Watch** *Withnail & I*, cult holiday disaster movie.

o **Listen** *Definitely Maybe*, landmark album from Manchester bad boys Oasis.

o **Log on** *Visit Britain* (www. visitbritain.com), Britain's official tourism website; large and comprehensive.

Need to Know

Currency
Pound; also called 'pound sterling' (£)

Language
English; also Scottish Gaelic and Welsh

ATMs
Widely available.

Visas
Not required for most citizens of Europe, Australia, NZ, USA and Canada.

Mobile Phones
Phones from most other countries operate in Britain but attract roaming charges. Local SIM cards cost from £10; SIM and basic handset around £30.

Wi-Fi
Most hotels and B&Bs, and many cafes, offer wi-fi. Wi-fi hot spots are common in the cities.

Driving
Traffic drives on the left; steering wheels are on the right side of the car. Most rental cars have manual gears (stick shift).

Tipping
Optional, but 10% in restaurants and cafes is standard. No need to tip in bars.

When to Go

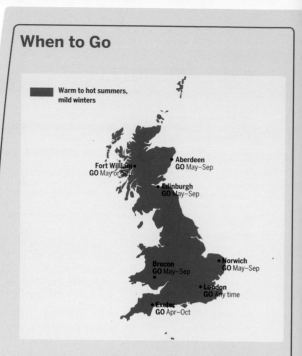

Warm to hot summers, mild winters

Fort William GO May or Sep
Aberdeen GO May–Sep
Edinburgh GO May–Sep
Brecon GO May–Sep
Norwich GO May–Sep
London GO Any time
Exeter GO Apr–Oct

High Season
(Jun–Aug)
○ Weather at its best; accommodation rates at their peak.

○ Roads are busy, especially in seaside areas, national parks and popular cities such as Oxford, Bath, Edinburgh and York.

Shoulder
(Mar–May & Sep–Oct)
○ Crowds reduce; prices drop.

○ Weather often good; March to May is a mix of sunny spells and showers; September to October can feature balmy Indian summers.

Low Season
(Nov–Feb)
○ Wet and cold. Snow falls in mountain areas, especially up north.

○ Opening hours reduced October to Easter; some places shut for winter. Big-city sights (particularly London's) operate all year.

Advance Planning

○ **Two months before** Book train tickets, hotels and car hire to get the best deals. In popular areas such as London, Bath, York and Edinburgh, the earlier you book the better.

○ **One month before** Reserve tables at high-profile restaurants, and book hotels and B&Bs in other areas.

○ **Two weeks before** Buy tickets online for big-ticket sights such as the Tower of London and the London Eye.

○ **One week before** Check the weather forecast. Then ignore it.

Your Daily Budget

Budget less than £50
- Dorm beds: £10–25
- Cheap meals in cafes and pubs: £5–9
- Long-distance coach: £10–30 (200 miles)

Midrange £50–100
- Midrange hotel or B&B: £60–130 (London £90–180) per double room
- Main course in midrange restaurant: £9–18
- Long-distance train: £15–50 (200 miles)
- Car hire: from £30 per day

Top End more than £100
- Four-star hotel room: from £130 (London £180)
- Three-course meal in a good restaurant: around £40 per person

Exchange Rates

Australia	A$1	65p
Canada	C$1	63p
Europe	€1	86p
Japan	¥100	68p
New Zealand	NZ$1	53p
USA	US$1	63p

For current exchange rates see www.xe.com.

What to Bring
- **Comfortable shoes** You'll be doing a lot of walking, so a pair of sturdy, comfy shoes is indispensable. If you're planning on hiking, bring a pair of proper waterproof boots.
- **Waterproof jacket and an umbrella** The British weather is famously fickle, so come prepared.
- **Small day pack** For carrying the waterproofs when the sun shines.
- **Good manners** The Brits are big fans of politeness. Keep the volume down, be respectful of others' opinions and whatever you do – don't skip queues.

Arriving in Britain

London Heathrow

Train The fast Heathrow Express (www.heathrowexpress.com; £18) trains run to London Paddington every 15 minutes.

Underground The Piccadilly Line connects all terminals to central London; cheaper (£5.30) but much slower.

Taxi A taxi to central London will cost between £50 and £80.

London Gatwick

Train Gatwick Express (www.gatwickexpress.com) runs to London Victoria every 15 minutes.

Getting Around
- **Train** Britain's comprehensive rail network connects major cities and towns. Peak times are the most expensive.
- **Car** Britain's roads are extensive and generally of a high standard. Motorways link major cities. Traffic can be a problem.
- **Local buses** Useful for reaching smaller towns, villages and rural sights.

Accommodation
- **Hotels** Britain has a huge and varied choice of hotels, although you'll pay a premium in London and other popular spots.
- **B&Bs** The traditional British bed-and-breakfast offers comfort and good value. The best places can match the standards of boutique hotels.
- **Inns** Many pubs and inns also offer accommodation, especially in rural areas.

Be Forewarned
- **Costs** Britain can be pricey; cut costs by staying in B&Bs, prebooking train and admission tickets online, and travelling outside peak times. Many tourist offices offer discount cards covering local attractions.
- **Driving** Petrol is expensive in Britain, and traffic jams are a fact of life during rush hour – especially in the cities.
- **School holidays** Things are busier and prices head upwards during school holidays, especially at Christmas, Easter and in July and August.

London & Around

When it comes to must-see sights, there's simply nowhere quite like London. This sprawling, stately city has been at the centre of British history for 2000 years, and it shows no sign of slowing down just yet. With its world-class theatres, landmark museums, iconic architecture and nonstop nightlife, London is truly a city that never sleeps, and you could spend your whole trip here and never run out of things to see and do. Its recent role as host of the 2012 Olympic Games simply adds to the interest, with the action centring on the newly created Queen Elizabeth Olympic Park.

Unfortunately, all this prestige comes at a price. London is by far the most expensive city in Britain, so it's well worth taking advantage of some of the city's free sights while you're here – many of its top museums, galleries and green spaces don't charge a penny.

London also makes an ideal base for day trips, with the lively coastal city of Brighton, the academic centre of Cambridge and the royal palaces of Hampton Court and Windsor Castle all within easy reach.

Green Park (p61)

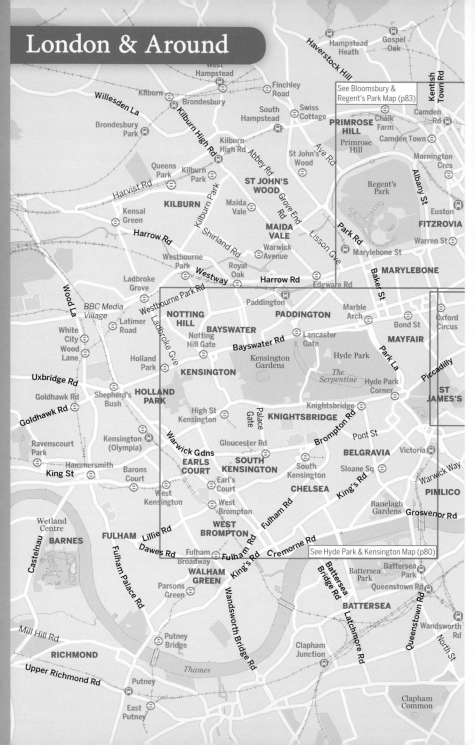

London & Around

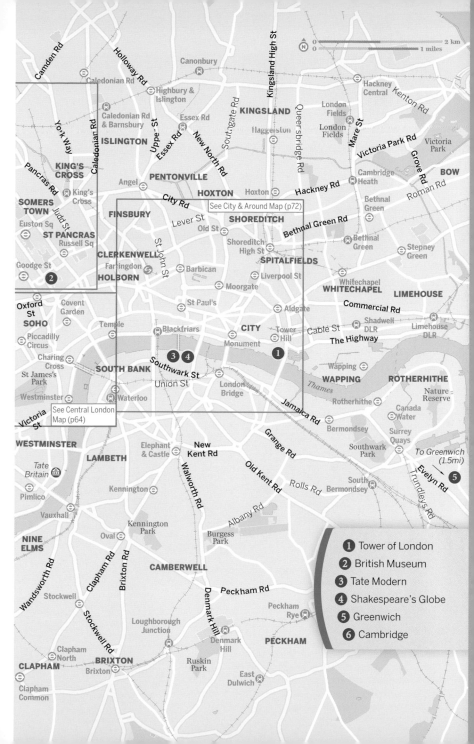

See City & Around Map (p72)

See Central London Map (p64)

To Greenwich (1.5mi)

1 Tower of London
2 British Museum
3 Tate Modern
4 Shakespeare's Globe
5 Greenwich
6 Cambridge

London & Around Highlights

TETRA IMAGES/GETTY IMAGES ©

① Tower of London

London's famous Tower has variously been a castle, palace and prison over almost 1000 years of history. Equally famous are the Yeoman Warders (or 'Beef-eaters') who guard the tower. To qualify, all Beefeaters must have served at least 22 years in the armed forces and earned a Good Conduct Medal. Above: White Tower; Top Right: Beefeater with raven; Bottom Right: Imperial State Crown

Need to Know

PHOTO OP From atop the battlements **DID YOU KNOW?** The Yeomans' ceremonial outfits cost around £7000 **For further coverage, see p68**

Tower of London Don't Miss List

BY ALAN KINGSHOTT, CHIEF YEOMAN WARDER AT THE TOWER OF LONDON

1 A TOWER TOUR
To understand the Tower and its history, a guided tour with one of the Yeoman Warders is essential. Very few people appreciate that the Tower is actually our home as well; all the Warders live inside the outer walls. The Tower is rather like a miniature village – visitors are often rather surprised to see our washing hanging out beside the castle walls!

2 CROWN JEWELS
Visitors often think the Crown Jewels are the Queen's personal jewellery collection. They're not, of course; the Crown Jewels are actually the ceremonial regalia used during the Coronation. The highlights are the Sceptre and the Imperial State Crown, which contains the celebrated diamond known as the Star of Africa. People are often surprised to hear that the Crown Jewels aren't insured (as they could never be replaced).

3 WHITE TOWER
The White Tower is the original royal palace of the Tower of London, but it hasn't been used as a royal residence since 1603. It's the most iconic building here. Inside you can see exhibits from the Royal Armouries, including a suit of armour belonging to Henry VIII.

4 RAVENS
A Tower legend states that if its resident ravens ever left, the monarchy would topple – a royal decree states that we must keep a minimum of six ravens at any time. We currently have nine ravens, looked after by the Ravenmaster and his two assistants.

5 CEREMONY OF THE KEYS
We hold three daily ceremonies: the 9am Official Opening, the Ceremony of the Word (when the day's password is issued), and the 10pm Ceremony of the Keys, when the gates are locked after the castle has closed. Visitors are welcome to attend the last, but must apply directly to the Tower in writing.

British Museum

The British Museum (p82) is one of London's great wonders, with hundreds of galleries containing Egyptian, Etruscan, Greek, Roman, European and Middle Eastern artifacts. Among the must-sees are the Rosetta Stone, the controversial Parthenon Sculptures, and the Anglo-Saxon Sutton Hoo burial relics. Great Court, British Museum

Tate Modern

This abandoned power station (p73) was once an eyesore, but the inspired decision to transform it into a gallery in the late 1990s helped reinvigorate the nation's interest in modern art. Spread out over five floors, the permanent collection takes in everyone from Andy Warhol to Pablo Picasso, but it's the exhibitions in the Turbine Hall that inevitably spark the most excitement. Best of all, it's free.

Shakespeare's Globe

4

The original theatre where William Shakespeare premiered some of his plays burned down in 1613, but this modern-day reconstruction (p74) used traditional materials and building techniques to bring the Bard's open-air playhouse back to vivid life.

It offers a fascinating insight into Shakespeare's theatrical world – you can take a tour or, better still, join the 'groundlings' for a performance.

5

Greenwich

It's worth making the time for a trip down-river to glorious Greenwich. In days gone by, this elegant area was the centre of British maritime power, and relics of the nation's illustrious seafaring heritage linger on at the National Maritime Museum (p85) and the Old Royal Naval College (p84). At the Royal Observatory (p85) the universal coordinate of Greenwich Mean Time was first established. Royal Observatory

6

Cambridge

The lovely university city of Cambridge is a day trip from London, and no visit is complete without taking a punt (flat-bottomed boat) along the river by the picturesque 'Backs' (p119), the green lawns that run behind the city's finest colleges. Finish your cruise with a pint in one of the city's many historic pubs. Punting on the River Cam

London & Around's Best...

City Views

○ **The Shard** (p75) Survey the scene from the capital's tallest skyscraper

○ **London Eye** (p74) Ride the pods on London's giant wheel

○ **Greenwich Royal Observatory** (p85) The heart of this historic maritime complex

○ **Westminster Cathedral** (p65) Climb the tower for views of Old London Town

○ **Tower Bridge** (p68) Get another perspective on the River Thames

Things for Free

○ **British Museum** (p82) London's flagship repository

○ **National Gallery** (p66) Marvel at the artistic masterpieces

○ **Tate Modern** (p73) Thanks to Mr Tate, another great gallery

○ **Covent Garden** (p67) The perfect spot to wander, window-shop and watch street-art performers

○ **Changing of the Guard** (p63) Classic daily London event outside Buckingham Palace

Green Spaces

○ **Hyde Park** (p79) London's largest green space, with paths, lawns, fountains and lakes

○ **Regent's Park** (p81) Huge park, best known as the home of London Zoo

○ **Hampstead Heath** (p85) A slice of the countryside in north London, with cross-city views

○ **Kew Gardens** (p85) Browse the rare flora of the Royal Botanical Collection

Need to Know

Traditional Pubs

○ **Princess Louise** (p95) Victorian classic, arguably London's most beautiful pub

○ **Lamb & Flag** (p95) Everyone's favourite in Covent Garden

○ **George Inn** (p96) London's last surviving galleried coaching inn

○ **Ye Olde Cheshire Cheese** (p95) An atmospheric icon of Fleet St

ADVANCE PLANNING

○ **Two months before** Reserve your hotel room and arrange theatre tickets.

○ **Two weeks before** Book a table at high-profile restaurants.

○ **One week before** Prebook online for top sights such as the London Eye, Madame Tussauds, St Paul's Cathedral and the Tower of London.

RESOURCES

○ **Visit London** (www.visitlondon.com) The official tourist website.

○ **BBC London** (www.bbc.com/london) London-centric low-down from the BBC.

○ **Evening Standard** (www.thisislondon.co.uk) Latest news from the city's daily rag.

○ **Urban Path** (www.urbanpath.com) Online guide to 'nice things' – events, restaurants, hotels, spas and shops.

GETTING AROUND

○ **Bus** Excellent network across the capital, though the famous red double-deckers are not so common these days.

○ **Underground train** London's 'tube' is the speediest way to get around town.

○ **Waterbus** Useful and scenic way to get between riverside points.

BE FOREWARNED

○ **Exhibitions** High-profile seasonal exhibitions at museums and galleries often charge extra and are sold out weeks ahead.

○ **Restaurants** You'll need to book for the big-name establishments.

○ **Public transport** All-day Travelcards and Oyster cards offer the best value.

○ **Rush hour** Morning peak hour won't impact travellers much; during the evening rush, find a nice pub and wait until it's over.

Left: London Eye (p74); **Above:** Covent Garden (p67)

London Walking Tour

This walk takes you through the West End of London, and features some of the capital's major attractions and icons.

WALK FACTS

- **Start** Covent Garden
- **Finish** Trafalgar Sq
- **Distance** 2.5 miles
- **Duration** Three hours

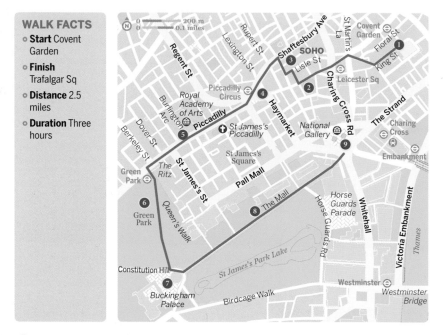

❶ Covent Garden Piazza

Yes it's touristy, but this wonderful square (designed by Inigo Jones), and former market hall, is a good place to start. Grab a coffee from one of the many open-air cafes to fuel you up for the walk, and sip it while watching the never-ending stream of buskers and street performers.

❷ Leicester Square

A walk down King St and over Charing Cross Rd brings you to Leicester Sq. Dominated by enormous nightclubs and cinemas, this is where movies premiere and stars make handprints in the pavement. It's a London landmark, but – to be blunt – not especially scenic.

❸ Chinatown & Theatreland

Head north, across Lisle St – the heart of London's Chinatown – to reach Shaftesbury Ave – the heart of London's theatreland and home to some of the West End's most prestigious theatres.

❹ Piccadilly Circus

Westwards down Shaftsbury Ave brings you to Piccadilly Circus, with the famous **Eros statue** at its centre. The Circus is always hectic and traffic-choked, with the buildings cloaked in massive flashing ads, but this is an icon of London, so it's worth making the stop.

5 Piccadilly

Running west from Piccadilly Circus is the elegant street of Piccadilly. It's lined with upmarket stores, including those on highly exclusive **Burlington Arcade**, thanks to the proximity of aristocratic neighbourhoods St James's and Mayfair.

6 Green Park

Walk past the **Ritz**, one of London's fanciest hotels, and turn left into Green Park for a chance to catch your breath, or rest your legs on one of the park benches under some stunning oak trees and olde-worlde street lamps.

7 Buckingham Palace

A stroll south through Green Park leads to one of London's best-known addresses: Buckingham Palace, the Queen's residence in London. If you made an early start, you might be here for the **changing of the guard** at 11.30am.

8 The Mall

With your back to Buckingham Palace you can march down The Mall, a grand avenue alongside **St James's Park**, where royal processions often take place and the Queen's limousine or carriage is escorted by her guards.

9 Trafalgar Square

The Mall leads you under **Admiralty Arch** and pops you out at Trafalgar Sq, with its fountains and statues, dominated by **Nelson's Column**. The square is also sur-rounded by grand buildings, including the **National Gallery** – where a seat on the steps outside the entrance is the perfect place to end your walk.

London in...

TWO DAYS

Start with our walking tour around the **West End**. In the afternoon, tick off more icons – **Westminster Abbey** and the **Houses of Parliament**, and the instantly recognisable tower of **Big Ben**. Cross Westminster Bridge to reach the **London Eye**, then spend the late afternoon at the **British Museum**. Day two starts at **St Paul's Cathedral**, followed by crossing the Millennium Bridge to the **Tate Modern**. From here stroll along the riverside walkways to reach **Tower Bridge**, then cross to visit the **Tower of London**.

FOUR DAYS

Day three could start with a morning of browsing – in the **Tate Gallery** or **National Gallery** if you're artistically inclined, or in the famous stores of **Regent Street** or **Kensington** if you're more retail minded. Then spend the afternoon enjoying the maritime splendours of **Greenwich**. Day four is for day trips: leave the capital behind for an excursion to **Hampton Court Palace**, **Windsor Castle** or **Canterbury Cathedral**.

Ritz Hotel

Discover London & Around

LONDON

POP: 7.82 MILLION

Everyone comes to London with a preconception shaped by a multitude of books, movies, TV shows and songs. Whatever yours is, prepare to have it exploded by this endlessly fascinating, amorphous city. You could spend a lifetime exploring it and find that the slippery thing's gone and changed on you. One thing is constant: that great serpent of a river enfolding the city in its sinuous loops, linking London both to the green heart of England and the world.

 Sights

The city's main geographical feature is the murky Thames, which snakes around but roughly divides the city into north and south. The old City of London (note the big 'C') is the capital's financial district, covering roughly a square mile bordered by the river and the many gates of the ancient (long-gone) city walls: Newgate, Moorgate etc. The areas to the east of the City are collectively known as the East End. The West End, on the City's other flank, is effectively the centre of London nowadays.

Westminster & St James's

Purposefully positioned outside the old City (London's fiercely independent burghers preferred to keep the monarch and parliament at arm's length), Westminster has been the centre of the nation's political power for nearly a millennium.

Westminster Abbey
DAVID TOMLINSON/GETTY IMAGES ©

WESTMINSTER ABBEY   Church

(Map p64; ☎020-7222 5152; www.westminster-abbey.org; 20 Dean's Yard; adult/child £15/6, tours £3; ⏱9.30am-4.30pm Mon, Tue, Thu & Fri, to 7pm Wed, to 2.30pm Sat; ⊖Westminster) Westminster Abbey is simply one of London's most imposing treasures. Every monarch since William the Conqueror has been crowned here, with the exception of a couple of unlucky Eds who were murdered (Edward V) or abdicated (Edward VIII) before the magic moment. Look out for the strangely underwhelming **Coronation Chair**.

Though a mixture of architectural styles, it is considered the finest example of Early English Gothic in existence. Apart from the royal graves, keep an eye out for the many famous commoners interred here, especially in **Poets' Corner**, where you'll find the resting places of Chaucer, Dickens, Hardy, Tennyson, Dr Johnson and Kipling as well as memorials to the other greats (Shakespeare, Austen, Brontë etc). Elsewhere you'll find the graves of Handel and Sir Isaac Newton.

Parts of the Abbey complex are free to visitors. This includes the **Cloister** and the 900-year-old **College Garden**. Free concerts are held here from 12.30pm to 2pm on Wednesday from mid-July to mid-August.

Verger-led tours are held several times a day (except Sunday) and are limited to 25 people per tour; call ahead to secure your place. Of course, admission to the Abbey is free if you wish to attend a service. On weekdays, Matins is at 7.30am, Holy Communion at 8am and 12.30pm, and Choral Evensong at 5pm. There are services throughout the day on Sunday.

HOUSES OF PARLIAMENT   Historic Building

(Map p64; www.parliament.uk; Parliament Sq; ⊖Westminster) Photos just don't do justice to the ornate stonework and golden filigree of Charles Barry and Augustus Pugin's neo-Gothic masterpiece (1840). Officially called the **Palace of Westminster**, the oldest part is **Westminster Hall** (1097), which is one of only a few sections that survived a catastrophic fire in 1834.

The palace's most famous feature is its clock tower, aka **Big Ben** (Map p64). Ben is actually the 13-ton bell, named after Benjamin Hall, who was commissioner of works when the tower was completed in 1858.

At the business end, parliament is split into two houses. The green-hued **House of Commons** is the lower house, where the 650 elected Members of Parliament sit. Traditionally the home of hereditary bluebloods, the scarlet-decorated **House of Lords** now has peers appointed through various means.

Parliamentary recesses (ie MP holidays) last for three months over summer and a couple of weeks over Easter and Christmas. When parliament is in recess there are guided **tours** (☎0844 847 1672; www.ticketmaster.co.uk/housesofparliament; 75min tours adult/child £15/6) of both chambers and other historic areas.

BUCKINGHAM PALACE   Palace

(Map p64; ☎020-7766 7300; www.royalcollection.org.uk; Buckingham Palace Rd; tours adult/child £17/9.75; ⏱late Jul-Sep; ⊖Victoria) Built in 1703 for the Duke of Buckingham, Buckingham Palace replaced St James's Palace as the monarch's official London residence in 1837. To know if she's at home, check whether the yellow, red and blue standard is flying.

Nineteen lavishly furnished State Rooms – hung with artworks by the likes of Rembrandt, van Dyck, Canaletto, Poussin and Vermeer – are open to visitors when HRH (Her Royal Highness) takes her holidays. The two-hour tour includes the **Throne Room**, with his-and-hers pink chairs initialed 'ER' and 'P'. Access is by timed tickets with admission every 15 minutes (audioguide included).

CHANGING OF THE GUARD
At 11.30am daily from May to July (on alternate days, weather permitting, for the rest of the year), the old guard (Foot Guards of the Household Regiment) comes off duty to be replaced by the new guard on the forecourt of Buckingham Palace.

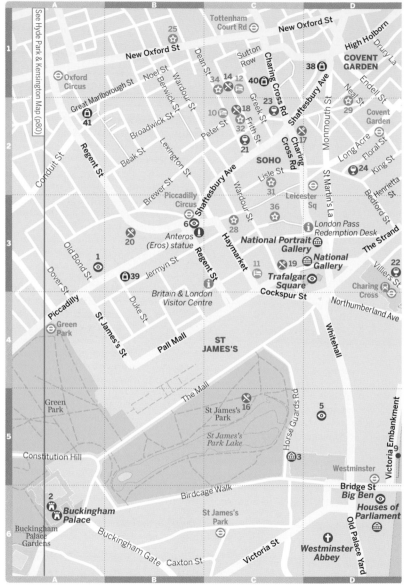

ROYAL MEWS

(Map p80; www.royalcollection.org.uk; Buckingham Palace Rd; adult/child £8/5; ⏰10am-5pm Apr-Oct, to 4pm Mon-Sat Nov-Dec) Indulge your Cinderella fantasies while inspecting the exquisite state coaches in the

Royal Mews, a working stable looking after the royals' immaculately groomed horses and opulent vehicles they use for getting from A to B. Highlights include the magnificent gold coach of 1762 and the 1910 Glass Coach (Prince William

WESTMINSTER CATHEDRAL Church

(www.westminstercathedral.org.uk; Victoria St; tower adult/child £5/2.50; ☉7am-7pm; ⊖Victoria) Begun in 1895, this neo-Byzantine cathedral is still a work in progress, with new sections completed as funds allow. The distinctive 83m red-brick and white-stone **tower** offers splendid views of London and, unlike St Paul's dome, you can take the lift.

NO 10 DOWNING STREET Historic Building

(Map p64; www.number10.gov.uk; 10 Downing St; ⊖Westminister) It's typically British that the official seat of the prime minister is a nondescript Georgian townhouse in Whitehall. The street was cordoned off with a rather large iron gate during Margaret Thatcher's tenure, so you can't get up close.

CHURCHILL MUSEUM & CABINET WAR ROOMS Museum

(Map p64; www.iwm.org.uk/cabinet; Clive Steps, King Charles St; adult/child £15/free; ☉9.30am-6pm; ⊖Westminster) Winston Churchill coordinated the Allied resistance against Nazi Germany on a Bakelite telephone from this underground military HQ during WWII. The Cabinet War Rooms remain much as they were when the lights were flicked off in 1945.

West End

A strident mix of culture and consumerism but more a concept than a fixed geographical area, the West End is synonymous with roof-raising musicals, bright lights, outstanding restaurants and indefatigable bag-laden shoppers. It casts its net around Piccadilly Circus and Trafalgar Sq to the south, Regent St to the west, Oxford St to the north and Covent Garden to the east and the Strand to the southeast.

Mayfair, west of Piccadilly Circus, hogs all of the most expensive streets from the Monopoly board. The elegant bow of **Regent Street** and frantic **Oxford Street** are the city's main shopping strips. At the heart of the West End lies **Soho**, a boho grid of narrow streets and squares

and Catherine Middleton actually used the 1902 State Landau for their wedding in 2011).

Central London

hiding gay bars, strip clubs, cafes and advertising agencies.

PICCADILLY CIRCUS   Square
(Map p64; Piccadilly Circus; ⊖Piccadilly Circus) Designed in the 1820s and named after the street Piccadilly (heading west to Hyde Park Corner from the square) at its confluence with the grand sweep of Regent St and Shaftesbury Ave, Piccadilly Circus is today a tumult of stop-start traffic, blinking neon advertisement panels and camera-toting visitors from all four corners of the globe.

TRAFALGAR SQUARE   Square
(Map p64; ⊖Charing Cross) Trafalgar Sq is the public heart of London, hosting rallies, marches and feverish New Year's festivities. The square is one of the world's grandest public places, with Admiral Nelson surveying his fleet from the 43.5m-high **Nelson's Column** at its heart, erected in 1843 to commemorate his 1805 victory over Napoleon off Spain's Cape Trafalgar.

FREE **NATIONAL GALLERY**   Gallery
(Map p64; www.nationalgallery.org.uk; Trafalgar Sq; ⊙10am-6pm Sat-Thu, to 9pm Fri; ⊖Charing Cross) Gazing grandly over Trafalgar Sq through its Corinthian columns, the National Gallery is the nation's most important repository of largely premodern art. Four million visitors flock annually to admire its 2300-plus Western European

paintings, spanning the eras from the 13th to the early 20th centuries.

FREE NATIONAL PORTRAIT GALLERY Gallery

(Map p64; www.npg.org.uk; St Martin's Pl; ◷10am-6pm Sat-Wed, to 9pm Thu & Fri; ⊖Charing Cross) This fascinating gallery is like stepping into a picture book of English history. Founded in 1856, the permanent collection (around 11,000 works) starts with the Tudors on the 2nd floor and descends to contemporary figures (from pop stars to scientists), including Marc Quinn's *Self*, a frozen self-portrait of the artist's head cast in blood and re-created every five years.

COVENT GARDEN PIAZZA Historic Area

(Map p64; ⊖Covent Garden) London's first planned square, Covent Garden Piazza now hosts bands of tourists shopping in quaint old arcades, and ringing street entertainers and buskers.

SIR JOHN SOANE'S MUSEUM Museum

(Map p64; www.soane.org; 13 Lincoln's Inn Fields; tours £5; ◷10am-5pm Tue-Sat, 6-9pm 1st Tue of month; ⊖Holborn) One of the most atmospheric and intriguing of London's museums, this was the remarkable home of architect and collector extraordinaire Sir John Soane (1753–1837). Among his eclectic acquisitions are an Egyptian sarcophagus, dozens of Greek and Roman antiquities and the original *Rake's Progress*, William Hogarth's set of caricatures telling the story of a late-18th-century London cad. Tours (£10) are held at 11am on Saturdays but bookmark the evening of the first Tuesday of each month when the house is candlelit and even more magical (queues are long).

BURLINGTON ARCADE Shopping Arcade

(Map p64; 51 Piccadilly; ⊖Green Park) The well-to-do Burlington Arcade, built in 1819, is famously patrolled by the Burlington Beadles, uniformed guards who constitute one of the world's smallest private police forces.

The City

It's only in the last 250 years that the City has gone from being the very essence of London and its main population centre to just its central business district.

Trafalgar Square

TOWER OF LONDON   Fortress

(Map p72; ☎0844 482 7777; www.hrp.org.uk;
Tower Hill; adult/child £20.90/10.45, audio guides
£4/3; ⏰9am-5.30pm Tue-Sat, from 10am Sun &
Mon, until 4.30pm Nov-Feb; ⊖Tower Hill) One
of London's four World Heritage Sites
(joining Westminster Abbey, Kew Gardens
and Maritime Greenwich), the Tower
offers a window on to a gruesome and
quite compelling history. A former royal
residence, treasury, mint and arsenal, it
became most famous as a prison when
Henry VIII moved to Whitehall Palace in
1529 and started meting out his preferred
brand of punishment.

The most striking building is indeed
the central **White Tower**, with its solid
Romanesque architecture and four
turrets. Today it houses a collection from
the Royal Armouries, including Henry
VIII's commodious suit of armour. To the
north stands **Waterloo Barracks**, which
now contains the spectacular and newly
redisplayed **Crown Jewels**, including
the platinum crown of the late Queen
Mother, set with the 105-carat **Koh-i-
Noor** (Mountain of Light) diamond, and
the **Imperial State Crown**. On the far
side of the White Tower rises the **Bloody
Tower**, where the 12-year-old Edward V
and his little brother were held 'for their
own safety' and later murdered, probably
by their uncle, the future Richard III. Sir
Walter Raleigh did a 13-year stretch here,
when he wrote his *History of the World*.

On the small green in front of the
Chapel Royal of St Peter ad Vincula
stood Henry VIII's **scaffold**, where seven
people, including Anne Boleyn and her
cousin Catherine Howard (Henry's
second and fifth wives) were beheaded.

Look out for the latest in the Tower's
long line of famous ravens, which legend
says could cause the kingdom to fall
should they leave (their wings are clipped
in case they get any ideas).

To get your bearings, take the hugely
entertaining free guided tour with any of
the Beefeaters (Yeoman Warders). Hour-
long tours leave every 30 minutes from
the bridge near the main entrance; the
last tour's an hour before closing. Book
online for cheaper rates for the Tower.

TOWER BRIDGE   Bridge

(Map p72; ⊖Tower Hill) London was still a
thriving port in 1894 when elegant Tower
Bridge was built. Designed to be raised
to allow ships to pass (it still lifts around
1000 times a year), electricity has
now replaced the original steam
power. A lift leads up from the
northern tower to the **Tower
Bridge Exhibition** (Map p72;
www.towerbridge.org.uk; adult/
child £7/3; ⏰10am-5.30pm
Apr-Sep, 9.30am-5pm Oct-Mar;
⊖Tower Hill) 42m above
the water, from where
you can walk along the
east- and west-facing
walkways.

FREE MUSEUM OF
LONDON   Museum
(Map p72; www.museumoflon
don.org.uk; 150 London Wall;
⏰10am-6pm; ⊖Barbican)

Tower Bridge

CHRIS MELLOR/GETTY IMAGES © MILLENNIUM BRIDGE ARCHITECT SIR NORMAN FOSTER

Don't Miss **St Paul's Cathedral**

Dominating the City with one of the world's largest church domes (around 65,000 tons' worth), St Paul's Cathedral was designed by Christopher Wren after the Great Fire and built between 1675 and 1710. As part of the 300th anniversary celebrations, St Paul's underwent a £40 million renovation project that gave the church a deep clean.

Inside, 30m above the main area, is the first of three domes (actually a dome inside a cone inside a dome) supported by eight huge columns. The walkway around its base, 257 steps up a staircase on the western side of the southern transept, is called the **Whispering Gallery**, because if you talk close to the wall, your words will carry to the opposite side 32m away. A further 119 steps brings you to the **Stone Gallery**, 152 iron steps above which is the **Golden Gallery** at the top, rewarded with unforgettable views of London.

The **Crypt** has memorials to up to 300 military demigods, including Wellington, Kitchener and Nelson, whose body lies below the dome. But the most poignant memorial is to Wren himself. On a simple slab bearing his name, a Latin inscription translates as: 'If you seek his memorial, look about you'.

Free guided tours leave the tour desk four times daily at 10.45am, 11.15am, 1.30pm and 2pm (90 minutes). Evensong takes place at 5pm (3.15pm on Sunday).

NEED TO KNOW

Map p72; www.stpauls.co.uk; St Paul's Churchyard; adult/child £12.50/4.50; ⊘8.30am-4pm Mon-Sat; Θ St Paul's

Catching this riveting museum early on in your stay helps peel back the layers of historical London for valuable perspectives on this great city. While the Lord Mayor's ceremonial coach is the centrepiece, an effort has been made to create an immersive experience: you can enter reconstructions of an 18th-century debtors' prison, a Georgian pleasure garden and a Victorian street.

Tower of London

Tackling the Tower

Although it's usually less busy in the late afternoon, don't leave your assault on the Tower until too late in the day. You could easily spend hours here and not see it all. Start by getting your bearings with the hour-long Yeoman Warder (Beefeater) tours; they are included in the cost of admission, entertaining and the only way to access the **Chapel Royal of St Peter ad Vincula** ❶, which is where they finish up.

When you leave the chapel, the **Tower Green scaffold site** ❷ is directly in front. The building immediately to your left is Waterloo Barracks, where the **Crown Jewels** ❸ are housed. These are the absolute highlight of a Tower visit, so keep an eye on the entrance and pick a time to visit when it looks relatively quiet. Once inside, take things at your own pace. Slow-moving travelators shunt you past the dozen or so crowns that are the treasury's centrepiece, but feel free to double-back for a second or even third pass – particularly if you ended up on the rear travelator the first time around. Allow plenty of time for the **White Tower** ❹, the core of the whole complex, starting with the exhibition of royal armour. As you continue onto the 2nd floor, keep an eye out for **St John's Chapel** ❺. The famous **ravens** ❻ can be seen in the courtyard around the White Tower. Head next through the towers that formed the **Medieval Palace** ❼, then take the **East Wall Walk** ❽ to get a feel for the castle's mighty battlements. Spend the rest of your time poking around the many, many other fascinating nooks and crannies of the Tower complex.

BEAT THE QUEUES

Buy your fast-track ticket in advance online or at the City of London Information Centre in St Paul's Churchyard.

Palacepalooza An annual Historic Royal Palaces membership allows you to jump the queues and visit the Tower (and four other London palaces) as often as you like.

Chapel Royal of St Peter ad Vincula

This chapel serves as the resting place for the royals and other members of the aristocracy who were executed on the small green out front. Several notable identities are buried under the chapel's altar.

Tower Green scaffold site

Seven people, including three queens (Anne Boleyn, Catherine Howard and Jane Grey), lost their heads here during Tudor times, saving the monarch the embarrassment of public executions on Tower Hill. The site now features a sculpture by Brian Catling.

Beauchamp Tower

Main Entrance

Bell Tower

White Tower

Much of the White Tower is taken up with this exhibition of 500 years of royal armour. Look for the virtually cuboid suit made to match Henry VIII's bloated body, complete with an oversized armoured pouch to protect his, ahem, crown jewels.

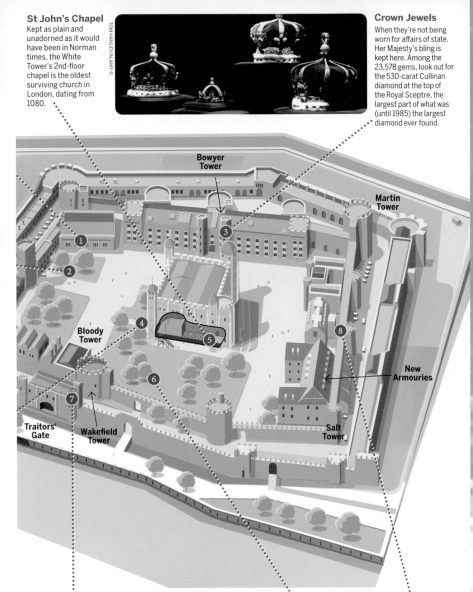

St John's Chapel
Kept as plain and unadorned as it would have been in Norman times, the White Tower's 2nd-floor chapel is the oldest surviving church in London, dating from 1080.

Crown Jewels
When they're not being worn for affairs of state, Her Majesty's bling is kept here. Among the 23,578 gems, look out for the 530-carat Cullinan diamond at the top of the Royal Sceptre, the largest part of what was (until 1985) the largest diamond ever found.

Bowyer Tower

Martin Tower

Bloody Tower

New Armouries

Traitors' Gate

Wakefield Tower

Salt Tower

Medieval Palace
This part of the Tower complex was commenced around 1220 and was home to England's medieval monarchs. Look for the recreations of the bedchamber of Edward I (1272–1307) in St Thomas' Tower and the throne room on the upper floor of the Wakefield Tower.

Ravens
This stretch of green is where the Tower's famous ravens are kept, fed on raw meat and blood-soaked bird biscuits. According to legend, if the birds were to leave the Tower, the kingdom would fall.

East Wall Walk
Follow the inner ramparts, starting from the 13th-century Salt Tower, passing through the Broad Arrow and Constable Towers, and ending at the Martin Tower, where the Crown Jewels were once stored.

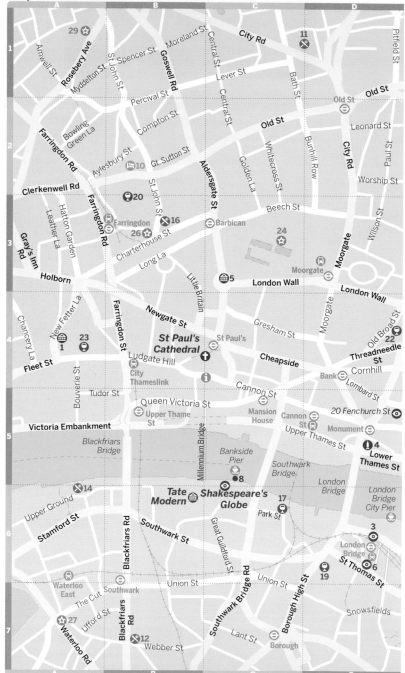

MONUMENT   Monument

(Map p72; www.themonument.info; Monument St; adult/child £3/1; ⏰9.30am-5.30pm; ⊖Monument) Designed by Wren to commemorate the Great Fire, the towering Monument is 60.6m high, the exact distance from its base to the bakery on Pudding Lane where the blaze began. Corkscrew your way up the 311 tight spiral steps (claustrophobes beware) for some of London's best wraparound views and twist down again to collect a certificate commemorating your climb.

DR JOHNSON'S HOUSE   Museum

(Map p72; www.drjohnsonshouse.org; 17 Gough Sq; adult/child £4.50/1.50; ⏰11am-5.30pm Mon-Sat May-Sep, to 5pm Mon-Sat Oct-Apr; ⊖Chancery Lane) The Georgian house where Samuel Johnson and his assistants compiled the first English dictionary (between 1748 and 1759) is full of prints and portraits of friends and intimates, including the good doctor's Jamaican servant to whom he bequeathed this grand residence.

South Bank

Londoners once crossed the river to the area controlled by the licentious bishops of Southwark for all manner of bawdy frolicking frowned upon in the City. It's a much more seemly area now, but the frisson of theatre and entertainment remains.

FREE **TATE MODERN**   Gallery

(Map p72; www.tate.org.uk; Queen's Walk; ⏰10am-6pm Sun-Thu, to 10pm Fri & Sat; ⊖Southwark) One of London's most popular attractions, this outstanding modern and contemporary art gallery is housed in the creatively revamped **Bankside Power Station** south of the Millennium Bridge. A spellbinding synthesis of funky modern art and capacious industrial brick design, the eye-catching result is one of London's must-see sights. Tate Modern has also been extraordinarily successful in bringing challenging work to the masses while a stunning extension is under construction, aiming for a 2016 completion date.

City & Around

The multimedia guides (£3.50) are worthwhile and there are free 45-minute guided tours of the collection's highlights (Level 3 at 11am and midday; Level 5 at 2pm and 3pm). Note the late night opening hours on Friday and Saturday.

SHAKESPEARE'S GLOBE   Historic Building
(Map p72; ☏020-7401 9919; www.shakespeares -globe.org; 21 New Globe Walk; adult/child £11/7; ☉10am-5pm; ☻London Bridge) The original Globe – known as the 'Wooden O' after its circular shape and roofless centre – was erected in 1599. Rival to the Rose Theatre, all was well but did not end well when the Globe burned down within two hours during a performance in 1613 (a stage cannon ignited the thatched roof). Its present-day incarnation is the vision of American actor and director Sam Wana-maker, who sadly died before the opening night in 1997.

Admission includes the **exhibition hall** and **guided tour** of the theatre (departing every 15 to 30 minutes), faithfully reconstructed from oak beams, handmade bricks, lime plaster and thatch.

From April to October plays are performed. As in Elizabethan times, seatless 'groundlings' can watch in all-weather conditions (£5; seats are £15 to £39) for the best views.

LONDON EYE   Viewpoint
(Map p64; ☏0871 781 3000; www.londoneye. com; adult/child £18/9.50; ☉10am-8pm; ☻Waterloo) This 135m-tall, slow-moving Ferris-wheel-like attraction is the tallest in the western hemisphere. Passengers ride in enclosed egg-shaped pods; the wheel takes 30 minutes to rotate completely, offering 25-mile views on clear days. Save money and shorter queues by buying tickets on line, or cough up

an extra £10 to show off your fast-track swagger. Alternatively, visit before 11am or after 3pm to avoid peak density.

THE SHARD   Landmark
(Map p72; www.the-shard.com; 32 London Bridge St; ⊖London Bridge) Puncturing the skies above London, the dramatic splinterlike form of The Shard – the tallest building in Western Europe – has rapidly become an icon of town. Approaching completion at the time of writing, the tower will boast the rooms-with-a-view, five-star Shangri-La Hotel, restaurants and a 360-degree **viewing gallery** in the clouds, accessible via high-speed lifts.

FREE **IMPERIAL WAR MUSEUM**   Museum
(www.iwm.org.uk; Lambeth Rd; ⊙10am-6pm; ⊖Lambeth North) Fronted by a pair of intimidating **15in naval guns** that could lob a 1938lb shell over 16 miles, this riveting museum is housed in what was once Bethlehem Royal Hospital, known as Bedlam. There's not just Lawrence of Arabia's 1000cc motorbike here, but a **German V-2 rocket**, a **Sherman tank**, a lifelike replica of **Little Boy** (the atom bomb dropped on Hiroshima), a **P-51 Mustang**, a **Focke-Wulf Fw 190** and other classic fighter planes dangling from the ceiling plus a re-created **WWI trench** and WWII bomb shelter as well as a **Holocaust exhibition**.

HMS BELFAST   Ship
(Map p72; http://hmsbelfast.iwm.org.uk; Queen's Walk; adult/child £13/free; ⊙10am-5pm; ⊖London Bridge) White ensign flapping on the Thames breeze, HMS *Belfast* is a magnet for naval-gazing kids. This large, light cruiser served in WWII, helping sink the German battleship *Scharnhorst* and shelling the Normandy coast on D-Day. Explore the nine decks and see the engine room, gun decks, galley, chapel, punishment cells, canteen and dental surgery.

LONDON DUNGEON   Offbeat Sight
(Map p72; ☎020-7403 7221; www.thedungeons.com; 28-34 Tooley St; adult/child £20/15; ⊙10.30am-5pm, extended hours during holidays; ⊖London Bridge) Older kids love the London Dungeon, as the terrifying queues during school holidays and weekends attest. It's all spooky music, macabre hangman's drop-rides, fake blood and actors dressed up as torturers and gory criminals (including Jack the Ripper and Sweeney Todd).

SEA LIFE   Aquarium
(Map p64; ☎0871 663 1678; www.sealife.co.uk/london; County Hall; adult/child £18/13; ⊙10am-6pm; ⊖Waterloo) Within imposing **County Hall**, this is one of the largest aquariums in Europe, with all sorts of aquatic (many endangered) creatures from the briny deep grouped into different zones (coral cave, rainforest, River Thames), culminating with the shark walkway. Check the website for shark-feeding times and book online for a 10% discount.

Pimlico

The origins of its name highly obscure, Pimlico is a grand part of London, bordered by the Thames but lacking a strong sense of neighbourhood, becoming prettier the further you stray from Victoria station.

Tate-a-Tate

Whisking art lovers between London's Tate galleries, the colourful **Tate Boat** (Map p72; www.thamesclippers.com) stops en route at the London Eye. Services from Bankside Pier run from 9.57am to 4.44pm daily at 40-minute intervals (10.20am to 4.27pm from Millbank Pier). One-way tickets are £5.50 (children £2.80), with discounts available for Travelcard holders.

The River Thames

A Floating Tour

London's history has always been determined by the Thames. The city was founded as a Roman port nearly 2000 years ago and over the centuries since then many of the capital's landmarks have lined the river's banks. A boat trip is a great way to experience the attractions.

There are piers dotted along both banks at regular intervals where you can hop on and hop off the regular services to visit places of

interest. The best place to board is Westminster Pier, from where boats head downstream, taking you from the City of Westminster, the seat of government, to the original City of London, now the financial district and dominated by a growing band of skyscrapers. Across the river, the once shabby and neglected South Bank now bristles with as many top attractions as its northern counterpart.

In our illustration we've concentrated on the top highlights you'll enjoy at a fish's-eye view

St Paul's Cathedral

Though there's been a church here since AD 604, the current building rose from the ashes of the 1666 Great Fire and is architect Christopher Wren's masterpiece. Famous for surviving the Blitz intact and for the wedding of Charles and Diana, it's looking as good as new after a major clean-up for its 300th anniversary.

Blackfriars

Somerset House

This grand neoclassical palace was once one of many aristocratic houses lining the Thames. The huge arches at river level gave direct access to the Thames until the Embankment was built in the 1860s.

3 Temple

Blackfriars Pier

Blackfriars Bridge

Charing Cross

Savoy Pier

Waterloo Bridge

Victoria Embankment Gardens

National Theatre

Embankment

OXO Tower

Southbank Centre

London Eye

Built in 2000 and originally temporary, the Eye instantly became a much-loved landmark. The 30-minute spin takes you 135m above the city from where the views are unsurprisingly amazing.

2

Waterloo Millennium Pier

Westminster Pier

Houses of Parliament

Rebuilt in neo-Gothic style after the old palace burned down in 1834, the most famous part of the British parliament is the clocktower. Generally known as Big Ben, it's named after Benjamin Hall who oversaw its construction.

Westminster

1

Westminster Bridge

as you sail along. These are, from west to east, the Houses of **Parliament** ❶, the **London Eye** ❷, **Somerset House** ❸, **St Paul's Cathedral** ❹, **Tate Modern** ❺, **Shakespeare's Globe** ❻, the **Tower of London** ❼ and **Tower Bridge** ❽.

Apart from covering this central section of the river, boats can also be taken upstream as far as Kew Gardens and Hampton Court Palace, and downstream to Greenwich and the Thames Barrier.

BOAT HOPPING

Thames Clippers hop-on/hop-off services are aimed at commuters but are equally useful for visitors, operating every 15 minutes on a loop from piers at Embankment, Waterloo, Blackfriars, Bankside, London Bridge and the Tower. Other services also go from Westminster. Oyster cardholders get a discount off the boat ticket price.

The Gherkin

Tower of London
It's not the tallest building in London anymore, but with the Crown Jewels and execution site, the 900-year-old Tower still overshadows the city's other attractions. From the river you can clearly see Traitors' Gate through which enemies of the crown entered the prison.

Cannon St

Monument

Millennium Bridge

Southwark Bridge

Bankside Pier

London Bridge

Southwark Cathedral

London Bridge Pier

HMS Belfast

Tower Pier

London Bridge

Tate Modern
Directly across the river from St Paul's, this cathedral of modern art is the biggest in the world. Built as a power station in the late 1940s, its industrial architecture is as popular with visitors as the paintings on the walls.

DOUG McKINLAY / GETTY IMAGES ©

Shakespeare's Globe
The reconstructed Globe stands on the river a few hundred metres from where the original stood (and burnt down in 1613 during a performance). The life's work of American actor Sam Wanamaker, the theatre runs a hugely popular season from April to October each year.

DOUG McKINLAY / GETTY IMAGES ©

City Hall

Tower Bridge
It might look as old as its namesake neighbour but one of the world's most iconic bridges was only completed in 1894. Not to be confused with London Bridge upstream, this one's famous raising bascules allowed tall ships to dock at the old wharves to the west and are still lifted up to 1000 times a year.

FREE **TATE BRITAIN** Museum
(www.tate.org.uk; Millbank; ⏰10am-5.40pm;
🚇Pimlico) The more elderly and venerable
of the two Tate siblings, this riverside Portland stone edifice celebrates paintings from
1500 to the present, with works from Blake,
Hogarth, Gainsborough, Barbara Hepworth,
Whistler, Constable and Turner – in particular – whose light-infused visions dominate
the **Clore Gallery**. Free one-hour thematic
tours held at 11am, noon, 2pm and 3pm
from Monday to Friday (noon and 3pm on
Saturday and Sunday) are eye-opening
but don't overlook **Late at Tate** night (first
Friday of the month), when the gallery stays
open till 10pm.

Chelsea & Kensington

Known as the royal borough, Chelsea
and Kensington lay claim to the highest
income earners in the UK (shops and
restaurants will presume you are among
them).

FREE **VICTORIA &
ALBERT MUSEUM** Museum
(V&A; Map p80; www.vam.ac.uk; Cromwell Rd;
⏰10am-5.45pm Sat-Thu, to 10pm Fri; 🚇South
Kensington) This outstanding museum
boasts an unparalleled collection specialising in decorative art and design with
some 4.5 million objects from Britain and
around the globe. Part of Albert's legacy
to Londoners in the wake of the Great
Exhibition of 1851, the museum is a bit
like the nation's attic, spread generously
through nearly 150 galleries. Highlights
of the world's greatest collection of
decorative arts include the **Ardabil Carpet** (Room 42, Level 1), the sumptuous
China Collection and **Japan Gallery**
(Rooms 44 and 47e, Level 1), **Tipu's Tiger**
(Room 41, Level 1), the astonishing **Cast
Courts** (Room 46a, Level 1), the **Raphael
Cartoons** (Room 48a, Level 1), the hefty
Great Bed of Ware (Room 57, Level 2)
and the stunning **Jewellery Gallery**
(Rooms 91–93, Level 3). You'll need to
plan as the museum is epic, but it's open

late on Friday evenings, when there are smaller crowds.

FREE NATURAL HISTORY MUSEUM   Museum

(Map p80; www.nhm.ac.uk; Cromwell Rd; ⏰10am-5.50pm; ⊖South Kensington) A sure-fire hit with kids of all ages, this splendid museum is crammed with fascinating discoveries, starting with the giant diplodocus skeleton that greets you in the main hall. In the dinosaur gallery, the fleshless fossils are brought to robotic life with the roaring 4m-high animatronic Tyrannosaurus rex. The other galleries are equally impressive.

FREE SCIENCE MUSEUM   Museum

(Map p80; www.sciencemuseum.org.uk; Exhibition Rd; ⏰10am-6pm; ⊖South Kensington) With seven floors of interactive and educational exhibits, this scientifically spellbinding museum will mesmerise even the most precocious of young

Einsteins. Some children head straight for voice warpers, lava lamps, boomerangs, bouncy globes and alien babies in the ground-floor shop, and stay put. Highlights include the **Energy Hall** on the ground floor, the riveting **Flight Gallery** on the 3rd floor and the **flight simulator**. There's also a 450-seat **Imax cinema**.

HYDE PARK   Park

(Map p80; ⏰5.30am-midnight; ⊖Marble Arch, Hyde Park Corner or Queensway) At 145 hectares, Hyde Park is central London's largest open space. The 1851 Great Exhibition was held here, and during WWII the park became an enormous potato field. These days, it serves as an occasional concert venue and a full-time green space for fun and frolics. There's boating on the **Serpentine** for the energetic, while **Speakers' Corner** (Map p80; Park Lane; ⊖Marble Arch) is for oratorical acrobats on Sundays, maintaining a tradition begun in 1872 as a response to rioting.

Hyde Park & Kensington

KENSINGTON PALACE   Palace
(Map p80; www.hrp.org.uk/kensingtonpalace; Kensington Gardens; adult/child £14.50/free; ⊙10am-6pm; ⊖High St Kensington) Kensington Palace (1605) became the favourite royal residence under the joint reign of William and Mary and remained so until the death of George II (in 1762 George III bought Buckingham Palace for his wife, Charlotte). In popular imagination it's most associated with three intriguing princesses: Victoria (who was born here in 1819 and lived here with her domineering mother until her accession to the throne), Margaret (sister of the current queen, who lived here until her 2002 death) and, of course, Diana. The building underwent magnificent restoration work totalling £12 million and reopened in early 2012.

KENSINGTON GARDENS   Gardens
(Map p80; ⊙dawn-dusk; ⊖High St Kensington) Blending in with Hyde Park, these royal gardens are part of Kensington Palace and hence popularly associated with Princess Diana. Diana devotees can visit the **Diana, Princess of Wales Memorial Fountain** (Map p80; ⊖Knightsbridge).

The gardens also house the **Serpentine Gallery** (Map p80; www.serpentinegallery.org; admission free; ⊙10am-6pm; ⊖Lancaster Gate or Knightsbridge), one of London's edgiest contemporary art spaces.

KING'S ROAD   Street
(Map p80; ⊖Sloane Sq) Named after King Charles II who would return to Hampton Court Palace along a farmer's track here after amorous interludes with Nell Gwyn, this street was almost synonymous with

Hyde Park & Kensington

London fashion during the '60s and '70s. Near the Sloane Sq end, the **Saatchi Gallery** (Map p80; www.saatchi-gallery.co.uk; Duke of York's HQ, King's Rd; ◷10am-6pm; ◉Sloane Sq) serves up stimulating temporary exhibitions of contemporary art.

Marylebone

Not as exclusive as its southern neighbour Mayfair, hip Marylebone has one of London's most pleasant high streets and the famous, if rather disappointing, Baker St, strongly associated with Victorian-era sleuth Sherlock Holmes (there's a museum and gift shop at his fictional address, 221B).

REGENT'S PARK   Park
(Map p83; ◉Regent's Park) A former royal hunting ground, Regent's Park was designed by John Nash early in the 19th century, although what was actually laid out is only a fraction of the celebrated architect's grand plan. Nevertheless,

it's one of London's most lovely open spaces – at once serene and lively, cosmopolitan and local – with football pitches, tennis courts, a boating lake, London Zoo (below), and Regent's Canal along its northern side.

LONDON ZOO   Zoo
(Map p83; www.londonzoo.co.uk; Outer Circle, Regent's Park; adult/child £18/14; ◷10am-5.30pm Mar-Oct, to 4pm Nov-Feb; ◉Camden Town) These famous zoological gardens have come a long way since being established in 1828, with massive investment making conservation, education and breeding the name of the game. Highlights include **Penguin Beach**, **Gorilla Kingdom**, **Animal Adventure** (the new childrens' zoo) and **Butterfly Paradise**. Feeding sessions or talks take place during the day.

MADAME TUSSAUDS   Museum

(Map p83; ☎0870 400 3000; www.madame-tus
sauds.co.uk; Marylebone Rd; adult/child £26/22;
⏰9.30am-5.30pm; ⊖Baker St) Tickets may
cost a (wax) arm and a (wax) leg and the
crowds can be as awesome as the exhibits, but the opportunity to pose beside
Posh and Becks has clear-cut kudos.
Most of the life-size wax figures – such as
Leonardo DiCaprio – are fantastically lifelike and as close to the real thing as most
of us will get.

Tickets are cheaper when ordered
online; combined tickets with London Eye
and London Dungeon are also available
(adult/child £65/48).

Bloomsbury & St Pancras

With the University of London and British
Museum within its genteel environs, it's
little wonder that Bloomsbury has attracted a lot of very clever, bookish people
over the years.

The conversion of spectacular St
Pancras station into the Eurostar terminal
and a ritzy apartment complex is reviving
the area's fortunes.

Emirates Air Line Cable Car

Destined to become a sight in its
own right and capable of ferrying
2400 people per hour across the
Thames in either direction, the new
Emirates Air Line Cable Car (adult/
child single £4.30/2.20, return £8.60/4.40;
⏰7am-9pm Mon-Fri, from 8am Sat, from
9am Sun Apr-Sep, shorter hours rest of the
year) links together the Greenwich
Peninsula and the Royal Docks in
a five- to 10-minute journey. Oyster
card and Travelcard holders get a
discount for journeys. Arriving at
Royal Docks, you can hop on the
Docklands Light Railway (DLR) at
Royal Victoria DLR station, while
in Greenwich, the underground
interchange is with North
Greenwich Station.

FREE BRITISH MUSEUM   Museum

(Map p83; ☎020-7323 8000; www.british
museum.org; Great Russell St; ⏰10am-5.30pm
Sat-Wed, to 8.30pm Thu & Fri; ⊖Russell Sq)
The country's largest museum and one
of the oldest and finest in the world, this
famous museum boasts vast Egyptian,
Etruscan, Greek, Roman, European and
Middle Eastern galleries, among many
others.

Among the must-sees are the **Rosetta
Stone**, the key to deciphering Egyptian
hieroglyphics, discovered in 1799; the
controversial **Parthenon Sculptures**,
stripped from the walls of the Parthenon
in Athens by Lord Elgin (the British
ambassador to the Ottoman Empire),
and which Greece wants returned; the
stunning **Oxus Treasure** of 7th- to 4th-
century-BC Persian gold; and the Anglo-
Saxon **Sutton Hoo** burial relics.

The **Great Court** was restored and
augmented by Norman Foster in 2000
and now has a spectacular glass-and-
steel roof, making it one of the most
impressive architectural spaces in the
capital. In the centre is the **Reading
Room**, with its stunning blue-and-gold
domed ceiling, where Karl Marx wrote the
Manifesto of the Communist Party.

You'll need multiple visits to savour
even the highlights here; happily there
are 15 half-hour free 'Eye Opener' tours
between 11am and 3.45pm daily, focusing
on different parts of the collection. Other
tours include the 90-minute highlights
tour at 10.30am, 1pm and 3pm daily
(adult/child £8/5), and audioguides are
available (£4.50).

BRITISH LIBRARY   Library

(Map p83; www.bl.uk; 96 Euston Rd; ⏰9.30am-
6pm Mon & Wed-Fri, to 8pm Tue, to 5pm Sat,
11am-5pm Sun; ⊖King's Cross St Pancras) For
visitors, the real highlight is a visit to
the **Sir John Ritblat Gallery** where the
most precious manuscripts, spanning
almost three millennia, are held. Here
you'll find the *Codex Sinaiticus* (the first
complete text of the New Testament), a
Gutenberg Bible (1455), the stunningly
illustrated Jain sacred texts, Leonardo
da Vinci's notebooks, a copy of the

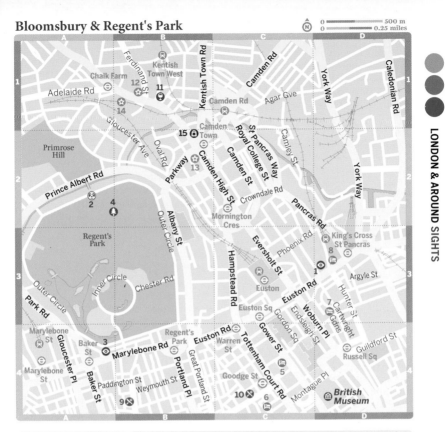

Bloomsbury & Regent's Park

Magna Carta (1215), explorer Captain Scott's final diary, Shakespeare's First Folio (1623) and the lyrics to 'A Hard Day's Night' (scribbled on the back of Julian Lennon's birthday card) plus original scores by Handel, Mozart and Beethoven.

Pound Savers

The **London Pass** (www.londonpass. com; per 1/2/3/6 days £46/61/66/89) is a smart card that gains you fast-track entry to 55 different attractions, including pricier ones such as the Tower of London and St Paul's Cathedral. Passes can be booked online and collected from the **London Pass Redemption Desk** (11a Charing Cross Rd; ⊖Leicester Sq) (check online for opening hours) opposite the Garrick Theatre.

If you're a royalty buff, taking out an annual membership to the **Historic Royal Palaces** (www.hrp.org. uk; individual/joint membership £43/65) allows you to jump the queues and visit the Tower of London, Kensington Palace, Banqueting House, Kew Palace and Hampton Court Palace as often as you like.

**CHARLES DICKENS
MUSEUM**   Museum
(www.dickensmuseum.com; 48 Doughty St; adult/ child £6/3; ⏱10am-5pm Mon-Sat, 11am-5pm Sun; ⊖Russell Sq) The handsome four-storey house narrowly escaped demolition and opened as a museum in 1925. Shut for most of 2012 for much-needed refurbishment, Dickens' sole surviving London residence is where his work really flourished – *The Pickwick Papers*, *Nicholas Nickleby* and *Oliver Twist* were all written here.

The East End & Docklands

**⊘QUEEN ELIZABETH
OLYMPIC PARK**   Park
(www.london2012.com/olympic-park; ⊖Stratford) From 2008, a huge, once-contaminated and largely neglected swath of industrial East London was ambitiously regenerated and transformed into London's Olympic Park for the 2012 Games. Complementing its iconic sporting architecture, the Olympic Park was thoughtfully designed with a diverse mix of wetland, woodland, meadow and other wildlife habitats as an environmentally fertile legacy for the future. The signature buildings are the sustainably built **Olympic Stadium**, the uplifting **Aquatics Centre** and the cutting-edge **Velodrome**. The twisted, abstract tangle of metal overlooking everything is the **ArcelorMittal Orbit**, aka the 'Hubble Bubble Pipe', a 115m-high observation tower which opened during the games.

Panoramic views of the Olympic Park can also be had from the **View Tube** (www. theviewtube.co.uk; The Greenway; ⏱9am-5pm; ⓇDLR Pudding Mill Lane) on the Greenway, next to the park.

Greenwich

Greenwich (*gren*-itch) straddles the hemispheres and the ages, retaining its own sense of identity based on historic associations with the sea and science and possessing an extraordinary cluster of buildings that have earned 'Maritime Greenwich' its place on Unesco's World Heritage list.

Greenwich is easily reached on the Docklands Light Railway (DLR) or via train from London Bridge. **Thames River Services** (www.thamesriverservices. co.uk; single/return £9.50/12.50) has boats departing from Westminster Pier (single/return £10/13, one hour, every 40 minutes), or alternatively take the cheaper Thames Clippers ferry.

**FREE OLD ROYAL
NAVAL COLLEGE**   Historic Building
(www.oldroyalnavalcollege.org; 2 Cutty Sark Gardens; ⏱10am-5pm; ⓇDLR Cutty Sark) Designed by Wren, the Old Royal Naval College is a magnificent example of monumental classical architecture. Parts are now used by the University of Greenwich and Trinity College of Music, but you can visit the **chapel** and the extraordinary **Painted Hall**, which took artist Sir James Thornhill 19 years to complete.

Yeomen-led tours of the complex leave at 2pm daily, taking in areas not otherwise open to the public (£6, 90 minutes).

FREE NATIONAL MARITIME
MUSEUM   Museum
(☎020-8858 4422; www.nmm.ac.uk; Romney
Rd; ☺10am-5pm; ⓡDLR Cutty Sark) With its
newly opened **Sammy Ofer Wing**, the
National Maritime Museum houses a
splendid collection of nautical paraphernalia recounting Britain's brine-soaked
seafaring history. Exhibits range from
Miss Britain III (the first boat to top
100mph on open water) from 1933, the
19m-long **golden state barge** built in
1732 for Frederick, Prince of Wales, hum-
dingers such as **Cook's journals** and **Nelson's uniform**, complete with bullet hole
and interactive plus educational displays.

ROYAL
OBSERVATORY   Historic Building
(☎020-8858 4422; www.rmg.co.uk; adult/child
£7/2; ☺10am-5pm; ⓡDLR Cutty Sark) Rising
south of Queen's House, idyllic **Greenwich Park** climbs up the hill, affording
stunning views of London from the Royal
Observatory, which Charles II had built in
1675 to help solve the riddle of longitude.

Success was confirmed in 1884 when
Greenwich was designated as the prime
meridian of the world, and Greenwich
Mean Time (GMT) became the universal
measurement of standard time.

Hampstead & Highgate
These quaint and well-heeled villages, perched on hills north of
London, are home to a litany
of celebrities.

HAMPSTEAD
HEATH   Park
(ⓡGospel Oak or Hamp-
stead Heath) With its
320 hectares of rolling
meadows and wild
woodlands, Hamp-
stead Heath is a mil-
lion miles away – well,
approximately four –
from central London. A
walk up **Parliament Hill**
affords one of the most

spectacular views of the city, and on summer days it's a choice spot for picnickers.

Outside Central London
KEW GARDENS   Gardens
(www.kew.org.uk; Kew Rd; adult/child £14/
free, Kew Explorer adult/child £4/1; ☺9.30am-
6.30pm Apr-Aug, earlier closing other months;
ⓡKew Bridge, ☻Kew Gardens) In 1759
botanists began rummaging around the
world for specimens they could plant in
the 3-hectare plot known as the Royal
Botanic Gardens. They never stopped
collecting, and the gardens, which have
bloomed to 120 hectares, provide the
most comprehensive botanical collection
on Earth (including the world's largest collection of orchids). The beautiful
gardens are now recognised as a Unesco
World Heritage Site.

You can easily spend a whole day
wandering around, but if you're pressed
for time, the **Kew Explorer** (adult/child
£4/1) is a hop-on/hop-off road train that
leaves from Victoria Gate and takes in the
gardens' main sights.

Kew Gardens
LATITUDESTOCK/GETTY IMAGES ©

The gardens are easily reached by tube, but you might prefer to take a cruise on a riverboat from the **Westminster Passenger Services Association** (☎020-7930 2062; www.wpsa.co.uk), which runs several daily boats from April to October, departing from Westminster Pier (return adult/child £18/9, 90 minutes).

HAMPTON COURT PALACE
Palace

(www.hrp.org.uk/HamptonCourtPalace; adult/child £14/7; ⏰10am-6pm Apr-Oct, to 4.30pm Nov-Mar; ℝHampton Court) Built by Cardinal Thomas Wolsey in 1514 but coaxed from him by Henry VIII just before Wolsey (as chancellor) fell from favour, Hampton Court Palace is England's largest and grandest Tudor structure.

Take a themed tour led by costumed historians or, if you're in a rush, visit the highlights: **Henry VIII's State Apartments**, including the Great Hall with its spectacular hammer-beamed roof; the **Tudor Kitchens**, staffed by 'servants'; and the **Wolsey Rooms**. You could easily spend a day exploring the palace and its 60 acres of riverside gardens, especially if you get lost in the 300-year-old **maze**.

Hampton Court is 13 miles southwest of central London and is easily reached by train from Waterloo. Alternatively, the riverboats that head from Westminster to Kew continue here (return adult/child £22.50/11.25, three hours).

Tours

One of the best ways to orient yourself when you first arrive in London is with a 24-hour hop-on/hop-off pass for the double-decker bus tours. The buses loop around interconnecting routes throughout the day, providing a commentary as they go, and the price includes a river cruise and three walking tours. Save a few pounds by booking online.

ORIGINAL TOUR
Bus Tours

(www.theoriginaltour.com; adult/child/family £26/13/91; ⏰every 20min 8.30am-5.30pm)

BIG BUS TOURS
Bus Tours

(☎020-7233 9533; www.bigbustours.com; adult/child £26/10)

LONDON WALKS
Walking Tours

(☎020-7624 3978; www.walks.com) Harry Potter tours, ghost walks and the ever popular Jack the Ripper tours.

LONDON MYSTERY WALKS
Walking Tours

(☎07957 388280; www.tourguides.org.uk)

CITY CRUISES
Ferry Tours

(Map p64; ☎020-7740 0400; www.citycruises.com; single/return trips from £8/10.50, day pass £13.50) Ferry service between Westminster, Waterloo, Tower and Greenwich piers.

CAPITAL TAXI TOURS
Taxi Tours

(☎020-8590 3621; www.capitaltaxitours.co.uk; 2hr day tour per taxi £165, by night 2½hr tour per taxi £235) Takes up to five people on a variety of tours with Blue Badge, City of London and City of Westminster registered guides/drivers, cheeky Cockney Cabbie option and foreign-language availability.

🛏 Sleeping

When it comes to finding a place for a good night's kip, London is one of the most expensive places in the world. 'Budget' is pretty much anything below £90 per night for a double; at the top end, how does a £14000-per-night suite on Hyde Park Corner sound? Double rooms ranging between £90 and £180 per night are considered midrange; more expensive options fall into the top-end category.

West End

Like in Monopoly, land on a Mayfair hotel and you may have to sell your house, or at least remortgage.

HAYMARKET HOTEL
Hotel £££

(Map p64; ☎020-7470 4000; www.haymarkethotel.com; 1 Suffolk Pl; r £318-408, ste from £492; ❄🛰🛜; ⊖Piccadilly Circus) An exquisite place to hang your well-trimmed hat, the Tim and Kit Kemp–designed Haymarket is a superstylish and eye-catching treat, with a knockout swimming pool bathed in serene mood lighting.

HAZLITT'S Historic Hotel ££££
(Map p64; ☎020-7434 1771; www.hazlittshotel. com; 6 Frith St; s £206, d/ste from £259/646; ❄☏; ⊖Tottenham Court Rd) Envelop yourself in Georgian finery at this lovely 1718 house and journey back to the days of four-poster beds, claw-foot baths and panelled walls.

**DEAN STREET
TOWNHOUSE** Boutique Hotel ££££
(Map p64; ☎020-7434 1775; www.deanstreet townhouse.com; 69-71 Dean St; r £160-310; ❄☏; ⊖Tottenham Court Rd) This Soho gem of a 39-bedroom boutique hotel enjoys a delightful boudoir atmosphere with choice rooms – everything faultlessly in its place – from 'tiny' options upwards.

SAVOY Hotel ££££
(Map p64; ☎020-7836 4343; Strand; ☏☒; ⊖Charing Cross) A night surrounded by the Edwardian and art deco grandeur of the iconic Savoy is never a casual choice, considering the sudden stupefying hole in your bank balance, but as one of life's memorable treats, you can't go wrong.

South Bank

Immediately south of the river is a great spot for reaching the central sights, while gauging the personality of London south of the river.

KENNINGTON B&B B&B ££
(☎020-7735 7669; www.kenningtonbandb. com; 103 Kennington Park Rd; d £120-150; ☏; ⊖Kennington) With gorgeous bed linen and well-preserved Georgian features, this lovely B&B is very tasteful in virtually every regard, from the shining, tiled shower rooms and Georgian shutters to the fireplaces and cast-iron radiators.

CAPTAIN BLIGH GUESTHOUSE B&B ££
(☎020-7928 2735; www.captainblighhouse. co.uk; 100 Lambeth Rd; s £63-75, d £85-90; ⊖Lambeth North) With helpful but non-intrusive owners, this late-18th-century property opposite the Imperial War

> # Booking Services
>
> **At Home in London** (☎020-8748 1943; www.athomeinlondon.co.uk) For B&Bs.
>
> **British Hotel Reservation Centre** (☎020-7592 3055; www.bhrconline.com) Hotels.
>
> **London Homestead Services** (☎020-7286 5115; www.lhslondon.com) B&Bs.
>
> **LondonTown** (☎020-7437 4370; www. londontown.com) Hotel and B&Bs.
>
> **Uptown Reservations** (☎020-7937 2001; www.uptownres.co.uk) Upmarket B&Bs.
>
> **Visit London** (☎per min 10p 0871 222 3118; www.visitlondonoffers.com) Hotels.

Museum has shipshape and quiet rooms with kitchen. The downside is there's a minimum four-night-stay policy, no credit cards, one night's nonrefundable deposit and you'll need to book way ahead. No lift.

Pimlico & Belgravia

LIME TREE HOTEL B&B ££
(Map p80; ☎020-7730 8191; www.limetreehotel. co.uk; 135-137 Ebury St; s £99, d £150-175; @☏; ⊖Victoria) A smartly renovated Georgian town-house hotel with a beautiful back garden to catch the late afternoon rays. The three 'C's: cosy, congenial and clean.

LUNA SIMONE HOTEL B&B ££
(☎020-7834 5897; www.lunasimonehotel. com; 47-49 Belgrave Rd; s £70-75, d £95-120; @; ⊖Pimlico) Rooms are quite compact but clean and calming at this central, welcoming hotel; the ones at the back are quieter. Belgrave Rd follows on from Eccleston Bridge, directly behind Victoria Station.

B+B BELGRAVIA B&B ££
(Map p80; ☎020-7259 8570; www.bb-belgravia. com; 64-66 Ebury St; d £99, studio £99-135, apt from £225; @☏; ⊖Victoria) This lovely

place marries contemporary chic with Georgian elegance; rooms are neat and although not very spacious, fine studio rooms with compact kitchens are along the road at No 82.

Knightsbridge

Named after a bridge over the River Westbourne, Knightsbridge is where you'll find some of London's best-known department stores and some top hotels.

LEVIN HOTEL   Hotel £££
(Map p80; ☏020-7589 6286; www.thelevin hotel.co.uk; 28 Basil St; r from £305; ✳🖥; ⊖Knightsbridge) As close as you can get to sleeping in Harrods, the 12-room Levin knows its market. Despite the baby-blue colour scheme, there's a subtle femininity to the decor, although it's far too elegant to be flouncy.

KNIGHTSBRIDGE HOTEL   Hotel £££
(Map p80; ☏020-7584 6300; www.knights bridgehotel.com; 10 Beaufort Gardens; s/d from £235/282; P✳@🖥; ⊖Knightsbridge) Another Firmdale property, the six-floor Knightsbridge is on a quiet, tree-lined cul-de-sac very close to Harrods.

Chelsea & Kensington

Well-turned-out Chelsea and Kensington offer easy access to the museums, natty shopping choices and some of London's best-looking streets.

NUMBER SIXTEEN   Hotel £££
(Map p80; ☏020-7589 5232; www.numbersix teenhotel.co.uk; 16 Sumner Pl; s from £168, d £222-360; ✳@🖥; ⊖South Kensington) It's four properties in one delightful whole and a stunning place to stay, with 42 individually designed rooms, a cosy drawing room, a fully stocked library and simply idyllic back garden.

GORE   Hotel £££
(Map p80; ☏020-7584 6601; www.gorehotel. com; 190 Queen's Gate; r from £205; @🖥; ⊖Gloucester Rd) A short stroll from the Royal Albert Hall, the Gore serves up British grandiosity (antiques, carved four-posters, polished mahogany, a secret bathroom in the Tudor room) in 50 individually furnished, magnificent rooms.

ASTER HOUSE   B&B ££
(Map p80; ☏020-7581 5888; www.asterhouse. com; 3 Sumner Pl; s £144. d £216-300; ✳@; ⊖South Kensington) The Singaporean owners certainly know how to keep things clean and shipshape at this charming and well-priced house hotel with a delightful plant-filled Orangerie and ducks in the garden.

Notting Hill, Bayswater & Paddington

Don't be fooled by Julia Roberts and Hugh Grant's shenanigans, Notting Hill and the areas immediately north of Hyde Park are as shabby as they are chic.

Scruffy Paddington has lots of cheap hotels, with a major strip of unremarkable ones along Sussex Gardens that may be worth checking if you're short on options.

VANCOUVER STUDIOS   Apartment ££
(Map p80; ☏020-7243 1270; www.vancouver studios.co.uk; 30 Prince's Sq; apt £89-170; @🖥; ⊖Bayswater) It's the addition of kitchenettes and a self-service laundry that differentiate these smart, reasonably priced studios and three-bedroom apartment (sleeping from one to six people) from a regular Victorian town-house hotel. In spring the garden is filled with colour and fragrance.

NEW LINDEN HOTEL   Boutique Hotel ££
(Map p80; ☏020-7221 4321; www.newlinden. co.uk; Herford Rd, near Leinster Sq; s/d from £79/105; 🖥; ⊖Bayswater) Cramming in a fair amount of style for little whack, this terrace house hotel exudes a modern and cool feel. The quiet location, helpful staff and monsoon shower heads in the deluxe rooms make this an excellent proposition.

Fitzrovia

SANDERSON   Hotel £££
(☏020-7300 1400; www.sandersonlondon.com; 50 Berners St; r from £253; @🖥; ⊖Goodge St) Liberace meets Philippe Starck in an

18th-century French bordello – and that's just the reception.

CHARLOTTE STREET HOTEL Hotel £££
(Map p83; ☎ 020-7806 2000; www.charlotte streethotel.com; 15-17 Charlotte St; d £300, ste from £492; ✳ ☎; ❸ Goodge St) Another of the Firmdale clan, this one's a favourite with media types, with a small gym and a screening room.

Bloomsbury & St Pancras

One step from the West End and crammed with Georgian town-house conversions, these are more affordable neighbourhoods.

ST PANCRAS RENAISSANCE LONDON HOTEL Luxury Hotel £££
(Map p83; ☎ 020-7841 3540; www.marriott. co.uk; Euston Rd; d from £295; ✳ ☎ ⚟; ❸ King's Cross St Pancras) It's an alluring (but expensive) proposition staying in this iconic George Gilbert Scott–designed Gothic masterpiece. Rooms are stylishly modern, dining in the Marcus Wareing–run restaurant is excellent and you can toast the former booking-office architecture from the 29m-long bar.

ARRAN HOUSE HOTEL B&B ££
(Map p83; ☎ 020-7636 2186; www.arran hotel-london.com; 77-79 Gower St; s/d/ tr/q £70/110/128/132, without bathroom £60/80/105/111; @ ☎; ❸ Goodge St) Period features such as cornicing and fireplaces, gorgeous gardens out back for a summer drink and a cosy lounge with two computers pushes this welcoming hotel from the average to the appealing. Squashed en suites or shared bathrooms are the trade-off for these reasonable rates.

HARLINGFORD HOTEL B&B ££
(Map p83; ☎ 020-7387 1551; www.harlingford hotel.com; 61-63 Cartwright Gardens; s/d/ tr £86/115/130; ☎; ❸ Russell Sq) This family-run Georgian 43-room hotel sports refreshing, upbeat decor: bright-green mosaic-tiled bathrooms (with trendy sinks), fuchsia bedspreads and colourful paintings in a neighbourhood of stiff competition. It's all stairs and no lift; request a 1st-floor room.

Hampton Court Palace (p86)

Clerkenwell & Farringdon

 ZETTER HOTEL & TOWNHOUSE Boutique Hotel £££ (Map p72; 020-7324 4444; www.thezetter. com; 86-88 Clerkenwell Rd; d from £222, studio £294-438; ❄ 🛜; Farringdon) Guided by a sustainable ethos (water is supplied by its own bore hole), the 59-room Zetter is lovely, from the fine furnishings to the cutting-edge facilities. The rooftop studios with private patios and long views are the icing on this cake.

Hoxton, Shoreditch & Spitalfields

HOXTON HOTEL Hotel ££ (Map p72; 020-7550 1000; www.hoxtonhotels. com; 81 Great Eastern St; d & tw £59-199; @ 🛜; Old St) Book three months ahead (sign up on the website) and you can, if fortunate, nab a room for £1; you'll also need to book early for £49 to £69 deals. The reasonably sized rooms all have comfy beds, quality linen and TVs that double as computers.

Airports

YOTEL Hotel £ (020-7100 1100; www.yotel.com; s/d £69/85, or per 4hr £29/45 then per additional hour £8; @ 🛜) Gatwick (South Terminal); Heathrow (Terminal 4) The best news for early-morning flyers since coffee-vending machines, Yotel's smart 'cabins' offer pint-sized luxury: comfy beds, soft lights, internet-connected TVs, monsoon showers and fluffy towels.

🍴 Eating

Dining out in London has become so fashionable that you can hardly open a menu without banging into some celebrity chef or other. The range and quality of eating options has increased exponentially over the last few decades.

Westminster & St James's

INN THE PARK British ££ (Map p64; 0207-451 9999; www.innthepark. com; St James's Park; mains £9.50-18.50; 8am-6pm, to 11pm in spring & summer; Charing Cross or St James's Park) Enjoying a fine location within one of London's best-looking and grandest parks, this Oliver Peyton wooden restaurant rewards diners with fine cuisine and delicious views (especially from the terrace). Book ahead for dinner.

West End

Mayfair, Soho and Covent Garden are the gastronomic heart of London, with a blinding choice of restaurants and cuisines at budgets to suit booze hounds, theatre-goers or determined grazers.

TAMARIND Indian ££ (Map p80; 020-7629 3561; www.tamarindrestau rant.com; 20 Queen St; mains £6.95-28; lunch Sun-Fri,

Hoxton street scene

dinner daily; ⊖Green Park) A mix of spicy Moghul classics and new creations keep this award-winning Michelin-starred Indian basement restaurant a popular and refreshingly authentic choice.

NATIONAL DINING ROOMS   British ££
(Map p64; ☎020-7747 2525; www.peytonand byrne.co.uk; Sainsbury Wing, National Gallery; mains £14.50-19.50; ☺10am-5pm Sat-Thu, to 8.30pm Fri; ⊖Charing Cross) It's fitting that this acclaimed restaurant should celebrate British food, being in the National Gallery and overlooking Trafalgar Sq.

GREAT QUEEN STREET   British ££
(Map p64; ☎020-7242 0622; 32 Great Queen St; mains £9-19; ☺lunch daily, dinner Mon-Sat; ⊖Holborn) Her claret-coloured walls and mismatched wooden chair, convey cosiness and tie-loosening informality, but the daily-changing, seasonal menu is still the very best of British, and booking is a must.

VEERASWAMY   Indian ££
(Map p64; ☎020-7734 1401; www.veeraswamy. com; 99 Regent St; mains £15-30, pre- & post-theatre 2/3 courses £18/21; ⊖Piccadilly Circus) Since 1926 Veeraswamy has occupied this prime 1st-floor location, with windows overlooking Regent St – making it Britain's longest-running Indian restaurant. Enter via Swallow St.

MOOLI'S   Indian £
(Map p64; www.moolis.com; 50 Frith St; roti wrap £5; ☺noon-10pm Mon-Wed, to 11.30pm Thu-Sat, closed Sun; ⊖Tottenham Court Rd) This snacktastic Soho 'Indian street food' eatery will have you drooling over the homemade rotis packed with scrumptious fillings (meat, paneer, chickpeas), graded through the chilli spectrum.

WILD HONEY   Modern European ££
(Map p80; ☎020-7758 9160; www.wildhoney restaurant.co.uk; 12 St George St; mains £15-24; ⊖Oxford Circus) If you fancy a relatively affordable meal within the oak-panelled ambience of a top Mayfair restaurant, Wild Honey offers excellent lunch and pretheatre set menus (respectively, £21.95 and £22.95 for three courses).

L'ATELIER DE JOËL ROBUCHON   French ££
(Map p64; ☎020-7010 8600; www.joel-robu chon.com; 13 West St; mains £16-34; ⊖Leicester Sq) Superchef Robuchon has 25 Michelin stars to his name – and two of them are derived from this, his London flagship. Degustation (£125) and set lunch and pretheatre menus (two/three courses £22/27) are available.

ARBUTUS   Modern European ££
(Map p64; ☎020-7734 4545; www.arbutus restaurant.co.uk; 63-64 Frith St; mains £14-20; ⊖Tottenham Court Rd) Focusing on seasonal produce, inventive dishes and value-for-money set meals, Anthony Demetre's Michelin-starred brainchild just keeps getting better.

South Bank

Popular restaurants make the most of the iconic riverside views but scouting around turns up gems all over the place.

LAUGHING GRAVY   British ££
(Map p72; ☎020-7998 1707; www.thelaughing gravy.co.uk; 154 Blackfriars Rd; mains £8.50-17.50; ☺11am-late Mon-Fri, 5.30pm-late Sat, noon-6pm Sun; ⊖Southwark) Recently steered in a lucrative fresh direction by new owners, this restaurant is a Southwark gem, with a sure-fire menu combining locally sourced food and culinary talent, plus splendid roasts on Sunday and attentive service all round.

OXO TOWER RESTAURANT & BRASSERIE   Fusion £££
(Map p72; ☎020-7803 3888; www.harveynichols. com/restaurants/oxo-tower-london; Barge House St; mains £18-26; ☺lunch & dinner; ⊖Waterloo) The extravagant views are the big drawcard, so skip the restaurant and head for the slightly less extravagantly priced brasserie, or if you're not hungry, the bar. Set-price menus (two/three courses £22.50/26.50) are offered at lunchtime, before 6.15pm and after 10pm.

MAGDALEN   Modern British ££
(Map p72; ☎020-7403 1342; www.magdalen restaurant.co.uk; 152 Tooley St; mains £14-18, lunch 2/3 courses £16/19; ☺lunch Mon-Fri,

dinner Mon-Sat; ⊖London Bridge) This lovely Tooley St restaurant hits the spot for anyone determined to savour some of London's best Modern British fare.

Knightsbridge

DINNER BY HESTON BLUMENTHAL
Modern British £££

(Map p80; ☎0207-201 3833; www.dinnerby heston.com; Mandarin Oriental Hyde Park, 66 Knightsbridge; set lunch £28, mains £32-72; ⊖Knightsbridge) The sumptuously presented Dinner is a gastronomic tour de force, ushering diners on a tour of British culinary history (with inventive modern inflections).

MARCUS WAREING AT THE BERKELEY
French £££

(Map p80; ☎020-7235 1200; www.marcus-wareing.com; Berkeley Hotel, Wilton Pl; 3-course lunch/dinner £38/80; ⊖Knightsbridge) Wareing runs this one-time Gordon Ramsay restaurant under his own name, and its reputation for exquisite food and exemplary service has only been enhanced.

Chelsea & Kensington

These highbrow neighbourhoods harbour some of London's very best (and priciest) restaurants.

TOM'S KITCHEN
Modern European ££

(Map p80; ☎020-7349 0202; www.tomskitchen.co.uk; 27 Cale St; breakfast £4-15, mains £13.90-30; ☉breakfast Mon-Fri, lunch & dinner daily; ⊖South Kensington) Celebrity chef Tom Aikens' restaurant keeps the magic flowing through the day, with award-winning breakfasts and pancakes drawing acclaim and crowds to its informal, but engaging, dining setting.

ORSINI
Italian ££

(Map p80; www.orsiniristorante.com; 8a Thurloe Pl; snacks £2-6, mains £9-16; ☉8am-10pm; ⊖South Kensington) Marinated in authentic Italian charm, this tiny family-run eatery serves excellent espresso and deliciously fresh baguettes stuffed with Parma ham and mozzarella.

Left: Oxo Tower Restaurant & Brasserie (p91); Below: St John (p94)

(LEFT) CATH HARRIES/ALAMY ©; (BELOW) BRUNO EHRS/CORBIS ©

GORDON RAMSAY
French £££

(Map p80; ☎ 020-7352 4441; www.gordonramsay.com; 68 Royal Hospital Rd; 3-course lunch/dinner £45/90; ⊖Sloane Sq) One of Britain's finest restaurants and London's longest-running with three coveted Michelin stars. You'll need to book ahead and hop into your best togs: jeans and T-shirts don't get past the door. And if you've seen the chef in action, you'll know not to argue.

Notting Hill, Bayswater & Paddington

Notting Hill teems with good places to eat, from cheap takeaways to atmospheric pubs and restaurants worthy of the fine-dining tag. Queensway has the best strip of Asian restaurants this side of Soho.

TAQUERÍA
Mexican £

(Map p80; www.taqueria.co.uk; 139-143 Westbourne Grove; tacos from £4.10; ⊗lunch & dinner; ⊖Notting Hill Gate) Its sustainable credentials are as exacting and appealing as its authentic soft-corn, freshly made tortillas – this place instantly elbows other Mexican restaurants into the Tex-Mex shade.

GEALES
Seafood ££

(Map p80; ☎ 020-7727 7528; www.geales.com; 2 Farmer St; 2-course lunch £10, mains £10-18; ⊗closed lunch Mon; ⊖Notting Hill Gate) Frying fish since 1939, Geales' fish is highly succulent, although chips disappointingly cost extra (outside of the set lunch) in what should be a classic combination.

Marylebone

You won't go too far wrong planting yourself on a table anywhere along Marylebone's charming High St.

PROVIDORES & TAPA ROOM
Fusion £££
(Map p83; ☎020-7935 6175; www.theprovi
dores.co.uk; 109 Marylebone High St; 2/3/4/5
courses £30/43/53/60; ⊖Baker St) New
Zealand's most distinctive culinary export
since kiwi fruit, chef Peter Gordon works
his fusion magic here, matching his
creations with NZ wines.

LOCANDA LOCATELLI
Italian ££
(Map p80; ☎020-7935 9088; www.locanda
locatelli.com; 8 Seymour St; mains £11-30;
⊖Marble Arch) Known for its sublime but
pricey pasta dishes, this dark but quietly
glamorous restaurant in an otherwise
unremarkable hotel is one of London's
hottest tables.

Fitzrovia
Tucked away behind busy Tottenham
Court Rd, Fitzrovia's Charlotte and
Goodge Sts form one of central London's
most vibrant eating precincts.

HAKKASAN
Chinese £££
(☎7927 7000; www.hakkasan.com; 8 Hanway
Pl; mains £9.50-42; ⊖Tottenham Court Rd)
Michelin-starred Hakkasan – hidden
down a lane like all fashionable haunts
should be – elegantly pairs fine Chinese
dining with stunning design and some
persuasive cocktail chemistry.

SALT YARD
Spanish, Italian ££
(Map p83; ☎020-7637 0657; www.saltyard.
co.uk; 54 Goodge St; tapas £4-8; ⊖Goodge St)
Named after the place where cold meats
are cured, this softly lit joint serves delicious Spanish and Italian tapas.

Clerkenwell & Farringdon
Clerkenwell's hidden gems are well worth
digging for. Pedestrianised Exmouth
Market is a good place to start.

BISTROT BRUNO LOUBET
French ££
(Map p72; ☎020-7324 4455; www.bistrot
brunoloubet.com; 86-88 Clerkenwell Rd; mains
£12-17; ⏱breakfast, lunch & dinner; ☎; ⊖Far-
ringdon) Facing onto St John's Sq, this
elegant restaurant from Bruno Loubet
at the Zetter (p90) matches top-quality
ingredients and inventive taste
combinations with impeccable execution, in the food, cocktails and the home-
infused aperitifs.

ST JOHN
British ££
(Map p72; ☎020-7251 0848; www.
stjohnrestaurant.com; 26 St John
St; mains £14-22; ⊖Farringdon)
Bright whitewashed brick
walls, high ceilings and simple wooden furniture keep
diners free to concentrate
on the world-famous
nose-to-tail offerings.

MODERN PANTRY
Fusion ££
(Map p72; ☎020-7553
9210; www.themodernpan
try.co.uk; 47-48 St John's Sq;
mains £15-22; ⏱breakfast,
lunch & dinner; ☎; ⊖Far-
ringdon) One of London's

Lamb & Flag traditional London pub
NIGEL JAMES/ALAMY ©

most talked-about eateries, this three-floor Georgian town house in the heart of Clerkenwell has a cracking, innovative all-day menu.

Hoxton, Shoreditch & Spitalfields

From the hit-and-miss Bangladeshi restaurants of Brick Lane to the Vietnamese strip on Kingsland Rd, and the Jewish, Spanish, French, Italian and Greek eateries in between, the East End's cuisine is as multicultural as its residents.

POPPIES Fish & Chips **£**
(Map p72; www.poppiesfishandchips.co.uk; 6-8 Hanbury St; mains £6-11; ⏰11am-11pm, to 10.30pm Sun; 🛜; 🚉Shoreditch High St, 🚇Shoreditch High St) Frying since 1945, this fantastic Spitalfields chippie is a retro delight, a throwback to the 1950s with iconic jukebox, wall-to-wall memorabilia, waitresses in pinnies and hairnets, and classic fish and chips (plus jellied eels).

FIFTEEN Italian **££**
(Map p72; 📞0871 330 1515; www.fifteen.net; 15 Westland Pl; breakfast £2-8.50, trattoria £6-11, restaurant £11-25; ⏰breakfast, lunch & dinner; 🛜; 🚇Old St) Jamie Oliver's culinary philanthropy started at Fifteen, set up to give unemployed young people a shot at a career. The Italian food is beyond excellent, and, surprisingly, even those on limited budgets can afford a visit.

 **Drinking**

As long as there's been a city, Londoners have loved to drink – and, as history shows, often immoderately.

West End

GORDON'S WINE BAR Bar
(Map p64; www.gordonswinebar.com; 47 Villiers St; 🚇Embankment) What's not to love about this cavernous, candlelit wine cellar that's practically unchanged for the last 120 years? Get here before the office crowd (generally around 6pm) or forget about getting a table.

FRENCH HOUSE Bar
(Map p64; 49 Dean St; 🚇Leicester Sq) French House is Soho's legendary boho boozer with a history to match: the meeting place of the Free French Forces during WWII, De Gaulle is said to have knocked back shots here, while Dylan Thomas, Peter O'Toole, Brendan Behan and Francis Bacon all conspired to drink the place dry.

LAB Cocktail Bar
(Map p64; www.lab-townhouse.com; 12 Old Compton St; 🚇Leicester Sq) The decor of the London Academy of Bartending has been left behind, but a frisson of creativity runs through the cocktail menu and LAB's mixologists can have your taste-buds singing.

PRINCESS LOUISE Pub
(208 High Holborn; 🚇Holborn) This late-19th-century Victorian boozer is arguably London's most beautiful pub. Spectacularly decorated with fine tiles, etched mirrors, plasterwork and a gorgeous central horseshoe bar, it gets packed with the after-work crowd.

LAMB & FLAG Pub
(Map p64; 33 Rose St; 🚇Covent Garden) Everyone's Covent Garden 'find', this historic pub is often as jammed with punters as it is packed with history.

The City

VERTIGO 42 Bar
(Map p72; 📞020-7877 7842; www.vertigo42.co.uk; Tower 42, Old Broad St; 🚇Liverpool St) Book a two-hour slot in this 42nd-floor champagne bar (no shorts, caps or flip-flops) with vertiginous views across London from the former National Westminster Tower. Reservations only.

YE OLDE CHESHIRE CHEESE Pub
(Map p72; Wine Office Crt, 145 Fleet St; ⏰Mon-Sat; 🚇Holborn) Rebuilt six years after the Great Fire, this hoary pub was popular with Dr Johnson, Thackeray, Dickens and the visiting Mark Twain. Touristy but always atmospheric and enjoyable for a pub meal.

South Bank

GEORGE INN — Pub

(Map p72; www.nationaltrust.org.uk/main/w-georgeinn; 77 Borough High St; ⊖London Bridge) This glorious old boozer is London's last surviving galleried coaching inn, dating from 1676 and now a National Trust property.

ANCHOR — Pub

(Map p72; 34 Park St; ⊖London Bridge) This 18th-century riverside boozer replaced the 1615 original where Samuel Pepys witnessed the Great Fire.

Chelsea & Kensington

BIBENDUM OYSTER BAR — Bar

(Map p80; www.bibendum.co.uk; 81 Fulham Rd; ⊖South Kensington) Slurp up some bivalves and knock back a champers in the glorious foyer of the standout art nouveau/deco Michelin House (1911).

Notting Hill, Bayswater & Paddington

CHURCHILL ARMS — Pub

(Map p80; 119 Kensington Church St; ⊖Notting Hill Gate) Adorned with a gob-smacking array of flower baskets and Union Jacks, this magnificent old boozer on Kensington Church St is a London classic, famed for its atmosphere, Winston memorabilia, knick-knacks and attached conservatory serving fine Thai food.

Camden Town

LOCK TAVERN — Pub

(Map p83; www.lock-tavern.co.uk; 35 Chalk Farm Rd; ⊖Camden Town) The archetypal Camden pub, the Lock has both a rooftop terrace and a beer garden and attracts an interesting crowd with its mix of ready conviviality and regular live music.

Clerkenwell & Farringdon

JERUSALEM TAVERN — Pub

(Map p72; www.stpetersbrewery.co.uk; 55 Britton St; 🛜; ⊖Farringdon) Pick a wood-panelled cubbyhole to park yourself in at this tiny 1720 coffee-shop-turned-inn (named after the Priory of St John of Jerusalem) and choose from a selection of St Peter's fantastic beers and ales, brewed in North Suffolk.

Cargo (p98)

Hoxton, Shoreditch & Spitalfields

BOOK CLUB — Bar

(Map p72; ☎020-7684 8618; www.wearetbc.com; 100 Leonard St; ⊙8am-midnight Mon-Wed, 8am-2am Thu & Fri, 10am-2am Sat & Sun; ⏾; ⊖Old St) A cerebral/creative vibe animates this fantastic one-time Victorian warehouse in Shoreditch that hosts cultural events (life drawing, workshops, dance lessons) and DJ nights to complement the drinking, enthusiastic table-tennis playing and pool-playing shenanigans.

TEN BELLS — Pub

(Map p72; cnr Commercial & Fournier Sts; ⊖Liverpool St) The most famous Jack the Ripper pub, Ten Bells was patronised by his last victim before her grisly end, and possibly by the slayer himself. Admire the wonderful 18th-century tiles and ponder the past over a pint.

 # Entertainment

Theatre

London is a world capital for theatre across the spectrum from mammoth musicals to thoughtful drama for the highbrow crowd.

On performance days, you can buy half-price tickets for West End productions (cash only) from the official agency **tkts** (Map p64; www.tkts.co.uk; Leicester Sq; ⊙10am-7pm Mon-Sat, noon-4pm Sun; ⊖Leicester Sq) on the south side of Leicester Sq. The booth is the one with the clocktower; beware of touts selling dodgy tickets. For a comprehensive look at what's being staged and where, visit www.officiallondontheatre.co.uk, www. theatremonkey.com or http://london. broadway.com.

NATIONAL THEATRE — Theatre

(Map p64; ☎020-7452 3000; www.national theatre.org.uk; Upper Ground; ⊖Waterloo) Flagship South Bank venue with three theatres and excellent-value tickets for classic and contemporary productions.

ROYAL COURT THEATRE — Theatre

(Map p80; ☎020-7565 5000; www.royal courttheatre.com; Sloane Sq; ⊖Sloane Sq) Progressive theatre and champion of new talent.

OLD VIC — Theatre

(Map p72; ☎0844 871 7628; www.oldvictheatre. com; The Cut; ⊖Waterloo) Kevin Spacey continues his run as artistic director (and occasional performer) at this venue, which features classic, highbrow drama.

DONMAR WAREHOUSE — Theatre

(Map p64; ☎0844 871 7624; www.donmarware house.com; 41 Earlham St; ⊖Covent Garden) A not-for-profit company that has forged itself a West End reputation.

Nightclubs

Clubland is no longer confined to the West End, with megaclubs scattered throughout the city wherever there's a venue big enough, cheap enough or quirky enough to hold them.

FABRIC — Club

(Map p72; www.fabriclondon.com; 77a Charter-house St; admission £8-18; ⊙10pm-6am Fri, 11pm-8am Sat, 11pm-6am Sun; ⊖Farringdon) Consistently rated by DJs as one of the world's greatest, Fabric's three dance floors occupy a converted meat cold-store opposite the Smithfield meat market.

PLASTIC PEOPLE — Club

(Map p72; www.plasticpeople.co.uk; 147-149 Curtain Rd; admission £5-10; ⊙10pm-3.30am Fri & Sat, to 2am Sun; ⊖Old St) Taking the directive 'underground club' literally, Plastic People provides a low-ceilinged subterranean den of dubsteppy, wonky, funky, no-frills fun times.

MINISTRY OF SOUND — Club

(☎7740 8600; www.ministryofsound.com; 103 Gaunt St; admission £13-22; ⊙11pm-6.30am Fri & Sat; ⊖Elephant & Castle) Where the global brand started, it's London's most famous club and still packs in a diverse crew with big local and international names.

CARGO Club
(Map p72; www.cargo-london.com; 83 Rivington St; admission free-£16; ⊖Old St) A popular club with a courtyard where you can simultaneously enjoy big sounds and the great outdoors. Also hosts live bands.

Rock, Pop & Jazz
Big-name gigs sell out quickly, so check www.seetickets.com before you travel.

O2 ACADEMY BRIXTON Live Music
(☏box office 0844 477 2000; www.o2academybrixton.co.uk; 211 Stockwell Rd; ⊖Brixton) This Grade II–listed art deco venue is always winning awards for 'best live venue' (something to do with the artfully sloped floor, perhaps) and hosts big-name acts in a relatively intimate setting (5000 capacity).

JAZZ CAFÉ Live Music
(Map p83; www.jazzcafe.co.uk; 5 Parkway; ⊖Camden Town) Jazz is just one part of the picture at this intimate club that stages a full roster of rock, pop, hip hop and dance, including famous names.

Abbey Road

Beatles aficionados can't possibly visit London without making a pilgrimage to **Abbey Road Studios** (3 Abbey Rd) in St John's Wood. The fence is covered with decades of fans' graffiti. Stop-start local traffic is long accustomed to groups of tourists lining up on the zebra crossing to reenact the cover of the fab four's 1969 masterpiece and penultimate swan song *Abbey Road*. In 2010 the crossing received the accolade of Grade II listed status. To get here, take the tube to St John's Wood, cross the road, follow Grove End Rd to its end and turn right.

BARFLY Live Music
(Map p83; ☏0207-691 4245; www.barflyclub.com; 49 Chalk Farm Rd; ⊖Chalk Farm) This grungy, indie-rock Camden venue hosts small-time artists looking for their big break.

RONNIE SCOTT'S Jazz
(Map p64; ☏020-7439 0747; www.ronniescotts.co.uk; 47 Frith St; ⊖Leicester Sq) London's legendary jazz club has been pulling in jazz titans since 1959.

100 CLUB Live Music
(Map p64; ☏020-7636 0933; www.the100club.co.uk; 100 Oxford St; ⊖Oxford Circus) Hosting live music for 70 years, this legendary London venue once showcased the Stones and was at the centre of the punk revolution.

ROUNDHOUSE Live Music
(Map p83; ☏0844 482 8008; www.roundhouse.org.uk; Chalk Farm Rd; ⊖Chalk Farm) Built in 1847 as a railway shed, Camden's Roundhouse has been an iconic concert venue since the 1960s (capacity 3300), hosting the likes of the Rolling Stones, Led Zeppelin and The Clash. Theatre and comedy are also staged.

Classical Music
ROYAL ALBERT HALL Concert Venue
(Map p80; ☏020-7589 8212; www.royalalberthall.com; Kensington Gore; ⊖South Kensington) This landmark elliptical Victorian arena – classically based on a Roman amphitheatre – hosts classical concerts and contemporary artists, but is best known as the venue for the annual classical-music festival, the Proms.

BARBICAN Arts Centre
(Map p72; ☏0845 121 6823; www.barbican.org.uk; Silk St; ⊖Barbican) Home to the excellent **London Symphony Orchestra** (www.lso.co.uk), this famously hulking complex (named after a Roman fortification) has a rich program of film, music, theatre, art and dance including concerts.

SOUTHBANK CENTRE Concert Venue
(Map p64; ☏0844 875 0073; www.southbankcentre.co.uk; Belvedere Rd; ⊖Waterloo) Home

DEGAS JEAN-PIERRE/HEMIS/CORBIS ©

to the **London Philharmonic Orchestra** (www.lpo.co.uk), **Sinfonietta** (www.londonsinfonietta.org.uk) and the **Philharmonia Orchestra** (www.philharmonia.co.uk), among others, this centre hosts classical, opera, jazz and choral music in three premier venues: the Royal Festival Hall, the smaller Queen Elizabeth Hall and the Purcell Room.

Opera & Dance

ROYAL OPERA HOUSE   Opera, Dance
(Map p64; ☎020-7304 4000; www.roh.org.uk; Bow St; tickets £5-195; ⊖Covent Garden) Covent Garden is synonymous with opera thanks to this world-famous venue, which is also the home of the Royal Ballet, Britain's premier classical ballet company. Backstage tours take place three times a day on weekdays and four times on Saturdays (£10.50, book ahead).

SADLER'S WELLS   Dance
(Map p72; ☎0844 412 4300; www.sadlerswells.com; Rosebery Ave; tickets £10-49; ⊖Angel) A glittering modern venue that was, in fact, first established in the 17th century, Sadler's Wells has been given much credit for bringing modern dance to the mainstream.

Comedy

COMEDY STORE   Comedy
(Map p64; ☎0844 847 1728; www.thecomedystore.co.uk; 1a Oxendon St; admission from £20; ⊖Piccadilly Circus) One of London's first comedy clubs, featuring the capital's most famous improvisers, the Comedy Store Players, on Wednesdays (8pm) and Sundays (7.30pm).

SOHO THEATRE   Comedy
(Map p64; ☎020-7478 0100; www.sohotheatre.com; 21 Dean St; tickets around £10-20; ⊖Tottenham Court Rd) This is where grown-up comedians graduate to once crowds start paying attention.

Cinemas

Glitzy premieres usually take place in one of the mega multiplexes in Leicester Sq.

ELECTRIC CINEMA   Cinema
(Map p80; ☎020-7908 9696; www.electriccinema.co.uk; 191 Portobello Rd; tickets £8-15; ⊖Ladbroke Grove) Getting Londoners buzzing since 1911, at the Electric you can grab a glass of wine from the bar, head to your leather sofa (£30) and snuggle down for a flick. Check out the **Electric Brasserie** (Map

p80; 📞020-7908 9696; www.electricbrasserie.com; 191 Portobello Rd; breakfasts £5.50-13.50, mains £9-36; 🚇Ladbroke Grove) next door.

BFI SOUTHBANK
Cinema

(Map p64; 📞020-7928 3232; www.bfi.org.uk; Belvedere Rd; tickets £9; 🕐11am-11pm; 🚇Waterloo) A film-lover's fantasy, screening some 2000 flicks a year, from classics to foreign art house.

BFI IMAX
Cinema

(Map p64; 📞020-7199 6000; www.bfi.org.uk/imax; Waterloo Rd; tickets £9-16; 🚇Waterloo) Watch 3D movies and cinema releases on the UK's biggest screen: 20m high (nearly five double-decker buses) and 26m wide.

PRINCE CHARLES
Cinema

(Map p64; www.princecharlescinema.com; Leicester Pl; 🚇Leicester Sq) West End cinema ticket prices are eye-watering, so wait till the first-runs have finished and come here, central London's cheapest picturehouse.

🔒 Shopping

From world-famous department stores to quirky backstreet retail revelations, London is a mecca for shoppers with an eye for style and a card to exercise.

West End

Oxford St is the place for high street fashion, while Regent St cranks it up a notch. Carnaby St is no way near the hip hub it was in the 1960s, but the lanes around it still have some interesting boutiques. Bond St has designers galore, Savile Row is all about bespoke tailoring and Jermyn St is the place for smart clothes (particularly shirts).

SELFRIDGES
Department Store

(Map p80; www.selfridges.com; 400 Oxford St; 🚇Bond St) Famed for its innovative window displays (especially at yuletide) the funkiest of London's one-stop shops bursts with fashion labels and tempts with an unparalleled food hall and Europe's largest cosmetics department.

FORTNUM & MASON
Department Store

(Map p64; www.fortnumandmason.com; 181 Piccadilly; 🚇Piccadilly Circus) It's the byword for quality and service from a bygone era, steeped in 300 years of tradition. The old-world basement food hall is where Britain's elite come for their pantry provisions and epicurean morsels.

LIBERTY
Department Store

(Map p64; www.liberty.co.uk; Great Marlborough St; 🚇Oxford Circus) An irresistible blend of contemporary styles and indulgent pampering in a mock-Tudor fantasyland of carved dark wood.

FOYLE'S
Books

(Map p64; www.foyles.co.uk; 113-119 Charing Cross Rd; 🚇Tottenham Court Rd) Flogging books since 1906, Foyles is a bookselling institution and retail landmark.

BENJAMIN POLLOCK'S TOY SHOP
Toys

(Map p64; www.pollocks-coventgarden.co.uk; 1st fl, Covent Garden Market; 🚇Covent Garden) You can turn up all sorts of treasures at this gem of a traditional toy shop.

FORBIDDEN PLANET
Comics, Sci-Fi

(Map p64; 179 Shaftesbury Ave; 🚇Tottenham Court Rd) Forbidden Planet is a mecca for collectors of comics, manga, *Star Trek* figurines, horror and fantasy literature, sci-fi and *Star Wars* memorabilia.

Knightsbridge, Kensington & Chelsea

HARRODS
Department Store

(Map p80; www.harrods.com; 87 Brompton Rd; 🚇Knightsbridge) Simultaneously stylish and garish, Harrods is an obligatory stop for visitors, cash-strapped and big, big spenders alike. The spectacular food hall is a sight in itself.

HARVEY NICHOLS
Department Store

(Map p80; www.harveynichols.com; 109-125 Knightsbridge; 🚇Knightsbridge) London's temple of high fashion, jewellery and perfume.

ℹ Information

Dangers & Annoyances

Considering its size and wealth disparities, London is generally safe. That said, keep your wits about you and don't flash your cash unnecessarily. When travelling by tube, choose a carriage with other people in it and avoid deserted suburban stations. Following reports of robberies and sexual attacks, shun unlicensed or unbooked minicabs.

Watch out for pickpockets on crowded tube trains, night buses and streets.

When using ATMs, guard your PIN details carefully. Don't use an ATM that looks like it's been tampered with as there have been incidents of card cloning.

Internet Resources

Evening Standard (www.thisislondon.com)

Londonist (www.londonist.com)

Time Out (www.timeout.com/london)

View London (www.viewlondon.co.uk)

Media

Two free newspapers bookend the working day (*Metro* in the morning and the *Evening Standard* in the evening), both available from tube stations. Published every Wednesday, *Time Out* (£2.99) is the local listing guide par excellence.

Toilets

If you're caught short around London, public toilets can be elusive. Only a handful of tube stations have them, but the bigger National Rail stations usually do (often coin-operated). If you can face five floors on an escalator, department stores are a good bet.

Tourist Information

Britain & London Visitor Centre (www. visitbritain.com; 1 Regent St; ⊘9am-6.30pm Mon-Fri, 10am-4pm Sat & Sun; ⊖Piccadilly Circus) Books accommodation, theatre and transport tickets; has *bureau de change*, international telephones and internet terminals.

♥ If You Like...
Markets

1 CAMDEN MARKET
(Map p83; www.camdenmarkets.org; Camden High St; ⊘10am-5.30pm; ⊖Camden Town) London's best-known street market, but the capital has lots more places to browse for bargains.

2 COLUMBIA ROAD FLOWER MARKET
(Map p72; Columbia Rd; ⊘8am-3pm Sun; ⊖Old St) The best place for East End barrow-boy banter ('We got flowers cheap enough for ya muvver-in-law's grave'). Unmissable.

3 PORTOBELLO ROAD MARKET
(Map p80; www.portobellomarket.org; Portobello Rd; ⊘8am-6.30pm Mon-Wed, Fri & Sat, to 1pm Thu; ⊖Notting Hill Gate or Ladbroke Grove) One of London's most famous street markets, in Notting Hill. New and vintage clothes are its main attraction, with antiques at its south end and food at the north.

4 OLD SPITALFIELDS MARKET
(Map p72; www.oldspitalfieldsmarket.com; 105a Commercial St; ⊘10am-4pm Mon-Fri, 11am-5pm Sat, 9am-5pm Sun; ⊖Liverpool St) It's housed in a Victorian warehouse, but the market's been here since 1638. Thursdays are devoted to antiques and vintage clothes, Fridays to fashion and art, but Sunday's the big day, with a bit of everything.

5 BRICK LANE MARKET
(Map p72; www.visitbricklane.org; Brick Lane; ⊘8am-2pm Sun; ⊖Liverpool St) An East End pearler, this is a sprawling bazaar featuring everything from fruit and veggies to paintings and bric-a-brac.

6 GREENWICH MARKET
(www.greenwichmarket.net; College Approach; ⊘10am-5.30pm Wed, Sat & Sun; ℝDLR Cutty Sark) Rummage through antiques, vintage clothing and collectables (Thursday and Friday), arts and crafts (Wednesday and weekends), or just chow down in the food section.

Right: Camden Market (p101);
Below: Toy soldiers, Portobello Road Market (p101)

City of London Information Centre
(☎ 020-7332 1456; www.visitthecity.co.uk; St Paul's Churchyard; ⏰ 9.30am-5.30pm Mon-Sat, 10am-4pm Sun; ⊖ St Paul's) Tourist information, fast-track tickets to City attractions and guided walks (adult/child under 12 £7/free).

ⓘ Getting There & Away

Air

There are a number of London airports; see Getting Around for details.

Bus

Most long-distance coaches leave London from Victoria Coach Station.

Train

London's main-line terminals are all linked by the tube and each serve different destinations. Most stations have left-luggage facilities (around £4) and lockers, toilets (20p) with showers (around £3), newsstands and bookshops, and a range of eating and drinking outlets.

- **Charing Cross** Canterbury.
- **Euston** Manchester, Liverpool, Carlisle, Glasgow.
- **King's Cross** Cambridge, Hull, York, Newcastle, Scotland.
- **Liverpool Street** Stansted airport, Cambridge.
- **London Bridge** Gatwick airport, Brighton.
- **Marylebone** Birmingham.
- **Paddington** Heathrow airport, Oxford, Bath, Bristol, Exeter, Plymouth, Cardiff.
- **St Pancras** Gatwick and Luton airports, Brighton, Nottingham, Sheffield, Leicester, Leeds, Paris.
- **Victoria** Gatwick airport, Brighton, Canterbury.
- **Waterloo** Windsor, Winchester, Exeter, Plymouth.

ℹ Getting Around

To/From the Airports

GATWICK

There are **National Rail** (www.nationalrail.co.uk) services between Gatwick's South Terminal and Victoria station (from £13.50, 37 minutes), running every 15 minutes during the day and hourly through the night. Other trains head to London St Pancras International (from £10, 66 minutes). If you're racing to make a flight, the **Gatwick Express** (☎0845 850 1530; www. gatwickexpress.com) departs Victoria every 15 minutes from 5am to 11.45pm (one way/ return £18.90/33.20, 30 minutes, first/last train 3.30am/12.32am).

Gatwick's taxi partner, **Checker Cars** (www. checkercars.com), has a counter in each terminal. Fares are quoted in advance (about £95 for the 65-minute ride to central London).

HEATHROW

The cheapest option is the Underground (the tube). The Piccadilly line is accessible from every terminal (£5.30, one hour to central London, departing from Heathrow every five minutes from around 5am to 11.30pm).

You might save some time on the considerably more expensive Heathrow Express, an ultramodern train to Paddington station (one way/return £18/34, 15 minutes, every 15 minutes 5.12am to 11.48pm). You can purchase tickets on board (£5 extra), from self-service machines (cash and credit cards accepted) at both stations, or online.

There are taxi ranks for black cabs outside every terminal; a fare to the centre of London will cost between £50 and £85.

LONDON CITY

The DLR connects London City Airport to the tube network, taking 22 minutes to reach Bank station (£4.30). A black taxi costs around £25 to/from central London.

London's Oyster Diet

To get the most out of London, you need to be able to jump on and off public transport like a local, not scramble to buy a ticket at hefty rates each time. The best and cheapest way to do this is with an Oyster card, a reusable smartcard on which you can load either a season ticket (weekly/monthly £29/112) or prepaid credit. The card itself is £5, which is fully refundable when you leave.

London is divided into concentric transport zones, although most places are in Zones 1 and 2. All you need to do is touch your card to the yellow sensors on the station turnstiles or at the front of the bus.

If you opt for pay as you go, the fare will be deducted from the credit on your card at a much lower rate than if you were buying a one-off paper ticket. An Oyster bus trip costs £1.35 as opposed to £2.30 for an individual fare, while a Zone 1 tube journey is £2 as opposed to £4.30. Even better, in any single day your fares will be capped at the equivalent of the Oyster day-pass rate for the zones you've travelled in (Zones 1–2 peak/off-peak £8.40/7).

Stansted

The Stansted Express connects with Liverpool Street station (one way/return £21.50/29.50, 46 minutes, every 15 minutes 6am to 12.30am).

A taxi cab to/from central London costs about £100.

Bicycle

Operating 24 hours a day and already clocking in over 11 million cycle hires, the excellent **Barclays Cycle Hire Scheme** (www.tfl.gov.uk) allows you to hire a bike from one of 400 docking stations around London. The access fee is £1 for 24 hours or £5 per week; after that, the first 30 minutes is free (making the bikes perfect for short hops), or £1/4/6/15 for one hour/90 minutes/two hours/three hours.

Car

London's streets can be congested beyond belief. If you drive into central London from 7am to 6pm on a weekday, you'll need to pay a £10 per day congestion charge (visit www.tfl.gov.uk for payment options) or face a hefty fine. If you're hiring a car to continue your trip from London, take the tube to Heathrow and pick it up from there.

Public Transport

TFL (www.tfl.gov.uk), the city's public transport provider, is the glue that binds the network together.

BOAT

Passengers with daily, weekly or monthly travelcards (including on Oyster) get a third off all fares.

Thames Clippers runs regular commuter services between Embankment, Waterloo, Blackfriars, Bankside, London Bridge, Tower, Canary Wharf, Greenwich, North Greenwich and Woolwich piers (adult/child £6/3) from 7am to midnight (from 9.30am weekends).

Leisure services include the Tate-to-Tate boat (p75) and Westminster–Greenwich services. There are also boats to Kew Gardens and Hampton Court Palace.

BUS

Travelling around London by double-decker bus is a great way to get a feel for the city, but it's usually slower than the tube. Heritage 'Routemaster' buses with conductors operate on route 9 (from Aldwych to Royal Albert Hall) and 15 (between Trafalgar Sq and Tower Hill); these are the only buses without wheelchair access. In 2012 a brand-new fleet of freshly designed hybrid diesel/electric hop-on/hop-off (and wheelchair-accessible) Routemasters began running on route 38 between Victoria and Hackney.

Buses run regularly during the day, while less-frequent night buses (prefixed with the letter 'N') wheel into action when the tube stops. Single-journey bus tickets (valid for two hours) cost £2.30 (£1.35 on Oyster, capped at £4.20 per day); a weekly pass is £18.80. Buses stop on request, so clearly signal the driver with an outstretched arm.

LONDON UNDERGROUND, DLR & OVERGROUND

'The tube', as it's universally known, extends its subterranean tentacles throughout London and into the surrounding counties, with services running every few minutes from roughly 5.30am to 12.30am (from 7am to 11.30pm Sunday). The DLR links the City to Docklands, Greenwich and London City Airport.

TAXI

London's famous black cabs are available for hire when the yellow light above the windscreen is lit. Fares are metered, with flag fall of £2.20 and the additional rate dependent on time of day, distance travelled and taxi speed. A 1-mile trip will cost between £5.20 and £8.40. To order a black cab by phone, try **Dial-a-Cab** (📞**020-7253 5000; www. dialacab.co.uk**); you must pay by credit card and will be charged a premium.

Licensed minicabs operate via agencies (most busy areas have a walk-in office with drivers waiting). They're a cheaper alternative to black cabs and quote trip fares in advance. To find a local minicab firm, visit www.tfl.gov.uk.

AROUND LONDON

Canterbury

POP 43,400

Canterbury tops the charts for English cathedral cities and is one of southern England's top attractions. Many consider the World Heritage–listed cathedral that dominates its centre to be one of Europe's finest, and the town's narrow medieval alleyways, riverside gardens and ancient city walls are a joy to explore.

◎ Sights

CANTERBURY CATHEDRAL Church (www.canterbury-cathedral.org; adult/concession £8/7, tour adult/child £5/3, audiotour adult/concession £3.50/2.50; ⊙9am-5pm Mon-Sat, 12.30-2.30pm Sun) A rich repository of more than 1400 years of Christian history, the Church of England's mother ship is a truly extraordinary place with an absorbing history. The spot in the northwest transept where Archbishop Thomas Becket met his grisly end has drawn pilgrims for more than 800 years and is marked by a flickering candle and striking modern altar.

The doorway to the crypt is beside the altar. This cavernous space is the cathedral's highlight, the only survivor from the cathedral's last devastating fire

Thomas Becket stained glass window, Canterbury Cathedral
NEIL HOLMES/GETTY IMAGES ©

Canterbury

Canterbury

Top Sights
Canterbury Cathedral	C2
Canterbury Heritage Museum	B3
St Augustine's Abbey	D3

Activities, Courses & Tours
1	Canterbury Guided Tours	C2
2	Canterbury Historic River Tours	B2

Sleeping
3	Abode Canterbury	B2
4	Cathedral Gate Hotel	C2

Eating
5	Boho	B2
6	Deeson's	C2
7	Goods Shed	B1

in 1174, which destroyed the rest of the building.

The wealth of detail in the cathedral is immense and unrelenting, so it's well worth joining a one-hour tour (three daily, Monday to Saturday from Easter to October), or taking a 40-minute self-guided audiotour.

CANTERBURY HERITAGE MUSEUM Museum
(www.canterbury-museums.co.uk; Stour St; adult/child £8/free; ☉10am-5pm) A fine 14th-century building, once the Poor Priests' Hospital, now houses the city's captivating museum, which houses a jumble of exhibits dating from pre-Roman times to the assassination of Becket, and from the likes of Joseph Conrad to locally born celebs. The building also houses the **Rupert Bear Museum** (Rupert's creator,

Mary Tourtel, was born in Canterbury) and a gallery celebrating another old-time children's favourite, *Bagpuss*.

ST AUGUSTINE'S ABBEY · Ruin
(EH; adult/child £4.90/2.90; ⊙10am-6pm Jul & Aug, to 5pm Wed-Sun Apr-Jun) An integral but often overlooked part of the Canterbury World Heritage Site, St Augustine's Abbey was founded in AD 597, marking the re-birth of Christianity in southern England. Later requisitioned as a royal palace, it fell into disrepair and only stumpy founda-tions remain.

 ## Tours

CANTERBURY HISTORIC
RIVER TOURS · Boat Tours
(☎07790 534744; www.canterburyrivertours.co.uk; adult/child £8/4.50; ⊙10am-5pm Mar-Oct) Knowledgable guides double up as energetic oarsmen on these fascinating River Stour minicruises, which depart from behind the Old Weaver's House on St Peter's St.

CANTERBURY GUIDED
TOURS · Walking Tours
(☎01227-459779; www.canterburyguidedtours.com; adult/child/concession £6.50/4.50/6; ⊙11am Feb-Oct, plus 2pm Jul-Sep) Guided walking tours leave from opposite the cathedral entrance.

 ## Sleeping

ABODE CANTERBURY · Hotel £££
(☎01227-766266; www.abodehotels.co.uk; 30-33 High St; r from £135; 🛜) The 72 rooms at this supercentral sleepery, the only boutique hotel in town, are graded from 'comfortable' to 'fabulous', and for the most part live up to their names. There's a splendid champagne bar, restaurant and tavern, too.

CATHEDRAL GATE HOTEL · Hotel ££
(☎01227-464381; www.cathgate.co.uk; 36 Burgate; s/d £70/105, without bathroom £48/80; 🛜) Predating the spectacular cathedral

gate it adjoins, this quaint 15th-century hotel is a medieval warren of steep stair-cases and narrow passageways leading to 27 pleasingly old-fashioned rooms with angled floors, low doors and cockeyed walls.

 ## Eating

DEESON'S · British ££
(☎01227-767854; 25-27 Sun St; mains £4.50-16) Put the words 'local', 'seasonal' and 'tasty' into a make-believe restaurant search engine and this superb British eatery would magically pop up first for Canterbury.

BOHO · International £
(43 St Peter's St; snacks £3-10; ⊙9am-6pm Mon-Sat, 10am-5pm Sun) This hip eatery in a prime spot on the main drag is extraor-dinarily popular and you'd be lucky to get a table on busy shopping days. Boho doesn't do bookings, so be prepared to queue.

GOODS SHED · Market Restaurant ££
(☎01227-459153; Station Rd West; mains £12-20; ⊙market 9am-7pm Tue-Sat, 10am-4pm Sun, restaurant breakfast, lunch & dinner Tue-Sat, lunch Sun) Farmers market, food hall and fabulous restaurant rolled into one, this converted warehouse by the Canterbury West train station is a hit with everyone from self-caterers to sit-down gourmets.

Canterbury Attractions Passport

The **Canterbury Attractions Passport** (adult/child £19/15.25) gives entry to the cathedral, St Augustine's Abbey, the Canterbury Tales and any one of the city's museums. It's available from the tourist office (p108).

ⓘ Information

ⓘ Getting There & Away

There are two train stations, Canterbury East for London Victoria and Canterbury West for London's Charing Cross and St Pancras stations.

Train

Canterbury connections:

Dover Priory £7.50, 25 minutes, every 30 minutes

London St Pancras High-speed service, £31.80, 1 hour, hourly

London Victoria/Charing Cross £26.80, 1¾ hour, two to three hourly

ⓘ Getting Around

Car parks are dotted along and just inside the walls, but to avoid heavy traffic day trippers may prefer to use one of three Park & Ride sites, which cost £2.50 per day and connect to the centre by bus every eight minutes (7am to 7.30pm Monday to Saturday).

Leeds Castle

For many people, the immense moated **Leeds Castle** (www.leeds-castle.com; adult/child £19.75/12.50; ⏱10am-6pm Apr-Sep, to 5pm Oct-Mar) is the world's most romantic castle, and it's certainly one of the most visited in Britain.

The castle was transformed over the centuries from fortress to lavish palace. Its last owner, the high-society hostess Lady Baillie, modernised some rooms for use as a princely family home and party pad, to entertain the likes of Errol Flynn, Douglas Fairbanks and JFK. Highlights include Queen Eleanor's medieval bathroom, King Henry VIII's ebony-floored banquetting hall and the boardroom where, in 1978, Israeli and Egyptian negotiators met for talks prior to the Camp David Accords. Since Lady Baillie's death in 1974, a private trust has managed the property.

The castle's vast estate offers enough attractions of its own to justify a day trip: peaceful walks, an aviary, falconry demonstrations and a restaurant. You'll also find plenty of kiddie and toddler attractions, as well as a hedge maze, overseen by a grassy bank from where fellow travellers can shout encouragement or mischevious misdirections.

Leeds Castle is just east of Maidstone. Trains run from London Victoria to Bearsted (£19.60, one hour) and from there you catch a special shuttle coach to the castle (£5 return), but only between March and October and on winter weekends.

The White Cliffs

Immortalised in song, literature and film, these resplendent cliffs are embedded in the British national consciousness, acting as a big, white 'Welcome Home' sign to generations of travellers and soldiers.

The cliffs rise 100m high and extend 10 miles either side of Dover, but it is the 6-mile stretch east of town – properly known as the Langdon Cliffs – that especially captivates visitors' imaginations. The chalk here is about 250m deep and the cliffs are about half a million years old, formed when the melting ice caps of northern Europe gouged a channel between France and England.

The Langdon Cliffs are managed by the National Trust, which has a **tourist office** (☎01304-202756; ⏱9.30am-5.30pm Mar-Oct, 10.30am-4pm Nov-Feb) and **car park** (non-members per park per day £3) 2 miles east of Dover along Castle Hill Rd and the A258 road to Deal, or off the A2 past the Eastern Docks. From the tourist office, follow the stony path east along the clifftops for a bracing 2-mile walk to the stout Victorian **South Foreland Lighthouse** (NT; www.nationaltrust.org.uk; adult/child £4/2; ⏱guided tours 11am-5.30pm Fri-Mon mid-Mar–Oct). This was the first lighthouse to be powered by electricity and is the site of the first international radio transmissions, in 1898.

To see the cliffs in all their full-frontal glory, **Dover White Cliffs Tours** (☎01303-271388; www.doverwhiteclifftours.com; adult/child £8/4; ☉daily Jul & Aug, Sat & Sun Apr-Jun & Sep-Oct) runs 40-minute sightseeing trips at least three times daily from the Western Docks.

South Downs National Park

After decades of campaigning, planning and deliberation, the **South Downs National Park**, comprised of over 600 sq miles of rolling chalk downs stretching west from Eastbourne for about 100 miles, finally came into being in March 2010.

From **Beachy Head**, the stunning **Seven Sisters Cliffs** undulate their way west. A clifftop path (a branch of the South Downs Way) rides the waves of chalk as far as picturesque Cuckmere Haven. Along the way, you'll stumble upon the tiny seaside hamlet of Birling Gap, where you can stop for a drink, snack or ice cream. The secluded beach is a suntrap popular with locals and walkers taking a breather.

Beachy Head is off the B2103, from the A259 between Eastbourne and Newhaven.

Brighton & Hove

POP 247,800

Raves on the beach, Graham Greene novels, mods and rockers in bank-holiday fisticuffs, naughty weekends for Mr and Mrs Smith, classic car runs from London, the United Kingdom's biggest gay scene and the Channel's best clubbing – this city by the sea evokes many images for the British. One thing is certain: with its bohemian, cosmopolitan, hedonistic vibe, Brighton is where England's seaside experience goes from cold to cool.

◉ **Sights**

ROYAL PAVILION Palace
(www.royalpavilion.org.uk; Royal Pavilion Gardens; adult/child £9.80/5.60; ☉9.30am-5.45pm Apr-Sep, 10am-5.15pm Oct-Mar) The city's must-see attraction is the Royal Pavilion, the glittering party pad and palace of Prince George, later Prince Regent and then King George IV. It's one of the most opulent buildings in England, certainly the finest example of early-19th-century chinoiserie anywhere in Europe and an apt symbol of Brighton's reputation for decadence. The dragon-themed banqueting hall must be the most incredible in all England; more dragons and snakes writhe in the music room, with its ceiling of 26,000 gold scales; and the then state-of-the-art kitchen must have wowed Georgians with its automatic spits and hot tables.

FREE **BRIGHTON MUSEUM & ART GALLERY** Museum
(www.brighton-hove-museums.org.uk; Royal Pavilion Gardens; ☉10am-5pm Tue-Sun) Set in the Royal Pavilion's renovated stable block, this museum and art gallery has a glittering collection of 20th-century art and design, including a crimson Salvador Dalí sofa modelled on Mae West's lips.

BRIGHTON PIER Amusement Park
(www.brightonpier.co.uk; Madeira Dr) This grand, century-old pier is the place to experience Brighton's tackier side. There are plenty of stomach-churning fairground rides and dingy amusement arcades to keep you amused, and candy floss and Brighton rock to chomp on while you're doing so.

Look west and you'll see the sad remains of the **West Pier** (www.westpier.co.uk), a skeletal iron hulk that attracts flocks of starlings at sunset. It's a sad end for this Victorian marvel, on which the likes of Charlie Chaplin and Stan Laurel once performed.

Brighton & Hove

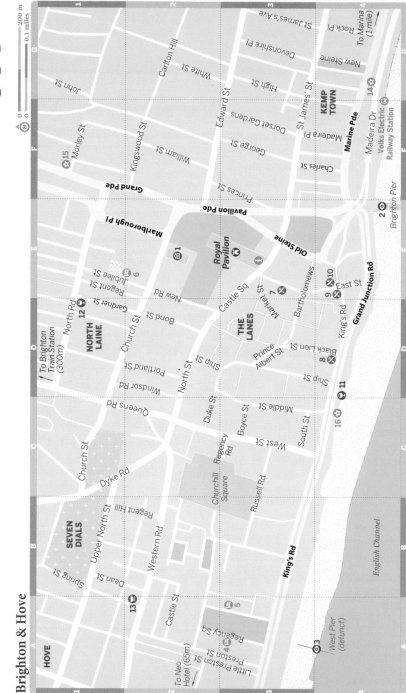

HOVE

SEVEN DIALS

NORTH LAINE

THE LANES

KEMP TOWN

Royal Pavilion

English Channel

West Pier (defunct)

Brighton Pier

Churchill Square

Regency Sq

To Neo Hotel (65m)

To Brighton Train Station (300m)

To Brighton Train Station (300m)

To Marina (1 mile)

Volks Electric Railway Station

Streets:
Spring St, Dean St, Castle St, Upper North St, Regent Hill St, Western Rd, Church St, Dyke Rd, Queens Rd, Windsor Rd, Portland St, Church St, North Rd, Gardner St, Regent St, Jubilee St, New Rd, North St, Bond St, Ship St, Duke St, Regency Rd, Boyce St, Middle St, West St, South St, Russell Rd, King's Rd, Little Preston St, Preston St, Castle St, Ship St, Prince Albert St, Black Lion St, Market St, Castle Sq, Bartholomews, East St, King's Rd, Grand Junction Rd, Morley St, John St, Kingswood St, William St, George St, Princes St, Grand Pde, Pavilion Pde, Marlborough Pl, Old Steine, Edward St, Dorset Gardens, High St, White St, Carlton Hill, Devonshire Pl, St James's Ave, St James's St, Charles St, Madeira Pl, Marine Pde, Madeira Dr, New Steine, Rock Pl

Map numbers: 1, 2, 3, 5, 6, 7, 8, 9, 10, 11, 12, 13, 14, 15, 16

0 200 m
0 0.1 miles

Brighton & Hove

 Festivals & Events

There's always something fun going on in Brighton, from **Gay Pride** (www.brighton pride.org) to food and drink festivals. The showpiece is May's three-week-long **Brighton Festival** (☎01273-709709; www. brightonfestival.org). The biggest arts festival in Britain after Edinburgh, it draws theatre, dance, music and comedy performers from around the globe.

 **Sleeping**

Despite a glut of hotels in Brighton, prices are relatively high and you'd be wise to book well ahead for summer weekends and for the Brighton Festival in May. Expect to pay up to a third more across the board at weekends.

HOTEL UNA   Boutique Hotel **££**
(☎01723-820464; www.hotel-una.co.uk; 55-56 Regency Sq; s £55-75, d £115-150; ✳🛜) All of the 19 generous rooms here wow guests with their bold-patterned fabrics, super-sized leather sofas, in-room free-standing baths and vegan/veggie/carnivorous breakfast in bed. All this plus a cool cocktail bar and lots of time-warp period features make the Una our numero uno.

HOTEL PELIROCCO   Theme Hotel **££**
(☎01273-327055; www.hotelpelirocco.co.uk; 10 Regency Sq; s £59-65, d £99-145, ste from £249; 🛜) One of Brighton's sexiest and nultiest places to stay, the Pelirocco takes the theme concept to a new level and has become the ultimate venue for a flirty rock-and-roll weekend. Flamboyant rooms, some designed by artists, others by local sponsors, include the Soviet-chic room with vodka bottles frozen into the walls, the Pin-up Parlour dedicated to Diana Dors, and the Pretty Vacant double, a shrine to the Sex Pistols.

NEO HOTEL   Boutique Hotel **££**
(☎01273-711104; www.neohotel.com; 19 Oriental Pl; d from £100; 🛜) You won't be surprised to learn the owner of this gorgeous hotel is an interior stylist. The nine rooms could have dropped straight from the pages of a design magazine, each finished in rich colours and tactile fabrics, with bold floral and Asian motifs and black-tiled bathrooms. Reception is not open 24 hours.

MYHOTEL   Hotel **££**
(☎01273-900300; www.myhotels.com; 17 Jubilee St; r from £89; P@🛜) With trendsetting rooms looking like space-age pods with curved white walls, floor-to-ceiling observation windows and suspended flatscreen TVs, enlivened by the odd splash of neon orange or pink, there's nothing about this place.

Brighton Pier (p109)

H & D ZIELSKE/LOOK-FOTO/GETTY IMAGES ©

Eating

TERRE À TERRE Vegetarian ££
(☎01273-729051; www.terreaterre.co.uk; 71 East St; mains £14; ⏱lunch & dinner Tue-Sun; 🖊) Even staunch meat eaters will rave about this legendary vegetarian restaurant. A sublime dining experience, from the vibrant modern space to the entertaining menus and inventive dishes packed with rich, robust flavours.

THE GINGERMAN Modern European £££
(☎01273-326688; 21a Norfolk Sq; 3-course menu £18; ⏱lunch & dinner Tue-Sun) Seafood from Hastings, Sussex beef, Romney Marsh lamb, local sparkling wines and countless other seasonal, local and British treats go into the adroitly flash-fried and slow-cooked dishes served at this snug, 32-cover eatery. Reservations are advised.

JB'S AMERICAN DINER Bistro £
(31 King's Rd; burgers £7, mains £6.50-12) The waft of hotdogs as you push open the door, the shiny red-leather booths, the Stars and Stripes draped across the wall, the '50s soundtrack twanging in the background and the colossal portions of burgers, fries and milkshakes – in short, a hefty slab of authentic Americana teleported to Brighton seafront.

ENGLISH'S OYSTER BAR Seafood ££
(www.englishs.co.uk; 29-31 East St; mains £11-25) An almost 70-year-old institution and celebrity haunt, this Brightonian seafood paradise dishes up everything from Essex oysters to locally caught lobster and Dover sole.

SCOOP & CRUMB Ice Cream £
(5-6 East St; snacks £3-5, sundaes £2.50-6; ⏱10am-6pm Sun-Fri, to 7pm Sat) This ice-cream parlour belongs to the city's artisan ice-cream producer, and the sundaes (more than 50 types) are second to none.

 Drinking

Outside London, Brighton's nightlife is the best in the south, with its unique mix of seafront clubs and bars.

DORSET Pub
(www.thedorset.co.uk; 28 North Rd; 🛜) In fine weather this laid-back Brighton institution throws open its doors and windows and spills tables onto the pavement.

TALK OF TEA Teahouse
(www.talkoftea.co.uk; 26 Spring St; ⊙8.30am-6pm Mon-Sat, 10am-4pm Sun; 🛜) This sparkling new teahouse will leave you with a classic black, white, green, herbal or fruit dilemma, as it stocks Brighton's biggest selection of teas (almost 60).

COALITION Bar
(171-181 Kings Rd Arches) On a summer's day, there's nowhere finer to sit and watch the world go by than at this popular beach bar, diner and club. All sorts happen here, from comedy to live music, to club nights.

 **Entertainment**

Nightclubs

When Britain's top DJs aren't plying their trade in London, Ibiza or Ayia Napa, chances are you'll spy them here. All of Brighton's clubs open until 2am, and many as late as 5am.

TUBE Club
(Kings Rd Arches) Twin giant brick subterranean tunnels, with bars at the front and back, playing funky house, '70s, R&B and disco to a stylish and attitude-free crowd.

PSYCHOSOCIAL Club
(www.psychosocialbrighton.com; 1-2 Morley St) This club specialises in everything and nothing, from punk to tropical nights, stand-up comedy to live music, and rap to lesbian satire.

CONCORDE 2 Club
(www.concorde2.co.uk; Madeira Dr) Brighton's best-known and best-loved club is a disarmingly unpretentious den, where DJ Fatboy Slim pioneered the Big Beat Boutique and still occasionally graces the decks.

🔒 Shopping

Whatever item you yearn for, old or new, you'll probably find it in Brighton. The tightly packed Lanes is the most popular shopping district, its every twist and turn jam-packed with jewellers and gift shops, coffee shops and boutiques selling everything from antique firearms to hard-to-find vinyls. There's another, less-claustrophobic shopping district in North Laine, a series of partially pedestrian thoroughfares north of the Lanes, including Bond, Gardner, Kensington and Sydney Sts, lined with retro-cool boutiques and bohemian cafes.

ⓘ Information

Brighton City Guide (www.brighton.co.uk)
Tourist office (📞01273-290337; www.visitbrighton.com; Royal Pavilion Shop;

Gay & Lesbian Brighton

Perhaps it's Brighton's long-time association with the theatre but the city has been a gay haven for more than 100 years. With upwards of 25,000 gay men and about 15,000 lesbians living here, it is the most vibrant queer community in the country outside London.

Kemptown (aka Camptown), on and off St James' St, is where it's all at. The old Brunswick Town area of Hove is a quieter alternative to the traditionally cruisy (and sometimes seedy) scene in Kemptown.

For up-to-date information on gay Brighton, check out www.gay.brighton.co.uk and www.realbrighton.com, or pick up the free monthly magazine *Gscene* (www.gscene.com) from the tourist office.

⊙ 9.30am-5.30pm) Superbly run office with an accommodation booking service (£1.50), train and bus ticketing and a highly recommended (free) greeter scheme that offers expert guides who show visitors around the city.

visitbrighton.com (www.visitbrighton.com)

ℹ️ Getting There & Away

Brighton is 53 miles from London and transport between the two is fast and frequent. If arriving by car, parking is plentiful but pricey, and the city-centre traffic, bus-clogged lanes and road layouts are confusing.

Train

All London-bound services pass through Gatwick Airport (£9.50, 30–40 minutes, up to five hourly).

Chichester £11.60, 50 minutes, half-hourly

Eastbourne £9.50, 30–40 minutes, half-hourly

London St Pancras £15.40, 1¼ hours, half-hourly

London Victoria £16, 50 minutes, three-hourly

ℹ️ Getting Around

Most of Brighton can be covered on foot. The city operates a pay-and-display parking scheme. In the town centre, it's usually £3.50 per hour for a maximum stay of two hours.

Cab companies include **Brighton Streamline Taxis** (📞 01273-74 74 74) and **City Cabs** (📞 01273-205 205), and there's a taxi rank at the junction of East St and Market St.

Windsor & Eton

POP 30,568

Dominated by the massive bulk of Windsor Castle, these twin towns have a rather surreal atmosphere, with the morning pomp and ceremony of the changing of the guards in Windsor, and the sight of school boys dressed in formal tailcoats wandering the streets of tiny Eton.

◎ Sights

WINDSOR CASTLE Castle
(www.royalcollection.org.uk; adult/child £17/10; ⊙ 9.45am-5.15pm) The largest and oldest occupied fortress in the world, Windsor Castle is a majestic vision of battlements and towers used for state occasions and as the Queen's weekend retreat.

William the Conqueror first established a royal residence in Windsor in 1070;

Windsor streetscape looking toward Windsor Castle

Windsor & Eton

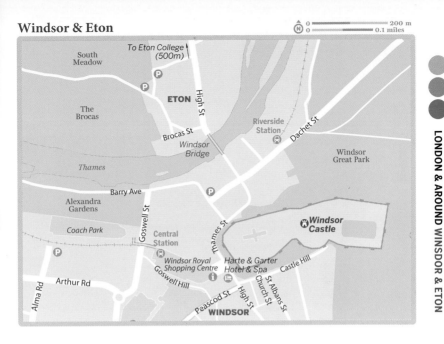

since then successive monarchs have rebuilt, remodelled and refurbished the castle complex to create the massive and sumptuous palace that stands here today. Join a free guided tour (every half-hour) or take a multilingual audio tour of the lavish state rooms and beautiful chapels. The State Apartments and St George's Chapel are closed at times during the year. If the Queen is in residence, you'll see the Royal Standard flying from the Round Tower.

A fabulous spectacle, with triumphant tunes from a military band and plenty of foot stamping, the **changing of the guard** (⏰11am Mon-Sat Apr-Jul, alternate days Aug-Mar) draws the crowds to the castle gates each day to watch the smartly attired lads in red uniforms and bear-fur hats do their thing. Stay to the right of the crowd for better views.

ETON COLLEGE   Notable Building
(www.etoncollege.com; adult/child £7/5.50; ⏰guided tours 2pm & 3.15pm daily during school hols, Wed, Fri, Sat & Sun during term time) Eton is the largest and most famous public (meaning very private) school

in England; it's only under the current headmaster that Eton has begun to accept applicants from state schools rather than just private schools. All the boys are boarders and must wear formal tailcoats, waistcoats and white collars to lessons (though the top hats went out in 1948). Fencing, shooting, polo and beagling are on the list of school sporting activities, and Eton very much embodies the old ideal of *mens sana in corpore sano* (a healthy mind in a healthy body).

Tours of Eton take in the **chapel**, the **cloisters**, the **Museum of Eton Life** – with a feature on Eton's star sport of rowing – the **lower school**, with names etched into its ancient desks by bored students, and the **school yard**, with a memorial to Etonians who died in the two world wars. You may recognise some of the buildings, as *Chariots of Fire*, *The Madness of King George*, *Mrs Brown* and *Shakespeare in Love* are just some of the movies that have been filmed here.

Buy tickets in advance at the tourist office, as they cannot be purchased at Eton itself.

Lego Buckingham Palace, Legoland Windsor

AFP/GETTY IMAGES ©

LEGOLAND WINDSOR
Amusement Park

(www.legoland.co.uk; Winkfield Rd; adult/child £43/34; ⏰from 10am Mar-early Nov) A fun-filled theme park of white-knuckle rides, Legoland is more about the thrills of scaring yourself silly than the joys of building your own castle from the eponymous bricks: the professionals have already done this for you, with almost 40 million Lego bricks transformed into some of the world's greatest landmarks. Book online to save £9 off the ticket prices.

 Sleeping

Windsor and Eton are easily doable as a day trip from London. If you wish to remain after the hordes of visitors have gone home, there's a good selection of quality hotels and B&Bs, but few budget options.

HARTE & GARTER HOTEL & SPA
Hotel ££

(☎01753-863426; www.foliohotels.com/harteandgarter; High St; d from £99; 🛜) Right opposite the castle, this Victorian hotel blends period style with modern furnishings.

High ceilings, giant fireplaces, decorative cornices and dark woods seamlessly combine with contemporary fabrics, plasma-screen TVs and traditional, cast-iron baths.

76 DUKE STREET
B&B ££

(☎01753-620636; www.76dukestreet.co.uk; 76 Duke St; s/d £80/100; P 🛜) Two immaculate, centrally located double rooms, presided over by a welcoming hostess who cooks up a superb breakfast. The second bedroom is only available if booked along with the first, so it's ideal for a family or two couples.

ℹ Information

Royal Windsor Information Centre (www.windsor.gov.uk; Old Booking Hall, Windsor Royal Shopping Arcade; ⏰9.30am-5pm Mon-Sat, 10am-4pm Sun)

ℹ Getting There & Away

Trains from Windsor Central station go to Slough, with regular connections to London Paddington (30 to 45 minutes). Trains from Windsor Riverside station go to London Waterloo (one hour). Services run half-hourly from both and tickets cost £8.50.

Cambridge

POP 108,863

Abounding with exquisite architecture, steeped in history and tradition and renowned for its quirky rituals, Cambridge is a university town extraordinaire. The tightly packed core of ancient colleges, the picturesque 'Backs' (college gardens) leading on to the river and the leafy green meadows that seem to surround the city give it a far more tranquil appeal than its historic rival Oxford.

The first Cambridge college, Peterhouse (never Peterhouse *College*), was founded in 1284, and in 1318 the papal bull by Pope John XXII declared Cambridge to be an official university.

 Sights

Most colleges close to visitors for the Easter term and all are closed for exams from mid-May to mid-June. Also, opening hours vary from day to day, so if you have your heart set on visiting a particular college, contact it for information in advance to avoid disappointment.

Cambridge University

KING'S COLLEGE CHAPEL
Chapel

(www.kings.cam.ac.uk/chapel; King's Pde; adult/child £7.50/free, Evensong free; ⊙9.45am-4.30pm Mon, from 9.30am Tue-Sun, Evensong 5.30pm Mon-Sat, 10.30am & 3.30pm Sun, term time only) In a city crammed with show-stopping architecture, this is the scene-stealer. Chances are you will already have seen it on a thousand postcards, tea towels and choral CDs before you catch your first glimpse of the grandiose King's College Chapel, but still it inspires awe. It's one of the most extraordinary examples of Gothic architecture in England, begun in 1446 as an act of piety by Henry VI and finished by Henry VIII around 1516. The vast 80m-long canopy is the work of John Wastell and is the largest expanse of fan vaulting in the world.

The thickly carved wooden stalls just beyond the screen are a stage for the chapel's world-famous **choir**. You can hear them in full voice during the magnificent **Evensong**.

Beyond the dark-wood choir, light suffuses the **high altar**, which is framed by Rubens' masterpiece *Adoration of the Magi* (1634) and the magnificent east window.

TRINITY COLLEGE
College

(www.trin.cam.ac.uk; Trinity St; adult/child £1.50/1; ⊙10.30am-4.30pm) The largest of Cambridge's colleges, Trinity is entered through an impressive Tudor gateway first created in 1546. The **Great Court** is the largest of its kind in the world. To the right of the entrance is a small tree, planted in the 1950s and reputed to be a descendant of the apple tree made famous by Trinity alumnus Sir Isaac Newton.

CHRIST'S COLLEGE
College

(www.christs.cam.ac.uk; St Andrew's St; admission free, Darwin room £2.50; ⊙9.30am-noon, Darwin room 10am-noon & 2-4pm) Over 500 years old and a grand old institution, Christ's is worth visiting if only for its gleaming Great Gate emblazoned with heraldic carving of spotted Beaufort yale (antelope-like creatures), Tudor roses and portcullis.

CORPUS CHRISTI COLLEGE
College

(www.corpus.cam.ac.uk; King's Pde; admission £2.50; ⊙10am-4.30pm) Entry to this illustrious college is via the so-called New Court, which dates back a mere 200 years. To your right is the door to the Parker Library, which holds the finest collection of Anglo-Saxon manuscripts in the world.

On the corner of Bene't St you'll find the college's new **Corpus Clock**. Made from 24-carat gold, it displays the time through a series of concentric LED lights. The clock is only accurate once every five minutes. At other times it slows or stops and then speeds up, which according to its creator, JC Taylor, reflects life's irregularity.

Cambridge

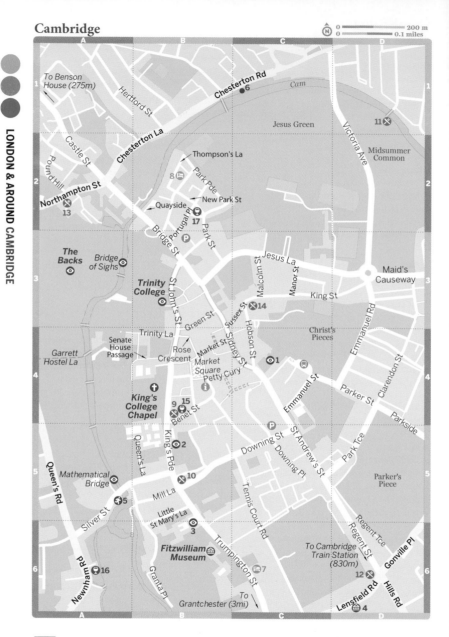

FREE **PETERHOUSE** College
(www.pet.cam.ac.uk; Trumpington St) The
oldest and smallest college, Peterhouse
is a charming place founded in 1284. Just
to the north is **Little St Mary's Church**,
which has a memorial to Peterhouse
student Godfrey Washington, great-uncle
of George. His family coat of arms was the
stars and stripes, the inspiration for the
US flag.

Cambridge

Other Sights

THE BACKS　　　　　　　　　　　Park

Behind the grandiose facades, stately courts and manicured lawns of the city's central colleges lies a series of gardens and parklands butting up against the river. Collectively known as the Backs, these tranquil green spaces and shimmering waters offer unparalleled views of the colleges and are often the most enduring image of Cambridge for visitors.

The fanciful **Bridge of Sighs** (built in 1831) at St John's is best observed from the stylish bridge designed by Wren just to the south. The oldest crossing is at **Clare College**, built in 1639 and ornamented with decorative balls. Most curious of all is the flimsy-looking wooden construction joining the two halves of Queen's College known as the **Mathematical Bridge**, first built in 1749. Despite what unscrupulous guides may tell you, it wasn't the handiwork of Sir Isaac Newton (he died in 1727), originally built without nails, or taken apart by academics who then couldn't figure how to put it back together.

FREE **FITZWILLIAM MUSEUM**　　Museum
(www.fitzmuseum.cam.ac.uk; Trumpington St; entry by donation, guided tour £5; ⊙10am-5pm Tue-Sat, noon-5pm Sun) Fondly dubbed 'the Fitz' by locals, this colossal neoclassical pile was one of the first public art museums in Britain, built to house the fabulous treasures that the seventh Viscount Fitzwilliam had bequeathed to his old university.

The lower galleries are filled with priceless treasures spanning the ancient world; look out for a Roman funerary couch, an inscribed copper votive plaque from Yemen (c100–200 AD), a figurine of Egyptian cat goddess Bastet, some splendid Egyptian sarcophagi and mummified animals, plus some dazzling illuminated manuscripts. The upper galleries showcase works by Leonardo da Vinci, Titian, Rubens, the Impressionists, Gainsborough and Constable, right through to Rembrandt and Picasso. You can join a one-hour **guided tour** of the museum at 2.30pm Saturday.

FREE **SCOTT POLAR RESEARCH INSTITUTE**　　　　Museum
(📞 guide Kay Smith 01223-336573, museum 01223-336540; www.spri.cam.ac.uk/museum; Lensfield Rd; ⊙10am-4pm Tue-Sat) The Scott Polar Institute, founded with part of the relief fund set up in the wake of the ill-fated Scott expedition to the South Pole, these days takes a lead role in climate-change research and has an excellent museum that focuses on polar exploration, charting the feats of the likes of Amundsen, Nansen and Scott himself.

 **Activities**

Punt hire costs £14 to £16 per hour, chauffeured trips of the Backs cost £10 to £12, and a return trip to Grantchester will set you back £20 to £30. All companies offer discounts if you prebook tickets online.

CAMBRIDGE
CHAUFFER PUNTS   Punting
(www.punting-in-cambridge.co.uk; Silver St Bridge)

GRANTA   Punting
(www.puntingincambridge.com; Newnham Rd)

 Tours

WALKING TOURS   Guided Tours
(☎01223-457574; tours@cambridge.gov.uk; Wheeler St; ☉1.30pm daily, sometimes extra tours at 10.30am, 11:30am & 14.30pm) The tourist office arranges these, as well as other less-frequent tours, such as colourful 'Ghost Tours' and 'Punt and Pint Tours'.

RIVERBOAT GEORGINA   Boat Tours
(☎01223-307694; www.georgina.co.uk) One-/ two-hour cruises (£6/12), with the option of including lunch or a cream tea.

 **Sleeping**

VARSITY HOTEL & SPA   Hotel £££
(☎01223-306030; www.thevarsityhotel.co.uk; Thompson's Lane; d/ste from £225/385; ☎) A celebration of Cambridge's august intellectual heritage, this hotel has an unparalleled location. The decor is understated, with lovely touches such as four-poster beds and floor-to-ceiling glass, monsoon showers and iPod docks. From the roof terrace there's a splendid view of the city.

HOTEL DU VIN
Hotel £££

(☎01223-227330; www.hotelduvin.com; Trumpington St; d from £150; @ ☎) This hotel chain really knows how to do things right. Its Cambridge offering has all the usual trademarks, from quirky but incredibly stylish rooms with monsoon showers and luxurious Egyptian cotton sheets, to the atmospheric vaulted cellar bar and the French-style bistro (mains £15 to £22).

HOTEL FELIX   Boutique Hotel £££
(☎01223-277977; www.hotelfelix.co.uk; Whitehouse Lane, Huntingdon Rd; s/d from £165/200; P @ ☎) Occupying a lovely grey-brick Victorian villa in landscaped grounds, the 52 rooms here embody designer chic, with minimalist style and touches such as Egyptian cotton bedding and rain showers in many rooms. The slick restaurant serves modern Mediterranean cuisine (mains £13 to £23). Follow Castle St and then Huntingdon Rd out of the city for about 1.5 miles.

BENSON HOUSE   B&B ££
(☎01223-311594; www.bensonhouse.co.uk; 24 Huntingdon Rd; d from £90; P ☎) Just a 15-minute walk from the city centre, the rooms at this B&B range from monochrome minimalism to muted classical elegance, and breakfast includes kippers.

Eating

MIDSUMMER HOUSE   Modern British £££
(☎01223-369299; www.midsummerhouse. co.uk; Midsummer Common; 3-/4-/5-course set menu £40/50/60, tasting menu £95; ☺lunch Wed-Sat, dinner Tue-Sat) In a Victorian villa backing onto the river, this place is sheer gastronomic delight. Chef Daniel's Michelin-starred creations are distinguished by depth of flavour, great technical skill and expert pairings of ingredients.

121

SIMON GREENWOOD/GETTY IMAGES ©

OAK BISTRO Modern British **££**
(📞01223-323361; www.theoakbistro.co.uk; 6 Lensfield Rd; mains £12-20, 2-/3-course set lunch £12/15; ⏱Mon-Sat) This great local favourite serves up simple, classic dishes with modern flair, such as tuna nicoise salad and slow-roasted lamb. Reservations essential even for lunch, due to its size and popularity.

STICKYBEAKS Cafe **£**
(www.stickybeakscafe.co.uk; 42 Hobson St; mains £3-7; ⏱8am-5.30pm Mon-Fri, 9am-5.30pm Sat, 10am-5pm Sun; ✈) Sip creamy hot chocolate, nibble on an array of cakes or tuck into some imaginative salads (couscous with pomegranate, puy lentils with goat's cheese) and sausage rolls with unusual chutney at this popular new cafe.

CHOP HOUSE Traditional British **££**
(http://www.cambscuisine.com/cambridge-chop-house; 1 Kings Pde; mains £9.50-24) If you're craving sausage and mash, a sizzling steak, suet pudding, fish pie or potted ham, look no further. Sister restaurant **St John's Chop House** (http://www.cambscuisine.com/st-johns-chop-house; 21-24 Northampton St) is located near the rear entrance to St John's College.

FITZBILLIES Bakery, Cafe **££**
(www.fitzbillies.co.uk; 52 Trumpington St; cafe mains £8-19; ⏱closed dinner Mon) Cambridge's oldest bakery, beloved by generations of students for its ultrasticky buns and quaint wood shopfront.

🍷 Drinking

MAYPOLE Pub
(www.maypolefreehouse.co.uk; 20a Portugal Pl) This friendly, locally popular traditional pub has hit on a winning formula: serve a good selection of real ales, not forgetting lesser-known beers from smaller breweries, throw in some great cocktails, and then, when it seemed that things couldn't get any better, add a successful beer festival in 2012 (set to become an annual event).

EAGLE Pub
(Bene't St) Cambridge's most famous pub has loosened the tongues and pickled the grey cells of many an illustrious academic; among them Nobel Prize–winning scientists Crick and Watson, who discussed their research into DNA here.

GRANTA   Pub

(☎01223-505016; Newnham Rd) If the exterior of this picturesque waterside pub, overhanging a pretty mill pond, looks strangely familiar, it could well be because it is the darling of many a TV director.

❶ Information

Tourist office (☎0871-266 8006; www. visitcambridge.org; Old Library, Wheeler St; ⊙10am-5.30pm Mon-Fri, to 5pm Sat, 11am-3pm Sun) Pick up a guide to the Cambridge colleges (£4.99) in the gift shop or a leaflet (£1.20) outlining two city walks. Download audio tours from the website or book slots on a plethora of tours. Rudimentary Cambridge map costs £1.

❶ Getting There & Away

Car

Cambridge's centre is largely pedestrianised and the car parks are expensive. Use one of the five free Park & Ride car parks on major routes into town. Buses (tickets £2.70) serve the city centre every 10 minutes between 7am and 7pm daily, then every 20 minutes until 10pm.

Train

The train station is off Station Rd, which is off Hills Rd. Destinations:

○ **Birmingham New Street** (£30, three hours, hourly)

○ **Ely** (£4, 15 minutes, three hourly)

○ **King's Lynn** (£9, 45 minutes, hourly)

○ **London Kings Cross** (£19, 50 minutes to 1¼ hours)

○ **Stansted** (£11, 30 minutes, hourly)

❶ Getting Around

Bicycle

Cambridge is very bike-friendly, and two wheels provide a great way of getting about town.

Cambridge Station Cycles (www.station cycles.co.uk; Station Building, Station Rd; per half-day/day/week £7/10/25) Near the train station.

City Cycle Hire (www.citycyclehire.com; 61 Newnham Rd; per half-/full day from £6/10, per week £17-22)

Bus

A free gas-powered City Circle bus runs around the centre, stopping every 15 minutes from 9am to 5pm, on Downing St, King's Pde and Jesus Lane. Dayrider passes (£3.30) offer unlimited travel on all buses within Cambridge for one day.

Oxford & Central England

Celebrated as the home of English academia, Oxford also sits slap bang at the very centre of England. With its dreaming spires and dazzling architecture, it opens a fascinating window on the nation's history, but it also provides an ideal gateway for exploring further afield.

Just beyond this studious city rise the tranquil hills and implausibly pretty villages of the Cotswolds, quintessential olde-worlde English villages, filled with flower-clad cottages, stone churches, frilly tearooms and antique shops. Nearby is Shakespeare's birthplace in Stratford-upon-Avon, now a point of pilgrimage for fans of the Bard. Further north the gentle landscape gives way to countryside with a slightly harder edge, with the rugged moors of the Peak District and Ironbridge Gorge, birthplace of the Industrial Revolution.

And then, of course, there are two of the nation's most impressive stately homes to discover, Blenheim Palace and Chatsworth House – both of which are a simply essential part of any English itinerary.

Main bridge, Chatsworth House (p164)

Oxford & Central England

Hull
M62
Humber
Grimsby
M180
Spurn
Head

NORTH

SEA

Lincoln

Skegness

Boston

The
Wash

Holkham
Burnham
Deepdale
Wells-next-
the-Sea

King's
Lynn

NORFOLK   Norwich

How Hill ▲

Great
Yarmouth

Peterborough   March

Great Ouse

Thetford
Forest
A11

Norfolk
Broads
National Park   Lowestoft

CAMBRIDGESHIRE

SUFFOLK

Huntingdon

Ely

Cambridge   Newmarket

Bury St
Edmunds

Stowmarket   Aldeburgh

Wellingborough

Lavenham
Haverhill   Long
Melford   Woodbridge

Milton
Keynes   A1

Saffron
Walden   Sudbury   Ipswich

Woburn

M11

Stansted
Airport

Luton

St Albans

Watford

Baintree

Harlow

Thames   M25

LONDON   M25

A325

M25

Maldon

Chelmsford

Brentwood
Basildon

Colchester   Felixstowe

ESSEX   A12

Southend-
on-Sea

Margate   Isle of
Thanet

Rochester

50 km
0
25 miles

53°N

52°N

① Oxford University
② Blenheim Palace
③ Stratford-upon-Avon
④ The Cotswolds
⑤ Ironbridge Gorge
⑥ Warwick Castle
⑦ Chatsworth House

Oxford & Central England Highlights

ALAN BLAIR/ALAMY STOCK IMAGES

1

Oxford University

Don't expect a neat, orderly campus here. Oxford University consists of 39 separate colleges scattered around the city, rubbing shoulders with other historic buildings and sometimes more workaday modern streets. Each college is a historic and architectural gem in its own right, so it's worth visiting as many as you can. Above: Radcliffe Camera (p139); Top Right: Bodleian Library detail; Bottom Right: Bridge of Sighs

Need to Know

TOP TIP Check opening hours; some colleges close for exams **BEST TIME TO VISIT** May or September **BEST PHOTO OP** Radcliffe Camera **For further coverage, see p138**

Oxford University Don't Miss List

PETER BERRY, WALKING-TOUR GUIDE, BLACKWELL BOOKSHOP

1 CHRIST CHURCH

I've been showing visitors around for over 15 years, and many people say how much they enjoy the vibrant atmosphere. Christ Church (along with **Magdalen College**) is the most popular sight, partly thanks to its links with Lewis Carroll. These spots can be crowded, but going with a guide helps you jump the queues and make the most of your time here.

2 EXETER COLLEGE

To escape the crowds (a little), I recommend seeing slightly less-well-known places such as Exeter College, which has the most beautiful chapel of all the Oxford colleges, containing an exquisite tapestry by Pre-Raphaelite artists William Morris and Edward Burne-Jones. Another favourite is **New College**, also with a beautiful chapel and a large section of the ancient City Walls.

3 BRIDGE OF SIGHS

Hertford College has academic buildings on each side of New College Lane joined by the ornate Bridge of Sighs, named after the famous bridge in Venice (although as that bridge led to a prison it had small windows – ours are much larger). Alumni here include authors Jonathan Swift and Evelyn Waugh.

4 BODLEIAN LIBRARY

The 17th-century Bodleian Library is one of the oldest libraries in the world. Priceless items stored here include the original manuscripts of Tolkien's *The Hobbit*. On the other side of Broad St is the 20th-century part of the library; not many people know an underground conveyor belt carries books between the two.

5 UNIVERSITY CHURCH OF ST MARY THE VIRGIN

Originally just for the university, the services are now open to 'town and gown' (locals and students). Climb the tower's 127 steps – there's no lift in this medieval building – for spectacular views of the 'dreaming spires' of Oxford and out to the **Cotswold Hills** beyond.

Blenheim Palace

This vast pile in the Oxfordshire countryside is the family seat of the dukes of Marlborough, but it's perhaps best known as the birthplace of Winston Churchill. Designed by Sir John Vanbrugh, the house is spectacular enough, but for many people it's the lavish grounds (partly designed by Lancelot 'Capability' Brown) that steal the show. Bottom: Italian Gardens; Top Right: Green Writing Room; Bottom Right: The Great Hall

Need to Know

TOP TIP Book online **BEST TIME TO VISIT** April or May **BEST PHOTO OP** 'Capability' Brown's cascade **For further coverage, see p142**

RELIGIOUS IMAGES/UIG/GETTY IMAGES ©

Blenheim Palace Don't Miss List

BY JOHN FORSTER, ARCHIVIST TO HIS GRACE THE DUKE OF MARLBOROUGH

1 THE GREAT HALL

The Great Hall is the first room visitors see, and its size, proportions and drama really establish the monumental purpose of the palace. Look out for the Victory Arch, the stone friezes by Grinling Gibbons, and the ceiling painting by Thornhill, which shows the kneeling duke presenting the battle plan of his victory at Blenheim to Britannia.

2 THE LONG LIBRARY

Though Sir John Vanbrugh was Blenheim's chief architect, he left his assistant Nicholas Hawksmoor to complete the Long Library. At 56m long, it's the second-longest private library in the country. The ceiling is particularly lovely, with its intricate stucco work and two false domes.

3 THE SALOON

In general the palace emphasises the duke's military achievements, but this room shows the virtues of peace. The wall and ceiling paintings depict the peaceful people of the four continents, while the duke's uplifted sword as he rides to victory is stayed by the hand of the figure of Peace.

4 THE BLENHEIM TAPESTRY IN THE GREEN WRITING ROOM

This is the most important of the 10 'Victory Tapestries' commissioned by the first duke to commemorate his exploits in the War of the Spanish Succession (1702–11). It's on a huge scale (7.62m x 4.42m), and even though it's over 300 years old, the details of the battle and its key protagonists (including the duke himself) remain perfectly clear.

5 THE TEMPLE OF DIANA

It's a five-minute walk from the palace to this 18th-century lakeside temple, where Winston Churchill proposed to his wife Clementine. Even today, it's a popular place for marriage proposals – very romantic!

TRAVEL IB/ALAMY ©

Shakespeare at Stratford-upon-Avon

What could be more English than taking in one of Shakespeare's play in the birthplace (p152) of the nation's best-known playwright? After visiting William's birthplace and his grave – and all the houses he's connected with in between – make sure you leave time to see the Royal Shakespeare Company in action. Royal Shakespeare Company Theatre (p155)

Exploring the Cotswolds

For a picture-perfect vision of rural England, there are few places finer than the quiet villages and winding lanes of the Cotswolds (p144). Filled with honey-stoned cottages, village greens and country pubs, they're the ideal place for leisurely exploration, either by bike, bus or car. Even in summer, it's usually possible to dodge the crowds and discover your own patch of olde-worlde England. Stow-on-the-Wold (p148)

Ironbridge Gorge

5

During the 18th and 19th centuries, the Midlands was the heart of the Industrial Revolution, and its towns and villages echoed to the sound of spinning looms and clattering mills. This river gorge (p157) – now a World Heritage Site – was the first place in Britain to perfect the art of smelting iron ore, and its period buildings have been turned into museums exploring the area's industrial past.

Warwick Castle

6

Founded in 1068 by William the Conqueror, immensely popular Warwick Castle (p151) is ruined enough to be romantic, but still well preserved enough to be impressive. With sumptuous interiors, landscaped gardens, waxwork-populated private apartments, towering ramparts, armoury displays, medieval jousting and a theme-park dungeon there's plenty to keep the family busy for a whole day.

Chatsworth House

7

In the heart of the Peak District National Park, the great stately home of Chatsworth House (p164) is known as the 'Palace of the Peak'. Inside, the lavish apartments and mural-painted staterooms are packed with paintings and priceless items of period furniture. The house sits in vast ornamental gardens and is surrounded by 25 sq miles of grounds, some landscaped by Lancelot 'Capability' Brown.

Oxford & Central England's Best...

Historic Churches

o **Christ Church Cathedral, Oxford** (p139) England's smallest cathedral in one of Oxford University's grandest colleges

o **Holy Trinity Church, Stratford-upon-Avon** (p153) William Shakespeare's final resting place with famous epitaph

o **Ely Cathedral** (p160) Marvel at the audacious architecture of the famous 'Ship of the Fens'

o **Lincoln Cathedral** (p159) Relive the climax of *The Da Vinci Code* at this wonderful cathedral

Architecture

o **Haddon Hall** (p148) The picture of a medieval manor – timbers, turrets and all

o **Iron Bridge** (p157) Arched bridge showcasing the new technology of cast iron

o **Burghley House** (p148) This magnificent house was state of the art in Elizabethan times

o **Warwick Castle** (p151) Classic medieval stronghold, which still hosts jousting tournaments

o **Radcliffe Camera** (p139) A Palladian dome with an unparalleled Oxford panorama

Natural Wonders

o **Peak District** (p161) England's oldest national park, with moors, valleys and lakes – but no peaks

o **Sherwood Forest** (p156) Famous as Robin Hood's hideout, this nature reserve is now a popular picnic spot

o **Peak Cavern** (p163) See stalagtites and stalagmites galore in this subterranean cavern, known locally as the Devil's Arse

o **River Avon** (p154) Cruise along this historic waterway from Shakespeare's home town

Country Towns

- **Stratford-upon-Avon** (p152) A delightful Midlands market town and birthplace of the Bard

- **Bakewell** (p165) Deep in the Peak District, famous for its eponymous pudding

- **Buxton** (p161) Former spa town, still with trappings of Regency elegance

- **Stow-on-the-Wold** (p148) A Cotswolds classic, famous for its large market square, surrounded by antique shops

- **Chipping Campden** (p146) Of all the pretty Cotswolds towns, this is the gem

Left: Burghley House (p148); **Above:** Fallow deer

Need to Know

ADVANCE PLANNING

- **Two months before** Book hotels in Oxford and the Cotswolds; reserve seats for the Royal Shakespeare Company in Stratford-upon-Avon.

- **One month before** Check opening times for Oxford colleges and the main Shakespeare attractions.

- **Two weeks before** Book tickets online for sights including Chatsworth House, Blenheim Palace and Warwick Castle.

RESOURCES

- **Oxford** (www.visitoxford.org)

- **The Cotswolds** (www.visitcotswolds.co.uk)

- **Heart of England** (www.visitheartofengland.com)

- **Peak District** (www.visitpeakdistrict.com)

- **Warwick, Stratford-upon-Avon, Coventry** (www.shakespeare-country.co.uk)

GETTING AROUND

- **Bus** Long-distance buses between main centres are good. Various companies offer services to the Cotswolds and Peak District villages.

- **Train** Connections between the major towns are fast and frequent, but to reach rural areas you'll have to take the bus.

- **Car** Easiest way of getting around the region, but cities and main motorways can get heavy with traffic. Oxford and other big cities have useful Park & Ride systems: park your car on the outskirts, take a shuttle bus into the centre.

BE FOREWARNED

- **Oxford** Many colleges are closed for the Easter term and summer exams. Check www.ox.ac.uk/colleges for full details of opening days and hours.

- **Major sights** Popular areas including Stratford-upon-Avon, Warwick, Oxford and the Peak District get busy in summer.

- **Royal Shakespeare Company** Tickets for major productions are often sold out months in advance, so book early.

Oxford & Central England Itineraries

Follow the three-day itinerary to explore the best of the Cotswolds. The five-day trip leads further north, through the Midlands and into the Peak District. Combine them for a longer tour of the whole region.

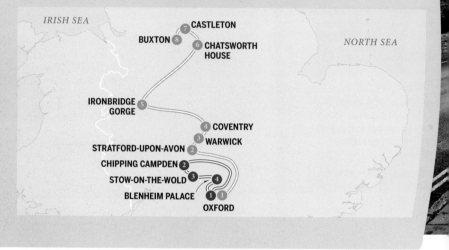

IRISH SEA

NORTH SEA

CASTLETON 7

BUXTON 8

6 **CHATSWORTH HOUSE**

IRONBRIDGE GORGE 5

4 **COVENTRY**

3 **WARWICK**

STRATFORD-UPON-AVON 2

CHIPPING CAMPDEN 2

STOW-ON-THE-WOLD 3

BLENHEIM PALACE 1

OXFORD

3 *DAYS*

OXFORD TO OXFORD
A Cotswolds Loop

Start your tour in the graceful city of **(1) Oxford**. It's easy to spend a day here, sauntering round the elegant colleges and other university buildings. Top sights include Christ Church, as well as architectural landmarks such as the Radcliffe Camera and Bodleian Library.

On your second day, head west into the rural landscape of the Cotswolds. This is an area famous for pretty towns and villages, but finest of them all is **(2) Chipping Campden**, with its graceful curving main street flanked by a wonderful array of stone cottages, quaint shops and historic inns. There's also a good selection of places to stay. Take a look at St James Church and the historic Market Hall, then enjoy an afternoon stroll in the surrounding countryside. Alternatively, visit **(3) Stow-on-the-Wold**, another classic Cotswolds town, its large market square featuring several antique shops.

Day three, and it's time to head back towards Oxford, stopping on the way at **(4) Blenheim Palace**, one of the region's greatest stately homes. Finish your tour with a good dinner at one of Oxford's excellent eateries.

OXFORD TO BUXTON

A Midlands Meander

5 DAYS

Start your tour in **(1) Oxford**, then head north to world-famous **(2) Stratford-upon-Avon**, birthplace of William Shakespeare. It's then a short hop to **(3) Warwick Castle**, for historical insights and family fun, possibly diverting to **(4) Coventry** for a moment of reflection at the famous cathedral. While fans of medieval monuments are never far from a highlight, if you're interested in more recent eras don't miss **(5) Ironbridge Gorge**, the crucible of the Industrial Revolution, now a World Heritage Site with several fascinating museums.

Then it's back to classic British history, and one of the country's finest stately homes, **(6) Chatsworth House**. Leave time to admire the stunning interiors and stroll in the ornamental gardens, famous for fountains and cascades, as well as exhibitions of contemporary sculpture. If time allows, take a longer stroll in the wilder landscape of the surrounding Peak District near **(7) Castleton**.

This tour ends in **(8) Buxton**, a picturesque sprawl of Georgian terraces, Victorian amusements and pretty parks.

Picturesque village, the Cotswolds (p144)
JOHN HAY/GETTY IMAGES ©

Discover Oxford & Central England

Village in the Cotswolds (p144)
FRANZ MARC FREI/GETTY IMAGES ©

OXFORD

POP 134,248

Oxford is a privileged place, one of the world's most famous university towns. The elegant honey-coloured buildings of the 39 colleges that make up the university wrap around tranquil courtyards along narrow cobbled lanes, and inside their grounds, a studious calm reigns.

Sights

If you have your heart set on visiting Oxford's iconic buildings, remember that not all are open to the public. For the colleges that are, visiting hours change with the term and exam schedule; check www.ox.ac.uk/colleges for full details of visiting hours and admission before planning your visit.

University Buildings & Colleges

CHRIST CHURCH College
(www.chch.ox.ac.uk; St Aldate's; adult/child £8/6.50; ⊙9am-5pm Mon-Sat, 2-5pm Sun) The largest of all of Oxford's colleges, and the one with the grandest quad, Christ Church is also its most popular. Its magnificent buildings, illustrious history and latter-day fame as a location for the *Harry Potter* films have tourists coming in droves. Over the years numerous luminaries have been educated here, including philosopher John Locke, poet WH Auden, Charles Dodgson (Lewis Carroll), and no less than 13 British prime ministers!

The main entrance is below the imposing **Tom Tower**, the upper part of which was designed by former student Sir Christopher Wren.

Immediately on entering is the 15th-century cloister, a relic of the ancient Priory of St Frideswide, whose shrine was once a focus of pilgrimage. From here, you go up to the **Great Hall**, the college's magnificent dining room, with its hammerbeam roof and imposing portraits of past scholars; it was replicated in the film studios as the dining hall at Hogwarts for the *Harry Potter* films.

Coming down the grand staircase, you'll enter **Tom Quad**, Oxford's largest and arguably most impressive quadrangle, and from here, **Christ Church Cathedral**, the smallest cathedral in England.

BODLEIAN LIBRARY   Library
(www.bodley.ox.ac.uk; Broad St; Divinity School adult/child £1/free, audioguide £2.50, library tours £6.50; ⏰9am-5pm Mon-Fri, to 4.30pm Sat, 11am-5pm Sun, library tours 10.30am, 11.30am, 1pm & 2pm Mon-Sat, 11.30am, 2pm & 3pm Sun) Oxford's Bodleian Library is one of the oldest public libraries in the world, the first of England's three copyright libraries (the other two are the British Library and the Cambridge University library) and quite possibly the most impressive library you'll ever see. It currently holds over 11 million items, 117 miles of shelving and has seating space for up to 2500 readers, with a staggering 4000 books and articles arriving *every week*, all of which need to be catalogued and stored.

Most of the rest of the library is closed to visitors, but **library tours** allow access to the medieval Duke Humfrey's library. The tour takes about an hour and is not suitable for children under 11 (for fear that they will run amok).

MAGDALEN COLLEGE   College
(www.magd.ox.ac.uk; High St; adult/child £5/4; ⏰noon-7pm) Set amid 40 hectares of lawns, woodlands, river walks and deer park, Magdalen (*mawd*-len), founded in 1458, is one of the wealthiest and most beautiful of Oxford's colleges. The fantastic gargoyles and grotesques along the frontage here are said to have inspired CS Lewis' stone statues in *The Chronicles of Narnia*.

RADCLIFFE CAMERA   Library
(Radcliffe Sq; extended tours £13) The Radcliffe Camera is the quintessential Oxford landmark and one of the city's most photographed buildings. The spectacular circular library/reading room, filled with natural light, was built between 1737 and 1749 in grand Palladian style, and has Britain's third-largest dome. In case you're wondering: no, you cannot enter disguised as a student; the only way to see the interior is to join one of the **extended tours** of the Bodleian Library. Tours take place at 9.15am Wednesday and Saturday and at 11.15am and 1.15pm most Sundays.

NEW COLLEGE   College
(www.new.ox.ac.uk; Holywell St; admission £3; ⏰11am-5pm Mar-Sep) This 14th-century college was the first in Oxford for undergraduates and is a fine example of the glorious Perpendicular style.

MERTON COLLEGE   College
(www.merton.ox.ac.uk; Merton St; admission £2, guided tour £2; ⏰2-5pm Mon-Fri, 10am-5pm Sat & Sun, guided tour 45min) Founded in 1264, Merton is the oldest college and was the first to adopt collegiate planning, bringing scholars and tutors together into a formal community and providing a planned residence for them. Its distinguishing architectural features include the large gargoyles whose expressions suggest that they're about to throw up, and the charming 14th-century **Mob Quad** – the first of the college quads.

FREE ALL SOULS COLLEGE   College
(www.all-souls.ox.ac.uk; High St; ⏰2-4pm Mon-Fri) Much of the college facade dates from the 1440s and, unlike other older colleges, the front quad is largely unchanged in five centuries. Designed by Nicholas Hawksmoor in 1710, the college's twin towers were lambasted for ruining the Oxford skyline when first erected.

TRINITY COLLEGE   College
(www.trinity.ox.ac.uk; Broad St; adult/child £1.75/1; ⏰10am-noon & 2-4pm Sun-Fri, 2-4pm Sat) This small 16th-century college is worth a visit to see its exquisitely carved

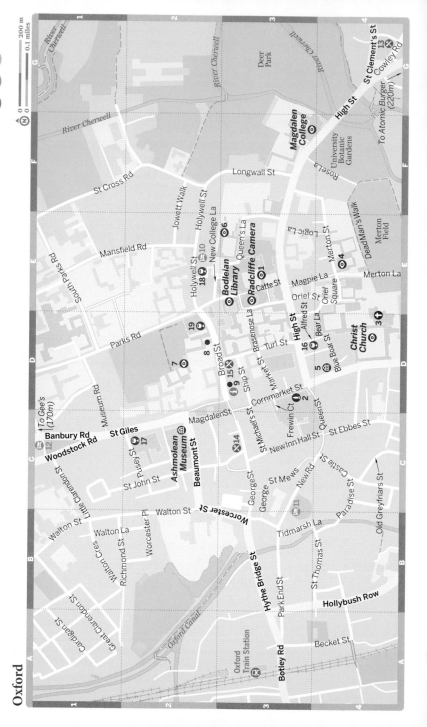

Oxford

200 m
0.1 miles

River Cherwell

River Cherwell

Deer Park

St Clement's St
13
Cowley Rd
To Atomic Burger (220m)

High St

Magdalen College

University Botanic Gardens

Rose La

Longwall St

St Cross Rd

Jowett Walk

Holywell St

Mansfield Rd

New College La

6

Bodleian Library

Radcliffe Camera

Queen's La

Catte St

1

Magpie La

Merton St

4

Merton La

DeadMan's Walk

Merton Field

Logic La

18
10

Holywell St

South Parks Rd

Parks Rd

19

7

8

Broad St

15

9

Ship St

Brasenose La

Turl St

Market St

Oriel St

Alfred St

Bear La

Oriel Square

High St

16

Blue Boar St

5

Christ Church

3

Museum Rd

To Gee's (170m)

Banbury Rd
12
Woodstock Rd

St Giles

17

St Pusey St

Ashmolean Museum

Beaumont St

St John St

Magdalen St

St Michael's St

Cornmarket St

New Inn Hall St

Frewin Ct

2

Queen St

St Ebbes St

14

George St

George St Mews

New Rd

Castle St

Paradise St

Old Greyfriars St

Walton St

Worcester St

Worcester Pl

Walton La

Walton Cres

Richmond St

Little Clarendon St

Great Clarendon St

Cardigan St

Hythe Bridge St

Oxford Canal

Park End St

St Thomas St

Tidmarsh La

11

Hollybush Row

Becket St

Botley Rd

Oxford Train Station

Oxford

chapel, one of the most beautiful in the city, and the lovely garden quad designed by Christopher Wren.

Other Sights

FREE ASHMOLEAN MUSEUM Museum
(www.ashmolean.org; Beaumont St; ☺10am-6pm Tue-Sun; 🚼) Britain's oldest public museum, and second in repute only to London's British Museum. Its collections, displayed in bright, spacious galleries within one of Britain's best examples of neo-Grecian architecture, span the world and include everything from Egyptian mummies and sarcophagi, Islamic and Chinese art, Japan's 'floating world' and examples of the earliest written languages to rare porcelain, tapestries and silverware, priceless musical instruments and extensive displays of European art (including works by Raphael and Michelangelo).

The Ashmolean has recently undergone a makeover, leaving it with new interactive features, a giant atrium, glass walls revealing galleries on different levels, and a beautiful rooftop restaurant.

FREE MUSEUM OF OXFORD Museum
(www.museumofoxford.org.uk; St Aldate's; ☺10am-5pm Tue-Sat) Though it often gets overlooked in favour of Oxford's other museums, this is an absorbing romp through the city's history. The reconstructions of period interiors, such as a 19th-century Jericho kitchen, are particularly good.

CARFAX TOWER Tower
(cnr Cornmarket & Queen Sts; adult/child £2.50/1.30; ☺10am-5.30pm) Oxford's central landmark, towering over what has been a crossroads for 1000 years, is the sole reminder of medieval St Martin's Church and offers good views over the city centre.

 Tours

TOURIST OFFICE Walking Tours
(☎01865-252200; www.visitoxfordandoxford shire.com; 15-16 Broad St; tours adult/child from £6/3.75; ☺9.30am-5pm Mon-Sat, 10am-4pm Sun) Runs tours of Oxford city and colleges (10.45am and 2pm year-round, 11am and 1pm July and August), *Inspector Morse* tours (1.30pm Saturday), family walking tours (1.30pm during school holidays), and a bewildering array of themed tours, including *Alice in Wonderland* and *Harry Potter*; check the website for exact dates.

RELIGIOUS IMAGES/UIG/GETTY IMAGES ©

Don't Miss **Blenheim Palace**

One of the country's greatest stately homes, Blenheim Palace is a monumental baroque fantasy designed by Sir John Vanbrugh and Nicholas Hawksmoor between 1705 and 1722. The land and funds to build the house were granted to John Churchill, Duke of Marlborough, by a grateful Queen Anne after his decisive victory at the 1704 Battle of Blenheim. Now a Unesco World Heritage Site, Blenheim (pronounced *blen*-num) is home to the 11th duke and duchess.

Highlights include the **Great Hall**, a vast space topped by 20m-high ceilings adorned with images of the first duke in battle; the opulent **Saloon**, the grandest and most important public room; the three **state rooms**, with their plush decor and priceless china cabinets; and the magnificent **Long Library**, which is 55m in length.

From the library, you can access the **Churchill Exhibition**, which is dedicated to the life, work and writings of Sir Winston, who was born at Blenheim in 1874. For an insight into life below stairs, the **Untold Story** exhibition explores the family's history through the eyes of the household staff.

If the crowds in the house become too oppressive, retire to the lavish gardens and vast parklands, parts of which were landscaped by Lancelot 'Capability' Brown.

Blenheim Palace is near the small town of Woodstock, 8 miles northwest of Oxford.

NEED TO KNOW

www.blenheimpalace.com; adult/child £20/10; ⊙10.30am-5.30pm mid-Feb–Oct

BILL SPECTRE'S GHOST TRAILS Walking Tours
(☎07941 041811; www.ghosttrail.org; adult/child £7/4; ⊙6.30pm Fri & Sat; 🚻) For an entertaining and informative look at Oxford's dark underbelly, join Victorian undertaker Bill Spectre on a tour of the city's's most haunted sites. The 1¾-hour tour departs from Oxford Castle Unlocked and the tourist office. Audience participation likely.

BLACKWELL — Walking Tours

(☎01865-333606; oxford@blackwell.co.uk; 48-51 Broad St; adult/child £7/6.50; ⊗mid-Apr–Oct) Oxford's most famous bookshop runs 1½-hour guided walking tours, including a literary tour (2pm Tuesday and 11am Thursday), a tour devoted to 'The Inklings' – an informal literary group whose membership included CS Lewis and JRR Tolkien (11.45am Wednesday), and a Historic Oxford tour (2pm Friday). Book ahead.

Sleeping

MALMAISON — Hotel £££

(☎01865-268400; www.malmaison-oxford.com; Oxford Castle; d/ste from £125/275; ☐@☎) This former Victorian prison next to Oxford Castle was converted into a sleek hotel with plush interiors, sultry lighting and giant beds, with each room made from three cells.

BATH PLACE HOTEL — Boutique Hotel ££

(☎01865-791812; www.bathplace.co.uk; 4-5 Bath Pl, Holywell St; s/d from £95/120) Comprising several 17th-century weavers' cottages surrounding a tiny, plant-filled courtyard right in the shadow of New College, this is one of Oxford's more unusual hotels.

OLD PARSONAGE HOTEL — Boutique Hotel £££

(☎01865-310210; www.oldparsonage-hotel.co.uk; 1 Banbury Rd; d from £225; ☐@☎) Wonderfully quirky, the Old Parsonage is a small boutique hotel in a 17th-century stone building covered with wisteria, with just the right blend of period charm and modern luxury. Oscar Wilde once made it his home.

Eating

GEE'S — Modern British ££

(☎01865-553540; www.gees-restaurant.co.uk; 61 Banbury Rd; mains £12-19) Set in a Victorian conservatory, this top-notch restaurant is popular with the visiting parents of university students, thanks to its creative menu of modern British and European dishes.

ATOMIC BURGER — American £

(www.atomicburger.co.uk; 96 Cowley Rd; mains £7-11; ⊗closed breakfast Mon-Fri) Fast food, but not as you know it. Try the inventive Messy Jessie, Dead Elvis, the barbeque ribs or nachos and curly fries, all washed down with mega shakes.

MISSING BEAN — Cafe £

(www.themissingbean.co.uk; 14 Turl St; mains £3-6; ⊗8am-6.30pm Mon-Fri, 10am-6.30pm Sat, 10.30am-5.30pm Sun; ☑) The fresh muffins, cakes and ciabatta sandwiches make this a great lunchtime stop.

JAMIE'S ITALIAN — Italian ££

(www.jamiesitalian.com; 24-26 George St; mains £9-19) Celebrity chef Jamie Oliver's restaurant serves up some excellent rustic Italian dishes at affordable prices, with the antipasti served on their trademark wooden planks.

CAFÉ COCO — Mediterranean ££

(www.cafe-coco.co.uk; 23 Cowley Rd; mains £6-10.50) This Cowley Rd institution is a hip hang-out, with classic posters on the walls and a bald plaster-cast clown in an ice bath.

Drinking

TURF TAVERN — Pub

(4 Bath Pl) Hidden down a narrow alleyway, this tiny medieval pub is one of the town's best loved and bills itself as 'an education in intoxication' (it's where president Bill Clinton 'did not inhale').

BEAR — Pub

(6 Alfred St) Arguably Oxford's oldest pub (there's been a pub on this site since 1242), this atmospherically creaky place requires tall people to duck their heads when passing through doorways.

WHITE HORSE — Traditional Pub

(www.whitehorseoxford.co.uk; 52 Broad St) This tiny old-world place – Oxford's smallest pub – was a favourite retreat for TV detective Inspector Morse, and it can get pretty crowded in the evening.

EAGLE & CHILD   Pub

(**49 St Giles**) Affectionately known as the 'Bird & Baby', this atmospheric place, dating from 1650, was once the favourite haunt of Tolkien and CS Lewis. Its wood-panelled rooms and good selection of real ales still attract a mellow crowd.

ℹ Information

Tourist office (☎01865-252200; www.visitoxford.org; 15-16 Broad St; ⏰9.30am-5pm Mon-Sat, 10am-4pm Sun)

ℹ Getting There & Away

Car

Driving and parking in Oxford is a nightmare. Use the five Park & Ride car parks on major routes leading into town. Parking is free and buses (10 to 15 minutes, every 10 minutes) cost £2.50.

Train

There are half-hourly services to London Paddington (£23, one hour) and roughly hourly trains to Birmingham (£16, 1¼ hours). Hourly services also run to Bath (£16, 1¼ hours) and Bristol (£22, one to two hours), but require a change at Didcot Parkway.

THE COTSWOLDS

Glorious villages riddled with beautiful old mansions of honey-coloured stone, thatched cottages, atmospheric churches and rickety almshouses draw crowds of visitors to the Cotswolds. The booming medieval wool trade brought the area its wealth and left it with such a proliferation of beautiful buildings that its place in history is secured for evermore.

ℹ Information

Cotswolds (www.the-cotswolds.org)

Cotswolds Tourism (www.cotswolds.com)

Minster Lovell

POP 1348

Set on a gentle slope leading down to the meandering River Windrush, Minster Lovell is a gorgeous village with a cluster of stone cottages nestled beside an ancient pub and riverside mill. One of William Morris' favourite spots, the village has changed little since medieval times. It's divided into two halves: Old Minster, recorded in the Domesday Book (1086), and the rather newer Minster Lovell, across the river. The main sight in Old Minster is **Minster Lovell Hall**, the 15th-century manor house that was home to Viscount Francis Lovell.

The revamped, luxurious **Old Swan & Minster Mill** (☎01993-774441; www.oldswanandminstermill.com; d from £165-350; P 🛜) has charming period-style rooms in the 17th-century Old Swan or sleek, contemporary design in the 19th-century converted mill, covered with creepers.

Burford

POP 1340

Slithering down a steep hill to a medieval crossing point on the River Windrush, the remarkable village of Burford is little changed since its glory days at the height of the wool trade.

👁 Sights & Activities

Burford's main attraction lies in its incredible collection of buildings, including the 16th-century **Tolsey House** (Toll House; High St; admission free; ⏰2-5pm Mon-Fri, 11am-5pm Sat & Sun Apr-Oct), where the wealthy wool merchants held their meetings. This quaint building perches on sturdy pillars and now houses a small museum on Burford's history. Just off the main street, you'll find the town's 14th-century **almshouses** and the **Church of St John the Baptist** (www.burfordchurch.org).

145

Sleeping & Eating

LAMB INN   Inn **£££**
(01993-823155; www.cotswold-inns-hotels.
co.uk/lamb; Sheep St; s/d from £120/160; P)
At this atmospheric 15th-century inn,
expect flagstone floors, beamed ceilings,
creaking stairs, a laid-back vibe downstairs, and luxurious period-style rooms
with antique furniture upstairs.

BULL   Hotel **££**
(01993-822220; www.bullatburford.co.uk;
High St; s/d from £70/75) You'll be following
in the footsteps of guests as illustrious
as Charles II if you stay at this distinguished hotel. The plusher rooms feature
four-poster beds and antique furniture,
and the restaurant is pure gourmet, with
beautifully executed dishes making the
most of local ingredients.

ANGEL   Modern British **££**
(01993-822714; www.theangelatburford.co.uk;
14 Witney St; mains £15.50-19) Set in a lovely
16th-century coaching inn, this atmospheric brasserie serves up an innovative
menu of modern British and European
food. There are three traditionally decorated rooms (double £100) upstairs if you
wish to linger.

HUFFKINS   Tearoom **££**
(www.huffkins.com; 98 High St; afternoon tea £16;
8am-5pm Mon-Sat, 10am-5pm Sun) Superb
tearoom serving some of the most
memorable scones you're likely to have.
Also a great place to stock up on local
chutneys and other produce.

Chipping Campden
POP 2206

An unspoiled gem in an area full of pretty
villages, Chipping Campden is a glorious
reminder of life in the Cotswolds in medieval times. The graceful curving main
street is flanked by a picturesque array
of wayward stone cottages, fine terraced
houses, ancient inns and historic homes,
many made of that honey-coloured stone
that the Cotswolds is so famous for.

Sights & Activities

Standing out from the splendour of other
historic buildings along the High St is the
highly photogenic 17th-century **Market
Hall**, with multiple gables and an
elaborate timber roof; this is where
dairy produce used to be sold.
Chipping Campden made
its fortune during the wool
boom, so it's little wonder
that one of the most
prominent buildings in
town is the 14th-century
Grevel House, former
home of successful wool
merchant William Gre-
vel. Nearby on Church
St is a remarkable row
of **almshouses** dating
from the 17th century,
and the Jacobean lodges
and gateways of the now-
ruined **Campden House**,

Market Hall, Chipping Campden
LAURIE NOBLE/GETTY IMAGES ©

a large and lavish 15th-century house, the remains of which you can see clearly from Shipston Rd. At the western end of High St is the 15th-century **St James'** (⏰10am-5pm Mon-Sat, 2-6pm Sun Mar-Oct); built in the Perpendicular style, it has a magnificent tower and some graceful 17th-century monuments.

The surviving **Court Barn Museum** (📞01386-841951; www.courtbarn.org.uk; Church St; adult/child £3.75/free; ⏰10am-5pm Tue-Sun Apr-Sep) is now a craft and design museum featuring work from the Arts and Crafts Movement, such as silverwork, pottery and hand-dyed cloth.

About 4 miles northeast, **Hidcote Manor Garden** (NT; www.nationaltrust.org.uk; Hidcote Bartrim; adult/child £10/5; ⏰10am-6pm) is one of the finest examples of Arts and Crafts landscaping in Britain, with outdoor 'rooms' filled with flowers and rare plants for the arboreally inclined.

🛏 Sleeping & Eating

COTSWOLD HOUSE HOTEL   Boutique Hotel **£££**
(📞01386-840330; www.cotswoldhouse.com; The Square; r £120-670; P @) This chic Regency townhouse-turned-boutique hotel has bespoke furniture, ultracomfortable king-sized beds, Frette linens, cashmere throws, private gardens and hot tubs.

EIGHT BELLS INN   B&B **££**
(📞01386-840371; www.eightbellsinn.co.uk; Church St; s/d from £65/85) This 14th-century inn is an atmospheric B&B featuring bright, modern rooms with iron bedsteads, soothing neutral decor and warm accents. The pub downstairs wins points for its flagstone floors and good, no-nonsense pub grub (two-/three-course menu £18/22) such as pork medallions with caramelised applies.

ℹ Information

Tourist office (📞01386-841206; www.chippingcampdenonline.org; High St; ⏰9.30am-5pm) Pick up a town trail guide (£1) for information on the most historic buildings and

to get you off the main drag and down some of the gorgeous back streets. If you're visiting on a Tuesday between July and September, it's well worth joining a guided tour at 2.30pm (suggested donation £3) run by the Cotswold Wardens.

Broadway
POP 2490

This pretty village, a quintessentially English place with a smattering of antique shops, tearooms and art galleries, has inspired writers, artists and composers in times past with its graceful, golden-hued cottages set at the foot of a steep escarpment. Take the time to wander down to the lovely 12th-century **Church of St Eadburgha**, a signposted 1-mile walk from town. Near here, a path leads uphill for 2 miles to **Broadway Tower** (www.broadwaytower.co.uk; adult/child £4.50/2.50; ⏰10.30am-5pm), a crenulated, 18th-century Gothic folly on the crest of the escarpment, for the all-encompassing views from the top.

For modern comfort within a 300-year-old exterior, try the wonderfully friendly **Crown & Trumpet** (📞01386-853202; www.cotswoldholidays.co.uk; Station Rd; d £60; P 🛜), the Broadway 'local' with five en suite rooms (complete with sloped floors, exposed beams and low ceilings) above the lively pub.

Winchcombe
POP 4379

Winchcombe is very much a working, living place, with butchers, bakers and small independent shops lining the main street. It was capital of the Saxon kingdom of Mercia and one of the most important towns in the Cotswolds until the Middle Ages.

⊙ Sights & Activities

SUDELEY CASTLE   Castle
(www.sudeleycastle.co.uk; adult/child £11/4.20; ⏰10.30am-5pm) The town's main attraction, this magnificent castle was once a favoured retreat of Tudor and Stuart monarchs. It once served as the home of Katherine Parr (Henry VIII's widow) and her second husband, Thomas Seymour.

If You Like...
Stately Homes

As well as showstoppers including Blenheim Palace (p142) and Chatsworth (p164), central England is home to a number of other lavish stately homes.

1 HARDWICK HALL
(NT; house & garden adult/child £11.50/5.80, garden only £5.80/free; ⏰house noon-4.30pm Wed-Sun, garden 9am-6pm daily) One of the most complete Elizabethan mansions in the country, Hardwick Hall featured all the latest mod-cons including fully glazed windows – a massive luxury in the 16th century. The hall is 10 miles southeast of Chesterfield, just off the M1.

2 HADDON HALL
(www.haddonhall.co.uk; adult/child £9.50/5.50; ⏰noon-5pm daily May-Sept, Sat-Mon Mar-Apr & Oct) Glorious Haddon Hall looks exactly like a medieval manor house should – all stone turrets, time-worn timbers and walled gardens. The house is 2 miles south of Bakewell on the A6.

3 BURGHLEY HOUSE
(www.burghley.co.uk; adult/child incl sculpture garden £13.80/7; ⏰11am-5pm Sat-Thu mid-Mar–late Oct) Lying just a mile south of Stamford in Essex, flamboyant Burghley House (pronounced 'bur-lee') was built by Queen Elizabeth's chief adviser William Cecil, whose descendants have lived here ever since.

4 SANDRINGHAM HOUSE
(www.sandringhamestate.co.uk; adult/child £11.50/5.50, gardens & museum only £8.50/4.50; ⏰11am-4.30pm Apr-Oct) The Queen's country estate is set in 25 hectares of landscaped gardens and lakes, and is open to the hoi polloi when the court is not at home. It's 6 miles northeast of King's Lynn off the B1440.

The house is still used as a family home and much of the interior is off limits to visitors, but you can get a glimpse of its grand proportions while visiting the exhibitions of costumes, memorabilia and paintings, and the surrounding gardens. For insight into real life in the castle, join one of the 'Connoisseur Tours' (£15, at 11am, 1pm and 3pm Tuesday, Wednesday and Thursday).

HAILES ABBEY   Ruin
(EH; www.english-heritage.org.uk; adult/child £4.40/2.20; ⏰10am-5pm) Just outside the town are the evocative ruins of this Cistercian abbey, once one of the country's main pilgrimage centres, due to a long-running medieval scam. The abbey was rumoured to possess a vial of Christ's blood, which turned out to be merely coloured water.

Sleeping & Eating

WHITE HART INN   Hotel ££
(☎01242-602359; www.whitehartwinchcombe.co.uk; r £79-119) An appealing central inn that caters well to walkers; choose one of the three cheaper 'rambler' rooms, with shared bathrooms and iron bedsteads, or go for greater luxury in a superior room.

WESTWARD AT
SUDELEY LODGE   B&B ££
(☎01242-604372; www.westward-sudeley.co.uk; Sudeley; s/d from £45/90; P) At this robust 18th-century hunting lodge that doubles as a warm family home, you get to stay in one of three rooms with sweeping views of the valley.

5 NORTH ST   Modern European £££
(☎01242-604566; www.5northstreet restaurant.co.uk; 5 North St; 2-/3-course lunch £23/27, 7-course tasting menu £64; ⏰lunch Wed-Sun, dinner Tue-Sat) From its splendid 400-year old timbered exterior to what you eventually find on your plate, this Michelin-starred restaurant is a treat from start to finish.

Stow-on-the-Wold
POP 2794

The highest town in the Cotswolds (244m), Stow is anchored by a large market square surrounded by handsome buildings and steep-walled alleyways, originally used to funnel the sheep into the fair. Today, it's famous for its twice-yearly

Stow Horse Fair (May and October) and attracting a disproportionate number of people from passing coach tours.

Sleeping & Eating

NUMBER 9
B&B ££

(01451-870333; www.number-nine.info; 9 Park St; s/d from £45/65;) Centrally located and wonderfully atmospheric, this friendly B&B is all sloping floors and exposed beams.

OLD BUTCHERS
Modern European ££

(01451-831700; www.theoldbutchers.com; 7 Park St; mains £15-26; closed Mon & Sun dinner) Simple, smart and sophisticated, this is Stow's top spot for dining, serving robust, local ingredients whipped up into sublime dishes with big flavours.

The Slaughters
POP 400

The picture-postcard villages of Upper and Lower Slaughter manage to maintain their unhurried medieval charm in spite of receiving a multitude of visitors. The village names have nothing to do with

abattoirs; they are derived from the Old English 'sloughtre', meaning slough or muddy place, but today the River Eye is contained within limestone banks and meanders peacefully through the village past the 17th-century Lower Slaughter Manor to the **Old Mill** (www.oldmill-lower slaughter.com; admission £2; 10am-6pm), which houses a small museum and an ice-cream parlour, famous for its fantastic organic ice cream.

Upper Slaughter is less visited than Lower Slaughter, and it's a pleasant stroll between the two villages. For eating or sleeping, you can do no better than **Lords of the Manor** (01451-820243; www. lordsofthemanor.com; Upper Slaughter; d £199-495;). The Michelin-starred restaurant is one of the best around (three-course menu £69), with imaginative, beautifully presented dishes.

Bibury
POP 1235

Once described by William Morris as 'the most beautiful village in England', Bibury is a Cotswold gem with a cluster of gorgeous riverside cottages and tangle of narrow streets flanked by wayward stone

Arlington Row, Bibury

Detour:
Woburn Abbey & Safari Park

Once a Cistercian abbey but dissolved by Henry VIII and awarded to the earl of Bedford, **Woburn Abbey** (www.woburn.co.uk; adult/child £13.50/6.50; ⏰11am-4pm Apr-Sep) is a wonderful country pile set within a 1200-hectare deer park. The opulent house displays paintings by Gainsborough, van Dyck and Canaletto.

On an equally grand scale is **Woburn Safari Park** (www.woburn.co.uk/safari; adult/child £20/15; ⏰10am-5pm), the country's largest drive-through animal reserve. Rhinos, tigers, lions, zebras, bison, monkeys, elephants and giraffes roam the grounds, while in the 'foot safari' area, you can see sea lions, penguins and lemurs.

For both attractions, buy a **passport ticket** (adult/child £22.50/15.50), which can be used on two separate days within any 12-month period.

The abbey and safari park are easily accessible by car off the M1 motorway.

buildings. The main attraction is **Arlington Row**, a stunning sweep of cottages, now thought to be the most photographed street in Britain. Also worth a look is the 17th-century **Arlington Mill**, just a short stroll away across Rack Isle, a wildlife refuge once used as a cloth-drying area.

Few visitors make it past these two sights, but for a glimpse of the real Bibury, venture into the village proper behind Arlington Row, where you'll find the Saxon **Church of St Mary**.

Kelmscott

Three miles east of Lechlade along the A417 lies the gorgeous Tudor pile **Kelmscott Manor** (☎01367-252486; www.kelmscottmanor.org.uk; adult/child £9/4.50; ⏰11am-5pm Wed & Sat Apr-Oct), once the summer home of William Morris, the poet, artist and founder of the Arts and Crafts Movement. The interior is true to his philosophy that one should not own anything that is neither beautiful nor useful, and the house contains many of Morris' personal effects, as well as fabrics and furniture designed by him and his associates.

Painswick

POP 1666

One of the most beautiful and unspoilt towns in the Cotswolds, hilltop Painswick is an absolute gem. Despite its obvious charms, Painswick sees only a trickle of visitors, so you can wander the narrow winding streets and admire the picture-perfect cottages, handsome stone town houses and medieval inns in your own good time.

Sights & Activities

Running downhill beside and behind the church is a series of gorgeous streetscapes. Look out for **Bisley St**, the original main drag, which was superseded by the now ancient-looking **New St** in medieval times. Just south of the church, rare **iron stocks** stand in the street.

ST MARY'S CHURCH   Church
The village centres on a fine, Perpendicular wool church, its pointy steeple fingering the sky, surrounded by tabletop tombs and exactly 99 clipped yew trees that resemble giant lollipops.

PAINSWICK ROCOCO GARDEN   Gardens
(www.rococogarden.co.uk; adult/child £6.50/3; ⏰11am-5pm mid-Jan–Oct; 👶) Just a mile north of town, the ostentatious Painswick Rococo Garden is the area's biggest attraction and the only garden of its type in England, designed by Benjamin Hyett in the 1740s and now restored to its former glory.

🛏 Sleeping

COTSWOLDS88 Boutique Hotel £££
(📞01452-813688; www.cotswolds88.com;
Kemps Lane; d £110-280; P 🛜) This is a
happy marriage of 18th-century architecture and a modern interior. The restaurant is one of the region's best, featuring
sophisticated yet playful fare.

CARDYNHAM HOUSE Hotel ££
(📞01452-814006; www.cardynham.co.uk;
Tibbiwell St; s/d from £65/87; 🕑closed Mon &
dinner Sun; 🛜) Choose the Shaker-style
New England room, the opulent Arabian
Nights room, the chintzy Old Tuscany
room or for a private pool and garden, the
Pool Room. Downstairs, the **Bistro (mains
£10-20)** serves Modern British cuisine.

THE MIDLANDS
Warwick
POP 25,434

Regularly name-checked by Shakespeare,
Warwick was the ancestral seat of the
earls of Warwick, who played a pivotal
role in the Wars of the Roses. Despite a
devastating fire in 1694, Warwick remains
a treasure house of medieval architecture
with rich veins of history and charming
streets, dominated by the soaring turrets
of magnificent Warwick Castle.

◉ Sights

WARWICK CASTLE Castle
(📞0870 442 2000; www.warwick-castle.co.uk;
castle adult/child £19.95/11.95, castle & dungeon
adult/child £27.45/19.45; 🕑10am-6pm Apr-Sep,
to 5pm Oct-Mar; P) Founded in 1068 by
William the Conqueror, the stunningly
preserved Warwick Castle is the biggest
show in town. The ancestral home of
the earls of Warwick, the castle remains
impressively intact, and the Tussauds
Group has filled the interior with noisy
attractions that bring the castle's rich history to life in a flamboyant but undeniably
family-friendly way.

As well as waxworks populating the
private apartments there are jousting
tournaments, daily trebuchet-firings,
themed evenings and a dungeon. Tickets
discounted if you buy online.

St Mary's Church, Painswick

🛏 Sleeping

ROSE & CROWN   Pub ££
(☎01926-411117; www.roseandcrownwarwick.
co.uk; 30 Market Pl; r incl breakfast from £75;
P@🛜≋) This convivial gastropub enjoys
a congenial location on the town square,
with five lovely, spacious and tastefully
decorated rooms, as well as great beer and
superior food (mains from £10.75).

PARK COTTAGE GUEST HOUSE   B&B ££
(☎01926-410319; www.parkcottagewarwick.
co.uk; 113 West St; s/d £52.50/70; P) Southwest of the centre, this stand-alone 16th-
century wattle-and-daub building once
served as the dairy for the castle. It has
seven pretty rooms, each with a teddy bear,
original floors and a courtyard garden.

🍴 Eating

TAILORS   Modern British £££
(☎01926-410590; www.tailorsrestaurant.co.uk;
22 Market Pl; 2-/3-course dinner £28/32.50;
🕙Tue-Sat) Set in a former gentlemen's tailor shop, this elegant eatery serves prime
ingredients – guinea fowl, pork belly and
lamb from named farms – presented
delicately in neat little towers.

MERCHANTS   Brasserie £
(☎01926-403833; www.merchantswarwick.
co.uk; Swan St; mains from £5; 🕙lunch & dinner
Mon-Sat) With a neat and appealing layout,
stylish leather furniture and chalk-board
menus, this black-fronted restaurant and
wine bar offers a fab selection of £5 main
courses.

ℹ Information

Tourist office (☎01926-492212; www.warwick-
uk.co.uk; Court House, Jury St; 🕙9.30am-
4.30pm Mon-Fri, from 10am Sat, 10am-4pm Sun)

ℹ Getting There & Away

Trains run to Birmingham (£7, 45 minutes, half-
hourly) Stratford-upon-Avon (£5.20, 30 minutes,
hourly) and London (£25, 1¾ hours, every 20
minutes), from the station northeast of the centre.

Stratford-upon-Avon
POP 22,187

The author of some of the most quoted
lines ever written in the English language,
William Shakespeare was born in Stratford in 1564 and died here in 1616, and
the five houses linked to his life form the
centrepiece of a tourist attraction that
verges on a cult of personality.

Experiences in this unmistakably Tudor
town range from the touristy (medieval
re-creations and Bard-themed tearooms)
to the humbling (Shakespeare's modest
grave in Holy Trinity Church) and the
sublime (taking in a play by the world-
famous Royal Shakespeare Company).

◎ Sights & Activities

**SHAKESPEARE'S
BIRTHPLACE**   Historic Home
(Henley St) Start your Shakespeare adventure at the house where the world's most
popular playwright supposedly spent his
childhood days. In fact, the jury is still out
on whether this really was Shakespeare's
birthplace, but devotees of the Bard

Shakespeare House Museums

Five of the most important buildings
associated with Shakespeare contain
museums that form the core of the
visitor experience at Stratford, run
by the Shakespeare Birthplace Trust.
You can buy individual tickets to
the **Shakespeare Houses** (☎01789-
204016; www.shakespeare.org.uk; all 5
properties adult/child £21.50/13.50, 3
in town houses £14/9; 🕙9am-5pm Apr-
Oct, hours vary Nov-Mar), but it's more
cost-effective to buy a combination
ticket either covering the three
houses in town, or all five properties.
Expect long queues throughout the
summer.

have been dropping in since at least the 19th century, leaving their signatures scratched onto the windows. Set behind a modern facade, the house contains restored Tudor rooms, live presentations from famous Shakespearean characters, and an engaging exhibition on Stratford's favourite son.

NASH'S HOUSE & NEW PLACE
Historic Site

(☎ 01789-292325; www.shakespeare.org.uk; cnr Chapel St & Chapel Lane) When Shakespeare retired, he swapped the bright lights of London for a comfortable town house at New Pl, where he died of unknown causes in April 1616. The house was demolished in 1759, but an attractive Elizabethan **knot garden** occupies part of the grounds. Recent finds are displayed in the adjacent **Nash's House**, where Shakespeare's granddaughter Elizabeth lived.

HALL'S CROFT
Historic Home

(☎ 01789-292107; Old Town) Shakespeare's daughter Susanna married respected doctor John Hall, and their handsome Jacobean town house stands south of the centre en route to Holy Trinity Church.

HOLY TRINITY CHURCH
Church

(☎ 01789-266316; www.stratford-upon-avon. org; Old Town; church admission free, Shakespeare's grave adult/child £1.50/50p; ◷ 8.30am-6pm Mon-Sat, 12.30-5pm Sun Apr-Sep, shorter hours Oct-Mar) The final resting place of the Bard is said to be the most visited parish church in England. Inside are handsome 16th- and 17th-century tombs (particularly in the Clopton Chapel), some fabulous carvings on the choir stalls and, of course, the grave of William Shakespeare, with its ominous epitaph: 'cvrst be he yt moves my bones'.

Shakespeare's Birthplace
EDUCATION IMAGES/UIG/GETTY IMAGES ©

ANNE HATHAWAY'S COTTAGE
Historic Home

(☎ 01789-292100; Cottage La, Shottery; adult/child £9/5) Before tying the knot with Shakespeare, Anne Hathaway lived in Shottery, a mile west of the centre, in this delightful thatched farmhouse.

MARY ARDEN'S FARM
Historic Home, Farm

(☎ 01789-293455; Station Rd, Wilmcote; adult/child £9.50/6.50) Shakespeare genealogists can trace the family tree to the childhood home of the Bard's mother at Wilmcote, 3 miles west of Stratford.

 Tours

Options include the popular and informative two-hour **guided town walks** (☎ 01789-292478; adult/child £5/2; ◷ 11am Mon-Wed, 2pm Thu-Sun) that depart from Waterside, opposite Sheep St, which is also the starting point for the spooky **Stratford Town Ghost Walk** (adult/child £6/3; ◷ 7.30pm Mon, Thu, Fri & Sat).

Stratford-upon-Avon

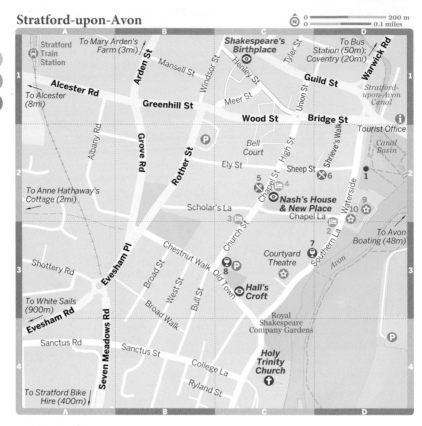

Stratford-upon-Avon

AVON BOATING   Boat Tours
(📞 01789-267073; www.avon-boating.co.uk; The Boathouse, Swan's Nest Lane; 30min river cruises adult/child £4.50/3) Runs river cruises that depart every 20 minutes from either side of the main bridge.

Sleeping

CHURCH STREET
TOWNHOUSE — Boutique Hotel £££

(☎ 01789-262222; www.churchstreettownhouse.com; 16 Church St; r £110-180; 🛜) The 12 rather decadent rooms at this exquisite boutique hotel are divine and very plush, some with free-standing bath and all with iPod dock, flatscreen TVs and luxurious furnishings.

SHAKESPEARE HOTEL — Hotel £££

(☎ 01789-294997; www.mercure.com; Chapel St; s/d £135/150; 🅿 @) With rooms named after the Bard's plays or characters and a hearty fire crackling in the hearth, the gorgeous Shakespeare offers the full Tudor-inn experience in a timbered medieval charmer on the main street. Car parking is £10 per guest.

ARDEN HOTEL — Hotel £££

(☎ 01789-298682; www.theardenhotelstratford.com; Waterside; r incl breakfast from £125; 🅿 @) Formerly the Thistle, this elegant property facing the Swan Theatre has been stylishly revamped, with a sleek brasserie and champagne bar, and rooms featuring designer fabrics and bathrooms full of polished stone.

WHITE SAILS — Guesthouse ££

(☎ 01789-264326; www.white-sails.co.uk; 85 Evesham Rd; r from £95) Plush fabrics, framed prints, brass bedsteads and shabby-chic tables and lamps set the scene at this gorgeous, intimate guest house on the edge of the countryside.

 Eating

CHURCH STREET
TOWNHOUSE — Bistro ££

(☎ 01789-262222; www.churchstreettownhouse.com; 16 Church St; mains from £11.50; ◷ 8am-10pm; 🛜) Open all day, this lovely restaurant is a fantastic place for immersing yourself in Stratford's historic charms, whether for breakfast, lunch or dinner. The food is delightful and the ambience impeccably congenial and well presented.

LAMBS — Modern European ££

(☎ 01789-292554; www.lambsrestaurant.co.uk; 12 Sheep St; mains £10.25-18.75; ◷ lunch Wed-Sun, dinner daily) Lambs swaps Shakespeare chintz in favour of venetian blinds and modern elegance but throws in authentic 16th-century ceiling beams for good measure.

EDWARD MOON'S — Modern British ££

(☎ 01789-267069; www.edwardmoon.com; 9 Chapel St; mains £10-15) Named after a famous travelling chef who cooked up the flavours of home for the British colonial service, this snug and just refurbished eatery serves delicious, hearty English dishes, many livened up with herbs and spices from the East.

 Drinking

DIRTY DUCK — Pub

(Waterside) Officially called the 'Black Swan', this enchanting riverside alehouse is a favourite thespian watering hole, boasting a roll call of former regulars (Olivier, Attenborough etc) that reads like an actors' *Who's Who*.

WINDMILL INN — Pub

(Church St) Ale was flowing here at the same time as rhyming couplets gushed from Shakespeare's quill – this pub with low ceilings has been around a while.

⭐ Entertainment

ROYAL SHAKESPEARE
COMPANY — Theatre

(RSC; ☎ 0844 800 1110; www.rsc.org.uk; Waterside; tickets £8-38) The three theatre spaces run by the world-renowned Royal Shakespeare Company have witnessed performances by such legends as Lawrence Olivier, Richard Burton, Judi Dench, Helen Mirren, Ian McKellan and Patrick Stewart. There are two grand stages in Stratford – Royal Shakespeare Theatre and the Swan Theatre on Waterside (both were extensively redeveloped between 2007 and 2010).

Detour:
Sherwood Forest National Nature Reserve

If Robin Hood wanted to hide out in Sherwood Forest today, he'd have to disguise himself and the Merry Men as day trippers on mountain bikes. Now covering just 182 hectares of old-growth forest, it's nevertheless a major destination for Nottingham city dwellers.

Until a proposed new visitor centre opens, the **Sherwood Forest visitor centre** (www.sherwoodforest.org.uk; Swincote Rd, Edwinstowe; parking £3; ⏱10am-5pm), on the B6034, is an uninspiring collection of faded late-20th-century buildings housing cafes, gift shops and 'Robyn Hode's Sherwode', with wooden cut-outs, murals and mannequins telling the tale of the famous woodsman. It's the departure point for walking trails passing such Sherwood Forest landmarks as the **Major Oak** (1 mile return), a broad-boughed oak tree (propped up by supporting rods) alleged to have sheltered Robin of Locksley. For informative guided walks try **Ezekial Bone Tours** (☎07941 210986; www.bonecorporation.co.uk; tours adult/child £8/4; ⏱Sat May-Sep). The week-long **Robin Hood Festival** (www.nottinghamcity.gov.uk) is a massive medieval re-enactment that takes place here every August.

ℹ Information

Tourist office (☎0870 160 7930; www.shakespeare-country.co.uk)

ℹ Getting There & Away

If you drive to Stratford, be warned that town car parks charge high fees, 24 hours a day.

Train

From Stratford train station, London Midland runs to Birmingham (£6.80, one hour, hourly), Chiltern Railways runs to London Marylebone (£25, 2¼ hours, four daily). The nostalgic **Shakespeare Express** (☎0121-708 4960; www.shakespeareexpress.com) steam train chugs twice every Sunday in July and August between Stratford and Birmingham Snow Hill; journey time is one hour.

ℹ Getting Around

A bicycle is handy for getting out to the outlying Shakespeare properties. **Stratford Bike Hire** (☎07711-776340; www.stratfordbikehire.com; 7 Seven Meadows Rd; per half-day/day from £7/13) will deliver to your accommodation.

Punts, canoes and rowing boats are available for hire from Avon Boating (p154) near Clopton Bridge.

Ironbridge Gorge

Strolling or cycling through the woods, hills and villages of this peaceful river gorge, it's hard to believe such a sleepy enclave could really have been the birthplace of the Industrial Revolution. Nevertheless, it was here that Abraham Darby perfected the art of smelting iron ore with coke in 1709, making it possible to mass-produce cast iron for the first time.

Abraham Darby's son, Abraham Darby II, invented a new forging process for producing single beams of iron, allowing Abraham Darby III to astound the world with the first-ever iron bridge, constructed in 1779. The bridge remains the focal point of this World Heritage Site, and 10 very different museums tell the story of the Industrial Revolution in the very buildings where it took place.

Sights

The Ironbridge museums are administered by the **Ironbridge Gorge Museum Trust** (☎01952-884391; www.ironbridge.org.uk), and all are open from 10am to 5pm from late March to early November, unless stated otherwise. You can buy tickets as you go, but the good-value **passport ticket** (adult/child £23.25/15.25) allows year-round entry to all of the sites.

MUSEUM OF THE GORGE   Museum
(☎01952-433424; The Wharfage; adult/child £3.60/2.35) Kick off your visit at the Museum of the Gorge, which offers an overview of the World Heritage Site using film, photos and 3D models.

IRON BRIDGE   Bridge
(toll house admission free) The flamboyant, arching and gravel-strewn Iron Bridge, which gives the area its name, was constructed to flaunt the new technology invented by the inventive Darby family. There's a small exhibition on the bridge's history at the former **tollhouse**.

BLISTS HILL
VICTORIAN TOWN   Museum
(☎01952-433424; Legges Way; adult/child £14.95/9.95) Set at the top of the Hay Inclined Plane (a cable lift that once transported coal barges uphill from the Shropshire Canal), Blists Hill is a lovingly restored Victorian village repopulated with townsfolk in period costume, busy with day-to-day chores. There's even a bank, where you can exchange your modern pounds for shillings to use at the village shops.

COALBROOKDALE
MUSEUM OF IRON   Museum
(Wellington Rd; adult/child £7.40/4.95) Set in the brooding buildings of Abraham Darby's original iron foundry, the Museum of Iron contains some excellent interactive exhibits. As well as producing the girders for the Iron Bridge, the factory became famous for heavy machinery and extravagant ornamental castings, including the gates for London's Hyde Park.

Combined tickets with Darby Houses also available.

DARBY HOUSES   Museum
(☎01952-433522; adult/child £4.75/3.25; ☺Apr-Oct) Just uphill from the Museum of Iron are these beautifully restored 18th-century homes, which housed generations of the Darby family in gracious but modest Quaker comfort.

COALPORT CHINA
MUSEUM & TAR TUNNEL   Museum
(museum adult/child £7.60/5.10, Tar Tunnel £2.60/2; ☺ Tar Tunnel Apr-Sep) Dominated by a pair of towering bottle kilns, the atmospheric old china works now contains an absorbing **museum** tracing the history of the industry, with demonstrations of traditional pottery techniques.

A short stroll along the canal brings you to the 200-year-old **Tar Tunnel**, an artificial watercourse that was abandoned when natural bitumen started trickling from its walls.

JACKFIELD TILE MUSEUM   Museum
(☎01952-433424; adult/child £7.60/5.10) Once the largest tile factory in the world, Jackfield was famous for its encaustic tiles, with ornate designs produced using layers of different coloured clay (the tiles are still produced here today for period restorations). Gas-lit galleries re-create ornately tiled rooms from past centuries, from Victorian public conveniences to fairy-tale friezes from children's hospital wards. Tours of the factory are held every Tuesday at 11.30am.

ENGINUITY   Museum
(Wellington Rd; adult/child £7.85/6.75) If the kids are starting to look glazed, recharge their batteries at this levers-and-pulleys science centre beside the Museum of Iron, where you can control robots, move a steam locomotive with your bare hands (and a little engineering know-how) and power up a vacuum cleaner with self-generated electricity.

Ironbridge Gorge

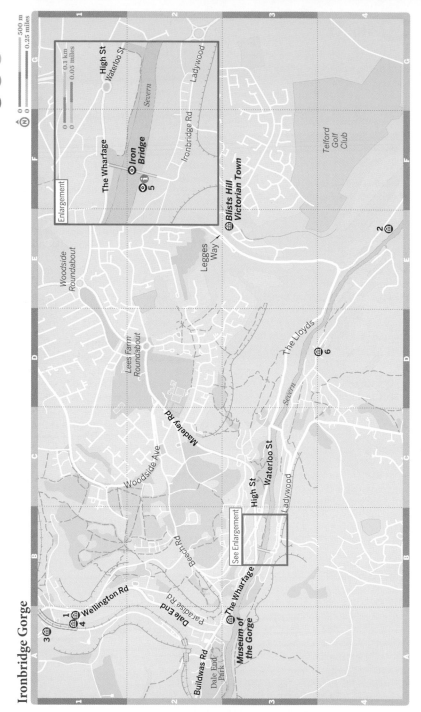

Ironbridge Gorge

. . . .

ⓘ Information

Tourist office (☏01952-884391; www.
visitironbridge.co.uk; The Wharfage; ⏱10am-
5pm) Located at the Museum of the Gorge.

. . . .

ⓘ Getting Around

At weekends and on bank holidays from Easter to
October, the Gorge Connect bus (free to Museum
Passport holders) runs from Telford bus station to
all of the museums on the north bank of the Severn.
A Day Rover pass costs £2.50/1.50 per adult/child.

Lincoln

POP 85,595

A bustling metropolis by Lincolnshire
standards, but a sleepy backwater compared with almost anywhere else, Lincolnshire's county town is a tangle of cobbled
medieval streets surrounding its colossal
12th-century cathedral. Ringed by historic
city gates (including the Newport Arch on
Bailgate, a relic from the original Roman
settlement), this is one of the Midlands'
most beautiful cities: the lanes that topple over the edge of Lincoln Cliff are lined
with Tudor town houses, ancient pubs and
quirky independent stores.

 Sights

LINCOLN CATHEDRAL   Church
(http://lincolncathedral.com; Minster Yard; adult/
child £6/1; ⏱7.15am-8pm Mon-Fri, to 6pm Sat
& Sun, evensong 5.30pm Mon-Sat, 3.45pm Sun)

Towering over Lincoln like a medieval skyscraper, Lincoln's magnificent cathedral
is a breathtaking representation of divine
power on Earth. The great tower rising
above the crossing is the third highest in
England at 83m, but in medieval times,
a lead-encased wooden spire added
a further 79m, topping even the great
pyramids of Giza.

Other interesting details include the
10-sided **chapterhouse** – where Edward I
held his parliament, and where the climax
of *The Da Vinci Code* was filmed in 2005.

Don't miss the one-hour **guided tours**,
which take place at least twice a day plus
less-frequent tours of the roof and the
tower. All are included in the admission
price.

LINCOLN CASTLE   Castle
(www.lincolnshire.gov.uk/lincolncastle; adult/
child £6/4; ⏱10am-6pm) One of the first
castles erected by the victorious William
the Conqueror to keep his new kingdom
in line, Lincoln Castle offers awesome
views over the city and miles of surrounding countryside. Highlights include the
chance to view one of the four surviving
copies of the **Magna Carta** (dated 1215),
and the grim **Victorian prison chapel**,
dating back to the days when this was the
county jailhouse and execution ground.

Free **guided tours** of the castle run
once or twice daily (weekends only in
December and January).

BISHOPS' PALACE   Historic Site
(EH; ☏01522-527468; www.english-heritage.
org.uk; adult/child £4.50/2.70; ⏱10am-5pm
Thu-Mon Apr-Oct, 10am-4pm Sat & Sun Nov-Mar)
Beside Lincoln Cathedral are the time-
ravaged but still imposing ruins of the
12th-century Bishops' Palace, gutted by
parliamentary forces during the Civil War.

 **Sleeping**

CASTLE HOTEL   Boutique Hotel **££**
(☏01522-538801; www.castlehotel.net; Westgate; s £90, d £110-120, incl breakfast; **P**🛜)
Each of the 18 rooms at this boutique
hotel have been exquisitely refurbished

If You Like…
Cathedrals

If you've been inspired by the majestic proportions of Lincoln Cathedral (p159), here are a few more English ecclesiastical wonders.

1 **ELY CATHEDRAL**
(www.elycathedral.org; tower tour Mon-Sat £6, Sun £8.50; ⊙7am-6.30pm, Evensong 5.30pm Mon-Sat, 4pm Sun, choral service 10.30am Sun) The stunning silhouette of Ely Cathedral is locally dubbed the 'Ship of the Fens' due to its visibility across the flat fenland for vast distances.

2 **COVENTRY CATHEDRAL**
(☏024-7652 1200; www.coventrycathedral. org.uk; Priory Row; adult/child under 7 £7/5; ⊙9am-5pm Mon-Sat, noon-3.45pm Sun) Coventry's original cathedral was destroyed by Nazi bombing during WWII, but was replaced by this modernist masterpiece designed by Sir Basil Spence.

3 **HEREFORD CATHEDRAL**
(☏01432-374200; www.herefordcathedral.org; 5 College Cloisters; cathedral entry by £5 donation, Mappa Mundi £6; ⊙9.15am-evensong, Mappa Mundi 10am-5pm Mon-Sat May-Sep, to 4pm Mon-Sat Oct-Apr, evensong 5.30pm Mon-Sat, 3.30pm Sun) Highlights of Hereford's cathedral are the 'chained library' and the magnificent Mappa Mundi, depicting the globe circa 1290.

4 **LICHFIELD CATHEDRAL**
(☏01543-306100; www.lichfield-cathedral.org; entry by donation; ⊙7.30am-6.15pm daily, to 5pm Sun low season) Crowned by three dramatic towers, Lichfield Cathedral is a stunning Gothic fantasy, constructed in stages from 1200 to 1350.

5 **WORCESTER CATHEDRAL**
(☏01905-732900; www.worcestercathedral. org.uk; entry by £5 donation, tower adult/child £4/2, tours £3/free; ⊙7.30am-6pm, tower 11am-5pm Apr-Oct, tours 11am & 2.30pm Mon-Sat Apr-Sep, Sat Oct-Mar, evensong 5.30pm Mon-Wed, Fri & Sat, 4pm Sun; ⊕) Rising above the River Severn, Worcester's majestic cathedral is best known as the final resting place of Magna Carta signatory King John.

in olive, truffle and oyster tones. Take advantage of the great-value dinner, bed and breakfast deals linked to its award-winning new restaurant **Reform** (☏01522 538801; www.castlehotel.net; The Castle Hotel, Westgate; mains £11.95-22.95; ⊙breakfast, lunch & dinner).

BAIL HOUSE B&B ££
(☏01522-541000; www.bailhouse.co.uk; 34 Bailgate; r from £89; P @ �ⓢ ⊠) Stone walls, worn flagstones, secluded gardens and one room with an extraordinary timber-vaulted ceiling are just some of the charms of this lovingly restored Georgian town house in central Lincoln.

Eating

BROWN'S PIE SHOP British ££
(☏01522-527330; www.brownspieshop. co.uk; 33 Steep Hill; takeaway pies £1.50-3, lunch mains £8.95-11.95, dinner mains £9.95-24.95; ⊙lunch & dinner Mon-Sat, noon-8pm Sun) This long-established pie shop is one of Lincoln's top tables, encompassing a smart upstairs dining room and cosy brick-lined basement.

WIG & MITRE Pub ££
(www.wigandmitre.com; 30 Steep Hill; mains £10-15; ⊙breakfast, lunch & dinner; ⊕) Civilised pub-restaurant the Wig & Mitre has an excellent menu yet retains the ambience of a friendly local.

OLD BAKERY Modern British ££
(☏01522-576057; www.theold-bakery.co.uk; 26-28 Burton Rd; mains £14-20.95; ⊙lunch Tue-Sun, dinner Tue-Sat) The menu at this eccentric foodie haven is built around impeccably presented local produce and – appropriately – freshly baked bread.

Information

Tourist office (☏01522-545458; www. visitlincoln.com; 9 Castle Hill; ⊙10.30am-4pm Mon-Sat)

ℹ Getting There & Away

Getting to and from Lincoln by rail usually involves changing trains.

Boston £12.30, 1¼ hours, every two hours, change at Sleaford

Cambridge £26.50, 2½ hours, hourly, change at Peterborough and Ely

Sheffield £13.10, one hour 20 minutes, hourly

PEAK DISTRICT

Rolling across the southernmost hills of the Pennines, the Peak District is one of the most beautiful parts of the country. Founded in 1951, the Peak District National Park was England's first national park and is Europe's busiest. But escaping the crowds is easy if you avoid summer weekends. Even at the busiest times, there are 555 sq miles of open English countryside in which to find your own viewpoint to soak up the glorious scenery.

Locals divide the Peak District into the Dark Peak – dominated by exposed moorland and gritstone 'edges' – and the White Peak, made up of the limestone dales to the south.

The Peak's most famous walking trail is the **Pennine Way**, which runs north from Edale for more than 250 miles, finishing in the Scottish Borders.

ℹ Information

The Peak District National Park Authority website (www.peakdistrict.gov.uk) is a goldmine of information on transport, activities and local events.

Buxton

POP 24,112

At the heart of the Peak District National Park (albeit outside the park boundary), Buxton is a picturesque sprawl of Georgian terraces, Victorian amusements and parks in the rolling hills of the Derbyshire dales. The town built its fortunes on its natural warm-water springs, which attracted health tourists in Buxton's heyday.

Detour:
Sulgrave Manor

The impressively preserved Tudor mansion **Sulgrave Manor** (www.sulgravemanor.org.uk; adult/child £8.25/4; ⏱11am-4pm Tue-Sun May-Oct, closed Nov-Apr) was built by Lawrence Washington in 1539 and the Washington family lived here for almost 120 years before Colonel John Washington, the great-grandfather of America's first president George Washington, sailed to Virginia in 1656.

Sulgrave Manor is southwest of Northampton, just off the B4525 near Banbury.

◉ Sights

Buxton's historic centre is a riot of Victorian pavilions, concert halls and glasshouse domes. Its most famous building is the flamboyant, turreted **Opera House** (www.buxtonoperahouse.org.uk; Water St), which hosts an impressive variety of stage shows.

The Opera House adjoins the equally flamboyant **Pavilion Gardens** (www.paviliongardens.co.uk; ⏱9.30am-5pm), dotted with domed pavilions.

Another piece of Victoriana, the **Devonshire Dome**, forms part of the University of Derby campus and is also home to **Devonshire Spa** (☎01332-594408; www.devonshire-spa.co.uk; 1 Devonshire Rd), which offers a full range of treatments, including one-hour body spa £38, ocean wrap £49 and day package from £65.

In Victorian times, spa activities centred on the extravagant **Buxton Baths** complex, built in grand Regency style in 1854.

At the base of the Slopes is the **Pump Room**, which dispensed Buxton's spring water for nearly a century. Modern-day

health-tourists queue up to fill bottles from a small spout known as **St Ann's Well**.

 Sleeping

OLD HALL HOTEL　　　Historic Hotel **££**
(📞01298-22841; www.oldhallhotelbuxton.co.uk; The Square; s/d incl breakfast from £65/85; @ 🛜) There is a tale to go with every creak of the floorboards at this history-soaked establishment, supposedly the oldest hotel in England.

ROSELEIGH HOTEL　　　B&B **££**
(📞01298-24904; www.roseleighhotel.co.uk; 19 Broad Walk; d from £78; P @ 🛜) This gorgeous family-run B&B in a Victorian house has lovingly decorated rooms, many with fine views out over the Pavilion Gardens.

VICTORIAN GUEST HOUSE　　　B&B **££**
(📞01298-78759; www.buxtonvictorian.co.uk; 3a Broad Walk; d from £82; P 🛜 👪) Overlooking the park, this elegant house has eight individually decorated bedrooms furnished

with Victorian and Edwardian antiques, and the home-cooked breakfasts are renowned.

Eating

COLUMBINE RESTAURANT　　　Modern British **££**
(📞01298-78752; 7 Hall Bank; mains £12.25-17.80; ⏱dinner Mon-Sat, closed Tue Nov-Apr) On the lane leading down beside the Town Hall, this understated restaurant is the top choice among in-the-know Buxtonites. Bookings recommended.

NAT'S KITCHEN　　　Modern British **£££**
(📞01298-214642; www.natskitchen.co.uk; 9-11 Market St; 2-/3-course menus £21/27.50; ⏱9am-11pm) A relaxing dining room full of natural wood tones provides the backdrop to some inventive Modern British cooking.

Left: Buxton Opera House (p161); **Below:** Ely Cathedral (p160)

(LEFT) CRAIG ROBERTS/GETTY IMAGES ©; (BELOW) PHOTOGRAPHY BY PAULGMCCABE/GETTY IMAGES ©

Information

Tourist office (www.visitpeakdistrict.com; Pavilion Gardens; ☻9.30am-5pm; 📶) Free hour-long Roman Buxton town walks depart at 11am and 2pm Saturday.

Castleton

POP 1200

Guarding the entrance to the forbidding Winnats Pass gorge, charming Castleton is a magnet on summer weekends for East Midlands visitors – try coming mid-week to enjoy the sights in relative peace and quiet.

👁 Sights

PEVERIL CASTLE Castle

(EH; adult/child £4.50/2.70; ☻10am-5pm Apr-Oct, 10am-4pm Sat & Sun Nov-Mar) Topping the ridge to the south of Castleton, this evocative castle has been so ravaged by the centuries that it almost looks like a crag itself. Constructed by William Peveril, son of William the Conqueror, the castle was used as a hunting lodge by Henry II, King John and Henry III, and the crumbling ruins offer swooping views over the Hope Valley.

FREE **CASTLETON MUSEUM** Museum

(📞01433-620679; Buxton Rd; ☻9.30am-5.30pm) Attached to the tourist office, the cute town museum has displays on everything from mining and geology to rock climbing, hang-gliding and the curious Garland Festival.

PEAK CAVERN Cave

(📞01433-620285; http://devilsarse.com; adult/child £8.75/6.75; ☻10am-4pm daily Apr-Oct, Sat & Sun Nov-Mar) Castleton's most convenient cave is easily reached by a pretty streamside walk from the village centre. It has the largest natural cave entrance in England, known (not so prettily) as the Devil's Arse. Dramatic limestone formations are lit with fibreoptic cables.

COLIN WESTON/GETTY IMAGES ©

Don't Miss **Chatsworth House**

Known as the 'Palace of the Peak', Chatsworth House has been occupied by the earls and dukes of Devonshire for centuries.

While the core of the house dates from the 16th century, Chatsworth was altered and enlarged over the centuries. The current building has a Georgian feel, dating back to the last overhaul in 1820. Inside, the lavish apartments and mural-painted staterooms are packed with priceless paintings and period furniture. Look out for the portraits of the current generation of Devonshires by Lucian Freud.

The house sits in 25 sq miles of grounds and ornamental gardens, some landscaped by Lancelot 'Capability' Brown.

Chatsworth is 3 miles northeast of Bakewell.

NEED TO KNOW
☎ 01246-582204; www.chatsworth.org; house & gardens adult/child £15/9, gardens only £10/6, playground £5, park free; ⏰ 11am-5.30pm mid-Mar–late Dec, closed late Dec–mid-Mar

SPEEDWELL CAVERN Cave
(☎ 01433-621888; www.speedwellcavern.co.uk; adult/child £9.25/7.25; ⏰ 9.30am-4pm) About half a mile west of Castleton at the mouth of Winnats Pass, this claustrophobe's nightmare is reached via an eerie boat ride through flooded tunnels, emerging by a huge subterranean lake called the Bottomless Pit.

 **Sleeping**

YE OLDE NAG'S HEAD HOTEL Pub £
(☎ 01433-620248; www.yeoldenagshead.co.uk; Cross St; d from £50; ☎) The cosiest of the 'residential' pubs along the main road, offering comfortable, well-appointed rooms (some with four-poster beds and jacuzzis), ale tasting trays and a popular restaurant, plus regular live music.

CAUSEWAY HOUSE B&B ££

(01433-623921; www.causewayhouse.co.uk; Back St; s/d from £33/65) The floors within this ancient stone cottage are worn and warped with age, but the quaint bedrooms are bright and welcoming.

 Eating & Drinking

1530 Italian ££

(01433-621870; www.1530therestaurant. co.uk; Cross St; mains £9-21.95; lunch & dinner Wed-Mon;) Crispy thin-crust pizzas and fresh pastas like king prawn, crab, crayfish and calamari linguine are the specialty of Castleton's swish new Italian flag-bearer.

YE OLDE CHESHIRE CHEESE INN Pub £

(01433-620330; www.cheshirecheeseinn. co.uk; How Lane; mains £7.95-10.95;) Tradition is everything at this well-known alehouse, set in a fine, old timbered building on the main road.

① Information

Tourist office (Buxton Rd; 9.30am-5.30pm Mar-Oct, 10am-5pm Nov-Feb)

Bakewell

POP 3979

The second-largest town in the Peak District, pretty Bakewell is a great base for exploring the White Peak. The town is ringed by famous walking trails and stately homes, but it's probably best known for its famous pudding (of which the Bakewell Tart is just a poor imitation).

 Sights

Up on the hill above Rutland Sq, **All Saints Church** (9am-4.45pm Apr-Oct, to 3.45pm Nov-Mar) is packed with ancient features, including a 14th-century font, a pair of Norman arches, some fine heraldic tombs and a collection of crude stone gravestones and crosses dating back to the 12th century.

Set in a time-worn stone house near the church, the **Old House Museum** (www. oldhousemuseum.org.uk; Cunningham Pl; adult/

child £3.50/2; 11am-4pm Apr-early Nov, closed early Nov-Mar) explores local history. Check out the Tudor loo and the displays on wattle and daub, a traditional technique for building walls using woven twigs and cow dung. Nearby, its recently opened collection **Spirit of the 1940s** (www. oldhousemuseum.org.uk; Matlock St; adult/child £2/50p, combined ticket with Old House Museum £5/2; 10.30am-4pm Fri-Mon Apr-early Nov, closed early Nov-Mar) incorporates an evocative '40s street scene, letters and photographs, and wartime memorabilia.

 **Sleeping**

RUTLAND ARMS HOTEL Hotel £££

(01629-812812; www.rutlandarmsbakewell. co.uk; The Square; s £88-118, d £140-165;) Jane Austen is said to have stayed in room 2 of this aristocratic, recently refurbished stone coaching inn while working on *Pride and Prejudice*.

MELBOURNE HOUSE B&B ££

(01629-815357; www.bakewell-accommo dation.co.uk; Buxton Rd; d from £60;) In a picturesque, creeper-covered building dating back more than three centuries, this inviting B&B is handily situated on the main road leading to Buxton.

 **Eating & Drinking**

PIEDANIEL'S French ££

(01629-812687; www.piedaniels-restaurant. com; Bath St; mains £16, 2-/3-course lunch Tue-Fri £13/15; Tue-Sat) Chefs Eric and Christiana Piedaniel's Modern French cuisine is the toast of the town. Weekday lunch menus are exceptional value.

CASTLE INN Pub

(01629-812103; www.castle-inn-bakewell. co.uk; Bridge St; mains £7.50-17;) The ivy-draped Castle Inn is one of the better pubs in Bakewell, with four centuries of practice in rejuvenating hamstrung hikers.

① Information

Tourist office (01629-813227; Bridge St; 9.30am-5pm Apr-Oct, from 10am Nov-Mar)

Bath & Southwest England

If it's scenic splendour you're after, the southwest serves it up in spades. From the grand cityscapes of Bristol, Bath and Exeter to Dartmoor's wild heaths and Cornwall's epic coastline, this is a region that never fails to inspire.

Fringed by craggy cliffs and golden beaches, swathed by great plains and stony moors, it offers a wealth of opportunity for hiking, biking and other fresh-air pursuits. It's also awash with architecture: cathedrals and abbeys, stately homes and castles – as well as the mysterious stone circles of Avebury and Stonehenge.

But the southwest also has an eye to the future, with a growing number of cutting-edge restaurants and cultural sights, including the gigantic greenhouses of the Eden Project, Bath's futuristic bath complex and Bristol's new M Shed Museum. In fact, there's so much to see and do, you'll be hard pressed to fit it all into one visit.

Roman Baths (p189), Bath
PETER PHIPP/GETTY IMAGES ©

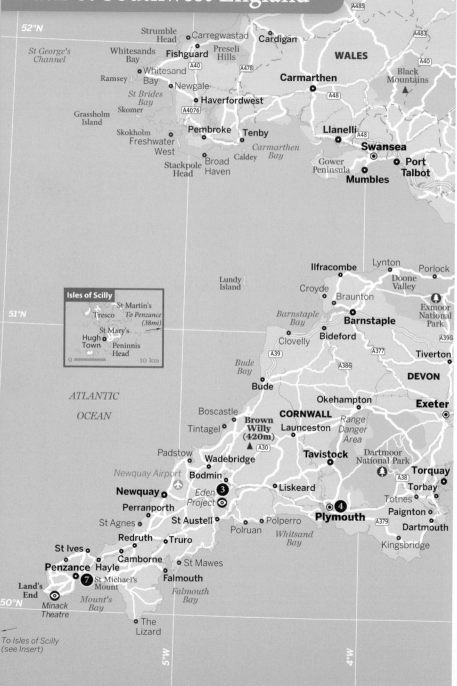

Bath & Southwest England

WALES

St George's Channel

Strumble Head
Carregwastad
Cardigan
Whitesands Bay
Fishguard
Preseli Hills
Ramsey
Whitesand Bay
Newgale
Carmarthen
St Brides Bay
Grassholm Island
Skomer
Haverfordwest
Skokholm
Freshwater West
Pembroke
Tenby
Llanelli
Swansea
Stackpole Head
Broad Haven
Caldey
Carmarthen Bay
Gower Peninsula
Mumbles
Port Talbot

Black Mountains

Lundy Island

Ilfracombe
Lynton
Porlock
Doone Valley
Croyde
Braunton
Barnstaple Bay
Barnstaple
Exmoor National Park
Clovelly
Bideford
Tiverton

DEVON

Bude Bay
Bude
Okehampton
Exeter
Boscastle
Brown Willy (420m)
CORNWALL
Launceston
Range Danger Area
Tintagel
Padstow
Wadebridge
Tavistock
Dartmoor National Park
Torquay
Newquay Airport
Bodmin
Liskeard
Torbay
Newquay
③
Eden Project
Totnes
Paignton
Perranporth
Plymouth ●④
Dartmouth
St Agnes
St Austell
Polruan
Polperro
Whitsand Bay
Kingsbridge
Redruth
Truro
St Ives
Camborne
St Mawes
Penzance
Hayle
Falmouth
Land's End
⑦
St Michael's Mount
Falmouth Bay
Minack Theatre
Mount's Bay
The Lizard

ATLANTIC

OCEAN

Isles of Scilly
St Martin's
Tresco
To Penzance (38mi)
St Mary's
Hugh Town
Peninnis Head
0   10 km

To Isles of Scilly
(see Insert)

52°N

51°N

50°N

5°W

4°W

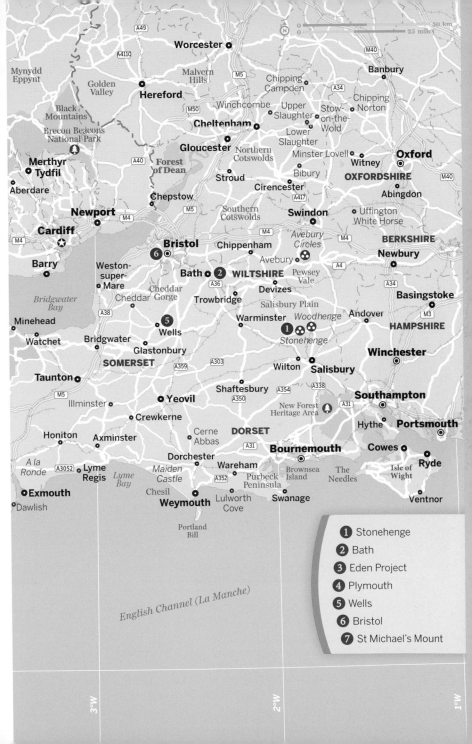

Bath & Southwest England Highlights

TETRA IMAGES/CORBIS ©

① Stonehenge

The great stone circle of Stonehenge is Britain's most iconic archaeological site, a compelling ring of mono-lithic boulders that has been attracting a steady stream of pilgrims, poets and philosophers for the last 5000 years. Above: Stonehenge; Top Right: Summer Solstice celebration; Bottom Right: Stonehenge

Need to Know

LOCATION Eighty miles southwest of London **TOP TIP** Avoid crowds with an Access Visit **BEST PHOTO OP** Sunrise or sunset **For further coverage, see p184**

Local Knowledge

Stonehenge Don't Miss List

BY PAT SHELLEY, GUIDE, SALISBURY & STONEHENGE GUIDED TOURS

1 THE MAIN CIRCLE

Stonehenge covers a large area but the focal point is, of course, the main circle of stones, including the distinctive trilithons – 'gateways' of two vertical stones with a lintel across the top. I've been running tours here for a few years – for me, nowhere sums up the magic and mystery of ancient Britain better than Stonehenge.

2 INSIDE THE CIRCLE

The main stones are fenced off, and you can't get very close – the only way to actually see inside the circle is on a special access tour, which you need to reserve in advance. It's also worth taking the informative audiotour. Soon, the site will hopefully also have a brand-new visitor centre which will provide background on the monument's history.

3 THE SLAUGHTER STONE

Look out for the Slaughter Stone, once thought to be a Neolithic altar for human sacrifice. In reality it's a toppled monolith; over the centuries iron ore has mixed with rain in holes in the stone to give the appearance of blood.

4 THE CURSUS & THE AVENUE

I recommend this short walk to see the route to Stonehenge Neolithic people would have used. Walk northeast along the bridleway from the car park to reach the Cursus, a long ditchlike earthwork that runs in an east–west line. Turn right to meet the Avenue, an ancient path leading back towards Stonehenge. Watching the giant stones looming up ahead is an unforgettable experience.

5 WOODHENGE & THE BARROWS

About 2 miles northeast of the stone circle, Woodhenge is an even older site where archaeologists are still discovering new evidence. There's not much to see, but it was featured on a TV show in the US called *Secrets of Stonehenge*, so many people want to visit. In the area surrounding Woodhenge and Stonehenge, the many hillocks or 'barrows' are ancient burial mounds.

Bath's Royal Crescent

Often described as Britain's most beautiful city, Bath owes its beauty to two pioneering 18th-century architects, John Wood the Elder and the Younger. Their work transformed Bath from a sleepy spa town to a triumph of the Georgian Age, and the Royal Crescent is their masterpiece. Below: Royal Crescent; Top Right: Spiral Staircase, Beckford's Tower; Bottom Right: Ballroom, Assembly Rooms

Need to Know

CROWDS Avoid July and August **TOP TIP** Don't miss the fashion rooms **BEST PHOTO OP** The top of Beckford's Tower **For further coverage, see p188**

SIMON GREENWOOD/GETTY IMAGES ©

Bath's Architecture Don't Miss List

BY DR AMY FROST, BATH PRESERVATION TRUST

1 THE ROYAL CRESCENT

The elegant proportions of the Royal Crescent display all the qualities that British architects sought to perfect in the 18th century. Go around the back however, and it's another story. The uniform facades conceal a mix and match of features – each house is different inside because they were built by different craftsman for different clients.

2 THE CIRCUS

The Circus is much more decorative than the Royal Crescent, from the Masonic symbols above the doorways to the acorns that run along the rooflines. Its design was inspired by Rome's Coliseum, but its architect, John Wood the Elder, was also fascinated by stone circles – so it's really ancient Rome meets Stonehenge.

3 THE ASSEMBLY ROOMS

Life in Georgian Bath was all about being part of the social elite, and the Assembly Rooms were the place to be seen. The grandest of the interiors is the Ballroom, with a balcony for musicians and a fabulous set of 18th-century English chandeliers. In the Tea Room some of the stone is slightly pink, showing the damage caused by fire when the Rooms were bombed in 1942.

4 UPPER BOROUGH WALLS

Most of Bath's medieval wall was lost during the building boom of the 18th century. But on Upper Borough Walls you will find a rare surviving fragment. You're actually walking alongside the battlements, almost two storeys above the original ground level of the medieval city. The Georgians literally built on top of it.

5 BECKFORD'S TOWER

On the outskirts of Bath is a 120ft-high tower built by William Beckford, once the wealthiest man in England and an eccentric writer and collector. Beckford built the Tower as an escape from life in the city, and from the top you get a sweeping panoramic view of the valley in which Bath sits. The wonderful spiral staircase is the tower's crowning glory.

173

Eden Project

Record producer turned eco-champion Tim Smit has transformed an old clay pit near St Austell in Cornwall into the space-age Eden Project (p206), where the massive greenhouses (or 'biomes') – the largest in the world – re-create a range of natural habitats, from tropical rainforest to dry desert. The rest of the site explores all the hot-topic issues surrounding climate change, sustainability and environmental protection. Tropical Dome, Eden Project

3

DOUG MCKINLAY/GETTY IMAGES ©

4

Plymouth

In a region famous for picturesque gems, gritty Plymouth (p200) often gets over-looked – but this historic harbour is well worth a look. The centre was practically flattened during WWII, but along the quaysides you'll discover a rich nautical history: Sir Francis Drake spied the Spanish Armada from Plymouth Hoe in 1588, and the Pilgrim Fathers' *Mayflower* set sail for America from the Barbican in 1620. Smeaton's Tower, Plymouth Hoe, Plymouth

TONY HOWELL/GETTY IMAGES ©

TREVOR NORMAN/GETTY IMAGES ©

Wells

5

The pretty little market town of Wells qualifies as England's smallest city thanks to the magnificent monument of Wells Cathedral (p195), which sits in the centre beside the grand Bishop's Palace (p195) – still the ecclesiastical seat of the Bishop of Bath and Wells. Ancient buildings and cobbled streets radiate out from the cathedral green to a marketplace that has been the bustling heart of Wells for some nine centuries. Wells Cathedral, Wells

JAMES OSMOND/GETTY IMAGES ©

SIMON BRADFIELD/GETTY IMAGES ©

6

Bristol

During the 18th and 19th centuries, Bristol (p185) was one of Britain's most important ports, and its streets are lined with spectacular architecture, best seen around the genteel suburb of Clifton and its famous suspension bridge. The city's also known for its culture and museums – don't miss a visit to the SS *Great Britain*, a ground-breaking trans-Atlantic liner that's been restored to its former glory. Georgian terrace, Bristol

7

St Michael's Mount

Looming from the sea near the historic town of Penzance, the unmistakable silhouette of St Michael's Mount (p208) is one of Cornwall's most iconic landmarks: a 12th-century abbey set on a craggy island connected to the mainland by a cobbled causeway covered at high tide. Highlights include the original armoury, the priory church and the abbey's subtropical gardens, which teeter dramatically above the sea.

BATH & SOUTHWEST ENGLAND HIGHLIGHTS ●●● 175

Bath & Southwest England's Best...

Cathedrals & Abbeys

○ **Salisbury Cathedral** (p182) Climb the tallest spire of any English cathedral

○ **Winchester Cathedral** (p180) Plain on the outside, but the interior is awe-inspiring

○ **Wells Cathedral** (p195) A medieval gem in this miniature city

○ **Bath Abbey** (p188) The last great medieval church raised in England

○ **Glastonbury Abbey** (p197) Evocative ruins and legendary burial place of King Arthur

Iconic Landmarks

○ **St Michael's Mount** (p208) Cornwall's island-topped abbey, star of a thousand postcards

○ **Eden Project** (p206) The world's largest greenhouses in a former Cornish claypit

○ **Royal Crescent** (p188) The epitome of Georgian architecture in beautiful Bath

○ **Clifton Suspension Bridge** (p186) Brunel's 19th-century masterpiece over the Avon Gorge

Artistic Links

○ **Tate St Ives** (p206) Home to Barbara Hepworth's studio and an offshoot of the Tate Gallery

○ **Minack Theatre** (p208) Catch a play at this amazing clifftop theatre

○ **Greenway** (p197) Visit Agatha Christie's summer hideaway

○ **Bristol** (p185) Guerrilla graffiti artist Banksy's home town

○ **Jane Austen Centre** (p191) Enjoy afternoon tea at this literary museum in Bath

Views

○ **Dartmoor** (p199) An otherworldly landscape of moors and tors

○ **Cheddar Gorge** (p196) Wander the clifftops of England's deepest gorge

○ **Glastonbury Tor** (p196) Legends swirl around this mystical hill in the heart of Somerset

○ **Land's End** (p208) Stirring coastal scenery at the very edge of England

Need to Know

ADVANCE PLANNING

○ **Two months before** Book hotels in popular spots such as Bath; reserve a Special Access Visit at Stonehenge.

○ **One month before** Arrange car hire and book train tickets.

○ **Two weeks before** Buy tickets online for major sights such as the Roman Baths, SS *Great Britain* and the Eden Project.

RESOURCES

○ **Southwest England** (www.visitsouthwest.com)

○ **Bath** (www.visitbath.co.uk)

○ **Somerset** (www.visitsomerset.co.uk)

○ **Wiltshire** (www.visitwiltshire.co.uk)

○ **Devon** (www.visitdevon.co.uk)

○ **Cornwall** (www.visitcornwall.com)

GETTING AROUND

○ **Bus** Long-distance buses between main towns and cities are good. Local buses are infrequent in some rural areas.

○ **Train** Connections between the major towns are fast and frequent, and there are several scenic branch lines.

○ **Car** The easiest way to get around, but beware of traffic jams, especially in summer. Bigger cities have Park & Ride systems, where you can park your car safely and catch a bus to the centre.

BE FOREWARNED

○ **High season** The southwest counties (especially Devon and Cornwall) are packed in July and August, when thousands of families head for the beach.

○ **Bath** Crowds are a fact of life in Bath, and can be oppressive in summer. Spring and autumn are less hectic.

○ **Minor roads** Many of the southwest's minor roads are narrow, winding and tricky to navigate. GPS can be more of a hindrance than a help.

Left: Cloister, Salisbury Cathedral (p182);
Above: Cheddar Gorge (p196)

Bath & Southwest England Itineraries

Our suggested three-day loop from Bath takes in two spectacular medieval cathedral towns and the prehistoric icon of Stonehenge. The five-day trip saunters through the southwest, via the key highlights.

BATH TO BATH
Historical Highlights

3 DAYS

Start your tour in the beautiful city of **(1) Bath**. A day here should include a visit to the Roman Baths, which give the city its name – go early or late in the day to avoid the crowds. Other sights include Bath Abbey and the fabulous Georgian architecture around the centre, especially the Royal Crescent and the nearby Circus.

Then it's off for a day trip to nearby **(2) Bristol**, a historic harbour city with a wealth of fascinating sights. Factor in the SS *Great Britain*, a wander around Clifton and the Suspension Bridge, and a visit to the new M Shed Museum – and leave

plenty of time for lunch at one of the city's excellent eateries.

Head onwards into Wiltshire for a stop to see the mighty cathedral spire in **(3) Salisbury** en route to one of England's most unmistakable landmarks, the trilithons of **(4) Stonehenge**. True fans of ancient Britain might like to divert via the southwest's other great stone circle at **(5) Avebury** – it's even bigger than Stonehenge, and has a pub in the middle. From here it's a short loop back to Bath.

BATH TO ST IVES
The Way Out West

5 DAYS

Start your tour with a couple of days in **(1) Bath**, admiring the elegant architecture and historic sites, then head south to the little city of **(2) Wells**, where the star of the show is the medieval gem of Wells Cathedral.

It's then a short hop to visit the nearby caves of **(3) Cheddar Gorge** and the grassy hump of **(4) Glastonbury Tor**, the supposed burial site of King Arthur, and the focal point for a whole host of other myths and legends.

Detour west for a spectacular drive across the wild moors and lonely tors of **(5) Dartmoor**, the southwest's largest and wildest national park.

Soon after you'll cross the border into Cornwall, once an independent Celtic kingdom, now known for its beautiful beaches and pretty seaside towns. Key sights include the crumbling castle of **(6) Tintagel**, the eco-domes of the **(7) Eden Project** and the iconic abbey of **(8) St Michael's Mount**. The artistic harbour of **(9) St Ives** makes an ideal base.

St Ives (p206), Cornwall

Discover Bath & Southwest England

At a Glance

○ **Hampshire & Wiltshire** (p180) Prehistoric remains and historic cities litter these ancient counties.

○ **Bristol** (p185) The southwest's biggest city, with culture and nightlife to match.

○ **Bath** (p188) Home to Britain's grandest Georgian architecture.

○ **Devon & Cornwall** (p198, p203) The far west of England, with miles of unspoilt coast and countryside.

Round Table, Winchester Cathedral
VISITBRITAIN/DANIEL BOSWORTH/GETTY IMAGES ©

HAMPSHIRE & WILTSHIRE

Winchester
POP 45,000

Calm, collegiate Winchester is a mellow must-see for all visitors. The past still echoes strongly around the flint-flecked walls of this ancient cathedral city.

◉ Sights

WINCHESTER CATHEDRAL   Church
(☎ 01962-857275; www.winchester-cathedral.org.uk; adult/child £6/free, incl tower tour £9/free; ⊙ 9am-5pm Sat, 12.30-3pm Sun) Winchester Cathedral is one of southern England's most awe-inspiring buildings. Its walls contain evidence of almost 1000 years of history, best experienced on one of the memorable tours of its sturdy tower. The cathedral's exterior features a fine Gothic facade, but it's the inside that steals the show with one of the longest **medieval naves** (164m) in Europe, and a fascinating jumble of features from all eras. **Jane Austen**, one of England's best-loved authors, is buried near the entrance in the cathedral's northern aisle. **Cathedral body tours** (free; ⊙ hourly 10am-3pm Mon-Sat) last one hour. **Tower and roof tours** (tickets £6; ⊙ 11.30am Sat & 2.15pm Mon, Wed, Fri & Sat Jun-Aug, 11.30am Sat & 2.15pm Wed & Sat Sep-May) clamber 213 steps up narrow stairwells, navigate an interior gallery high above the nave, visiting the bell chamber and going onto the roof for views as far as the Isle of Wight. For safety reasons these popular tours are only open to those aged 12 to 70. Book well in advance.

DAVID C TOMLINSON/GETTY IMAGES ©

Don't Miss **Stourhead**

Overflowing with vistas, temples and follies, Stourhead is landscape gardening at its finest. The Palladian house has some fine Chippendale furniture and paintings by Claude and Gaspard Poussin, but it's a sideshow to the magnificent 18th-century **gardens**, which spread out across the valley. A picturesque 2-mile circuit takes you past the most ornate follies, around the lake and to the Temple of Apollo; a 3½-mile side trip can be made from near the Pantheon to **King Alfred's Tower**, a 50m-high folly with wonderful views.

Stourhead is off the B3092, 8 miles south of Frome (in Somerset).

NEED TO KNOW

Stourhead (NT; ☎01747-841152; www.nationaltrust.org.uk; house or garden adult/child £7.50/4.10, house & garden £12.50/6.20; ⏰house 11am-5pm Fri-Tue mid-Mar–Sep, gardens 9am-dusk year-round; P); **King Alfred's Tower** (adult/child £3/1.50; ⏰noon-4pm school holidays only)

FREE ROUND TABLE &
GREAT HALL   Historic Building
(☎01962-846476; www.hants.gov.uk/greathall; Castle Ave; suggested donation £2; ⏰10am-5pm) Winchester's cavernous Great Hall is the only part of 11th-century Winchester Castle that Oliver Cromwell spared from destruction. Crowning the wall like a giant-sized dartboard of green and cream spokes is what centuries of mythology has dubbed King Arthur's Round Table.

It's actually a 700-year-old copy, but is fascinating nonetheless.

 **Sleeping**

WYKEHAM ARMS   Inn ££
(☎01962-853834; www.fullershotels.com; 75 Kingsgate St; s/d/ste £70/119/150; P) At 250-odd years old, the Wykeham bursts with history – it used to be a brothel and also put Nelson up for a night (some say

the events coincided). Creaking stairs lead to plush bedrooms that manage to be both deeply established but also on-trend; brass bedsteads meet jazzy throws, oak dressers sport stylish lights.

HOTEL DU VIN Historic Hotel £££
(☎01962-841414; www.hotelduvin.com; Southgate St; r £145-230; P@🛜) A glamorous, gorgeous oasis, boasting luxurious furnishings, ornate chaise longues and extravagant stand-alone baths.

 Eating

BLACK RAT Modern British ££
(☎01962-844465; www.theblackrat.co.uk; 88 Chesil St; mains £17-20; ⏲dinner daily, lunch Sat & Sun) The decor is casually countrified, the food is anything but. Accomplished cooking has won it a Michelin star – partly down to the intense flavours conjured from ingredients such as braised beef cheek, lamb rump and oxtail.

CHESIL RECTORY British ££
(☎01962-851555; www.chesilrectory.co.uk; 1 Chesil St; mains £16) Flickering candles and low beams lend this 15th-century restaurant a romantic feel. The two-course lunch and early-evening menu (£16, served 6pm to 7pm) is a steal.

🛈 **Information**

Tourist office (☎01962-840500; www.visitwinchester.co.uk; High St; ⏲10am-5pm Mon-Sat, plus 11am-4pm Sun May-Sep)

🛈 **Getting There & Away**

Trains leave every 30 minutes for London Waterloo (£30, 1¼ hours) and hourly for Portsmouth (£10.20, one hour). There are also fast links to the Midlands.

Salisbury

POP 39,730

Centred on a majestic cathedral that's topped by the tallest spire in England, the gracious city of Salisbury makes a charming base from which to discover the rest of Wiltshire.

◉ **Sights**

FREE **SALISBURY CATHEDRAL** Church
(☎01722-555120; www.salisburycathedral.org.uk; requested donation adult/child £5/3; ⏲7.15am-6.15pm) England is endowed with countless stunning churches, but few can hold a candle to the grandeur and sheer spectacle of Salisbury Cathedral. Built between 1220 and 1258, the structure bears all the hallmarks of the early English Gothic style, with an elaborate exterior decorated with pointed arches and flying buttresses, and a sombre, austere interior designed to keep its congregation suitably pious.

The best way to experience the cathedral, is on a 90-minute **tower tour** (☎01722-555156; adult/child £8.50/6.50; ⏲11am-2.30pm Apr-Sep, 1 per day Mon-Sat Nov-Mar); these see you climbing 332 vertigo-inducing steps to the base of the spire, for jaw-dropping views across the city and the surrounding countryside. Bookings are required.

CATHEDRAL CLOSE Historic Area
Salisbury's medieval cathedral close, a hushed enclave surrounded by beautiful houses, has an other-worldly feel. Many of the buildings date from the same period as the cathedral, although the area was heavily restored during an 18th-century clean-up by James Wyatt.

 **Sleeping**

ST ANN'S HOUSE B&B ££
(☎01722-335657; www.stannshouse.co.uk; 32 St Ann St; s/d £60/110) For some perfectly priced indulgence head to this sumptuous Georgian terrace, which overflows with antiques, fine silk and linen direct from Istanbul.

ROKEBY B&B ££
(☎01722-329800; www.rokebyguesthouse. co.uk; 3 Wain-a-long Rd; s £40-70, d £60-95; P🛜) Glinting bathrooms, satin cushions and gauzy throws lift this late-Victorian B&B above the rest. Rokeby is a mile northeast of the cathedral.

Salisbury

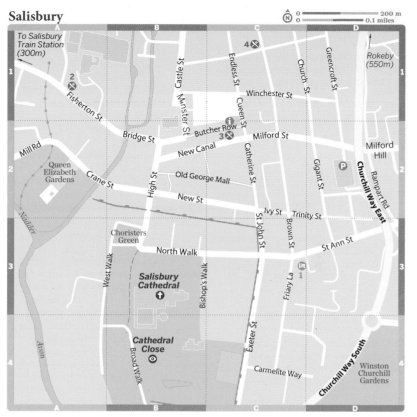

 Eating

ANOKAA
Indian **££**

(☏01722-414142; www.anokaa.com; 60 Fisherton St; mains £11-32; 🔊) Sophisticated, contemporary Indian cuisine makes this the top table in town. Wise locals head for the bargain buffet lunches (£9 per person).

PHEASANT
Pub **££**

(☏01722-322866; www.restaurant-salisbury.com; 19 Salt Lane; mains £7-15; ⏰food noon-9.30pm) Flying the flag for great British bar food, this chilled-out gastropub does the basics well; try the pheasant stuffed with bacon and leeks, and the gooey, crumbly Eton mess.

Salisbury

BIRD & CARTER
Deli, Cafe **£**

(3 Fish Row, Market Sq; snacks from £5; ⏰8.30am-6pm Mon-Sat, 10am-4pm Sun) This heavily beamed deli-cafe is piled high with local meats and cheeses – the New Forest Blue, Old Sarum and Nanny Williams come from just a few miles away.

① Information

Tourist office (☏01722-334956; www.
visitwiltshire.co.uk/salisbury; Fish Row, Market
Sq; ⊙9.30am-6pm Mon-Sat, 10am-4pm Sun Jun-
Sep, 9.30am-5pm Mon-Sat Oct-Apr)

① Getting There & Away

Trains run half-hourly from London Waterloo (£35,
1½ hours).

Bath £9, one hour

Bristol £11, 1¼ hours

Exeter £30, two hours

Stonehenge

This compelling ring of monolithic **stones**
(EH; ☏0870-333 1181; www.english-heritage.
org.uk; adult/child £6.90/3.50; ⊙9am-7pm)
has been attracting a steady stream of
pilgrims, poets and philosophers for the
last 5000 years and is easily Britain's
most iconic archaeological site.

The first phase of construction at
Stonehenge started around 3000 BC,
when the outer circular bank and ditch
were erected. A thousand years later, an
inner circle of granite stones, known as
bluestones, was added. It's thought these
mammoth 4-ton blocks were hauled from
the Preseli Mountains in South Wales,
some 250 miles away. Although no one
is entirely sure how the stones were
transported so far, it's thought a system
of ropes, sledges and rollers fashioned
from tree trunks was used.

Around 1500 BC, Stonehenge's main
stones were dragged to the site, erected
in a circle and crowned by massive
lintels to make the trilithons (two vertical
stones topped by a horizontal one). The
sarsen (sandstone) stones were cut from
rock found on the Marlborough Downs,
20 miles from the site. It's estimated
dragging one of these 50-ton stones
across the countryside would require
about 600 people.

Also around this time, the bluestones
from 500 years earlier were rearranged
as an inner **bluestone horseshoe** with
an **altar stone** at the centre. Outside this
the **trilithon horseshoe** of five massive
sets of stones was erected. Three of these
are intact; the other two have just a single
upright. Then came the major **sarsen
circle** of 30 massive vertical stones, of
which 17 uprights and six lintels remain.

SS *Great Britain*

Like many stone circles in Britain (including Avebury, 22 miles away), the inner horseshoes are aligned to coincide with sunrise at the midsummer solstice, which some claim supports the theory that the site was some kind of astronomical calendar.

A marked pathway leads around the henge, and although you can't walk freely in the circle itself, it's possible to see the stones fairly close up. An audioguide (in 10 languages) is included in the admission price.

 Tours

STONE CIRCLE ACCESS VISITS Walking Tours (01722-343830; www.english-heritage.org. uk; adult/child £14.50/7.50) Visitors normally have to stay outside the stone circle itself, but on these self-guided walks, you get to wander around the core of the site, getting up-close views of the iconic bluestones and trilithons. They take place in the evening or early morning so the quieter atmosphere and the slanting sunlight add to the effect. Each visit only takes 26 people; to secure a place book at least two months in advance.

Getting There & Away

The Stonehenge Tour (01722-336855; www. thestonehengetour.info; return adult/child £11/5) leaves Salisbury's railway and bus stations half-hourly from June to August, and hourly between September and May.

Taxis charge £40 to go to Stonehenge from Salisbury, wait for an hour and come back.

Avebury

While the tour buses head straight for Stonehenge, prehistoric purists make for the massive stone circle at Avebury. It's bigger, older and a great deal quieter, and a large section of the village is actually inside the stones – footpaths wind around them, allowing you to really soak up the extraordinary atmosphere.

With a diameter of about 348m, Avebury is the largest stone circle in

the world. It's also one of the oldest, dating from around 2500 to 2200 BC, between the first and second phase of construction at Stonehenge. The site originally consisted of an outer circle of 98 standing stones of up to 6m in length, many weighing 20 tons, which had been carefully selected for their shape and size. The stones were surrounded by another circle delineated by a 5m-high earth bank and ditch up to 9m deep. Inside were smaller stone circles to the north (27 stones) and south (29 stones).

In the Middle Ages, when Britain's pagan past was an embarrassment to the church, many of the stones were buried, removed or broken up. In 1934 wealthy businessman and archaeologist Alexander Keiller supervised the re-erection of the stones, and planted markers to indicate those that had disappeared; he later bought the site for posterity using funds from his family's marmalade fortune.

The site is 6 miles west of Marlborough on the A4361.

Bristol

Bristol might just be Britain's most over-looked city. While most visitors speed past en route to Bath without giving the south-west's biggest metropolis so much as a second glance, they're missing out on one of Britain's quirkiest and coolest cities.

Sights

SS GREAT BRITAIN Ship (www.ssgreatbritain.org; Great Western Dock, Gas Ferry Rd; adult/child/family £12.50/6.25/33.50; 10am-5.30pm Apr-Oct) Bristol's pride and joy is the mighty steamship SS *Great Britain*, designed by the genius engineer Isambard Kingdom Brunel in 1843. You can wander around the ship's impeccably refurbished interior, including the galley, surgeon's quarters, dining saloon and the great engine room, but the highlight is the amazing 'glass sea' on which the ship sits, enclosing an airtight dry dock

that preserves the delicate hull and allows visitors to see the ground-breaking screw propeller up close.

Tickets also allow admission to the neighbouring **Maritime Heritage Centre** (☏0117-927 9856; Great Western Dockyard, Gas Ferry Rd; ☉10am-5.30pm Apr-Oct, to 4.30pm Nov-Mar), which has exhibits relating to the ship's illustrious past and the city's boat-building heritage.

FREE M SHED　　　　　　　　Museum

(www.mshed.org; Princes Wharf; ☉10am-5pm Tue-Fri, to 6pm Sat & Sun) It's taken four years and £27 million to build, but Bristol's brand-new museum is finally open – and it's really rather brilliant. Lodged in a massive old warehouse overlooking the docks, it's a treasure trove of weird-and-wonderful memorabilia rummaging through the city's past. Best of all, it's free – although well worth the £2 suggested donation.

CLIFTON SUSPENSION BRIDGE　　Bridge

(www.cliftonbridge.org.uk) Clifton's most famous (and photographed) landmark is a

Brunel masterpiece, the 76m-high Clifton Suspension Bridge, which spans the Avon Gorge from Clifton over to Leigh Woods in northern Somerset.

It's free to walk or cycle across the bridge; car drivers pay a 50p toll. There's a **visitor information point** (visitinfo@clifton-suspension-bridge.org; ☉10am-5pm) near the tower on the Leigh Woods side. Free guided tours (£3) of the bridge take place at 3pm on Saturdays and Sundays from Easter to October.

 **Sleeping**

HOTEL DU VIN　　　　　　　Hotel £££

(☏0117-925 5577; www.hotelduvin.com; Narrow Lewins Mead; r £145-215; [P][☎]) If expense is no object, there's only one choice in Bristol, and that's this indulgently elegant warehouse conversion. Occupying an old sugar store, it's a mix of industrial chic and sleek minimalism, complete with

Left: Avebury Stone Circle (p185); **Below:** Clifton Suspension Bridge

(LEFT) CHRIS WARREN/GETTY IMAGES ©; (BELOW) MARK BOLTON/GETTY IMAGES ©

giant futon beds, claw-foot baths and frying-pan showerheads.

NUMBER 38 — B&B ££££

(0117-946 6905; www.number38clifton.com; 38 Upper Belgrave Rd, Clifton; d £138; P) Perched on the edge of the Downs, this super new B&B puts most of the city's hotels to shame in terms of designer decor. It's really handy for Clifton and Whiteladies Rd, but a long walk from the centre, so it might not be ideal for everyone.

Eating

MUSET BY RONNIE — British ££

(0117-973 7248; www.ronnies-restaurant. co.uk; 12-16 Clifton Rd; 2-/3-course lunch menu £13/16, dinner menu £19/22, mains £13-21) Chef Ron Faulkner trained under big names including Anton Mosimann and Ed Baines, and his Brit-meets-Mediterranean blend

has earned him local fans as well as critical acclaim.

RIVERSTATION — British ££

(0117-914 4434; www.riverstation.co.uk; 2-/3-course lunch £12.75/15.50, dinner mains £14.50-19.75) It's been around for many years now, but this riverside bistro is as reliable as ever, turning out some of the city's best European cuisine. Head upstairs for dining, downstairs for coffee – and ask for a window table to make the most of the harbour views.

GLASSBOAT — French ££

(0117-929 0704; www.glassboat.co.uk; Welsh Back; 2-/3-course lunch menu £15/20, dinner mains £15.50-22; lunch Tue-Fri & Sun, dinner Mon-Sat) You couldn't ask for a more romantic place for dinner than this double-decked river barge, with its candlelit tables and watery views.

ℹ️ Information

Bristol Tourist Information Centre (☎0333-321 0101; www.visitbristol.co.uk; E-Shed, 1 Canons Rd; ☺10am-6pm)

ℹ️ Getting There & Away

Bristol is an important rail hub, with regular services to London provided by **First Great Western** (www.firstgreatwestern.co.uk) and services to northern England and Scotland mainly covered by **Cross Country** (www.crosscountrytrains.co.uk).

DESTINATION	DETAILS
Birmingham	£47, 1½hr, hourly
Edinburgh	£136.50, 6½hr, hourly
Exeter	£25, 1hr, hourly
Glasgow	£136.50, 6½hr, hourly
London Paddington	£39, 1¾hr, hourly
Penzance	£42, 5½ hr, hourly
Truro	£42, 5hr, hourly

SOMERSET
Bath

POP 90,144

Britain's littered with beautiful cities, but precious few can hold a candle to Bath. Founded on top of a network of natural hot springs, Bath's heyday really began during the 18th century, when local entrepreneur Ralph Allen and his team of father-and-son architects, John Wood the Elder and Younger, turned this sleepy backwater into the toast of Georgian society, and constructed fabulous landmarks such as the Circus and Royal Crescent.

◉ Sights & Activities

BATH ABBEY   Church
(www.bathabbey.org; requested donation £2.50; ☺9am-6pm Mon-Sat, 1-2.30pm & 4.30-5.30pm Sun) Looming above the centre of the city, Bath's huge abbey church was built between 1499 and 1616, making it the last great medieval church raised in England. Its most striking feature is the west facade, where angels climb up and down stone ladders, commemorating a dream of the founder, Bishop Oliver King. Among those buried here are Sir Isaac Pitman (who devised the Pitman method of shorthand) and the celebrated *bon viveur* Beau Nash.

ROYAL CRESCENT
Historic Neighbourhood
(Royal Crescent) Bath is rightly celebrated for its glorious Georgian architecture, and it doesn't get any grander than on Royal Crescent, a semicircular terrace of majestic tow houses overlooking the green sweep of Royal Victoria Park. They were designed by John Wood

Bath Abbey
GRAHAM BELL/GETTY IMAGES ©

SIMON GREENWOOD/GETTY IMAGES ©

Don't Miss **Roman Baths**

Ever since the Romans arrived in Bath, life in the city has revolved around the three geothermal springs that bubble up near the abbey. In typically ostentatious style, the Romans constructed a glorious complex of bathhouses above these thermal waters to take advantage of their natural temperature, a constant 46°C when they emerge.

The heart of the complex is the **Great Bath**, a large lead-lined pool filled with steaming, geothermally-heated water from the so-called 'Sacred Spring' to a depth of 1.6m. Further bathing pools and changing rooms are situated to the east and west, with excavated sections revealing the hypocaust system that would have kept the bathing rooms balmy.

You can usually avoid the worst crowds by buying tickets in advance online, visiting early on a midweek morning, and by avoiding July and August. Admission includes an audioguide in a choice of eight languages, featuring a special commentary by the bestselling author Bill Bryson.

NEED TO KNOW

www.romanbaths.co.uk; Abbey Churchyard; adult/child £12/7.80; ⏲9am-6pm

the Younger (1728–82) and built between 1767 and 1775.

For a glimpse into the splendour and razzle-dazzle of Georgian life, head for the beautifully restored house at **No 1 Royal Crescent** (www.bath-preservation-trust.org.uk; 1 Royal Cres; adult/child £6.50/2.50; ⏲10.30am-5pm Tue-Sun late Feb–mid-Dec), given to the city by the shipping magnate Major

Bernard Cayzer, and since restored using only 18th-century materials.

A walk east along Brock St from the Royal Crescent leads to the **Circus**, a ring of 33 houses divided into three terraces. Plaques on the houses commemorate famous residents such as Thomas Gainsborough, Clive of India and David Livingstone.

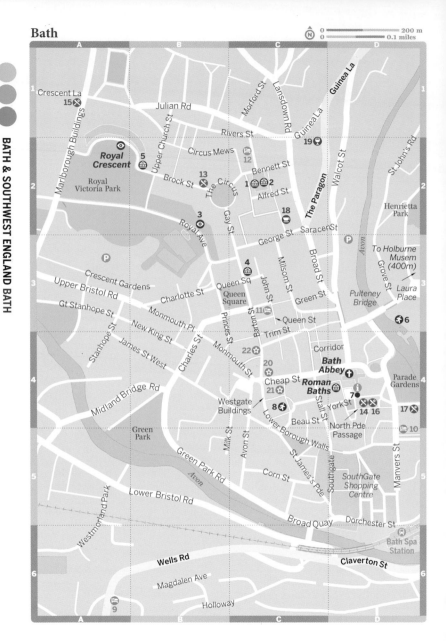

To the south along Gravel Walk is the **Georgian Garden**, restored to resemble a typical 18th-century-town house garden.

ASSEMBLY ROOMS Historic Building (NT; www.nationaltrust.org.uk/main/w-bath assemblyrooms; 19 Bennett St; adult/child £2/ free; ⏱10.30am-6pm) Opened in 1771, the city's glorious Assembly Rooms were where fashionable Bath socialites once

Bath

◉ Top Sights
Bath Abbey	D4
Roman Baths	D4
Royal Crescent	A2

◎ Sights
1	Assembly Rooms	C2
2	Fashion Museum	C2
3	Georgian Garden	B2
4	Jane Austen Centre	C3
5	No 1 Royal Crescent	B2

◈ Activities, Courses & Tours
6	Boat Trips	D3
7	Jane Austen's Bath Walking Tours	D4
8	Thermae Bath Spa	C4

⊜ Sleeping
9	139 Bath	A6

10	Halcyon	D5
11	Haringtons Hotel	C3
12	Queensberry Hotel	C2

✖ Eating
13	Circus	B2
14	Demuth's	D4
15	Marlborough Tavern	A1
16	Sally Lunn's	D4
17	Sotto Sotto	D4

❑ Drinking
18	Same Same But Different	C2
19	Star Inn	C2

❂ Entertainment
20	Komedia	C4
21	Little Theatre Cinema	C4
22	Theatre Royal	C4

gathered to waltz, play cards and listen to the latest chamber music. You're free to wander around the rooms, as long as they haven't been reserved for a special function.

FREE HOLBURNE MUSEUM — Gallery
(www.holburne.org; Great Pulteney St; temporary exhibitions incur fee; ⊙10am-5pm) Sir William Holburne, the 18th-century aristocrat, aesthete and art fanatic, amassed a huge collection which now forms the core of the Holburne Museum, in a lavish mansion at the end of Great Pulteney St. Fresh from a three-year refit, the museum houses an impressive roll-call of works by artists including Turner, Stubbs, William Hoare and Thomas Gainsborough, as well as a fine collection of 18th-century majollica and porcelain.

JANE AUSTEN CENTRE — Museum
(www.janeausten.co.uk; 40 Gay St; adult/child £7.45/4.25; ⊙9.45am-5.30pm) Bath is known to many as a location in Jane Austen's novels, including *Persuasion* and *Northanger Abbey*. This museum houses a small collection of memorabilia relating to the writer's life in Bath, and costumed guides bring the era to life. There's also a Regency tearoom which serves crumpets and cream teas in suitably frilly surrounds.

FASHION MUSEUM — Museum
(www.fashionmuseum.co.uk; Assembly Rooms, Bennett St; adult/child £7.25/5.25; ⊙10.30am-5pm) In the basement of the Assembly Rooms, this museum contains a wonderful collection of costumes worn from the 16th to late 20th centuries.

AMERICAN MUSEUM IN BRITAIN — Museum
(www.americanmuseum.org; Claverton Manor; adult/child £8/4.50; ⊙noon-5pm) Britain's largest collection of American folk art, including Native American textiles, patchwork quilts and historic maps, is housed in a fine mansion a couple of miles from the city centre. Several rooms have been re-created in period style, including a 17th-century Puritan house, an 18th-century tavern and a New Orleans boudoir c 1860.

BOAT TRIPS — Cruises
Various cruise operators offer boat trips up and down the River Avon from the landing station underneath Pulteney Bridge, including the open-top **Pulteney Cruisers** (☎01225-312900; www.bathboating.com; adult/child £8/4), the **Pulteney Princess** (☎07791-910650; www.pulteneyprincess.co.uk; adult/child £8/3) or **Bath City Boat Trips** (☎07974-560197; www.bathcityboattrips.com; adult/child £6.95/4.95).

Tours

FREE MAYOR'S
GUIDE TOURS Walking Tours
(01225-477411; www.bathguides.org.uk;
10.30am & 2pm Sun-Fri, 10.30am Sat) Excellent historical tours provided free by the Mayor's Corp of Honorary Guides. Leave from outside the Pump Rooms. Extra tours at 7pm on Tuesdays and Thursdays May to September.

**JANE AUSTEN'S BATH
WALKING TOURS** Walking Tours
(01225-443000; adult/child £6/5; 11am Sat & Sun) A guided tour of the Georgian city, organised by the Jane Austen Centre. Tours leave from the Abbey Churchyard.

Sleeping

Bath gets incredibly busy, especially in the height of summer and at weekends, when prices are at a premium. Very few hotels have parking, although some offer discounted rates at municipal car parks.

QUEENSBERRY HOTEL Hotel £££
(01225-447928; www.thequeensberry.co.uk; 4 Russell St; d £150-270, ste £460;) It's a budget-buster, but the quirky Queensberry is undoubtedly one of Bath's best boutique spoils. Four Georgian town houses have been combined into one seamlessly stylish whole, but all the rooms are subtly different. The basement Olive Tree Restaurant is one of the town's top tables, too.

HALCYON Hotel ££
(01225-444100; www.thehalcyon.com; 2/3 South Pde; d £125-145;) Situated on a listed terrace off Manvers St, the heavily renovated Halcyon is all about style on a budget: whitewashed rooms, bright bed linen, Philippe Starck bath fittings and White Company smellies, along with a smart basement breakfast room and the brand-new Circo cocktail bar. The drawbacks? Rooms are spread out over three floors and there's no lift.

Thermae Bath Spa

Taking a dip in the Roman Baths might be off the agenda, but you can still sample the city's curative waters at **Thermae Bath Spa** (0844-888 0844; www.thermaebathspa.com; Bath St; 9am-10pm, last entry 7.30pm). Here the old **Cross Bath**, incorporated into an ultramodern shell of local stone and plate glass, is now the setting for a variety of spa packages. The New Royal Bath ticket includes steam rooms, waterfall shower and a choice of bathing venues – including the jaw-dropping open-air rooftop pool, where you can swim in the thermal waters in front of a backdrop of Bath's stunning cityscape.

139 BATH B&B ££
(01225-314769; www.139bath.co.uk; 139 Wells Rd; r £120-195; P) It's a bit out of the centre, but this swish B&B really sets the pace. It's been thoughtfully designed throughout, with swirly fabrics, contemporary colour schemes and supremely comfy beds, plus lots of little spoils such as cafetière coffee, Molton Bown bath products and a generous buffet breakfast (two four-poster rooms even have jacuzzis).

HARINGTONS HOTEL Hotel ££
(01225-461278; www.haringtonshotel.co.uk; Queen St; d £88-168) Bath's classical trappings aren't to everyone's taste, so things are kept modern and minimal at this city-centre crash pad: clean lines, crisp colour schemes and LCD TVs, although some of the rooms are shoebox-sized.

 Eating

**MENU GORDON
JONES** Gourmet British ££
(01225-480871; www.menugordonjones.co.uk; 2 Wellsway; 5-course lunch £30, 6-course dinner

£40) Gordon Jones is the name to watch in Bath. The multicourse 'surprise menus' are dreamt up by Jones on the day, and showcase his taste for experimentation, both in terms of ingredients (smoked eel, seagull's eggs, samphire) and presentation (test tubes, edible cups, slate plates).

CIRCUS   Modern British ££

(01225-466020; www.thecircuscafeand restaurant.co.uk; 34 Brock St; mains lunch £5.50-10, dinner £11-14; 10am-midnight Mon-Sat) It's not quite the locals' secret it once was, but the Circus is still one of Bath's best. Installed in a converted town house between the Circus and the Royal Crescent, it's the model of a modern Brit bistro: chef Ali Golden has a taste for hearty dishes such as rabbit pie and roast guinea fowl, all seasonally inspired, impeccably presented and reassuringly generous.

MARLBOROUGH TAVERN   Pub ££

(01225-423731; www.marlborough-tavern. com; 35 Marlborough Buildings; mains £12-17) Bath certainly isn't short on gastropubs, but the Marlborough is still very much top of the class. Chef Richard Knighting previously worked in Michelin-starred restaurants, and it shows: his menu is a mix of heartwarming classics and cheffy showiness, and rarely fails to hit the mark.

DEMUTH'S   Vegetarian ££

(01225-446059; www.demuths.co.uk; 2 North Pde Passage; lunch £4.95-11, dinner £14.50-17;) Even the most committed of carnivores can't fail to fall for this long-established veggie restaurant, which consistently turns out some of the city's most creative food – from cheddar soufflé served with figs, walnut purée and spring greens, to a port-poached pear baked with fennel seeds and ewe's cheese.

SOTTO SOTTO   Italian ££

(01225-330236; 10a North Pde; pasta £9, mains £13-17) Authentic Italian food served in a lovely cellar setting complete with barrel-brick roof.

SALLY LUNN'S   Tearoom £

(4 North Pde Passage; lunch mains £5-6, dinner mains from £8) This fabulously frilly tearoom occupies one of Bath's oldest houses, and makes the perfect venue for classic cream tea (served in proper bone china), accompanied by finger sandwiches, dainty cakes and the trademark Sally Lunn's Bun.

Thermae Bath Spa

🍷 Drinking

SAME SAME BUT DIFFERENT   Cafe, Bar
(7a Prince's Buildings, Bartlett St; ⏰8am-6pm
Mon-Wed, 8am-11pm Thu-Sat, 10am-5pm Sun)
Boho hang-out for the town's trendies,
tucked down an alley off George St.

STAR INN   Pub
(www.star-inn-bath.co.uk; 23 The Vineyards) Not
many pubs are registered relics, but the
Star is – it still has many of its 19th-
century bar fittings. It's off The Paragon.

⭐ Entertainment

THEATRE ROYAL   Theatre
(www.theatreroyal.org.uk; Sawclose) This is
one of the southwest's classiest regional
theatres.

KOMEDIA   Cabaret, Comedy
(www.komedia.co.uk; 22-23 Westgate St) Live
comedy and cabaret at this Bath offshoot
of the Brighton-based original.

LITTLE THEATRE CINEMA   Cinema
(St Michael's Pl) Bath's excellent art house
cinema screens fringe films and foreign-
language flicks.

ℹ️ Information

Bath Visitor Centre (www.visitbath.co.uk; Abbey
Churchyard; ⏰9.30am-5pm Mon-Sat, 10am-4pm
Sun) Sells the Bath City Card (£3), which is valid
for three weeks and offers discounts at many
local shops, restaurants and attractions.

ℹ️ Getting There & Away

Bath Spa station is at the end of Manvers St.
Many services connect through Bristol (£9.90, 20
minutes, two or three per hour), especially to the
north of England.

London Paddington or **London Waterloo** £39,
1½ hours, half-hourly

Cardiff Central £18, one hour, hourly

Exeter £27.50, 1¼ hours, hourly

Salisbury £15.70, one hour, hourly

ℹ️ Getting Around

Bath has serious traffic problems (especially at
rush hour). **Park & Ride services** (📞01225-
464446; return Mon-Fri £3, Sat £2.50; ⏰6.15am-
7.30pm Mon-Sat) operate from Lansdown to the
north, Newbridge to the west and Odd Down
to the south. It takes about 10 minutes
to the centre; buses leave every 10 to
15 minutes. If you brave the city, the
best-value car park is underneath
the new SouthGate shopping
centre (two/eight hours £3/13,
after 6.30pm £2).

Wells

POP 10,406

With Wells, small is
beautiful. This tiny, picturesque metropolis is
England's smallest city,
and only qualifies for
the 'city' title thanks to a
magnificent medieval
cathedral, which sits in

Powderham Castle
NIGEL HICKS/GETTY IMAGES ©

the centre beside the grand Bishop's Palace.

Sights

WELLS CATHEDRAL · Church

(www.wellscathedral.org.uk; Cathedral Green; requested donation adult/child £6/3; ⏰7am-7pm) Wells' gargantuan Gothic cathedral (officially known as the Cathedral Church of St Andrew) sits plum in the centre of the city, surrounded by one of the largest cathedral closes anywhere in England. It was built in several stages between 1180 and 1508, and consequently showcases a range of different Gothic styles.

Dominated by its squat towers, the cathedral's most famous asset is its **west front**, an immense sculpture gallery decorated with more than 300 figures, built in the 13th century and restored in 1986. Inside, the cathedral's famous **scissor arches** separate the nave from the choir.

Other highlights include the elegant **Lady Chapel** (1326), the fan-vaulted **Chapter House** (1306) and the celebrated **chained library**, which contains books and manuscripts dating back to 1472. Outside, the cathedral's **Chain Bridge** enabled clerics to reach the cathedral without getting their robes wet.

Free guided tours usually run every hour from Monday to Saturday, but you'll need a photography permit (£3) to take pictures.

CATHEDRAL CLOSE · Historic Area

Wells Cathedral forms the centrepiece of a cluster of ecclesiastical buildings dating back to the Middle Ages. Facing the west front, on the left are the 15th-century **Old Deanery** and the **Wells & Mendip Museum** (www.wellsmuseum.org.uk; 8 Cathedral Green; adult/child £3/1; ⏰10am-5.30pm Easter-Oct, 11am-4pm Wed-Mon Nov-Easter), with exhibits on local life, cathedral architecture and the infamous Witch of Wookey Hole.

If You Like...
Castles

The southwest is home to an impressive array of historic castles and fortresses. Here are a few that are particularly worth seeking out.

1 **CORFE CASTLE**
(NT; ☎01929-481294; www.nationaltrust.org.uk; adult/child £7.72/3.86; ⏰10am-6pm Apr-Sep, to 4pm Oct-Mar) One of Dorset's most iconic landmarks, Corfe Castle was all but blown to bits during the English Civil War, and its fractured defences feel wonderfully atmospheric. It's 20 miles east of Dorchester.

2 **POWDERHAM CASTLE**
(☎01626-890243; www.powderham.co.uk; adult/child £10.50/8.50; ⏰11am-4.30pm Sun-Fri Apr-Oct) Powderham was built in 1391 and heavily remodelled in the Victorian era. It's still the home of the Earl of Devon and, despite its grandeur, sometimes it feels like you're wandering through someone's sitting room. It's 8 miles south of Exeter.

3 **PENDENNIS CASTLE**
(EH; ☎01326-316594; adult/child £5.40/2.70; ⏰10am-6pm Jul & Aug, to 5pm Apr-Jun & Sep, to 4pm Oct-Mar) This Tudor castle sits on Pendennis Point, just outside the Cornish seaport of Falmouth. Highlights include the atmospheric Tudor gun deck, a WWI guard house and the WWII-era Half-Moon Battery.

4 **TINTAGEL CASTLE**
(EH; ☎01840-770328; adult/child £5.20/2.60; ⏰10am-6pm Apr-Sep, to 5pm Oct, to 4pm Nov-Mar) This dramatic clifftop castle on the north Cornish coast is said to be King Arthur's legendary birthplace, but the ruins mostly date from the 13th century. It's about 22 miles northeast of Padstow.

BISHOP'S PALACE · Historic Building

(www.bishopspalacewells.co.uk; adult/child £6.35/2.70; ⏰palace 10am-6pm Apr-Dec, gardens Feb-Dec) Built for the bishop in the 13th century, this moat-ringed palace is purportedly the oldest inhabited building in England. The natural springs after which Wells is named bubble up in the palace's grounds.

Sleeping

BABINGTON HOUSE Luxury Hotel **£££**
(☎01373-812266; www.babingtonhouse.co.uk; near Frome; r £340-530; P🛜🏊) It's eye-poppingly pricey, but this lauded design hotel is without doubt one of Britain's most luxurious places to stay. There's a top-class restaurant, cool library, private 45-seat cinema and, of course, a spa in the old cow shed. It's 14 miles east of Wells.

BERYL B&B **££**
(☎01749-678738; www.beryl-wells.co.uk; Hawkers Lane; d £100-150; P🏊) This grand gabled mansion about a mile from Wells offers a taste of English eccentricity. Its every inch is crammed with antique atmosphere, and the rooms boast grandfather clocks, chaise longues and four-posters galore.

✗ Eating

GOODFELLOWS Bistro, Cafe **££**
(☎01749-673866; www.goodfellows.co.uk; 5 Sadler St; 3-course bistro dinner £39) Two eateries in one, both excellent. The continental-style **cafe** (menus £10-17; ⏱8.30am-4pm Mon & Tue, 8.30am-5pm & 6-10pm Wed-Sat) serves quick lunch food and patisseries made by the in-house pastry chef. For something more sophisticated, the seafood **bistro** (mains £11.50-23; ⏱noon-2pm Tue-Sat, 6.30-9.30pm Wed-Sat) offers a full line-up of fishy delights plus a choice of settings (downstairs for open-plan dining, upstairs for intimacy).

OLD SPOT British **££**
(☎01749-689099; www.theoldspot.co.uk; 12 Sadler St; 2-/3-course lunch £15.50/18.50, dinner mains £14-18.50; ⏱lunch Wed-Sun, dinner Tue-Sat) Hale and hearty classics form the core of Ian Bates' bistro. It's heavy on rich, meaty dishes such as duck terrine, pork fillet with lentils and black pudding, or guinea fowl with mushroom pithivier.

ℹ Information

Tourist office (☎01749-672552; www.wellstourism.com; Market Pl; ⏱9.30am-5.30pm Apr-Oct, 10am-4pm Nov-Mar)

196

Cheddar Gorge

Only marginally less touristy than their Wookey cousins, the massive cliffs of **Cheddar Gorge** (www.cheddarcaves.co.uk; Explorer Ticket adult/child £18.50/12; ⏱10am-5.30pm) are nonetheless a dramatic sight. This is England's deepest natural canyon, and in places the limestone cliffs tower 138m above the twisting road.

The gorge is famous for its bewildering network of subterranean caves, a few of which are open to the public. **Cox's Cave** and **Gough's Cave**, both lined with stalactites and stalagmites, are subtly illuminated to bring out the spectrum of colours in the rock. To explore the more-remote caverns, you'll need to organise a caving trip with **X-Treme** (☎01934-742343; www.cheddargorge.co.uk/x-treme; 1½hr trip adult/child £21/19); be prepared to get cold, wet and very muddy. Rock-climbing sessions are also available.

Cheddar gets extremely busy during summer and school holidays, when the gorge road turns into one long traffic jam. You can normally escape the worst crowds by climbing the 274-step staircase known as **Jacob's Ladder**, which leads to a spectacular viewpoint and a 3-mile cliff trail.

There's a 10% discount for online booking.

Glastonbury
POP 8429

Ley lines converge, white witches convene and every shop is filled with the aroma of smouldering joss sticks in good old Glastonbury, the southwest's undisputed capital of alternative culture.

◎ Sights

 GLASTONBURY TOR Landmark
(NT; www.nationaltrust.org.uk) This 160m-high grassy mound provides glorious views over the surrounding countryside, and a focal point for a bewildering array of myths. According to some it's the home of a faery king, while an old Celtic legend identifies it as the stronghold of Gwyn ap

Detour:
Greenway

The world-famous detective writer Agatha Christie was born in Torquay, and visiting her gorgeous summer house, **Greenway** (NT; ☎01803-842382; www.nationaltrust.org.uk; Greenway Rd, Galmpton; adult/child £9/5; ◷10.30am-5pm Wed-Sun Mar-Oct, plus Tue Aug; P), near Dartmouth is a unique experience. Part-guided **tours** allow you to wander between rooms where the furnishings and knick-knacks are much as she left them. So you can check out the piles of hats in the lobby, the books in her library and the clothes in her wardrobe, and listen to her speak (via a replica radio) in the drawing room. The gardens too are a delight: glorious woods hug the water, speckled with splashes of magnolias, daffodils and hydrangeas.

The property is hugely popular, entrance to the house is by timed ticket, and there are only a very limited number of parking places, which have to be booked well in advance. The best way to arrive is by boat or on foot. The **Greenway Ferry** (☎ 01803-882811; www.greenwayferry.co.uk) runs regularly from Dartmouth (adult/child return £7.50/5.50), Totnes (adult/child return £11/7.50) and Torquay (adult/child return £19/12). Times vary and it's best to book.

Nudd (ruler of Annwyn, the Underworld) – but the most famous legend identifies the tor as the mythic Isle of Avalon, where King Arthur was taken after being mortally wounded in battle by his nephew Mordred, and where Britain's 'once and future king' sleeps until his country calls again.

Whatever the truth of the legends, the tor has been a site of pilgrimage for many years, and was once topped by the medieval chapel of **St Michael**, although today only the tower remains.

It takes about 45 minutes to walk up and down the tor, plus an extra half hour to walk from town. The regular **Tor Bus** (adult/child £3/1.50; ◷half-hourly Apr-Sep) from Dunstan's car park stops at Chalice Well, near the start of the main trail on Well House Lane.

GLASTONBURY ABBEY
Ruins
(www.glastonburyabbey.com; Magdalene St; adult/child £6/4; ◷9am-8pm) The scattered ruins of Glastonbury Abbey give little hint that this was once one of England's great seats of ecclesiastical power.

The abbey was torn down following Henry VIII's Dissolution of the Monasteries in 1539, when the last abbot Richard Whiting was hung, drawn and quartered on the tor. Precious little remains of the original building, except for the nave walls, the ruined St Mary's chapel, and the remains of the crossing arches, which may have been scissor-shaped like those in Wells Cathedral. The grounds also contain a museum, cider orchard and herb garden, as well as the Holy Thorn tree, which supposedly sprung from Joseph's staff and mysteriously blooms twice a year, at Christmas and Easter.

ℹ Information
Glastonbury Tourist Office (☎01458-832954; www.glastonburytic.co.uk; The Tribunal, 9 High St; ◷10am-5pm)

Exmoor National Park

Barely 21 miles across and 12 miles north to south, Exmoor might be the little sister of England's national parks, but what she lacks in scale she more than makes up in scenery. Part wilderness expanse, part rolling fields, dotted with bottle green meadows, wooded coombes and crumbling cliffs, Exmoor seems to sum up everything that's green and pleasant about the English landscape.

It's a haven for ramblers, mountain bikers and horse riders, and it's also home to lots of rare wildlife, including some of England's largest herds of wild red deer; best spotted on a dawn safari.

Several companies offer 4WD 'safari' trips across the moor: the best season to visit is autumn, especially from October onwards, when the annual autumn 'rutting' season begins, and stags can be seen bellowing, charging and clashing horns in an attempt to impress their prospective mates. Standard 2½-hour safari trips cost around £25, although longer expeditions can usually be arranged with plenty of advance notice.

○ **Barle Valley Safaris** (☎01643-851386; www.exmoorwildlifesafaris.co.uk; safaris £30)

○ **Discovery Safaris** (☎01643-863080; www. discoverysafaris.com; safaris £20)

○ **Exmoor Safari** (☎01643-831229; www. exmoorsafari.co.uk; safaris £30)

○ **Red Stag Safari** (☎01643-841831; www. redstagsafari.co.uk; safaris £25-38)

ⓘ Information

Exmoor National Park (www.exmoor-nationalpark.gov.uk) The official NPA site.

DEVON
Exeter
POP 119,600

◉ Sights

EXETER CATHEDRAL Church
(☎01392-285983; www.exeter-cathedral.org.uk; The Close; adult/child £5/free; ⊗9.30am-4.45pm Mon-Sat) Magnificent in warm, honey-coloured stone, Exeter's Cathedral Church of St Peter is framed by lawns and wonky half-timbered buildings – a quintessentially English scene peopled by picnickers snacking to the sound of the bells.

Above the **Great West Front** scores of weather-worn figures line a once brightly painted screen that now forms England's largest collection of 14th-century sculpture. Inside, the ceiling is

Glastonbury Tor (p196)

Detour:
Dartmoor National Park

Dartmoor is an ancient, compelling landscape, so different from the rest of Devon that a visit feels like falling straight into Tolkien's *Return of the King*. Exposed granite hills (called tors) crest on the horizon, linked by swaths of honey-tinged moors. The centre of this 368-sq-mile wilderness is the higher moor; an elemental, treeless expanse. Moody and utterly empty, you'll either find its remote beauty exhilarating or chilling, or quite possibly a bit of both.

Steven Spielberg chose to film part of his WWI epic *War Horse* in this landscape; a century earlier it inspired Sir Arthur Conan Doyle to write *The Hound of the Baskervilles*.

Dartmoor is also a natural breakout zone with a checklist of charms: superb walking, cycling, riding, climbing and white-water kayaking; rustic pubs and fancy restaurants; wild camping nooks and country-house hotels – perfect boltholes when the fog rolls in.

Dartmoor National Park Authority (DNPA; ☏01822-890414; www.dartmoor.gov.uk) runs the **High Moorland Visitor Centre** (☏01822-890414; ◷10am-5pm Apr-Oct, to 4pm Nov-Mar) in Princetown. Other DNPA centres include those at **Haytor Vale** (☏01364-661520; Haytor Vale; ◷10am-5pm Easter-Oct, 10am-4pm Sat & Sun Nov & Dec) and **Postbridge** (☏01822-880272; ◷10am-5pm Easter-Oct, 10am-4pm Sat & Sun Nov & Dec). Dartmoor's official visitor website is www.dartmoor.co.uk.

mesmerising – the longest unbroken Gothic vaulting in the world, it sweeps up to meet ornate ceiling bosses in gilt and vibrant colours.

Free **guided tours** (◷11am & 12.30pm Mon-Sat, plus 2.30pm Mon-Fri) last 45 minutes. For a sensational view of Exeter Cathedral book one of the high-rise guided **walks** (☏01392-285983; www.exeter-cathedral.org.uk; adult/child £10/5; ◷2pm Tue-Thu, 11am Sat Apr-Sep). Climb 251 steps up a spiral staircase, head out onto the sweeping roof to stroll its length, then gaze down on the city from the top of the North Tower. They're popular so book two weeks ahead.

UNDERGROUND PASSAGES   Tunnels
(☏01392-665887; www.exeter.gov.uk/passages; Paris St; adult/child £5.50/4; ◷9.30am-5.30pm Mon-Sat, 10am-4pm Sun Jun-Sep, 11.30am-4pm Tue-Sun Oct-May) Prepare to crouch down, don a hard hat and possibly get spooked in what is the only publicly accessible system of its kind in England. These medieval vaulted passages were built to house pipes bringing fresh water to the city. Guides lead you on a scramble through

the network telling tales of ghosts, escape routes and cholera. The last tour is an hour before closing; they're popular – book ahead.

 Sleeping

ABODE, ROYAL CLARENCE   Hotel ££
(☏01392-319955; www.abodehotels.co.uk/exeter; Cathedral Yard; r £120-300; ⊚) This is the epitome of sink-into-it luxury. Exquisite room are categorised as Comfortable, Desirable, Enviable or Fabulous – either way they're a drop-dead gorgeous blend of Georgian grandeur and minimalist chic. Breakfast is not included.

RAFFLES   B&B £
(☏01392-270200; www.raffles-exeter.co.uk; 11 Blackall Rd; s/d £42/72; P) The antique-dealer owner has peppered each room of this late-Victorian town house with heritage features – look out for Bakelite radios, wooden plant stands and creaking trunks.

ST OLAVES   Hotel ££

(☎ 01392-217736; www.olaves.co.uk; Mary Arches St; d £80-125, ste £95-155, f £165; P)
This hotel's swirling spiral staircase is so beautiful it's tempting to sleep beside it. But if you did, you'd miss out on the 18th-century-with-contemporary-twist bedrooms: think rococo mirrors, brass bedsteads and plush furnishings.

Eating

MICHAEL CAINES   Fine Dining £££

(☎ 01392-223638; www.michaelcaines.com; Cathedral Yard; mains £25) Run by the eponymous, double-Michelin-starred chef, the food here is a complex blend of prime Westcountry ingredients and full-bodied French flavours.

@ANGELA'S   Modern British ££

(☎01392-499038; www.angelasrestaurant. co.uk; 38 New Bridge St; dinner mains £19; ⊘lunch Wed-Sat, dinner Tue-Sat) Dedication to sourcing local ingredients sometimes sees the chef at this smart bistro rising before dawn to bag the best fish at Brixham Market; his steamed John Dory with seared scallops is worth the trip alone. Wise foodies opt for the prebooked lunch (two/three courses £19/23).

HARRY'S   Bistro ££

(www.harrys-exeter.co.uk; 86 Longbrook St; mains £8-12; ⊘closed Sun) Harry's is the kind of welcoming neighbourhood eatery you wish was on your own doorstep but rarely is.

ℹ Information

Main tourist office (☎01392-665700; www. heartofdevon.com; Dix's Field; ⊘9am-5pm Mon-Sat Apr-Sep, 9.30am-4.30pm Oct-Mar)

ℹ Getting There & Away

Air

Exeter International Airport (www.exeter -airport.co.uk) has flights connecting with cities in Europe and the UK, including Glasgow, Manchester and Newcastle, plus the Channel Islands and the Isles of Scilly.

Train

Main-line and branch-line trains run from Exeter St David's and Exeter Central stations:

London Paddington £35, 2½ hours, half-hourly

Penzance £15, three hours, hourly

Plymouth £5, one hour, half-hourly

Plymouth

POP 256,000

If parts of Devon are nature programs or costume dramas, Plymouth is a healthy dose of reality TV. Its location, on the edge of a stunning natural harbour and just behind Dartmoor, brings endless possibilities for boat trips, sailing or hiking. Add a rich maritime history, one of the country's best aquariums and a playful 1930s lido, and you have a place to reconnect with the real before another foray into Devon's chocolate-box-pretty moors and shores.

Sights

PLYMOUTH HOE   Headland
Francis Drake supposedly spied the Spanish fleet from this grassy headland overlooking **Plymouth Sound** (the city's wide bay); the fabled bowling green on which he finished his game was probably where his **statue** now stands.

The red-and-white-striped former lighthouse, **Smeaton's Tower** (☎01752-304774; The Hoe; adult/child £2.50/1; ⊘10am-noon & 1-3pm Tue-Sat Apr-Oct), was built 14 miles offshore on the Eddystone Rocks in 1759, then moved to the Hoe in 1882. Climbing its 93 steps provides an illuminating insight into lighthouse keepers' lives and stunning views of the city, Dartmoor and the sea.

BARBICAN   Neighbourhood
(www.plymouthbarbican.com) To get an idea of what Plymouth was like before the Blitz, head for the Barbican, a district of cobbled streets and Tudor and Jacobean buildings, many now converted into galleries, antiques shops and restaurants.

Plymouth

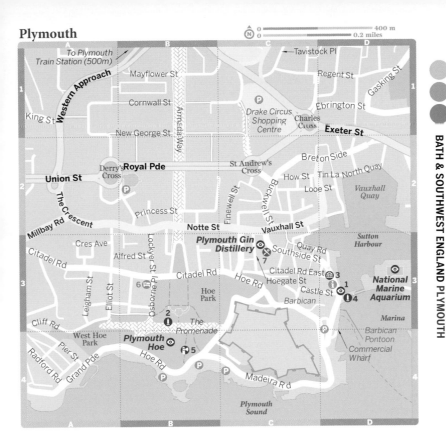

Plymouth

The Pilgrim Fathers' *Mayflower* set sail for America from here on 16 September 1620. The **Mayflower Steps** mark the approximate embarkation point – track down the passenger list displayed on the side of **Island House** nearby. Scores of other famous departures are also commemorated at the steps, including Captain James Cook's 1768 voyage of discovery, and the first emigrant ships to New Zealand.

PLYMOUTH GIN DISTILLERY Distillery (☎ 01752-665292; www.plymouthgin.com; 60 Southside St; tours £6; ☼ tours half-hourly 10.30am-4.30pm Mon-Sat, 11.30am-3.30pm Sun) This heavily beamed distillery is the oldest producer of gin in the world; it has been made here since 1793.

Below: Camel Trail cycle path; **Right:** Barbican (p200), Plymouth

(BELOW) WILL GRAY/JAI/CORBIS ©; (RIGHT) LEE PENGELLY/GETTY IMAGES ©

NATIONAL MARINE
AQUARIUM   Aquarium
(📞 0844 893 7938; www.national-aquarium.co.uk; Rope Walk; adult/child £12/8; 🕙10am-6pm Apr-Sep, to 5pm rest of year; **P**) The futuristic glass lines of this innovative aquarium are wittily sited next to the city's pungent Fish Market; an interesting dead-fish-live-fish juxtaposition. Walk-through glass arches ensure huge rays glide over your head, while the immense Atlantic Reef tank reveals just what's lurking a few miles offshore.

 **Sleeping**

ST ELIZABETH'S
HOUSE   Boutique Hotel £££
(📞 01752-344840; www.stelizabeths.co.uk; Longbrook St, Plympton St Maurice; d £90-199; **P**)
A manor house in the 17th century, this minihotel now oozes boutique chic. It's set in the suburb-cum-village of Plympton St Maurice, 5 miles east of Plymouth.

BOWLING GREEN Hotel £££
(📞 01752-209090; www.thebowl inggreenplymouth.com; 10 Osborne Pl; s/d/f £50/70/80; **P** 🛜) Some of the smart cream and white rooms in this family-run hotel look out onto the modern incarnation of Drake's famous bowling green.

 Eating

RIVER COTTAGE
CANTEEN & DELI   Modern British ££
(📞 01752-252702; www.rivercottage.net; Royal William Yard; mains £7-15; 🕙breakfast, lunch & dinner Tue-Sat, breakfast & lunch Sun; 🍽️)
Television-chef Hugh Fearnley-Whittingstall has long campaigned for local, sustainable, seasonal, organic produce, and that's exactly what you get here.

BARBICAN KITCHEN Modern British ££
(📞 01752-604448; www.barbicankitchen.com; 60 Southside St; mains £5-18) The bistro-style place has a wood and stone interior with bursts of shocking pink and lime. The

food is attention grabbing too – try the calves' livers with horseradish mash or maybe the honey, goat's cheese and apple crostini. It's all set in the atmospheric Plymouth Gin Distillery.

ℹ Information

Tourist office (☏ 01752-306330; www. visitplymouth.co.uk; 3 The Barbican; 🕙 9am-5pm Mon-Sat, 10am-4pm Sun Apr-Oct, 9am-5pm Mon-Fri, 10am-4pm Sat Nov-Mar)

ℹ Getting There & Away

Plymouth is on the intercity London Paddington–Penzance line; regular services include those to London (£40, 3½ to four hours, every 30 minutes), Bristol (£20, two hours, two or three per hour) and Exeter (£6.50, one hour, two or three per hour).

CORNWALL
Padstow
POP 3162

If anywhere symbolises Cornwall's recent renaissance, it's Padstow. This once-sleepy fishing port has been transformed into one of the county's most cosmopolitan corners thanks to celebrity chef Rick Stein, whose property portfolio encompasses several restaurants, shops and hotels around town, as well as a seafood school and fish-and-chip outlet.

◉ Sights & Activities

BEACHES Beach
Padstow is surrounded by fine beaches, including the so-called **Seven Bays**: Trevone, Harlyn, Mother Ivey's, Booby's, Constantine, Treyarnon and Porthcothan.

CAMEL TRAIL Cycling
The old Padstow–Bodmin railway was closed in the 1950s, and has now been turned into Cornwall's most popular bike trail. The main section starts in Padstow and runs east through Wadebridge (5.75 miles), but the trail runs on all the way to Poley Bridge on Bodmin Moor (18.3 miles).

Bikes can be hired from Padstow Cycle Hire (☎01841-533533; www.padstowcyclehire.com; South Quay; ⏰9am-5pm, to 9pm summer) or **Trail Bike Hire** (☎01841-532594; www.trailbikehire.co.uk; Unit 6, South Quay; ⏰9am-6pm) at the Padstow end, or from **Bridge Bike Hire** (☎01208-813050; www.bridgebikehire.co.uk) at the Wadebridge end, for around £12 to £15 per day.

🛏 Sleeping

TREANN HOUSE   B&B ££
(☎01841-553855; www.treannhousepadstow.com; 24 Dennis Rd; d £95-125; P) This stylish number makes a fancy place to stay. The three rooms are finished with stripped floors, crisp sheets and antique beds, and the Estuary Room has its own dinky balcony with a panorama over Padstow's rooftops.

TREVERBYN HOUSE   B&B £
(☎01841-532855; www.treverbynhouse.com; Station Rd; d £85-120; P) This town house offers four colour-themed rooms (pink, green, lilac or yellow) plus an extra-romantic turret hideaway.

🍴 Eating

PAUL AINSWORTH AT NO 6   British ££
(☎01840-532093; www.number6inpadstow.co.uk; 6 Middle St; dinner mains £22-27) Paul Ainsworth is the name to watch in Padstow – partly thanks to his recent TV appearances, but mainly because he's one of Cornwall's most talented young chefs. His flagship restaurant blends classic British and modern European, focusing on local goodies such as just-landed seafood, ham knuckle, squab pigeon and Cornish lamb.

SEAFOOD RESTAURANT   Seafood £££
(☎01841-532700; www.rickstein.com; Riverside; £22.50-62.50) Rick Stein's much-vaunted seafooderie needs no introduction – it's one of Britain's foremost fish addresses, with an expensive menu offering treats such as fresh Padstow lobster and sumptuous *fruits de mer*. You'll generally need to book months in advance.

MARGOT'S BISTRO   British ££
(☎01840-533441; margotspadstow.blogspot.com; 11 Duke St; mains £14.50-17.50; ⏰dinner Tue-Sat year-round, lunch Wed-Sat summer) While the food snobs head for Stein's, Margot's is where you'll be sent by the locals.

RICK STEIN'S CAFÉ   European ££
(☎01841-532700; Middle St; mains £10-18; ⏰closed Sun) Stein's backstreet bistro offers stripped-down samples of his trademark cuisine at more reasonable prices (you'll probably still need to book, though).

ℹ Information

Padstow Tourist Office (☎01841-533449; www.padstowlive.com; North Quay; ⏰10am-5pm Mon-Sat)

Newquay
POP 19,423

Bright, breezy and brash: that's Newquay, Cornwall's premier party town and the spiritual home of British surfing.

👁 Sights & Activities

NEWQUAY BEACHES   Beach
Newquay is set amid some of North Cornwall's finest beaches. The best known is **Fistral**, England's most famous surfing beach and the venue for the annual **Boardmasters** surfing festival.

Just below town are **Towan**, **Great Western** and **Tolcarne**, followed by nearby **Lusty Glaze**. North of Lusty Glaze is **Porth**, a long, narrow beach that's popular with families, followed a couple of miles later by the massive curve of **Watergate Bay**, home to Jamie Oliver's much-vaunted restaurant, Fifteen Cornwall. Two miles north brings you to **Mawgan Porth**, a horseshoe-shaped bay which often stays quieter than its neighbours.

NICK DOLDING/GETTY IMAGES ©

You'll find even more beaches to the southwest of Newquay, including the large, sandy beaches of **Crantock** (about 3 miles from town) and **Holywell Bay** (6 miles from town).

 Sleeping

SCARLET   Hotel £££
(01637-861600; www.scarlethotel.co.uk; r from winter/summer £195/295; P 🛜 🏊) For out-and-out luxury, Cornwall's fabulously chic new eco-hotel takes the crown. In a regal location above Mawgan Porth, it screams designer style, from the huge sea-view rooms with their funky furniture and minimalist decor to the luxurious spa, complete with meditation lounge, outdoor hot tubs and wild swimming pool. The restaurant's a beauty, too.

CARNMARTH HOTEL   Hotel ££
(01637-872519; www.carnmarth.com; Headland Rd; r £95-130; P) This decent midrange hotel is a short walk uphill from Fistral Beach, overlooking the golf course.

Eating

FIFTEEN CORNWALL   Italian £££
(01637-861000; www.fifteencornwall.com; Watergate Bay; lunch/dinner menu £28/60) Jamie Oliver's social-enterprise restaurant on Watergate Bay is where everyone wants to eat. It's a red-hot ticket: bookings essential.

BEACH HUT   Bistro ££
(01637-860877; Watergate Bay; mains £9.75-19.95; ⏲breakfast, lunch & dinner) If you can't get a table at Fifteen, head downstairs to this bistro by the sand.

ℹ Information

Newquay Tourist Office (01637-854020; www.visitnewquay.com; Marcus Hill; ⏱9.30am-5.30pm Mon-Sat, to 12.30pm Sun)

ℹ Getting There & Away

There are trains every couple of hours on the branch line between Newquay and Par (£4.30, 45 minutes) on the main London–Penzance line.

ARCHITECT: NICHOLAS GRIMSHAW, PHOTOGRAPHER: DOUG MCKINLAY/GETTY IMAGES ©

Don't Miss **The Eden Project**

The giant biomes of the Eden Project – the largest greenhouses in the world – have become one of Cornwall's most celebrated landmarks. Tropical, temperate and desert environments have been re-created inside the biomes, so a single visit can carry you from the steaming rainforests of South America to the dry deserts of Northern Africa.

In summer the biomes become a spectacular backdrop to a series of gigs known as the **Eden Sessions** (artists have included José Gonzalez, Goldfrapp and The Magic Numbers) and from November to February Eden transforms itself into a winter wonderland for the **Time of Gifts festival**, complete with a full-size ice rink.

It's informative, educational and enormous fun, but it does get busy. Booking online avoids the queues and gets a 10% to 15% discount.

There are regular buses from St Austel. If you're driving, follow signs from the A38.

NEED TO KNOW

✆01726-811911; www.edenproject.com; adult/child £23/9.50; ⏱10am-6pm Apr-Oct, to 4.30pm Nov-Mar

St Ives

POP 9870

Once a busy pilchard harbour, St Ives later became the centre of Cornwall's arts scene in the 1920s and '30s, and the town's cobbled streets are crammed with quirky galleries and crafts shops – although the outsider edge has been

somewhat dulled by the steady dribble of chain stores and generic restaurants.

 **Sights & Activities**

TATE ST IVES   Museum
(✆01736-796226; www.tate.org.uk/stives; Porthmeor Beach; adult/child £5.75/3.25;

⏱10am-5pm Mar-Oct, to 4pm Tue-Sun Nov-Feb)
Hovering like a concrete curl above Porthmeor Beach, this far-westerly outpost of the Tate focuses mainly on the work of the artists of the so-called 'St Ives School'. On the top floor there's a stylish cafe-bar which has a memorable panorama across St Ives.

A joint ticket with the Barbara Hepworth Museum costs adult/child £10/5.50.

BARBARA HEPWORTH MUSEUM　　　Museum
(☏01736-796226; Barnoon Hill; adult/child £5.50/3.25; ⏱10am-5pm Mar-Oct, 10am-4pm Tue-Sun Nov-Feb) Barbara Hepworth (1903–75) was one of the leading abstract sculptors of the 20th century, and a key figure in the St Ives art scene. Her studio on Barnoon Hill has remained almost untouched since her death, and the adjoining garden contains several of her most notable sculptures.

A joint ticket with the Tate St Ives costs adult/child £10/5.50.

Sleeping

BOSKERRIS　　　Hotel £££
(☏01736-795295; www.boskerrishotel.co.uk; Boskerris Rd; d £130-195; P🛜) It's a bit out of St Ives in nearby Carbis Bay, but this flashy guest house is worth the trip.

BLUE HAYES　　　Hotel £££
(☏01736-797129; www.bluehayes.co.uk; Trelyon Ave; r £110-240; P) Riviera luxury in a St Ives stunner, with manicured grounds, a balustraded breakfast terrace and five suite-sized rooms, most of which provide a memorable perspective along the St Ives coastline.

LITTLE LEAF GUEST HOUSE　　　B&B
(☏01736-795427; www.littleleafguesthouse. co.uk; Park Ave; r £80-115; 🛜) A tiny five-roomer, uphill from town. Rooms are sweet and simple, finished in creamy colours and pine furniture. Ask for room 2 or 5 if you're a sucker for a sea view.

Eating

SEAGRASS　　　Modern British ££
(☏01736-793763; www.seagrass-stives.com; Fish St; dinner mains £13.25-19.95; ⏱Tue-Fri) This vaunted restaurant on the 'front is overseen by Lee Groves, an ex-semi-finalist on *Masterchef: The Professionals*. The two-/three-course menu (served from Sunday to Thursday) is fab value at £15.95/19.95.

PORTHMINSTER BEACH CAFÉ　　　Bistro £££
(☏01736-795352; www.porthminstercafe. co.uk; Porthminster Beach; lunch £10.50-16.50, dinner £10-22; ⏱9am-10pm) For a seaside lunch there's nowhere better than this designer beach cafe, with its gorgeous suntrap terrace and Mediterranean-influenced menu.

ALBA　　　Seafood £££
(☏01736-797222; Old Lifeboat House; mains £11-18) Split-level sophistication next to the lifeboat house, serving top-quality seafood. With its banquette seats and sharp decor, it's stylish – especially if you get one of the prime tables next to the panoramic window.

BLAS BURGERWORKS　　　Cafe ££
(The Warren; burgers £5-10; ⏱dinner Tue-Sun) Imaginative burger joint with an eco-friendly, fair trade, 100% homemade manifesto.

ℹ Information

St Ives Tourist Office (☏01736-796297; www. stivestic.co.uk; Street-an-Pol; ⏱9am-5.30pm Mon-Fri, 9am-5pm Sat, 10am-4pm Sun)

ℹ Getting There & Away

The gorgeous branch line from St Ives is worth taking just for the coastal views: trains terminate at St Erth (£3, 14 minutes, half-hourly), where you can catch connections along the Penzance–London Paddington main line.

Sennen & Land's End

In the far west, the coastline peaks and plunges all the way into the sandy scoop of Sennen, which overlooks one of Penwith's most stunning stretches of sand on **Whitesand Bay** (pronounced Whitsand).

From here, there's a wonderful stretch of coast path that leads for about a mile and a half along the clifftops all the way to Land's End, the westernmost point of mainland England, where the coal-black cliffs plunge dramatically down into the pounding surf, and the views stretch all the way to the Isles of Scilly on a clear day. Unfortunately, the decision to build the **Legendary Land's End** (www.landsend-landmark.co.uk; adult/child £10/7; ⊙10am-5pm Mar-Oct) theme park just behind the headland in the 1980s hasn't done much to enhance the view.

Land's End is 9 miles from Penzance.

Minack Theatre

In terms of theatrical settings, the **Minack** (🖉01736-810181; www.minack.com) really has to take top billing. Carved directly into the crags overlooking Porthcurno Bay and the azure blue Atlantic, this amazing clifftop amphitheatre was the lifelong passion of local lady Rowena Cade, who dreamt up the idea in the 1930s and oversaw the theatre until her death in 1983. It's now a hugely popular place for alfresco theatre, with a 17-week season running from mid-May to mid-September: regulars bring wine, picnic supplies, wet-weather gear and – most importantly of all, considering the seats are carved out of granite – a very comfy cushion.

The Minack is 3 miles from Land's End and 9 miles from Penzance.

St Michael's Mount

Looming from the waters of Mount's Bay, this abbey-crowned, tidal **island** (NT; 🖉01736-710507; www.stmichaelsmount. co.uk; castle & gardens adult/child £8.75/4.25; ⊙house 10.30am-5.30pm Sun-Fri late Mar-Oct, gardens Mon-Fri Apr-Jun, Thu & Fri Jul-Sep) is one of Cornwall's most iconic sights. There's been a monastery on the island since at least the 5th century, but the present abbey was mostly built during the 12th century by the Benedictine monks of Mont St Michel. The abbey

Causeway, St Michael's Mount

later became the family seat of the St Aubyns (who still reside here), and is now under the stewardship of the National Trust.

Highlights include the rococo drawing room, the original armoury, the 14th-century priory church and the abbey's subtropical cliff gardens. Recent excavations have also uncovered important Bronze Age finds, including an axe-head, dagger and metal clasp, now on display inside the castle.

St Michael's Mount is connected to the mainland and the small seaside town of Marazion by a cobbled causeway. You can catch a ferry (adult/child £2/1) at high tide, but it's worth timing your arrival for low tide so you can walk across on the causeway, just as the monks and pilgrims did centuries ago.

Lost Gardens of Heligan

Cornwall's own real-life secret **garden** (☎01726-845100; www.heligan.com; adult/child £10/6; ◷10am-6pm Mar-Oct, to 5pm Nov-Feb). Formerly the family estate of the Tremaynes, the gardens fell into disrepair following WWI (when many staff were killed) and have since been restored to their former splendour by Tim Smit (the man behind the Eden Project) and a huge army of gardeners, horticultural specialists and volunteers. Among the treats in store at Heligan are a working kitchen garden, formal terraces, a secret grotto and a wild jungle valley – as well as the world's largest rhododendron, measuring an impressive 82ft from root to tip.

Heligan is 7 miles from St Austell.

York & Northern England

The old North–South divide may not be quite as pronounced as it once was, but there's definitely something different about England's northern half. Dominated by the twin cities of Manchester and Liverpool, this was once the epicentre of industrial England, and the landscape is littered with reminders of its historic past – not to mention its musical heritage, cultural prowess and world-famous football teams. Meanwhile, much older cities like York and Chester conceal medieval cathedrals and cobbled streets, still circled by their original city walls.

Beyond the cities the landscape takes on a noticeably wilder character around the national parks of the Yorkshire Dales and the Lake District, which have inspired generations of hikers, poets and artists alike. Even further north stretches the amazing Roman rampart of Hadrian's Wall, one of Britain's most impressive relics from the classical age.

Shambles (p225), York
TJ BLACKWELL/GETTY IMAGES ©

Grasmere (p252)

York & Northern England

Legend

1. York
2. Hill Top
3. Hadrian's Wall
4. Manchester
5. Yorkshire Dales
6. Liverpool
7. Castle Howard

Isle of Man

Point of Avre

Bride

IRISH SEA

ISLE OF MAN

Dalby

Douglas

20 km
10 miles

0   50 km
0   25 miles

56°N

55°N

54°N

53°N

NORTH SEA

IRISH SEA

Liverpool Bay

Barrow Island

Solway Firth

FIFE
Kinross
Crail
Kirkcaldy
Falkirk
A9
M9
EDINBURGH
A68
A702
Moorfoot Hills
M74
A74(M)
Moffat
Hawick
NORTHUMBERLAND
Crookham
Wooler
Bamburgh
Alnwick
A697
Rothbury
Simonside Hills
Morpeth
Dumfries
Border Forest Park
Northumberland National Park
Housesteads Roman Fort & Museum
Newcastle-upon-Tyne
Hadrian's Wall
Brampton
Hexham
Segedunum
Sunderland
Carlisle
Vindolanda Roman Fort & Museum
Seaham
Peterlee
CUMBRIA
The Pennines
Durham
Hartlepool
Workington
Penrith
Kirkby Stephen
Langdon Beck
Stockton-on-Tees
Middlesbrough
Keswick
Lake District National Park
A595
A66
Darlington
Whitby
Robin Hood's Bay
Windermere
Keld
Leyburn
Grosmont
North York Moors NP
Kendal
Thirsk
Helmsley
Scarborough
Isle of Man (see inset)
Yorkshire Dales National Park
Kilburn
Malton
Barrow-in-Furness
Ingleton
Cleveland Hills
Norton
Bridlington
Morecambe
Settle
A1
Castle Howard
Lancaster
Skipton
Harrogate
Great Driffield
M6
Ilkley
York
YORKSHIRE
Blackpool
Keighley
Beverley
Preston
Haworth
Burnley
Leeds
Selby
Hull
Blackburn
Halifax
Goole
Humber
Southport
Bolton
Wakefield
Scunthorpe
M180
Grimsby
Wigan
Huddersfield
Manchester
Doncaster
Liverpool
Warrington
Castleton
Rotherham
Gainsborough
A16
Birkenhead
Sheffield
Rhyl
Liverpool Airport
Manchester Airport
Buxton
Chesterfield
Lincoln
Burgh le Marsh
Colwyn Bay
Vale of Conwy
Clwydian Ranges
Chester
Peak District National Park
Sherwood Forest
Newark-on-Trent
Vale of Llangollen
Dovedale
The Wash
Coed-y-Brenin Forest
Wrexham
Stoke-on-Trent
Nottingham
Grantham
Berwyn Mountains
A49
A1
A458
Shrewsbury
Telford
Galley
Packington
Melton Mowbray
A38
M1
Llanidloes
Birmingham
M69
A1
A10
Coventry

York & Northern England Highlights

MARK SUNDERLAND/CORBIS ©

1
York

The ancient city of York is a medieval masterpiece, with narrow streets and twisting alleyways encircled by sturdy city walls, all crowned by the glorious architecture of the minster. With even older Roman and Viking heritage too, it's not surprising that York is bidding for Unesco World Heritage status. Above: King's Arms; Top Right: St Mary's Abbey; Bottom Right: York Minster

Need to Know
BEST PHOTO OP West face of the Minster, or on the City Walls **TOP TIP** Walk slowly and look up to see features **For further coverage, see p224**

York Don't Miss List

MARK GRAHAM, GUIDE WITH THE ORIGINAL GHOST WALK OF YORK

1 YORK MINSTER

The Minster is the best-known sight in York, and rightly so. I highly recommend going to the top of the **Lantern Tower** for spectacular views over the medieval streets surrounding the Minster, with the modern city beyond and the North York Moors visible 30 miles away. It's a stiff climb up 275 steps, but well worth the effort.

2 BOOTHAM BAR

In York, a 'bar' is a medieval gateway in the city walls and Bootham Bar is the oldest. To enjoy a great view of the city and a great sense of surrounding history, stop at the cafe in the square in front of **York Art Gallery**, opposite Bootham Bar. Beyond the city walls, you can see the massive towers of the Minster, while just to the right is the old **King's Manor** dating from the 15th century.

3 STROLLING THE STREETS

A great pleasure in York is just walking the old streets, admiring the architecture. My favourite strolls meander through the narrow 'gates' (streets) and 'snickelways' (alleys) from **Stonegate** – an old Roman road and one of the most beautiful streets in the city – to the best-known of York's medieval thoroughfares, the **Shambles**.

4 DRINKING IN HISTORY

Many of York's old pubs have historic links and many are haunted too. My favourites include the **Blue Bell** on Fossgate and the **Ye Olde Starre** on Stonegate. The **King's Arms** is famous as the pub that floods in winter, but its riverside tables are a great meeting spot in the summer.

5 ST MARY'S ABBEY

A beautiful little bit of medieval York that's often overlooked is the ruin of St Mary's Abbey, now sitting in the **Museum Gardens** near the Yorkshire Museum, on the western side of the city centre. The abbey dates from the 13th century and was mostly destroyed by Henry VIII in the Dissolution of the Monasteries in 1539.

Hill Top

The delightful cottage of Hill Top was Beatrix Potter's first house in the Lake District, and it features in lots of her books and illustrations, making it a must for Potter fans. Admission includes an informative guided tour with one of the house's guides, but half the fun is spotting all the tiny Potteresque details for yourself. Bottom: Hill Top Farm; Top Right: Beatrix Potter Gallery; Dottom Right: Tower Bank Arms

Need to Know

TICKETS Entry is timed to avoid overcrowding **WHEN TO VISIT** Saturday afternoon and Sundays are quietest **For further coverage, see p253**

2

ALAN NOVELLI/GETTY IMAGES ©

Local Knowledge

Hill Top Don't Miss List

BY JOANNE HUDSON, VISITOR SERVICES MANAGER AT HILL TOP

1 THE KITCHEN
Hill Top was Beatrix Potter's first house in the Lake District, and it features in lots of her books and illustrations. The kitchen is particularly interesting: here you can see the dresser from *Samuel Whiskers*, the grandfather clock from the *Tailor of Gloucester*, and the kitchen range from *Tom Kitten*.

2 THE RAT HOLE FROM SAMUEL WHISKERS
One of my favourite details at Hill Top is the rathole which features in *Samuel Whiskers*. Rats were a perennial problem at Hill Top – Beatrix caught 96 in her first year here alone!

3 THE GARDEN & VEGETABLE PATCH
Although it's probably not quite the same as it was in Beatrix's day, Hill Top's garden and vegetable patch are one of the highlights for many visitors. A version of it appeared as Mr McGregor's garden in *Peter Rabbit* and *Benjamin Bunny*. It looks particularly lovely in summer when the fruit trees are blossoming – and look out for the rhubarb patch where Jemima Puddleduck laid her eggs!

4 THE TOWER BANK ARMS
Just up the road from Hill Top is this lovely old inn, which has barely changed since the days when Beatrix lived here. The outside is almost exactly as it appears in *Jemima Puddleduck*. It serves really good food and feels lovely and cosy, especially if you can manage to get a spot by the fire.

5 THE BEATRIX POTTER GALLERY
In nearby Hawkshead, this gallery is housed inside the offices of the solicitor William Heelis, Beatrix's husband. It has an amazing collection of her illustrations, including many original watercolours from the books. The exhibition changes every year to focus on a different book, so there's always something new to see.

Hadrian's Wall

The awesome engineering project of Hadrian's Wall (p255) stretches for 117km across the north of England. Along the wall, several of the original garrison forts are still standing, including wonderful examples at Vindolanda and Housesteads, offering a unique insight into the day-to-day world of the soldiers and legionnaires who lived along this monument to Roman Britain.

3

ROGER COULAM/GETTY IMAGES ©

4 Manchester

Like many of northern England's cities, Manchester has enjoyed a new lease of life in recent years. One of its most interesting new additions is the striking Imperial War Museum North (p237), designed in typically imaginative style by the American architect Daniel Libeskind. For many, the city's key attraction is a structure of a different kind: Old Trafford football stadium (p238), home to Manchester United. Imperial War Museum North

PAUL THOMPSON/GETTY IMAGES © ARCHITECT: DANIEL LIBESKIND

Yorkshire Dales

5

The green valleys, high hills and limestone escarpments and 'pavements' of the Yorkshire Dales (p233) have been a magnet for fans of the great outdoors for many years. With a network of tracks and trails, this is the place to go for a walk, or rent a mountain bike, and shake off city life for an hour or two – or even a day or two.

6

Liverpool

Forever famous as the birthplace of The Beatles, and still with a healthy Fab Four heritage industry, the city of Liverpool (p242) is only now rediscovering and celebrating its (sometimes glorious, sometimes harsh) maritime past, spearheaded by a major renaissance on the Albert Dock, home to several fine museums, hotels and restaurants, and a clutch of classic buildings. Royal Liver Building (p245)

7

Castle Howard

The finest stately home in the north of England, and one of the best in the whole of Britain, the palatial edifice of Castle Howard (p231) was designed by the architect Sir John Vanbrugh for the third earl of Carlisle in the early 18th century, and it set the baroque benchmark for everyone else to follow. Surrounded by gardens and parkland, this is perhaps the quintessential English country estate.

York & Northern England's Best...

Wild Spots

○ **Lake District** (p250) The UK's favourite national park, famous for its natural scenery

○ **Yorkshire Dales** (p233) A bucolic landscape of hills, dales and rolling fields

○ **Hadrian's Wall** (p255) Look out across England's stormy northern frontier

Museums

○ **Imperial War Museum North** (p237) A Manchester must-see, and one of Britain's great modern museums

○ **Jorvik Viking Centre** (p225) Travel back in time to Viking York – sights, smells and all

○ **International Slavery Museum** (p243) This moving museum explores Liverpool's participation in the slave trade

○ **Chesters Roman Fort & Museum** (p254) This Roman cavalry fort has many fascinating architectural artefacts in its museum

Old-World Architecture

○ **York City Walls** (p225) Medieval battlements circling the city, with great views

○ **The Rows, Chester** (p242) Quirky two-tier shopping streets dating from Tudor times

○ **Fountains Abbey** (p232) Magnificent ruins of one of the north's great medieval abbeys

○ **Durham Cathedral** (p253) This truly mighty cathedral dates from the early Middle Ages

Need to Know

Timeless Towns & Villages

- **Chester** (p241) A hotch-potch of medieval buildings and cobbled lanes

- **Haworth** (p235) Wander the streets of the Brontës' home town

- **Durham** (p253) This ancient university town has history aplenty

- **Grasmere** (p252) Visit the former homes of William Wordsworth at this Lakeland village

ADVANCE PLANNING

- **Two months before** Book hotels, especially in popular areas such as the Lake District, York and the Yorkshire Dales.

- **One month before** Consider booking in advance for major sights such as Castle Howard, Hill Top and Jorvik. Book long-distance train tickets for the best deals.

- **One week before** Check the weather forecast if you plan to visit the Lake District or Yorkshire Dales, but remember conditions are always variable.

RESOURCES

- **Manchester** (www.visitmanchester.com)

- **Liverpool** (www.visitliverpool.com)

- **Northwest England** (www.visitnorthwest.com)

- **Lake District National Park** (www.lake-district.gov.uk)

- **Lake District** (www.golakes.co.uk)

- **Yorkshire** (www.visityorkshire.com)

- **Yorkshire Dales National Park** (www.yorkshiredales.org.uk)

- **Hadrian's Wall** (www.hadrians-wall.org)

GETTING AROUND

- **Bus** Good long-distance bus networks cover most of the north, but it's slower than train or car.

- **Train** Lots of regular links between the big cities, plus several scenic branch-lines.

- **Car** You'll regret taking a car into the cities – use Park & Ride schemes or other public transport instead.

BE FOREWARNED

- **Crowds** Be prepared for summer crowds and traffic jams, especially in the Yorkshire Dales and the Lake District.

- **Weather** Statistically speaking, the north is colder and wetter than most of the rest of England – come prepared.

- **Football** The beautiful game (also known as soccer) is practically a religion in Liverpool and Manchester; the cities can get rowdy on match days.

Left: Durham Cathedral (p253);
Above: Grasmere (p252)

(LEFT) CRAIG ROBERTS/GETTY IMAGES ©;
(ABOVE) RICHARD IANSON/GETTY IMAGES ©

York & Northern England Itineraries

The three-day loop takes in the verdant Yorkshire Dales and the stately Castle Howard. The five-day trip mixes modern cities with countryside and rich history.

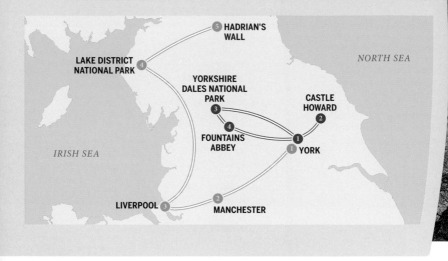

⑤ HADRIAN'S WALL

④ LAKE DISTRICT NATIONAL PARK

NORTH SEA

YORKSHIRE DALES NATIONAL PARK ③

④

CASTLE HOWARD ②

① YORK

FOUNTAINS ABBEY

IRISH SEA

LIVERPOOL ③

② MANCHESTER

---

3 DAYS

YORK TO YORK
Spirit of Yorkshire

In the historic city of **(1) York**, start with a walk around the city walls, via the ancient 'bars' (gateways). Then head for York Minster, the finest medieval cathedral in northern England, and some say in all of Europe. Other highlights include rickety looking buildings in the cobbled lanes around the Shambles.

On day two, take a trip to **(2) Castle Howard**, a stately home of theatrical grandeur and architectural audacity a few miles outside York, recognisable from its starring role in the TV series and film of *Brideshead Revisited*. Return to York in time for a late afternoon river cruise, or have fun on an evening ghost tour.

On day three, head into the **(3) Yorkshire Dales National Park**, for picturesque hills and a classic rural landscape. The wild valley of Ribblesdale is particularly scenic. If time allows, stop off at the classic ruins of **(4) Fountains Abbey**.

YORK TO HADRIAN'S WALL
Northern Highlights

5 DAYS

Start your tour with a couple of days in **(1) York**, admiring the elegant architecture and historic sites, then head southwest, across the Pennine Hills to **(2) Manchester**. Art and architecture fans will love the galleries, especially the imposing structure of the Imperial War Museum North. Fans of another kind will want to visit Old Trafford, home of Manchester United.

Then on to another great northern city: **(3) Liverpool**, famous as the birthplace of The Beatles. It's now rediscovering its maritime past, focused on the Albert Dock, with fine museums, restaurants, and some classic old buildings.

After the cities, it's time for a breath of fresh air – a short journey northwards takes you to the **(4) Lake District**. This is where you will find England's highest mountains and the region's most beautiful lakes, including Windermere and Grasmere.

From here it's easy to head north towards **(5) Hadrian's Wall**, the country's most impressive remains from the Roman era.

Yorkshire Dales National Park (p233)
DEREK CROUCHER/GETTY IMAGES ©

Discover York & Northern England

At a Glance

○ **Northwest England** (p237)
Home to the lively cities of Manchester and Liverpool.

○ **The Lake District** (p250) Britain's favourite national park, with literary connections and scenery galore.

○ **York** An ancient medieval city with a world-famous minster.

○ **Yorkshire Dales** (p233) Hills, villages and valleys characterise this national park.

○ **Hadrian's Wall** (p255) Vast Roman wall stretching for 72 miles across northern England.

YORK

POP 181,100

Nowhere in northern England says 'medieval' quite like York, a city of extraordinary cultural and historical wealth that has lost little of its pre-industrial lustre. A magnificent circuit of 13th-century walls enclose its medieval spider's web of narrow streets. At the heart of the city lies the immense, awe-inspiring minster, one of the most beautiful Gothic cathedrals in the world. York's long history and rich heritage is woven into virtually every brick and beam, and the modern, tourist-oriented city – with its myriad museums, restaurants, cafes and traditional pubs – is a carefully maintained heir to that heritage.

◎ Sights

If you plan on visiting a number of sights, you can save yourself some money by using a **York Pass** (www.yorkpass.com; 1/2/3 days adult £34/48/58, child £18/22/26). It gives you free access to more than 30 pay-to-visit sights in and around York, including York Minster, Jorvik and Castle Howard. You can buy it at the York tourist office (p230) or online.

FREE NATIONAL RAILWAY MUSEUM   Museum
(www.nrm.org.uk; Leeman Rd; ☉10am-6pm) York's National Railway Museum – the biggest in the world, with more than 100 locomotives – is so well presented and crammed with fascinating stuff that it's interesting even to folk whose eyes don't mist over at the thought of a 4-6-2 A1 Pacific class chuffing into a tunnel.

City Walls, York
VISITBRITAIN/BRITAIN ON VIEW/GETTY IMAGES ©

JORVIK VIKING CENTRE
Museum

(www.jorvik-viking-centre.co.uk; Coppergate; adult/child £9.25/6.25; ⏰10am-5pm Apr-Oct, to 4pm Nov-Mar) Interactive multimedia exhibits aimed at bringing history to life often achieve exactly the opposite, but the much-hyped Jorvik – after the minster, the most-visited attraction in town – manages to pull it off with aplomb. It's a smells-and-all reconstruction of the Viking settlement unearthed here during excavations in the late 1970s, brought to you courtesy of a 'time-car' monorail that transports you through 9th-century Jorvik.

You can reduce time waiting in the queue by booking your tickets online and choosing the time you want to visit (it costs £1 extra).

FREE CITY WALLS
Archaeological Site

(⏰8am-dusk) If the weather's good, don't miss the chance to walk the City Walls, which follow the line of the original Roman walls and give a whole new perspective on the city. Allow 1½ to two hours for the full circuit of 4.5 miles or, if you're pushed for time, the short stretch from Bootham Bar (Bootham) to Monk Bar (City Walls) is worth doing for the views of the minster. You can download a free guide to the wall walk from www.visityork.org/explore/walls.html.

YORKSHIRE MUSEUM
Museum

(www.yorkshiremuseum.org.uk; Museum St; adult/child £7.50/free; ⏰10am-5pm) Most of York's Roman archaeology is hidden beneath the medieval city, so the recently revamped displays in the Yorkshire Museum are invaluable if you want to get an idea of what Eboracum was like.

SHAMBLES
Street

(www.yorkshambles.com) The most-visited street in Europe is the narrow cobbled lane known as the Shambles, lined with 15th-century Tudor buildings that overhang so much they seem to meet above your head. The Shambles takes its name from the Saxon word *shamel*, meaning 'slaughterhouse' – in 1862 there were 26 butcher shops on this street.

YORK CASTLE MUSEUM
Museum

(www.yorkcastlemuseum.org.uk; Tower St; adult/child £8.50/free; ⏰9.30am-5pm) This excellent museum has displays of everyday life through the centuries, with reconstructed domestic interiors, a Victorian street and a less-than-homely prison cell where you can try out a condemned man's bed – in this case, that of highwayman Dick Turpin (he was imprisoned here before being hanged in 1739).

TREASURER'S HOUSE
Historic Building

(NT; www.nationaltrust.org.uk; Chapter House St; adult/child £6.30/3; ⏰11am-4.30pm Sat-Thu Apr-Oct, to 3pm Sat-Thu Nov) Home to York Minster's medieval treasurers, the Treasurer's House was substantially rebuilt in the 17th and 18th centuries. The 13 rooms house a fine collection of furniture and provide a clear insight into 18th-century life.

DIG
Museum

(www.digyork.com; St Saviour's Church, St Saviourgate; adult/child £5.50/5, Dig & Jorvik combined £13.25/10; ⏰10am-5pm, last admission 4pm, closed 24-26 Dec; 👪) Under the same management as Jorvik, Dig cashes in on the popularity of archaeology programs on TV by giving you the chance to be an 'archaeological detective', unearthing the secrets of York's distant past as well as learning something of the archaeologist's world – what they do, how they do it, and so on. Aimed mainly at kids, it's much more hands-on than Jorvik and a lot of its merit depends on how good – and entertaining – your guide is.

CLIFFORD'S TOWER
Castle

(EH; www.english-heritage.org.uk; Tower St; adult/child £4/2.40; ⏰10am-6pm Apr-Sep, to 5pm Oct) There's precious little left of York Castle except for this evocative stone tower, a highly unusual figure-of-eight design built into the castle's keep after the original one was destroyed in 1190 during anti-Jewish riots. There's not much to see inside, but the views over the city are excellent.

IVAN VDOVIN/GETTY IMAGES ©

Don't Miss York Minster

Not content with being Yorkshire's most important historic building, the remarkable York Minster is also the largest medieval cathedral in all of Northern Europe. Seat of the archbishop of York, primate of England, it is second in importance only to Canterbury, home of the primate of *all* England – the separate titles were created to settle a debate over whether York or Canterbury was the true centre of the English church.

But that's where Canterbury's superiority ends, for this is without doubt one of the world's most beautiful Gothic buildings. If this is the only cathedral you visit in England, you'll still walk away satisfied – so long as you have the patience to deal with the constant flow of school groups and organised tours that will inevitably clog up your camera's viewfinder.

The first church on this site was a wooden chapel built for the baptism of King Edwin of Northumbria on Easter Day 627, whose location is marked in the crypt. It was replaced with a stone church built on the site of a Roman basilica, parts of which can be seen in the foundations. The first Norman minster was built in the 11th century and again, you can see surviving fragments in the foundations and crypt.

The present minster, built mainly between 1220 and 1480, manages to encompass all the major stages of Gothic architectural development. The transepts (1220–55) were built in Early English style; the octagonal chapter house (1260–90) and nave (1291–1340) in the Decorated style; and the west towers, west front and central (or lantern) tower (1470–72) in Perpendicular style.

At the heart of York Minster is the massive tower, which is well worth climbing for its unparalleled views of York. You'll have to tackle a fairly claustrophobic climb of 275 steps and, most probably, a queue of people with cameras in hand.

NEED TO KNOW

www.yorkminster.org; Deangate; adult/child £9/free, combined ticket incl tower £14/3.50; ⊘9am-5.30pm Mon-Sat Apr-Oct, 9.30am-5.30pm Mon-Sat Nov-Mar, noon-5.30pm Sun year-round

Tours

GHOST HUNT OF YORK Walking Tours
(www.ghosthunt.co.uk; adult/child £5/3; ⏰tours 7.30pm; 👣) The kids will just love this award-winning and highly entertaining 75-minute tour laced with authentic ghost stories. It begins at the Shambles, whatever the weather (it's never cancelled) and there's no need to book, just turn up.

YORKWALK Walking Tours
(www.yorkwalk.co.uk; adult/child £5.50/3.50; ⏰tours 10.30am & 2.15pm Feb-Nov) Offers a series of two-hour themed walks on an ever growing list of themes, from the classics – Roman York, the snickelways (alleys) and City Walls – to specialised walks focused on chocolates and sweets, women in York, secret York and the inevitable graveyard, coffin and plague tour. Walks depart from Museum Gardens Gate on Museum St; there's no need to book.

YORKBOAT Boat Tours
(www.yorkboat.co.uk; King's Staith; adult/child £7.50/3.50; ⏰tours 10.30am, noon, 1.30pm & 3pm) Hour-long cruises on the River Ouse, departing from King's Staith and, 10 minutes later, Lendal Bridge.

FREE ASSOCIATION OF VOLUNTARY GUIDES Walking Tour
(http://avgyork.co.uk; ⏰tours 10.15am & 2.15pm Apr-Oct, also 6.45pm Jun-Aug, 10.15am Nov-Mar) Two-hour walking tours of the city, setting out from Exhibition Sq in front of York City Art Gallery.

Sleeping

Beds are hard to find in midsummer, even with the inflated prices of the high season. It's also worth looking at serviced apartments if you're planning to stay two or three nights. **In York Holidays** (☎01904-632660; www.inyorkholidays.co.uk) offers a good selection of places from about £100 a night for a two-person apartment.

MIDDLETHORPE HALL Hotel £££
(☎01904-641241; www.middlethorpe.com; Bishopthorpe Rd; s/d from £130/200; 🅿🛜) York's top spot is this breathtaking 17th-century country house set in 8 hectares of parkland, once the home of diarist Lady Mary Wortley Montagu. The rooms are divided between the main house, restored courtyard buildings and three cottage suites.

ELLIOTTS B&B B&B ££
(☎01904-623333; www.elliottshotel.co.uk; 2 Sycamore Pl; s/d from £55/80; 🅿@🛜) A beautifully converted 'gentleman's residence', Elliotts leans towards the boutique end of the guesthouse market, with stylish and elegant rooms and high-tech touches, such as flatscreen TVs and free wi-fi.

Jorvik Viking Centre (p225)
VISITBRITAIN/BRITAIN ON VIEW/GETTY IMAGES ©

York

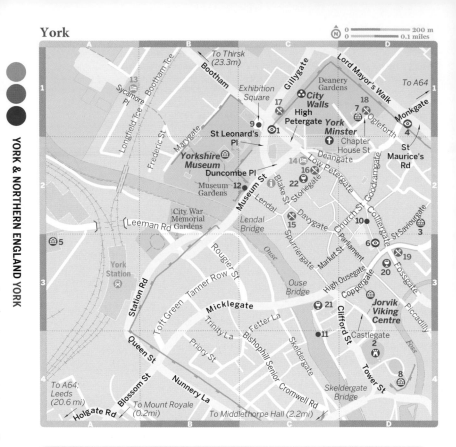

York

⊙ Top Sights

City Walls	C1
Jorvik Viking Centre	D3
York Minster	C2
Yorkshire Museum	B2

⊙ Sights

1	Bootham Bar	C1
2	Clifford's Tower	D4
3	Dig	D2
4	Monk Bar	D1
5	National Railway Museum	A3
6	Shambles	D3
7	Treasurer's House	D1
8	York Castle Museum	D4

⊙ Activities, Courses & Tours

9	Association of Voluntary Guides	C1
10	Ghost Hunt of York	D2
11	YorkBoat	C4
12	Yorkwalk	C2

⊜ Sleeping

13	Elliotts B&B	A1
14	Guy Fawkes Inn	C2

⊗ Eating

15	Bettys	C2
16	Betty's Stonegate	C2
17	Cafe No 8	C1
18	Grays Court	D1
19	J Baker's Bistro Moderne	D3

⊙ Drinking

20	Blue Bell	D3
21	King's Arms	C3
22	Ye Olde Starre	C2

RICHARD WATSON/GETTY IMAGES ©

GUY FAWKES INN
Inn ££

(☎01904-623716; www.gfyork.com; 25 High Petergate; s/d/ste from £65/90/200) Directly opposite the minster is this comfortable and atmospheric hotel, complete with gas lamps and log fires. The premises include a cottage reputed to be the birthplace of Guy Fawkes himself.

MOUNT ROYALE
Hotel £££

(☎01904-628856; www.mountroyale.co.uk; The Mount; s/d from £95/125; P🖥⊠) A grand, early 19th-century heritage-listed building converted into a superb luxury hotel, complete with a solarium, beauty spa and outdoor heated tub and swimming pool.

Eating

J BAKER'S BISTRO MODERNE
Modern British ££

(☎01904-622688; www.jbakers.co.uk; 7 Fossgate; 2-/3-course lunch £20/25, dinner £25/30; ⊘lunch & dinner Tue-Sat) Superstar chef Jeff Baker left a Michelin-starred eatery in Leeds to pursue his own vision of Modern British cuisine here. The ironic '70s-style decor (think chocolate/oatmeal/tango) with moo-cow paintings is echoed in the unusual menu, which offers witty gourmet interpretations of retro classics – try Olde York cheese and spinach pasties with dried grapes, capers and aged balsamic vinegar, or Whitby crab cocktail with apple 'textures' and curry-spiced granola.

CAFE NO 8
Bistro £

(☎01904-653074; www.cafeno8.co.uk; 8 Gillygate; mains £7-10, 2-course lunch £14; ⊘Mon-Fri 11am-10pm, Sat & Sun 10am-10pm; 🖥⊞) A cool little bistro with modern artwork mimicking the Edwardian stained glass at the front, No 8 offers a day-long menu of classic bistro dishes using fresh local produce, including smoked duck breast salad and cassoulet of Yorkshire pork and chorizo. Booking is recommended.

GRAYS COURT
Cafe £

(www.grayscourtyork.com; Chapter House St; mains £6-10; ⊘lunch) An unexpected find right in the heart of York, this 16th-century house has more of a country atmosphere. Enjoy gourmet coffee and cake in the sunny garden, or indulge in a light lunch in the historic setting of the oak-panelled Jacobean gallery (extra points if you grab the alcove table above the main door).

229

BETTYS
Tearoom **££**

(www.bettys.co.uk; St Helen's Sq; mains £6-13, afternoon tea £18; ⏰9am-9pm; 👪) Old-school-style afternoon tea, with white-aproned waitresses, linen tablecloths and a teapot collection ranged along the walls. No bookings are taken – queue for a table at busy times, or head to the nearby **Bettys Stonegate** (46 Stonegate; mains £6-13; ⏰10am-5.30pm Sun-Fri, 9am-5.30pm Sat; 👪).

 Drinking

BLUE BELL
Pub

(53 Fossgate) This is what a real English pub looks like – a tiny, wood-panelled room with a smouldering fireplace, decor (and beer and smoke stains) dating from c 1798, a pile of ancient board games in the corner, friendly and efficient bar staff, and Timothy Taylor and Black Sheep ales on tap. Bliss, with froth on top.

YE OLDE STARRE
Pub

(40 Stonegate) Licensed since 1644, this is York's oldest pub – a warren of small rooms and beer garden, with a half-dozen real ales on tap.

KING'S ARMS
Pub

(King's Staith) York's best-known pub in a fabulous riverside location, with tables spilling out onto the quayside.

ⓘ Information

York Tourist Office (☎01904-550099; www.visityork.org; 1 Museum St; ⏰9am-6pm Mon-Sat, 10am-5pm Sun Apr-Sep, shorter hours Oct-Mar)

ⓘ Getting There & Away

Car

A car is more hindrance than help in the city centre, so use one of the Park & Ride car parks at the edge of the city.

Train

York is a major railway hub, with frequent direct services to Birmingham (£45, 2¼ hours), Newcastle (£15, one hour), Leeds (£11, 30 minutes), London King's Cross (£80, two hours), Manchester (£15, 1½ hours) and Scarborough (£10, 50 minutes). There are also trains to Cambridge (£60, 2¾ hours), changing at Peterborough.

Traditional architecture, York

VERONICA GARBUTT/GETTY IMAGES ©

KARL BLACKWELL/GETTY IMAGES ©

Don't Miss Castle Howard

Stately homes may be two-a-penny in England, but you'll have to try pretty damn hard to find one as breathtakingly stately as Castle Howard, a work of theatrical grandeur and audacity set in the rolling Howardian Hills. This is one of the world's most beautiful buildings, instantly recognisable from its starring role in the 1980s TV series *Brideshead Revisited* and more recently in the 2008 film of the same name (both based on Evelyn Waugh's 1945 novel of nostalgia for the English aristocracy).

When the Earl of Carlisle hired his pal Sir John Vanbrugh to design his new home in 1699, he was hiring a bloke who had no formal training and was best known as a playwright. Luckily, Vanbrugh hired Nicholas Hawksmoor who had worked as Christopher Wren's clerk of works. Not only would Hawksmoor have a big part to play in the house's design, but he and Vanbrugh would later work wonders with Blenheim Palace. Today the house is still home to the Hon Simon Howard and his family and he can often be seen around the place.

As you wander about the peacock-haunted grounds, views open up over the hills, Vanbrugh's playful **Temple of the Four Winds** and Hawksmoor's stately **mausoleum**, but the great baroque house with its magnificent central cupola is an irresistible visual magnet. Inside, the house is full of treasures – the breathtaking **Great Hall** with its soaring Corinthian pilasters, Pre-Raphaelite stained glass in the chapel, and corridors lined with classical antiquities.

Castle Howard is 15 miles northeast of York, off the A64. There are several organised tours from York – check with the tourist office for up-to-date schedules.

NEED TO KNOW

www.castlehoward.co.uk; adult/child house & grounds £13/7.50, grounds only £8.50/6; ⊙house 11am-4.30pm Apr-Oct, grounds 10am-5.30pm Mar-Oct & 1st 3 weeks Dec, 10am-4pm Nov-Feb

YVAN TRAVERT/GETTY IMAGES ©

Don't Miss Fountains Abbey

Nestled in the secluded valley of the River Skell are two of Yorkshire's most beautiful attractions – an absolute must on any northern itinerary. The alluring and strangely obsessive water gardens of the **Studley Royal** estate were built in the 18th century to enhance the picturesque ruins of 12th-century Fountains Abbey. Together, they present a breathtaking picture of pastoral elegance and tranquillity that have made them a Unesco World Heritage Site and the most visited of all the National Trust's pay-to-enter properties.

After falling out with the Benedictines of York in 1132, a band of rebel monks came here to establish their own monastery. Struggling to make it alone, they were formally adopted by the Cistercians in 1135. By the middle of the 13th century, the new abbey had become the most successful Cistercian venture in the country. After the Dissolution, when Henry III confiscated church property, the abbey's estate was sold into private hands, and between 1598 and 1611 **Fountains Hall** was built using stone from the abbey ruins. The hall and ruins were united with the Studley Royal estate in 1768.

The remains of the abbey are impressively grandiose, gathered around the sunny Romanesque **cloister**, where the abbey's 200 lay brothers lived. Food and wool from the abbey's farms was stored in the huge vaulted **cellarium** that leads off the west end of the church. with a huge vaulted leading off the west end of the church. At the east end is the soaring **Chapel of Nine Altars** and on the outside of its northeast window is a Green Man carving (a pre-Christian fertility symbol).

Fountains Abbey is 4 miles west of Ripon off the B6265.

NEED TO KNOW

NT; www.fountainsabbey.org.uk; adult/child £9/4.85; ⊙10am-5pm Apr-Sep, to 4pm Oct-Mar

YORKSHIRE DALES NATIONAL PARK

The Yorkshire Dales – named from the old Norse word *dalr*, meaning 'valleys' – is the central jewel in the necklace of three national parks strung across northern England, with the dramatic fells of the Lake District to the west and the brooding heaths of the North York Moors to the east.

From well-known names such as Wensleydale and Ribblesdale to the obscure and evocative Langstrothdale and Arkengarthdale, the park's glacial valleys are characterised by a distinctive landscape of high heather moorland, stepped skylines and flat-topped hills. The Dales have been protected as a national park since the 1950s, assuring their status as a walker's and cyclist's paradise. But there's plenty for nonwalkers as well, from exploring the legacy of literary vet James Herriot of *All Creatures Great And Small* fame to sampling the favourite teatime snack of the British TV characters Wallace and Gromit at the Wensleydale Creamery.

The *Visitor* newspaper, available from tourist offices, lists local events and walks guided by park rangers, as well as many places to stay and eat. The official park website (www.yorkshiredales.org.uk) is also useful.

ℹ Getting There & Around

About 90% of visitors to the park arrive by car, and the narrow roads can become extremely crowded in summer.

By train, the best and most interesting access to the Dales is via the famous **Settle–Carlisle Line** (www.settle-carlisle.co.uk). Trains run between Leeds and Carlisle, stopping at Skipton, Settle, and numerous small villages, offering unrivalled access to the hills straight from the station platform.

Grassington

The perfect base for jaunts around the south Dales, Grassington's handsome Georgian centre teems with walkers and visitors throughout the summer months, soaking up an atmosphere that, despite the odd touch of faux rusticity, is as attractive and traditional as you'll find in these parts.

 Sleeping & Eating

DEVONSHIRE FELL　　　　Hotel **£££**
(☏ 01756-718111; www.devonshirefell.co.uk; Burnsall; s/d from £129/159; P @ 🛜) A sister property to Bolton Abbey's Devonshire Arms Country House Hotel, this former gentleman's club for mill owners has a much more contemporary feel, with beautiful modern furnishings crafted by local experts. It's 3 miles southeast of Grassington on the B6160.

ASHFIELD HOUSE　　　　B&B **££**
(☏ 01756-752584; www.ashfieldhouse.co.uk; Summers Fold; r from £96; P @ 🛜) A secluded 17th-century country house behind a walled garden, with exposed stone walls, open fireplaces and an all-round cosy feel. It's just off the main square.

COBBLESTONES CAFÉ　　　　Cafe **£**
(3 The Square; mains £3-6; ◷9.30am-5pm; 🐾) A cute little cafe, dog-friendly and popular with locals as well as visitors.

Ribblesdale & The Three Peaks

The village of Horton-in-Ribblesdale makes the best base for exploring. Scenic Ribblesdale cuts through the southwestern corner of the Yorkshire Dales National Park, where the skyline is dominated by a trio of distinctive hills known as the **Three Peaks** – Whernside (735m), Ingleborough (724m) and Pen-y-ghent (694m). Easily accessible via the Settle–Carlisle railway line, this is one of England's most popular areas for outdoor activities, attracting thousands of hikers, cyclists and cavers each weekend.

Detour: Harewood House

The great park, sumptuous gardens and mighty edifice of **Harewood House** (www.harewood.org; adult/child £14/7; ⏰grounds 10am-6pm, house noon-3pm Apr-Oct) are a classic example of a stately English pile. The house was built between 1759 and 1772 by the era's superstar designers: John Carr designed the exterior, Lancelot 'Capability' Brown laid out the grounds, Thomas Chippendale supplied the furniture (the largest commission he ever received, costing the unheard-of amount of £10,000), Robert Adams designed the interior, and Italy was raided to create an appropriate art collection. The superb terrace was added 100 years later by yet another top name, Sir Charles Barry, best known for rebuilding the Houses of Parliament.

Harewood is about 7 miles north of Leeds on the A61.

Sleeping & Eating

GOLDEN LION Inn £
(☎01729-860206; www.goldenlionhotel.co.uk; s/d from £40/65, dm £12) The Golden Lion is a lively pub that offers comfortable B&B rooms, a 40-bed bunkhouse, and three public bars where you can tuck into a bit of grub washed down with a pint of hand-pulled ale.

PEN-Y-GHENT CAFE Cafe £
(mains £3-6; ⏰9am-5.30pm Mon & Wed-Fri, 8.30am-5pm Sat & Sun) A traditional cafe run by the same family since 1965, the Pen-y-Ghent fills walkers' fuel tanks with fried eggs and chips, homemade scones and pint-sized mugs of tea. It also sells maps, guidebooks and walking gear.

Richmond
POP 8200

The handsome market town of Richmond is one of England's best-kept secrets, perched on a rocky outcrop overlooking the River Swale and guarded by the ruins of a massive castle. A maze of cobbled streets radiates from the broad, sloping market square (market day is Saturday), lined with elegant Georgian buildings and photogenic stone cottages, with glimpses of the surrounding hills and dales peeking through the gaps.

👁 Sights

Top of the pile is the impressive heap that is **Richmond Castle** (www.english-heritage.org.uk; Market Pl; adult/child £4.70/2.80; ⏰10am-6pm Apr-Sep, reduced hours at other times), founded in 1070 and one of the first castles in England since Roman times to be built of stone. The best part is the view from the top of the remarkably well-preserved 30m-high keep, which towers over the River Swale.

🛏 Sleeping

MILLGATE HOUSE B&B £££
(☎01748-823571; www.millgatehouse.com; Market Pl; r £110-145; P @) While the house itself is a Georgian gem crammed with period details, it is overshadowed by the multi-award-winning garden at the back, which offers superb views over the River Swale and the Cleveland Hills. If possible, book the garden suite.

FRENCHGATE HOTEL Hotel ££
(☎01748-822087; www.thefrenchgate.co.uk; 59-61 Frenchgate; s/d from £88/118; P) Nine elegant bedrooms occupy the upper floors of this converted Georgian town house, now a boutique hotel decorated with local art.

⚔ Eating & Drinking

RUSTIQUE French ££
(📞01748-821565; www.rustiqueyork.co.uk;
Chantry Wynd, Finkle St; mains £10-16; 🕙10am-9pm Mon-Sat, noon-9pm Sun) Tucked away in
an arcade, this cosy bistro has consistently impressed with its mastery of French
country cooking, from *confit de canard*
(duck slow roasted in its own fat) to *paupiette de poulet* (chicken breast stuffed with
brie and sun-dried tomatoes). Booking is
recommended.

CROSS VIEW TEAROOM Tearoom £
(www.crossviewtearooms.co.uk; 38 Market
Pl; mains £4-7; 🕙9am-5.30pm Mon-Sat) So
popular with locals that you might have
to queue for a table at lunchtime, the
Cross View is the place to go for a hearty
breakfast, homemade cakes, a hot lunch,
or just a nice cup of tea.

**SEASONS RESTAURANT
& CAFE** International ££
(www.restaurant-seasons.co.uk; Richmond
Station, Station Rd; mains £6-15; 🕙9am-9pm
Mon-Sat, to 7pm Sun) Housed in the restored
Victorian station building, this attractive
open-plan eatery shares space with a
boutique brewery, artisan bakery, ice-cream factory and cheesemonger – and
yes, all this local produce is on the menu.

Haworth
POP 6100

It seems that only Shakespeare himself is
held in higher esteem than the Brontë sisters – Emily, Anne and Charlotte – judging
by the 8 million visitors a year who trudge
up the hill from the train station to pay
their respects at the handsome parsonage
where the literary classics *Jane Eyre* and
Wuthering Heights were penned.

◉ Sights

FREE **HAWORTH PARISH
CHURCH** Church
(Church St; admission free; 🕙9am-5.30pm)
Your first stop should be Haworth Parish
Church, a lovely old place of worship built
in the late 19th century on the site of the
older church that the Brontë sisters knew,
which was demolished in 1879.

Harewood House

PETER RICHARDSON/CORBIS ©

BRONTË PARSONAGE
MUSEUM   Museum

(www.bronte.info; Church St; adult/child £7/3.60; ◷10am-5.30pm Apr-Sep, 11am-5pm Oct-Mar) Set in a pretty garden overlooking the church and graveyard, the house where the Brontë family lived from 1820 till 1861 is now a museum. The rooms are meticulously furnished and decorated exactly as they were in the Brontë era, including Charlotte's be droom with her clothes and writing paraphernalia. There's also an informative exhibition, which includes the fascinating miniature books the Brontës wrote as children.

🛏 Sleeping & Eating

OLD REGISTRY   B&B ££

(☎01535-646503; www.theoldregistryhaworth. co.uk; 2-4 Main St; r £75-120; 🛜) This place is a bit special. It's an elegantly rustic guest house where each of the carefully themed rooms has a four-poster bed, whirlpool bath or valley view.

AITCHES   B&B £

(☎01535-642501; www.aitches.co.uk; 11 West Lane; s/d from £40/60) A classy, stone-built Victorian house with four en suite rooms, each differently decorated with a pleasantly olde-worlde atmosphere.

WEAVER'S   British ££

(☎01535-643822; www.weaversmallhotel. co.uk; 15 West Lane; mains £15-20; ◷lunch Wed-Fri, dinner Tue-Sat) A stylish and atmospheric restaurant, Weaver's menu features local produce (such as slow-cooked shoulder of Pennine lamb with fennel seed and coriander stuffing), or simple lunches like an Ellison's pork pie with mushy peas and mint sauce (2-course lunch costs £16). Upstairs are three comfy bedrooms, two of which have views towards the moors.

HAWORTH OLD HALL   Pub ££

(☎01535-642709; www.hawortholdhall.co.uk; Sun St; mains £9-17) A 16th-century pub serving real ale and decent food.

ℹ Information

Tourist Office (☎01535-642329; www.haworth-village.org.uk; 2-4 West Lane; ◷9am-5.30pm Apr-Sep, to 5pm Oct-Mar)

Haworth Moor

MANCHESTER

POP 394,270

Raised on lofty ambition and not afraid to declare its considerable bona fides, Manchester is – by dint of geography and history – England's second city (apologies to Birmingham), although if you were to ask a Mancunian what it's like to be second they might reply: 'Don't know; ask a Londoner.'

Even accounting for northern bluster, the uncrowned capital of the north is well deserving of the title. It has a rich history and culture, easily explored in its myriad museums and galleries. And while history and heritage make the city interesting, its distractions of pure pleasure make Manchester fun: you can dine, drink and dance yourself into happy oblivion in the swirl of hedonism that is one of Manchester's most cherished characteristics.

 **Sights & Activities**

City Centre

FREE MUSEUM OF SCIENCE & INDUSTRY Museum

(MOSI; ☎0161-832 2244; www.msim.org.uk; Liverpool Rd; charges vary for special exhibitions; ⏱10am-5pm) The city's largest museum comprises 2.8 hectares in the heart of 19th-century industrial Manchester. If there's anything you want to know about the Industrial (and post-Industrial) Revolution and Manchester's key role in it, you'll find the answers among the collection of steam engines and locomotives, factory machinery from the mills, and the excellent exhibition telling the story of Manchester from the sewers up.

NATIONAL FOOTBALL MUSEUM Museum

(☎0161-605 8200; www.nationalfootball museum.com; Corporation St, Urbis, Cathedral Gardens; ⏱10am-5pm Mon-Sat, 11am-5pm Sun) It's the world's most popular game and Manchester is home to both the world's most popular and the world's richest teams, so it makes sense that a museum dedicated to the global charms of football should find its home here. Opened in July 2012, the museum is chock-a-block with the world's most extensive collections of memorabilia, trophies and other keepsakes of its storied past.

FREE MANCHESTER ART GALLERY Gallery

(☎0161-235 8888; www.manchestergalleries .org; Mosley St; ⏱10am-5pm Tue-Sun) A superb collection of British art and a hefty number of European masters are on display at the city's top gallery. The older wing, designed by Charles Barry (of Houses of Parliament fame) in 1834, has an impressive collection that includes 37 Turner watercolours, as well as the country's best collection of Pre-Raphaelite art. The newer gallery features a permanent collection of 20th-century British art starring Lucien Freud, Francis Bacon, Stanley Spencer, Henry Moore and David Hockney.

FREE JOHN RYLANDS LIBRARY Library

(☎0161-306 0555; www.library.manchester. ac.uk; 150 Deansgate; ⏱noon-5pm Mon & Sun, 10am-5pm Tue-Sat) Less a library and more a cathedral to books, Basil Champneys' stunning building is arguably the most beautiful library in Britain and one hell of a way for Rylands' widow to remember her husband, John.

Salford Quays

Just west of the city centre, and easily reached via Metrolink (£2), is Salford Quays, home to the city's big-ticket attractions and new hub of the BBC's northern HQ. Check out www.thequays. co.uk for more info.

FREE IMPERIAL WAR MUSEUM NORTH Museum

(☎0161-836 4000; www.iwm.org.uk/north; Trafford Wharf Rd; ⏱10am-5pm) War museums generally appeal to those with a fascination for military hardware and battle strategy (toy soldiers optional), but Daniel Libeskind's visually stunning

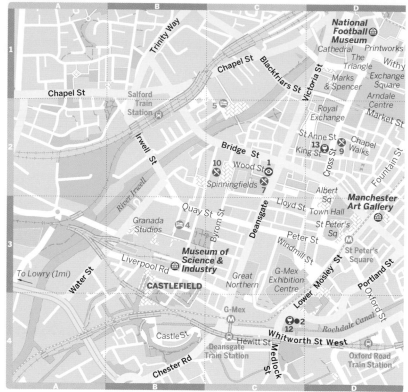

Imperial War Museum North takes a radically different approach. War is hell, it tells us, but it's a hell we revisit with tragic regularity.

The exhibits cover the main conflicts of the 20th century through a broad selection of displays, but the really effective bit comes every half-hour when the entire exhibition hall goes dark and one of three 15-minute films (*Children and War*, *The War at Home* or *Weapons of War*) is projected throughout.

Although the audiovisuals and displays are quite compelling, the extraordinary aluminium-clad building itself is a huge part of the attraction, and the exhibition spaces are genuinely breathtaking. Take the Metrolink to Harbour City or MediaCityUK.

OLD TRAFFORD (MANCHESTER UNITED MUSEUM & TOUR)　Stadium
(☎ 0161-868 8000; www.manutd.com; Sir Matt Busby Way; tour adult/child £15/10, museum adult/child £10.50/8.50; ☉ 9.30am-5pm, tour every 10 min except match days 9.40am-4.30pm, museum 9.30am-5pm) Home of the world's most famous club, the Old Trafford stadium is both a theatre and a temple for its millions of fans worldwide, many of whom come in pilgrimage to the ground to pay tribute to the minor deities disguised as highly paid footballers that play there. Take the Metrolink to Old Trafford.

THE LOWRY　Arts Centre
(☎ 0161-876 2020; www.thelowry.com; Pier 8, Salford Quays; ☉ 11am-8pm Tue-Fri, 10am-8pm Sat, 11am-6pm Sun & Mon) Looking more like a shiny steel ship than an arts centre, The

Manchester

Lowry is the quays' most notable success. The centre is also home to 300 beautifully humanistic depictions of urban landscapes by LS Lowry (1887–1976), who was born in nearby Stretford, and after whom the complex is named.

 **Sleeping**

City Centre

GREAT JOHN STREET HOTEL　　　　　Hotel £££
(☎0161-831 3211; www.greatjohnstreet.co.uk; Great John St; r £85-345; @ 🛜) This former schoolhouse is small but sumptuous – beyond the art deco lobby are the fabulous bedrooms, each an example of style and luxury.

ABODE　　　　　　　　　　Hotel ££
(☎0161-247 7744; www.abodehotels.co.uk; 107 Piccadilly St; r from £75; @ 🛜) Modern British style is the catchphrase at this converted textile factory. The original fittings have been combined successfully with 61 bedrooms divided into four categories of ever-increasing luxury: Comfortable, Desirable, Enviable and Fabulous, the latter being five seriously swanky top-floor suites.

LOWRY　　　　　　　　　Hotel £££
(☎0161-827 4000; www.roccofortecollection.com; 50 Dearman's Pl; r £120-950; P @ 🛜) Simply dripping with designer luxury and five-star comfort, Manchester's top hotel (not to be confused with the arts centre in Salford Quays) has fabulous rooms with enormous beds, ergonomically designed furniture, walk-in wardrobes, and bathrooms finished with Italian porcelain tiles and glass mosaics.

239

MALMAISON Hotel £££

(☎0161-278 1000; www.malmaison.com; Piccadilly St; r from £109; ☒Piccadilly Station)
Drop-dead trendy and full of crushed-red velvet, deep purples, art deco ironwork and signature black-and-white tiles, Malmaison Manchester follows the chain's quirky design style and passion for cool, although rarely at the expense of comfort: the rooms are terrific. The **Smoak Grill** (☎0161-278-1000; www.smoak-grill.com; mains £13-25) downstairs is hugely popular.

Eating

City Centre

AUSTRALASIA Modern Australian ££

(☎0161-831 0288; www.australasia.uk.com; 1 The Avenue, Spinningfields; mains £13-30, 2-/3-/4-course lunch £11/15/20) What should you do with the dusty old basement archive of the *Manchester Evening News*? Convert it into the city centre's best new restaurant, of course. The menu combines contemporary Australian cuisine with flavours of southeast Asia – the lunchtime selection of fresh sushi is particularly good, as are the specials.

THE OAST HOUSE International ££

(☎0161-829 3830; www.theoasthouse.uk.com; Crown Sq, Spinningfields; mains £9-15) An oast house is a 16th-century kiln used to dry out hops as part of the beer-making process. In Manchester, the Oast House is Tim Bacon's exciting new BBQ restaurant, a slice of medieval charm in the heart of (slightly) po-faced Spinningfields' contemporary designer chic. The kitchen is an outdoor covered grill, so staff have to shuttle the grilled delights (nothing fancy: burgers, kebabs, steaks and rotisserie chickens) to diners inside, but it works brilliantly.

SAM'S CHOP HOUSE British £

(☎0161-834 3210; www.samschophouse.co.uk; Back Pool Fold, Chapel Walks, off Cross St; mains £6-8) Arguably the city's top gastropub, Sam's is a Victorian classic that serves dishes straight out of a Dickens novel. The highlight is the crispy corned beef hash cake, which is salt-cured for 10 days on the premises. The owners also run Mr Thomas' Chop House (p241).

Old Trafford (p238)

RICHMOND TEA ROOMS   Cafe £

(0161-237 9667; www.richmondtearooms.
com; Richmond St; mains £5-8) You've never
seen Victorian tearooms like this. Or
maybe you have – in Tim Burton's *Alice
in Wonderland*. Bold, clashing colours,
a potpourri of period furniture and a
counter painted to resemble the icing on
a cake are just some of the features that
make the Richmond one of the city's best
new additions.

 **Drinking**

BLUU   Bar

(0161-839 7740; www.bluu.co.uk; Smithfield
Market Buildings, Thomas St; noon-midnight
Sun-Mon, to 1am Tue-Thu, to 2am Fri & Sat) Our
favourite of the Northern Quarter's collection of great bars. Bluu is cool, comfortable and comes with a great terrace on
which to enjoy a pint and listen to music
selected by folks with really good taste.

BRITONS PROTECTION   Pub

(0161-236 5895; 50 Great Bridgewater St;
mains £8) Whisky – 200 different kinds of
it – is the beverage of choice at this liver-
threatening, proper English pub that also
does Tudor-style meals (boar, venison
and the like).

ODD   Bar

(0161-833 0070; www.oddbar.co.uk; 30-32
Thomas St; 11am-11pm Mon-Sat, to 10.30pm
Sun) This eclectic little bar, with its oddball
furnishings, wacky tunes and anti-estab-
lishment crew of customers, is the perfect
antidote to the increasingly similar look of
so many modern bars.

MR THOMAS' CHOP HOUSE   Pub

(52 Cross St; mains £10) An old-style boozer
that is very popular for a pint as well as
a meal.

Information

Tourist Office (www.visitmanchester.com;
Piccadilly Plaza, Portland St; guided tours per
adult/child daily £6/5; 10am-5.15pm Mon-Sat,
10am-4.30pm Sun)

Getting There & Away

Air

Manchester Airport (0161-489 3000; www.
manchesterairport.co.uk), south of the city, is the
largest airport outside London and is served by 13
locations throughout Britain as well as more than
50 international destinations.

Train

Manchester Piccadilly (east of the Gay Village) is
the main station for trains to and from the rest of
the country, although Victoria station (north of
the National Football Museum) serves Halifax and
Bradford. The two stations are linked by Metrolink.

Liverpool Lime St £9.80, 45 minutes, half-
hourly

London Euston £131, three hours, seven daily

Getting Around

To/From the Airport

The airport is 12 miles south of the city. A train
to or from Victoria station costs £2, and a coach
is £3. A taxi is nearly four times as much in light
traffic.

Public Transport

For enquiries about local transport, including
night buses, contact Travelshop (0161-228
7811; www.gmpte.com; 9 Portland St, Piccadilly
Gardens; 8am-8pm).
Centreline bus 4 provides a free service around
the heart of Manchester every 10 minutes.
There are frequent Metrolink (www.metrolink.
co.uk) trams between Victoria and Piccadilly train
stations and G-Mex (for Castlefield), as well as
further afield to Salford Quays.

Chester

POP 80,130

Marvellous Chester is one of English
history's greatest gifts to the contemporary visitor. Its red-sandstone wall, which
today gift-wraps a tidy collection of Tudor
and Victorian buildings, was built during
Roman times.

⦿ Sights & Activities

FREE CITY WALLS   Landmark
A good way to get a sense of Chester's unique character is to walk the 2-mile circuit along the walls that surround the historic centre. Originally built by the Romans around AD 70, the walls were altered substantially over the following centuries but have retained their current position since around 1200. The tourist office's *Walk Around Chester Walls* leaflet is an excellent guide.

ROWS   Architecture
Chester's other great draw is the Rows, a series of two-level galleried arcades along the four streets that fan out in each direction from the **Central Cross**. The architecture is a handsome mix of Victorian and Tudor (original and mock) buildings that house a fantastic collection of individually owned shops.

CHESTER CATHEDRAL   Church
(☎01244-324 756; www.chestercathedral.com; 12 Abbey Sq; adult/child £6/2.50; ⊙9am-5pm Mon-Sat, 1-4pm Sun) Originally a Benedictine abbey built on the remains of an earlier Saxon church dedicated to St Werburgh (the city's patron saint), it was shut down in 1540 as part of Henry VIII's dissolution frenzy but reconsecrated as a cathedral the following year. Although the cathedral itself was given a substantial Victorian facelift, the 12th-century cloister and its surrounding buildings are essentially unaltered and retain much of the structure from the early monastic years.

❶ Getting There & Away

The train station is about a mile from the city centre via Foregate St and City Rd, or Brook St. City-Rail Link buses are free for people with rail tickets, and operate between the station and **Bus Stop A** (Frodsham St). Destinations:

Liverpool £4.35, 45 minutes, hourly

London Euston £65.20, 2½ hours, hourly

Manchester £12.60, one hour, hourly

LIVERPOOL
POP 469,020

Few English cities are as shackled by reputation as Liverpool, and none has worked so hard to outgrow the cliches that for so long have been used to define it.

A hardscrabble town with a reputation for wit and an obsessive love of football, Liverpool also has an impressive cultural heritage: it has more listed buildings than any other outside London, has recently undergone an impressive program of urban regeneration and its collection of museums and galleries is easily amongst the best in the country. And then there's the Beatles.

The main attractions are Albert Dock (west of the city centre), and the trendy Ropewalks area (south of Hanover St and west of the two cathedrals). Lime St station, the bus station and the Cavern Quarter – a mecca for Beatles fans – lie just to the north.

⦿ Sights

City Centre
LIVERPOOL CATHEDRAL   Church
(☎0151-709 6271; www.liverpoolcathedral.org.uk; Upper Duke St; visitor centre & tower admission £5; ⊙8am-6pm) Liverpool's Anglican cathedral is a building of superlatives. Not only is it Britain's largest church; it's also the world's largest Anglican cathedral, and it's all thanks to Sir Giles Gilbert Scott, who made its construction his life's work. The central bell is the world's third-largest (with the world's highest and heaviest peal), while the organ, with its 9765 pipes, is likely the world's largest operational model. Your ticket also gives you access to the cathedral's 101m **tower**, from which there are terrific views of the city and beyond – on a clear day you can see Blackpool Tower.

FREE WORLD MUSEUM   Museum
(☎0151-478 4399; www.liverpoolmuseums.org.uk/wml; William Brown St; ⊙10am-5pm) Natural history, science and technology are the themes of this sprawling museum,

STEPHEN SAKS/GETTY IMAGES ©

whose exhibits range from birds of prey to space exploration. It also includes the country's only free planetarium.

FREE **WALKER ART GALLERY**　Gallery
(☏0151-478 4199; www.liverpoolmuseums. org.uk/walker; William Brown St; ⊙10am-5pm) Touted as the 'National Gallery of the North', the city's foremost gallery is the national gallery for northern England, housing an outstanding collection of art from the 14th to the 21st centuries. Its strong suits are Pre-Raphaelite art, modern British art and sculpture – not to mention the rotating exhibits of contemporary expression.

METROPOLITAN CATHEDRAL OF CHRIST THE KING　Church
(☏0151-709 9222; www.liverpoolmetrocathedral. org.uk; Brownlow Hill; ⊙8am-6pm Mon-Sat, to 5pm Sun Oct-Mar) Known colloquially as Paddy's Wigwam, Liverpool's Catholic cathedral is a mightily impressive modern building that looks like a soaring concrete teepee, hence its nickname. It was completed in 1967 according to the design of Sir Frederick Gibberd after the original plans by Sir Edwin Lutyens, whose crypt is inside. The central tower frames the

world's largest stained-glass window, created by John Piper and Patrick Reyntiens.

LIVERPOOL WAR MUSEUM　Museum
(www.liverpoolwarmuseum.co.uk; 1 Rumford St; adult/child £6/4; ⊙10.30am-4.30pm Mon-Thu & Sat Mar-Oct) The secret command centre for the Battle of the Atlantic, the Western Approaches, was abandoned at the end of the war with virtually everything left intact. You can get a good glimpse of the labyrinthine nerve centre of Allied operations, including the all-important map room, where you can imagine playing a real-life, full-scale version of Risk.

Albert Dock

FREE **INTERNATIONAL SLAVERY MUSEUM**　Museum
(☏0151-478 4499; www.liverpoolmuseums.org. uk/ism; Albert Dock; admission free; ⊙10am-5pm) Museums are, by their very nature, like a still of the past, but the extraordinary International Slavery Museum resonates very much in the present. It reveals slavery's unimaginable horrors – including Liverpool's own role in the triangular slave trade – in a clear and uncompromising manner.

243

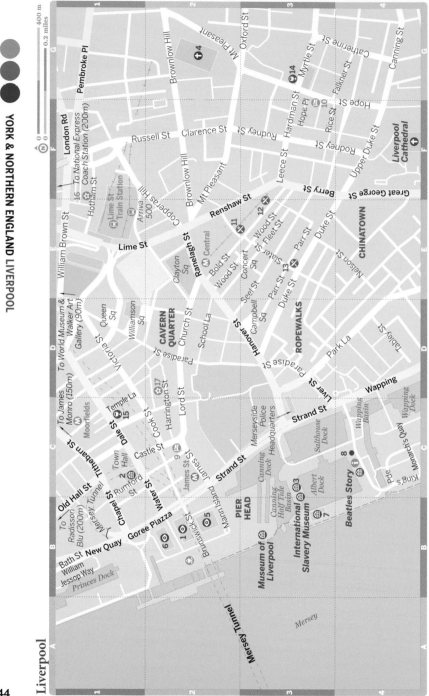

Liverpool

Liverpool

BEATLES STORY　　　　　Museum

(☎ 0151-709 1963; www.beatlesstory.com; Albert Dock; adult/student/child £12.95/9/7, incl Elvis & Us £15.95/12/7; ⊙ 9am-7pm, last admission 5pm) Liverpool's most popular museum won't illuminate any dark, juicy corners in the turbulent history of the world's most famous foursome – there's ne'er a mention of internal discord, drugs or Yoko Ono – but there's plenty of genuine memorabilia to keep a Beatles fan happy. Particularly impressive is the full-size replica Cavern Club (which was actually tiny) and the Abbey Rd studio where the lads recorded their first singles, while George Harrison's crappy first guitar (now worth half a million quid) should

inspire budding, penniless musicians to keep the faith.

FREE **MERSEYSIDE MARITIME MUSEUM**　　　　　Museum

(☎ 0151-478 4499; www.liverpoolmuseums.org.uk/maritime; Albert Dock; ⊙ 10am-5pm) The story of one of the world's great ports is the theme of this excellent museum and, believe us, it's a graphic and compelling page-turner. One of the many great exhibits is Emigration to a New World, which tells the story of nine million emigrants and their efforts to get to North America and Australia; the walk-through model of a typical ship shows just how tough conditions on board really were.

FREE **TATE LIVERPOOL**　　　　　Museum

(☎ 0151-702 7400; www.tate.org.uk/liverpool; Albert Dock; special exhibitions adult/child from £5/4; ⊙ 10am-5.50pm Tue-Sun) Touted as the home of modern art in the north, this gallery features a substantial checklist of 20th-century artists across its four floors, as well as touring exhibitions from the mother ship on London's Bankside.

North of Albert Dock

The area to the north of Albert Dock is known as **Pier Head**, after a stone pier built in the 1760s. This is still the departure point for ferries across the River Mersey, and was for millions of migrants their final contact with European soil.

The new **Museum of Liverpool** (☎ 0151-478 4545; www.liverpoolmuseums.org.uk; Pier Head; ⊙ 10am-5pm) is an impressive architectural interloper, but pride of place in this part of the dock still goes to the trio of Edwardian buildings known as the 'Three Graces', dating from the days when Liverpool's star was still ascending. The southernmost, with its dome mimicking St Paul's Cathedral, is the **Port of Liverpool Building**, completed in 1907. Next to it is the **Cunard Building**, in the style of an Italian palazzo, once HQ to the Cunard Steamship Line. Finally, the **Royal Liver Building** (pronounced *lie*-ver) was opened in 1911 as the head office of the Royal Liver Friendly Society.

(Never) Let it Be

They broke up more than 40 years ago and two of their members are dead, but the Beatles are bigger business than ever in Liverpool.

Most of the action centres around tiny Mathew St, site of the original Cavern Club, which is now the main thoroughfare of the 'Cavern Quarter'. Here you can shuck oysters in the Rubber Soul Oyster Bar, buy a George pillowcase in the From Me to You shop and put it on the pillows of the Hard Day's Night Hotel.

Wandering around Mathew St is plenty of fun – and the Beatles Shop is best for memorabilia – but if you really want a bit of Beatles lore, you'll have to visit the National Trust–owned **Mendips**, the home where John lived with his Aunt Mimi from 1945 to 1963 (which is also the time period covered by Sam Taylor-Wood's superb 2009 biopic of the young Lennon, *Nowhere Boy*) and **20 Forthlin Road**, the plain terraced home where Paul grew up; you can only do so by prebooked **tour** (NT; ☎0151-427 7231; www.nationaltrust.org.uk; pick-up Jury's Inn, 31 Keel Wharf, Wapping Dock; adult/child £20/5; ☉Wed-Sun Easter-Oct). Tours also leave from **Speke Hall** (NT; www.nationaltrust.org.uk; house & gardens adult/child £8.10/4, gardens only adult/child £4.95/2.60; ☉11am-5pm Wed-Sun).

Tours

BEATLES FAB FOUR
TAXI TOUR
Guided Tour

(☎0151-601 2111; www.thebeatlesfabfourtaxi tour.co.uk; 2-/3-hour £40/50) Themed tours of the city's mop-top landmarks – there's the three-hour original Lennon tour or the two-hour Epstein express tour. Pick-ups arranged when booking. Up to five people per tour.

LIVERPOOL BEATLES
TOUR
Guided Tour

(☎0151-281 7738; www.beatlestours.co.uk; tours from £50) Your own personalised tour of every bit of Beatles minutiae, from cradle to grave. Pick-ups are arranged upon booking.

MAGICAL MYSTERY
TOUR
Guided Tour

(☎0151-709 3285; www.beatlestour.org; per person £15.95; ☉2.30pm year-round, plus noon Sat Jul & Aug) Two-hour tour that takes in all Beatles-related landmarks – their birthplaces, childhood homes, schools and places such as Penny Lane and Strawberry Field – before finishing up in the Cavern Club (which isn't the original). Departs from opposite the tourist office on Albert Dock.

Sleeping

City Centre
HOPE STREET
HOTEL
Boutique Hotel **£££**

(☎0151-709 3000; www.hopestreethotel.co.uk; 40 Hope St; r/ste from £125/170; @ 🛜) Luxurious Liverpool's pre-eminent flag-waver is this stunning boutique hotel on the city's most elegant street. King-sized beds draped in Egyptian cotton; oak floors with underfloor heating; LCD wide-screen TVs; and sleek modern bathrooms (with luxe bath and beauty products) are but the most obvious touches of class at this supremely cool address. Breakfast, taken in the marvellous London Carriage Works, is not included.

RADISSON BLU
Hotel **££**

(☎0151-966 1500; www.radissonblu.co.uk; 107 Old Hall St; r from £89; @ 🛜) Funky ergonomic designer furniture in the lobby beneath a soaring nine-story atrium – there's something so appealing about Scandinavian corporate style, at least if you're a fan of contemporary decor.

62 CASTLE ST Boutique Hotel **££**
(☎ 0151-702 7898; www.62castlest.com; 62 Castle St; r from £69; P @ 🛜) This elegant property on (arguably) the city's most handsome street successfully blends the traditional Victorian features of the neo-classical building with a sleek, contemporary style. The 20 fabulously different suites come with HD plasma screen TVs, drench showers and luxe toiletries as standard.

Eating

MONRO Pub **££**
(☎ 0151-707 9933; www.themonro.com; 92 Duke St; 2-course lunch £11.95, dinner mains £14-20; ⏱ lunch & dinner) The Monro has fast become one of the city's favourite spots for lunch, dinner and, especially, weekend brunch – the constantly changing menu of classic British dishes made with ingredients sourced as locally as possible has transformed this handsome old pub into a superb dining experience. It's tough to find pub grub this good elsewhere, unless you go to its sister pub, the **James Monro** (☎ 0151-236 9700; www.thejamesmonro.com; 69 Tithebarn St; ⏱ lunch & dinner Tue-Sun).

ITALIAN CLUB Italian **£**
(☎ 0151-708 5508; www.theitalianclubliverpool.co.uk; 85 Bold St; mains £6-11; ⏱ 10am-7pm Mon-Sat) The Crolla family must have been homesick for southern Italy, so they opened this fabulous spot, adorned it with family pictures and began serving the kind of food relatives visiting from the home coun-

try would be glad to tuck into. They've been so successful that they recently opened **Italian Club Fish** (☎ 0151-707 2110; 128 Bold St; mains £8-14; ⏱ Tue-Sun), just down the street, specialising in, erm, fish.

LONDON CARRIAGE WORKS Modern British **£££**
(☎ 0151-705 2222; www.thelondoncarriageworks.co.uk; 40 Hope St; 2-/3-course meals £15/20, mains £15-27) Liverpool's dining revolution is being led by Paul Askew's award-winning restaurant, which successfully blends ethnic influences from around the globe with staunch British favourites and serves up the result in a beautiful dining room – actually more of a bright glass box divided only by a series of sculpted glass shards. Reservations are recommended.

Drinking

PHILHARMONIC Pub
(36 Hope St; ⏱ to 11.30pm) This extraordinary bar, designed by the shipwrights

Statue of John Lennon
GLENN BEANLAND/GETTY IMAGES ©

who built the *Lusitania,* is one of the most beautiful bars in all of England. The interior is resplendent with etched and stained glass, wrought iron, mosaics and ceramic tiling – and if you think that's good, just wait until you see inside the marble men's toilets, the only heritage-listed lav in the country.

RIGBY'S Pub
(21 Dale St) A traditional boozer that serves 'real ale' (ie a traditional brew with no extraneous carbon dioxide), Rigby's looks, feels and smells like an old-school pub.

⭐ Entertainment

Music
ACADEMY Live Music
(✆ 0151-794 6868; Liverpool University, 11-13 Hotham St) Good spot to see midsize bands on tour.

CAVERN CLUB Live Music
(✆ 0151-236 1965; www.cavernclub. org; 8-10 Mathew St) It's a reconstruction, and not even on the same spot, but the 'world's most famous club' is still a great spot to see local bands.

ℹ️ Information

There is a small **tourist office** (✆ 0151-707 0729; www.visitliverpool.com; Anchor Courtyard; ⏰ 10am-6pm) in Albert Dock, and a separate **accommodation hotline** (✆ 0845 601 1125; ⏰ 9am-5.30pm Mon-Fri, 10am-4pm Sat).

ℹ️ Getting There & Away

Air
Liverpool John Lennon Airport (✆ 0870 750 8484; www.liverpoolairport.com; Speke Hall Ave) serves a variety of international destinations as well as destinations in the UK (Belfast, London and the Isle of Man).

Train

Liverpool's main station is Lime St. It has hourly services to almost everywhere, including:

Chester £4.35, 45 minutes

London Euston £65.20, 3¼ hours

Manchester £9.80, 45 minutes

Wigan £5.40, 50 minutes

ⓘ Getting Around

To/From the Airport

The airport is 8 miles south of the centre. Arriva Airlink (www.arriva.co.uk; £2; ⏱6am-11pm) buses 80A and 180 depart from Paradise St Interchange, and Airportxpress 500 (www. arriva.co.uk; £2.50; ⏱5.15am-12.15am) buses leave from outside Lime St station. Buses from both stations take half an hour and run every 20 minutes. A taxi to the city centre should cost no more than £18.

Boat

The famous Mersey ferry (www.merseyferries. co.uk; adult/child £2.10/1.50) crossing for Woodside and Seacombe departs from Pier Head Ferry Terminal, next to the Royal Liver Building (to the north of Albert Dock).

Public Transport

Local public transport is coordinated by Merseytravel (www.merseytravel.gov.uk). Highly recommended is the Saveaway ticket (adult/ child £5/2.50) which allows for one day's off-peak (after 9.30am) travel on all bus, train and ferry services throughout Merseyside. Tickets are available at shops and post offices throughout the city.

Merseyrail (www.merseyrail.org) is an extensive suburban rail service linking Liverpool with the Greater Merseyside area. There are four stops in the city centre: Lime St, Central (handy for Ropewalks), James St (close to Albert Dock) and Moorfields (for the Liverpool War Museum).

THE LAKE DISTRICT

If you're a lover of the great outdoors, the Lake District is one corner of England where you'll want to linger. This sweeping panorama of slate-capped fells, craggy hilltops, misty mountain tarns and glittering lakes has been pulling in the crowds ever since the Romantics pitched up in the early 19th century, and it remains one of the country's most popular beauty spots.

Windermere & Bowness-on-Windermere

POP 8432

Of all England's lakes, none carries the cachet of Windermere. Stretching for 10.5 silvery miles from Ambleside to Newby Bridge, it's one of the classic Lake District vistas, and has been a centre for tourism since the first steam trains chugged into town in 1847.

The town itself is split between Windermere, 1.5 miles uphill from the lake, and bustling Bowness-on-Windermere (usually shortened to Bowness), with its touristy collection of teashops, ice-cream stalls and cruise boats.

 **Activities**

WINDERMERE LAKE CRUISES
Boat Tours

(☎015395-31188; www.windermere-lakecruises.co.uk) Top on the list of things to do in Windermere is to take a lake cruise. The first passenger ferry was launched back in 1845, and cruising on the lake is still a popular pastime: some of the vessels are modern, but there are a couple of period beauties dating back to the 1930s. Trips include the **Freedom of the Lake Ticket** (adult/child/family £17.75/8.90/48.50), with one day's unlimited travel on all routes.

 **Sleeping**

THE BOUNDARY
B&B ££

(☎015394-48978; www.theboundaryonline.co.uk; Lake Rd; d £100-180; P 🛜) Owners

Steve and Helen have given this Victorian house a sleek, boutique makeover: chic decor, monochrome colours, quirky furniture and all. Steve's a cricket obsessive, so all the rooms are named after famous batsmen.

WHEATLANDS LODGE
B&B ££

(☎015394-43789; www.wheatlandslodge-windermere.co.uk; Old College Lane; d £80-150; P 🛜) Between Bowness and Windermere, this detached house looks Victorian, but inside you'll find eight elegant, contemporary rooms with either a power shower or sit-down jacuzzi.

1 PARK ROAD
B&B ££

(www.1parkroad.com; 1 Park Rd; £76-104; P 🛜) It's the little treats that keep this cosy guest house a cut above: bath goodies from Pure Lakes and The White Company, iPod docks in every room, and home-made baked beans and marmalade on the breakfast table.

 Eating

MASON'S ARMS
Pub, Inn ££

(☎015395-68486; www.masonsarmsstrawberrybank.co.uk; Winster; mains £13-20, d £75-105) Three miles east of the lake, not far from Bowlands Bridge, the marvellous Mason's Arms is a local secret. The rafters, flagstones and cast-iron range haven't changed in centuries, but the food's up to date, and the patio has to-die-for views across fields and fells.

HOOKED
Seafood ££

(☎015394-48443; www.hookedwindermere.co.uk; Ellerthwaite Sq; mains £16.95-19.95; ◷dinner Tue-Sun) It's only been open since 2011, but this admirably simple seafood restaurant already has a loyal following.

ANGEL INN
Gastropub ££

(☎015394-44080; www.the-angelinn.com; Helm Rd; mains £10.95-16.50) This attractive pub is set on top of a grassy hummock behind the Bowness shoreline. It's more big-city-modern than backcountry-cosy: leather sofas, wooden floors and blackboards,

Lake District

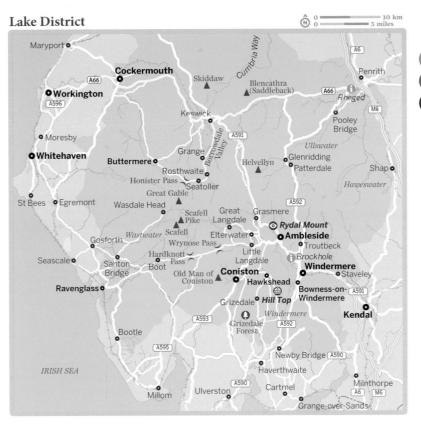

plus a gastropub menu of pork belly ballontine and honey-roasted chicken.

Information

Brockhole National Park Visitor Centre (015394-46601; www.lake-district.gov.uk; 10am-5pm Easter-Oct) Installed inside a 19th-century mansion 3 miles north of Windermere on the A591, this is the Lake District's flagship visitor centre, and also has a teashop, adventure playground and gardens.

Windermere Tourist Office (015394-46499; windermeretic@southlakeland.gov.uk; Victoria St; 9am-5.30pm Mon-Sat, 9.30am-5.30pm Sun Apr-Oct, shorter hours in winter)

Bowness Tourist Office (015394-42895; bownesstic@lake-district.gov.uk; Glebe Rd; 9.30am-5.30pm Easter-Oct, 10am-4pm Fri-Sun Nov-Easter)

Getting There & Away

Boat

The **Windermere Ferry** (car/bike/pedestrian £4.30/1/50p; 6.50am-9.50pm Mon-Fri, 9.10am-9.50pm Sat & Sun Mar-Oct, last ferry one hour earlier in winter) carries vehicles and pedestrians from Ferry Nab, just south of Bowness, across to Ferry House on the lake's west side. There's a ferry roughly every 20 minutes, although queues can be horrendous in summer.

Train

Windermere is the only town inside the national park accessible by train. It's on the branch line to Kendal and Oxenholme, from where there are frequent connections north and south.

DESTINATION	FARE (ONE WAY)	DURATION (HR)
Edinburgh	£55	2½
Glasgow	£43.40	2¾
Kendal	£4.20	15min
Lancaster	£12.60	45min
London	£92.10	3¼
Manchester Piccadilly	£32.40	1½-2
Oxenholme	£4.90	20min

Grasmere

POP 1458

Even without its Romantic connections, gorgeous Grasmere would still be one of the Lakes' biggest draws. It's one of the prettiest of the Lakeland hamlets, huddled at the base of a sweeping valley dotted with woods, pastures and slate-coloured hills, but most of the thousands of trippers come in search of its famous former residents: opium-eating Thomas de Quincey, unruly Coleridge and grand old man William Wordsworth.

 Sights

DOVE COTTAGE Historic Home
(015394-35544; www.wordsworth.org.uk; adult/child £7.50/4.50; 9.30am-5.30pm) This tiny, creeper-clad cottage on the edge of the village famously belonged to William Wordsworth. He arrived here with his sister Dorothy in 1799, before being joined in 1802 by his new wife, Mary, and soon after, three children: John, Dora and Thomas, who were born here in 1803, 1804 and 1806 respectively. Like nearby Rydal Mount, the cottage's cramped rooms are full of artefacts; keep your eyes peeled for the poet's passport, a pair of his spectacles and a portrait of his favourite dog Pepper, given to him by Sir Walter Scott. One upstairs bedroom was lined with newspaper by Wordsworth's sister Dorothy to try and keep out the draughts.

Entry is by timed ticket to avoid overcrowding, and includes a guided tour.

Next door, the **Wordsworth Museum & Art Gallery** houses one of the nation's main collections relating to the Romantic movement, including many original manuscripts.

ST OSWALD'S CHURCH Church
In the churchyard of this tiny chapel in the centre of Grasmere are the graves of many of the Wordsworths, including William, his wife Mary, sister Dorothy, and children Dora, Catherine and Thomas.

 **Sleeping**

MOSS GROVE ORGANIC Hotel £££
(015394-35251; www.mossgrove.com; r Sun-Thu £114-209, Fri & Sat £129-259; P) This eco-chic hotel champions its green credentials: sheep-wool insulation, organic paints, reclaimed timber beds, but for once, eco also equals elegance. Rooms are enormous, and bathrooms sparkle with sexy showers and underfloor heating. Breakfast is served buffet-style in the kitchen-diner downstairs.

HOW FOOT LODGE B&B ££
(015394-35366; www.howfoot.co.uk; Town End; d £72-8; P) Just a stroll from Dove Cottage, this stone house has six rooms finished in fawns and beiges; the nicest are the Deluxe Doubles, one with sun terrace and the other with private sitting room.

 Eating & Drinking

JUMBLE ROOM Restaurant £££
(015394-35188; Langdale Rd; dinner mains £14.50-26.50; lunch Fri-Sun, dinner Wed-Sun) Husband-and-wife team Andy and Crissy Hill have turned this village bistro into a much-loved dining landmark. It's a really fun and friendly place to dine.

SARAH NELSON'S GINGERBREAD SHOP Food
(www.grasmeregingerbread.co.uk; Church Stile; 12 pieces of gingerbread £4.95; 9.15am-5.30pm Mon-Sat, 12.30-5pm Sun) In business since 1854, this famous sweetshop makes Grasmere's essential souvenir: traditional

Detour:
Rydal Mount

William Wordsworth's best-known Lakeland residence is definitely Dove Cottage, but he actually spent much more time at **Rydal Mount** (www.rydalmount. co.uk; adult/child £6/2.50, gardens only adults £4; ⏰9.30am-5pm Mar-Oct, 11am-4pm Wed-Mon Nov & Feb), a much grander house halfway between Ambleside and Grasmere. This was the Wordsworth family's home from 1813 until the poet's death in 1850, and it's still owned by his descendants.

The house is a treasure trove of Wordsworth memorabilia. Downstairs you can wander around the library, dining room and drawing room (look out in the cabinets for William's pen, inkstand and picnic box, and a famous portrait of the poet by the American painter Henry Inman hanging above the fireplace). Upstairs are the family bedrooms and Wordsworth's attic study, containing his encyclopedia and a sword belonging to his brother John, who was lost in a shipwreck in 1805. Below the house is Dora's Field, which Wordsworth planted with daffodils in memory of his eldest daughter, who died from tuberculosis in 1847.

The house is 1.5 miles northwest of Ambleside, off the A591.

gingerbread with a half-biscuity, half-cakey texture, cooked according to a top-secret recipe by ladies in frilly pinafores and starched bonnets.

Hill Top

In the tiny village of Near Sawrey, 2 miles south of Hawkshead, the idyllic farmhouse of **Hill Top** (NT; ☎015394-36269; www.nationaltrust.org.uk/hill-top; adult/child £8/4; ⏰10am-5pm Sat-Thu mid-Feb–Oct, shorter hours outside summer) is a must for Beatrix Potter buffs: it was the first house she lived in after moving to the Lake District, and also where she wrote and illustrated many of her famous tales.

Purchased in 1905 (largely on the proceeds of her first bestseller, *The Tale of Peter Rabbit*), Hill Top is crammed with decorative details that fans will recognise from the author's illustrations.

Entry is by timed ticket, and the queues can be seriously daunting during the summer holidays.

Durham

POP 42,940

Consider the setting: England's most beautiful Romanesque cathedral, a masterpiece of Norman architecture and a resplendent monument to the country's ecclesiastical history; a huge castle; and, surrounding them both, a cobweb of cobbled streets usually full of upper-crust students attending Durham's other big pull, England's third university of choice (after Oxford and Cambridge). Welcome to Durham.

Sights

DURHAM CATHEDRAL　　Church
(www.durhamcathedral.co.uk; donation requested, guided tours adult/child £4/free; ⏰7.30am-6pm, tours 10.30am, 11am & 2pm Mon-Sat, Evensong 5.15pm Mon-Sat & 3.30pm Sun) This exquisite cathedral is the definitive structure of the Anglo-Norman Romanesque style, one of the world's greatest places of worship and, since 1986, a Unesco World Heritage Site. This was the first European cathedral to be roofed with stone-ribbed vaulting, which upheld the heavy stone roof and made it possible to build pointed transverse arches – the first in England, and a great architectural achievement.

One of the cathedral's most beautiful parts is the **Galilee Chapel**, dating from

If You Like...
Roman Ruins

The impressive fort at Housesteads (p255) is undoubtedly the wall's best-preserved site, but several more intriguing Roman ruins are within easy reach.

1 **CHESTERS ROMAN FORT & MUSEUM** (EH; ☎01434-681379; Chollerford; adult/child £4.80/2.40; ⏰10am-6pm Apr-Sep) The best-preserved remains of a Roman cavalry fort in England are at **Chesters**, set among idyllic green woods and meadows near the village of Chollerford. It's 5.5 miles from Hexham.

2 **VINDOLANDA ROMAN FORT & MUSEUM** (www.vindolanda.com; adult/child £6.25/3.75, with Roman Army Museum £9.50/5.25; ⏰10am-6pm Apr-Sep, to 5pm Feb, Mar & Oct) The extensive site of Vindolanda offers a fascinating glimpse into the daily life of a Roman garrison town. The time-capsule museum contains many fascinating Roman artefacts, while the rest of the site includes the fort, town, reconstructed turrets and temple. It's 1.5 miles north of Bardon Mill between the A69 and B6318.

3 **BIRDOSWALD ROMAN FORT** (EH; ☎016977-47602; adult/child £5.20/3.10; ⏰10am-5.30pm Mar-Oct) The remains of this once-formidable fort are on a minor road off the B6318, about 3 miles west of Greenhead; a fine stretch of wall extends from here to Harrow's Scar Milecastle.

1175, its northern side features rare surviving examples of 12th-century wall painting (thought to feature portraits of Sts Cuthbert and Oswald).

Other highlights include the 14th-century **Bishop's Throne**; the beautiful stone **Neville Screen** (1372–80), which separates the high altar from **St Cuthbert's tomb**; and the mostly 19th-century **Cloisters** where you'll find the **Monk's Dormitory**, now a library of 30,000 books and displaying Anglo-Saxon carved stones. Also worthwhile

are the **guided tours** and a visit during **Evensong** services.

The **tower** (£5) provides show-stopping vistas, but you've got to climb 325 steps to enjoy them.

DURHAM CASTLE   Castle
(www.dur.ac.uk; admission by guided tour only, adult/child £5/3.50; ⏰tours 2pm, 3pm & 4pm term time, 10am, 11am & noon during university holidays) Built as a standard motte-and-bailey fort in 1072, Durham Castle was the prince bishops' home until 1837, when it became the first college of the newly formed University of Durham. It remains a university hall, and you can stay here.

Highlights of the 45-minute tour include the groaning 17th-century **Black Staircase**, the 16th-century **chapel** and the beautifully preserved **Norman chapel** (1080).

 Sleeping

GADDS TOWNHOUSE   Boutique Hotel **£££**
(☎0191-384 1037; www.gaddstownhouse.com; 34 Old Elvet; d from £99) Possibly the north-east's most bizarre digs, the 11 rooms at this fun place leave few indifferent. Each room has a theme, with 'Le Jardin' featuring a shed and garden furniture, the 'Premiere' boasting a huge projection screen and popcorn machine, and the 'Edwardian Express' recreating a night in a yesteryear sleeper compartment. The restaurant is superb and some rooms have cathedral views.

CATHEDRAL VIEW   B&B **££**
(☎0191-386 9566; www.cathedralview.com; 212 Gilesgate; s/d from £70/85) Six large rooms decorated with lots of cushions and coor-dinated bed linen and window dressings make up the numbers, but it's the two at the back that are worth the fuss – the views of the cathedral are fantastic.

Eating

OLDFIELDS British ££
(www.oldfieldsrealfood.co.uk; 18 Claypath; mains
£12-19) With strictly seasonal menus that
use only local or organic ingredients
sourced within a 60-mile radius of Durham, this award-winning restaurant is one
of the county's finest, though it's not quite
as good as its Newcastle sister.

COTTONS Cafe £
(32 Silver St; snacks £2.50-5; ⊙9.30am-5.30pm
Mon-Sat, 11am-4.30 Sun) Down an inconspicu-
ous flight of steps two doors along from
the post office, this junk shop/art gallery/
tearoom hides in a brick-and-stone cellar
where a range of teas plus sandwiches,
jacket potatoes and cakes are served to
in-the-know punters.

ℹ Information

Tourist office (www.thisisdurham.com; Owen
Gate; ⊙9.30am-5.30pm Mon-Sat, 11am-4pm Sun)

ℹ Getting There & Away

Trains destination include:

Edinburgh £50.30, two hours, hourly

London King's Cross £103.60, three hours,
hourly

Newcastle £5.20, 15 minutes, five hourly

York £21.90, one hour, four hourly

HADRIAN'S WALL

Hadrian's Wall, named in honour of the
emperor who ordered it built, was one of
Rome's greatest engineering projects, a
spectacular 73-mile testament to ambition
and the practical Roman mind. Even today,
1900 years after the first stone was laid,
the sections that are still standing remain
an awe-inspiring sight, proof that when the
Romans wanted something done, they just
knuckled down and did it. When completed, the mammoth structure ran across the
narrow neck of the island, from the Solway
Firth in the west almost to the mouth of the
Tyne in the east.

Detour: Angel of the North

Nicknamed the Gateshead Flasher,
this extraordinary 200-tonne, rust-
coloured human frame with wings,
more soberly known as the **Angel of
the North**, has been looming over
A1(M) 5 miles south of Newcastle
since 1998. At 20m high and with a
wingspan wider than a Boeing 767,
Antony Gormley's most successful
work is the UK's largest sculpture
and the most viewed piece of public
art in the country, though Mark
Wallinger's *White Horse* in Kent may
pinch both titles soon.

A series of forts was developed along
the length of the wall, many of which are
still standing, including **Housesteads**
(EH; adult/child £6/3.60; ⊙10am-6pm Apr-
Sep), the wall's most dramatic site. The
remains here include an impressive
hospital, granaries, barrack blocks and
even communal flushable latrines. It's 2.5
miles north of Bardon Mill on the B6318,
and about 6 miles from Haltwhistle.

Carlisle, in the west, and Newcastle,
in the east, are obviously good starting
points, but Brampton, Haltwhistle,
Hexham and Corbridge all make good
bases. The B6318 follows the course of
the wall from the outskirts of Newcastle
to Birdoswald; from Birdoswald to Carlisle
it pays to have a detailed map.

ℹ Information

Hadrian's Wall Country (www.hadrians-wall.
org) The official portal for the whole of Hadrian's
Wall Country.

Northumberland National Park
Visitor Centre (☎01434-344396; www.
northumberlandnationalpark.org.uk; Once Brewed;
⊙9.30am-5.30pm Apr-Oct) Off the B6318.

Hadrian's Wall

Rome's Final Frontier

Of all Britain's Roman ruins, Emperor Hadrian's 2nd-century wall, cutting across northern England from the Irish Sea to the North Sea, is by far the most spectacular; Unesco awarded it world cultural heritage status in 1987.

We've picked out the highlights, one of which is the prime remaining Roman fort on the wall, Housesteads, which we've reconstructed here.

Housesteads' granaries
Nothing like the clever underground ventilation system, which kept vital supplies of grain dry in Northumberland's damp and drizzly climate, would be seen again in these parts for 1500 years.

Birdoswald Roman Fort
Explore the longest intact stretch of the wall, scramble over the remains of a large fort then head indoors to wonder at a full-scale model of the wall at its zenith. Great fun for the kids.

Housesteads Roman Fort
See Illustration Right

Chesters Roman Fort
Built to keep watch over a bridge spanning the River North Tyne, Britain's best-preserved Roman cavalry fort has a terrific bathhouse, essential if you have months of nippy northern winter ahead.

Hexham Abbey
This may be the finest non-Roman sight near Hadrian's Wall, but the 7th-century parts of this magnificent church were built with stone quarried by the Romans for use in their forts.

Housesteads' hospital
Operations performed at the hospital would have been surprisingly effective, even without anaesthetics; religious rituals and prayers to Aesculapius, the Roman god of healing, were possibly less helpful for a hernia or appendicitis.

Milecastle

North Gate

Interval Tower

Housesteads' latrines
Communal toilets were the norm in Roman times and Housesteads' are remarkably well preserved – fortunately no traces remain of the vinegar-soaked sponges that were used instead of toilet paper.

QUICK WALL FACTS & FIGURES
Latin name Vallum Aelium
Length 73.5 miles (80 Roman miles)
Construction date AD 122–128
Manpower for construction
Three legions (around 16,000 men)
Features At least 16 forts, 80 milecastles, 160 turrets
Did you know Hadrian's wasn't the only wall in Britain – the Antonine Wall was built across what is now central Scotland in the AD 140s, but it was abandoned soon after

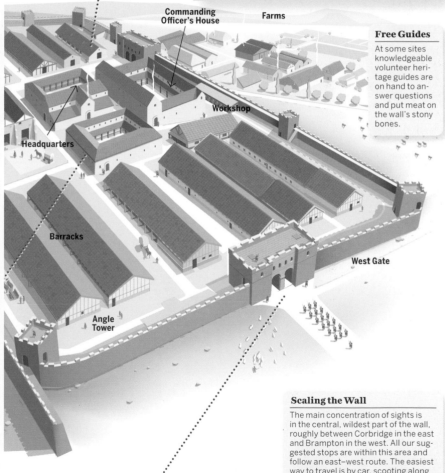

Commanding
Officer's House   Farms

Free Guides
At some sites knowledgeable volunteer heritage guides are on hand to answer questions and put meat on the wall's stony bones.

Workshop

Headquarters

Barracks

West Gate

**Angle
Tower**

Scaling the Wall
The main concentration of sights is in the central, wildest part of the wall, roughly between Corbridge in the east and Brampton in the west. All our suggested stops are within this area and follow an east–west route. The easiest way to travel is by car, scooting along the B6318, but special bus AD122 will also get you there. Hiking along the designated Hadrian's Wall Path (84 miles) allows you to appreciate the achievement up close.

Housesteads' gatehouses
Unusually at Housesteads neither of the gates faces the enemy, as was the norm at a Roman fort – builders aligned them east-west. Ruts worn by cart wheels are still visible in the stone.

Wales

Wales is a separate nation, with its own language and culture. And you can feel the difference as soon as you cross the border. Although this ancient Celtic country was under English rule from around 1300, the flame of independence never died, and in 1998 Wales finally regained control of its own destiny.

So after centuries of oppression and decades in the doldrums, Wales is now rediscovering itself with energy and determination. Cultural landmarks across the country have been restored; the capital city of Cardiff has decorated the once-abandoned waterfront with stunning new buildings; and even the summit of Snowdon, the highest peak in the land, has received a brand-new 21st-century visitor centre.

Whether you're marvelling at the medieval castles in the north, exploring pubs and shops in the south, or hiking airy clifftops in the west, you certainly won't regret spending some time in Wales.

Pembrokeshire Coast National Park (p277)
ANDREW BOXALL/GETTY IMAGES ©

Pembrokeshire Coast (p277)

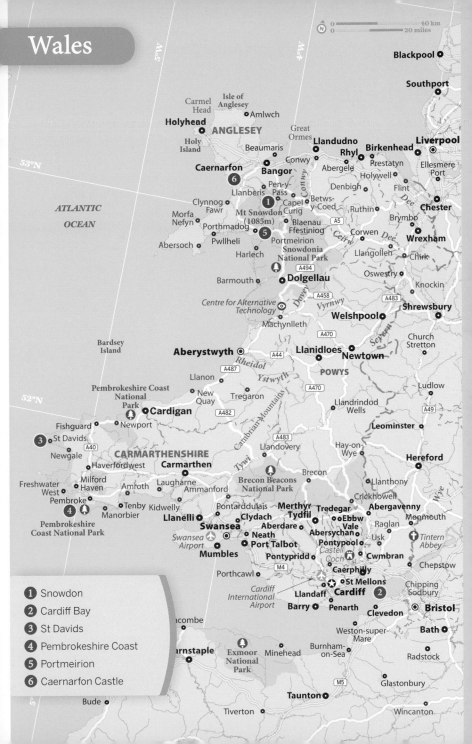

Wales

ATLANTIC OCEAN

Blackpool
Southport

Carmel Head
Isle of Anglesey
Amlwch
Holyhead
ANGLESEY
Great Ormes
Llandudno
Rhyl
Birkenhead
Liverpool
Holy Island
Beaumaris
Conwy
Abergele
Prestatyn
Ellesmere Port
Caernarfon
Bangor
Holywell
6
Pen-y-Pass
Denbigh
Flint
Chester
Clynnog Fawr
Llanberis
Capel Curig
Ruthin
Brymbo
1
Betws-y-Coed
Corwen
Wrexham
Morfa Nefyn
Mt Snowdon (1085m)
Blaenau Ffestiniog
A5
Dee
Porthmadog
5
Portmeirion
Corwen
Dee
Wrexham
Abersoch
Pwllheli
Snowdonia National Park
Llangollen
Chirk
Harlech
A494
Oswestry
Knockin
Barmouth
Dolgellau
A458
Vyrnwy
A483
Shrewsbury
Bardsey Island
Centre for Alternative Technology
Dovey
Welshpool
Machynlleth
A470
Church Stretton
Aberystwyth
Rheidol
A44
Llanidloes
Newtown
Llanon
A487
Ystwyth
POWYS
A470
Ludlow
Pembrokeshire Coast National Park
New Quay
Tregaron
A482
Llandrindod Wells
A49
Fishguard
Cardigan
Newport
Cambrian Mountains
Leominster
3 St Davids
A40
Llandovery
Hay-on-Wye
Hereford
Newgale
CARMARTHENSHIRE
Carmarthen
Tywi
Brecon
Llanthony
Haverfordwest
Crickhowell
Freshwater West
Milford Haven
Amroth
Laugharne
Ammanford
Brecon Beacons National Park
Abergavenny
Monmouth
Raglan
Pembroke
Tenby
Kidwelly
Pontarddulais
Merthyr Tydfil
Tredegar
Usk
Tintern Abbey
4
Manorbier
Llanelli
Clydach
Aberdare
Ebbw Vale
Pontypool
Chepstow
Pembrokeshire Coast National Park
Swansea
Neath
Abersychan
Castell Coch
Cwmbran
Swansea Airport
Port Talbot
Pontypridd
Caerphilly
Chipping Sodbury
Mumbles
Porthcawl
M4
Cardiff
2
Bristol
Cardiff International Airport
Llandaff
St Mellons
Clevedon
Barry
Penarth
Bath
Weston-super-Mare
ilfracombe
Radstock
Barnstaple
Exmoor National Park
Minehead
Burnham-on-Sea
Bude
Taunton
Glastonbury
Tiverton
Wincanton

1 Snowdon
2 Cardiff Bay
3 St Davids
4 Pembrokeshire Coast
5 Portmeirion
6 Caernarfon Castle

0   40 km
0   20 miles

53°N

52°N

Wales Highlights

PETER ADAMS/GETTY IMAGES ©

1

Snowdon

Dominating the map of North Wales is the spectacular mountainous landscape of Snowdonia, much of it protected as a national park. The region gets its name from Snowdon, the highest peak in Wales and the most popular spot for visitors. Above: Mt Snowdon; Top Right: Snowdon Mountain Railway; Bottom Right: Climbing Snowdon

Need to Know

LOCATION 120 miles north of Cardiff **WEATHER** Get a proper forecast before you visit **CLOTHING** Proper boots and waterproofs **For further coverage, see p284**

Snowdon Don't Miss List

SAM ROBERTS, SENIOR WARDEN (RETIRED) OF SNOWDONIA NATIONAL PARK

1 HIKE TO SNOWDON'S SUMMIT

I've lived in this area all my life, and as a Welshman I'm naturally proud of my homeland. My favourite hike up to Snowdon's summit is the **Rhyd-Ddu Path**; it's on the western side of the mountain which sees fewer visitors. Alternatively, take the Snowdon Sherpa bus to **Pen-y-Pass**, reach the summit from there and descend on the **Llanberis Path**.

2 LLANBERIS PATH

This is one of the most popular walking trails up the mountain, starting from **Llanberis**. You can stroll up just for a short distance, or it's easy enough to go all the way to the summit. On your way back down the Llanberis Path, enjoy a drink and a warm welcome at my favourite cafe, **Penceunant Tearoom**.

3 SNOWDON MOUNTAIN RAILWAY

If you can't hike up to the summit, or haven't got time, you can take a ride on the unique Snowdon Mountain Railway, built in the 19th century for Victorian tourists and still working today. Be aware that queues at the ticket office in Llanberis can be long on sunny days in the summer, so I recommend booking ahead if you can.

4 HAFOD ERYRI

Not only does a railway run up Snowdon, you can get a cup of tea at the top as well! Hafod Eryri was built in 2009 and is the highest cafe in Wales. It can be very busy, but to escape the crowds you need walk only a short distance back down the mountain. If you get a return ticket on the train, the half hour allowed at the top is not really enough; I recommend train up, walk down.

5 PEN-Y-GWYRD HOTEL

To immerse yourself in Snowdon tradition and atmosphere, stay a night at this historic hotel (p285). It's been a base for hikers and mountaineers for more than a century.

263

Cardiff Bay

The Welsh capital city is buzzing with confidence, and nowhere is this more apparent than the revitalised waterfront of Cardiff Bay (p271). Once a derelict dock and down-at-heel neighbourhood called Tiger Bay, now it's home to a collection of fascinating structures including the historic Pierhead building, the new Wales Millennium Centre (p274) and the Senedd (p271; the Assembly Building for Wales's devolved government) – not to mention several film locations for *Doctor Who*.

St Davids

It's little more than a village but St Davids ranks as Britain's smallest city thanks to the presence of a magnificent 12th-century cathedral (p278) that marks the burial place of the nation's patron saint. The burial place has been a place of pilgrimage for some 1400 years, and today St Davids still attracts many visitors, as it makes a good base for exploring this beautiful corner of West Wales. St Davids Cathedral

Pembrokeshire Coast

4

At the end of the peninsula that makes up the southwest part of Wales is the old county of Pembrokeshire (p277), edged on two sides by the sea, and some of the most beautiful stretches of coastline in Britain. It's protected as a national park, and provides excellent hiking, surfing and wildlife-watching opportunities – as well as bucket-and-spade beaches perfect for family holidays.

Baby seal, Pembrokeshire Coast National Park

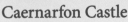

5

Portmeirion

Perhaps the wackiest attraction in Wales is the seaside fantasy land of Portmeirion (p287), an Italianate village perched above the sea, created by the eccentric architect Sir Clough Williams-Ellis in the early 20th century. Brimming with follies, colonnades, pastel-coloured palaces and other architectural oddities, with nods to styles as varied as Moorish and Greek, it provided the perfect setting for the classic cult TV series *The Prisoner* in the 1960s.

6

Caernarfon Castle

One of an 'iron ring' of fortresses built by (English) King Edward I to control Wales in the late 13th century, Caernarfon Castle (p286) was a military stronghold, seat of government and royal palace. It is dramatic and unusual thanks to colour-banded masonry and polygonal towers, supposedly inspired by the ancient walls of Constantinople. Today, it's a Unesco World Heritage Site.

Wales' Best…

Castles

o **Cardiff Castle** (p270) Roman foundations, Norman additions, Victorian frills – the capital's stronghold has a chequered past

o **Conwy Castle** (p286) Part of the English 'iron ring' that controlled North Wales for centuries

o **Caernarfon Castle** (p286) Yet another 'magnificent badge of our subjection', as Welsh writer Thomas Pennant put it

o **Beaumaris Castle** (p286) Moody fortress situated on the island of Anglesey, which once guarded the Welsh coastline

Architecture

o **Cardiff Bay** (p271) Victorian Gothic splendour at the Pierhead and modernist style at the Millennium Centre

o **Portmeirion** (p287) Bizarre fantasy land of follies, colonnades and architectural oddities

o **St Davids Cathedral** (p278) Small maybe, but one of the loveliest cathedrals in Wales

o **Erddig** (p290) This country house near Llangollen is among the finest in Wales

Culture Spots

o **Hay-on-Wye** (p280) Self-proclaimed secondhand bookshop capital of the world, and home of the Hay Literary Festival

o **Wales Millennium Centre, Cardiff** (p274) The capital's stunning centre for music and the performing arts

o **Tintern Abbey** (p275) Evocative ruins in the Wye Valley, and the inspiration for poets and artists through the centuries

o **Laugharne** (p276) The ramshackle hut where Dylan Thomas penned some of his finest poems

Natural Beauty

o **Pembrokeshire** (p277)
In the far west of Wales, a beautiful rural area with a dramatic coastline

o **Snowdonia** (p281) The largest national park in Wales, home to the mighty peak of Snowdon

o **Gower Peninsula** (p275)
This sea-fringed headland makes a lovely detour from Cardiff

o **Ramsey Island**
(p278) Wildlife-spotting opportunities aplenty on this island near St Davids

ADVANCE
PLANNING

Need to Know

ADVANCE PLANNING

o **Six months before**
Make accommodation plans if you're interested in the Hay Literary Festival, the Eisteddfod or other major events.

o **Two months before**
Book long-distance train and bus tickets for the best deals.

o **Two weeks before**
Confirm opening times and prices for the major sights.

RESOURCES

o **Wales** (www.visitwales.co.uk)

o **Cardiff** (www.visitcardiff.com)

o **Snowdonia** (www.visitsnowdonia.info)

o **Snowdonia National Park** (www.eryri-npa.co.uk; www.pembrokeshirecoast.org.uk)

o **Pembrokeshire** (www.visitpembrokeshire.com)

o **South Wales** (www.visitsouthwales.com)

GETTING AROUND

o **Bus** Long-distance buses between main centres are good; local buses are infrequent in some rural areas.

o **Train** Wales has useful railways through the south and north of the country, plus a number of scenic branch lines.

o **Car** Gives you maximum freedom, but many roads are narrow and twisting; don't aim on getting anywhere in a hurry.

BE FOREWARNED

o **Festivals**
Accommodation is practically impossible to find during major events such as the Eisteddfod and the Hay Festival. If you're not coming for the festivals, you're better off avoiding these towns at these times.

o **Welsh** In some parts of Wales (but not all) the first language is Welsh. Trying a few words can help break the ice, but remember not everyone's a Welsh-speaker! Try: *sul mae* (pronounced 'sit mai') – hello; *bore da* ('boray da') – good morning; *diolch* ('dee-olkh') – thanks; and *hwyl fawr* ('hueyl vowrr') – goodbye.

Left: Hay-on-Wye (p280);
Above: Dylan Thomas boathouse, Laugharne (p276)

(LEFT) VISITBRITAIN/BRITAIN ON VIEW/GETTY IMAGES ©;
(ABOVE) ROBERT MORRIS/ALAMY ©

267

Wales Itineraries

Our three-day trip runs along the southern edge of Wales, while the five-day option heads up through the borders to the mountains and castles of the north. The routes intersect at Cardiff.

3 DAYS

BRISTOL TO ST DAVIDS

City to Coast

From southwest England's largest city, **(1) Bristol**, head across the Severn Bridge into Wales and start your tour with a visit to the Wye Valley and the romantic ruins of **(2) Tintern Abbey**, immortalised in a William Wordsworth poem.

Continue west to **(3) Cardiff**, the dynamic Welsh capital. The city has plenty of diversions, especially around revitalised Cardiff Bay, which is home to the Wales Millennium Centre and the Welsh Parliament building. Rugby fans may want to visit the Millennium Stadium in the city centre, and everyone should catch the sunset from Cardiff Castle.

After the city, head out along the south coast into the national park of the **(4) Pembrokeshire Coast**, known for its stunning coastal scenery, clifftop walks and world-class surf. Wind your way along the coast all the way to the tiny city of **(5) St Davids** and its fine cathedral.

Top Left: North Beach, Pembrokeshire Coast (p277);
Top Right: Caernarfon (p286)

(TOP LEFT) HUW JONES/GETTY IMAGES ©; (TOP RIGHT) JIM RICHARDSON/CORBIS ©

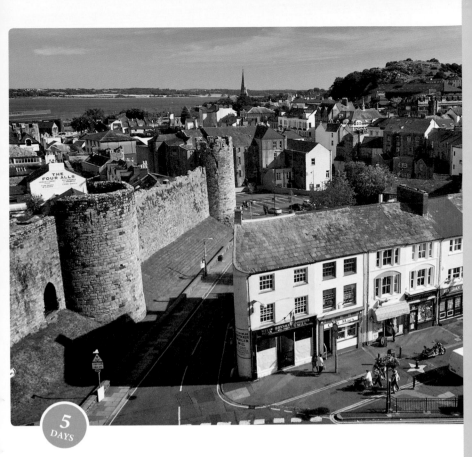

5 DAYS

CARDIFF TO CAERNARFON

Welsh Wonders

Start your tour in **(1) Cardiff**, the capital of Wales. On day two head north via the impressive monuments of **(2) Caerphilly** and **(3) Castell Coch**, both awash with local history. A little further north is the eccentric border town of **(4) Hay-on-Wye**, famous for its population of over 30 secondhand bookshops, and its celebrated annual literary festival.

Next stop is the coastal town of Machynlleth and the nearby **(5) Centre for Alternative Technology**, where you can check out a selection of ingenious solutions tackling our future energy needs. Then it's on into the mountainous landscape of Snowdonia National Park, centring on the windswept peak of **(6) Snowdon**, where you'll find hiking trails aplenty and a historic mountain railway.

On the edge of the park sit four sturdy fortresses, together forming a World Heritage Site. Base yourself in **(7) Caernarfon**, and make day trips to visit nearby Conwy Castle and Harlech Castle. Finish up with some more outlandish architecture at **(8) Portmeirion**, a fantasy land of turrets, follies and multicoloured buildings made famous by *The Prisoner*.

Discover Wales

Gower Peninsula (p275)
THOMAS STANKIEWICZ/GETTY IMAGES ©

CARDIFF (CAERDYDD)

POP 324,800

The capital of Wales since only 1955, Cardiff has embraced its new role with vigour, emerging as one of Britain's leading urban centres in the 21st century. Caught between an ancient fort and an ultramodern waterfront, this compact city seems to have surprised even itself with how interesting it has become. This new-found confidence is infectious; people now travel to Cardiff for a good night out, bringing with them a buzz that reverberates through the streets.

 Sights

Central Cardiff

CARDIFF CASTLE   Castle

(www.cardiffcastle.com; Castle St; adult/child £11/8.50, incl guided tour £14/11; ⊙9am-5pm) The grafting of Victorian mock-Gothic extravagance onto Cardiff's most important historical relics makes Cardiff Castle the city's leading attraction. It's far from a traditional Welsh castle, more a collection of disparate castles scattered around a central green, which encompass practically the entire history of Cardiff. The most conventionally castlelike bits are the 12th-century motte-and-bailey **Norman keep** at its centre and the 13th-century **Black Tower**, which forms the entrance gate. A 50-minute guided tour takes you through the interiors of this flamboyant fantasy world.

FREE **NATIONAL MUSEUM CARDIFF**   Museum

(www.museumwales.ac.uk; Gorsedd Gardens Rd; ⊙10am-5pm Tue-Sun) Cardiff's Civic

Centre is an early-20th-century complex of neobaroque buildings in gleaming white Portland stone, set around green lawns and colourful flower beds. They include the **City Hall**, police headquarters, law courts, crown offices, Cardiff University and this excellent museum, one of Britain's best, which covers natural history, archaeology and art.

MILLENNIUM STADIUM   Stadium
(☎029-2082 2228; www.millenniumstadium.com; Westgate St; tours adult/child £7.50/4.95; ⏱10am-5pm) The spectacular Millennium Stadium squats like a stranded spaceship on the River Taff's east bank. It's well worth taking a tour – you get to run through the players' tunnel and sit in the VIP box.

Cardiff Bay

CARDIFF BAY WATERFRONT   Waterfront
Lined with important national institutions, Cardiff Bay is where the modern Welsh nation is put on display in an architect's playground of interesting buildings, large open spaces and public art. Since 1987 the area has been completely redeveloped.

DOCTOR WHO UP CLOSE   Exhibition
(☎0844 801 3663; www.doctorwhoexhibitions.com; Porth Teigr; adult/child £15/11; ⏱10am-5pm Wed-Mon, daily school holidays) The huge success of the reinvented classic TV series *Doctor Who*, produced by BBC Wales, has brought Cardiff to the attention of sci-fi fans worldwide. Capitalising on Time Lord tourism, this interactive exhibition is located right next to the BBC studios where the series is filmed – look for the Tardis hovering outside.

FREE **SENEDD (NATIONAL ASSEMBLY BUILDING)**   Notable Building
(☎0845 010 5500; www.assemblywales.org; ⏱10.30am-4.30pm Fri-Mon, 8am-end of business Tue-Thu) Designed by Lord Richard Rogers (the architect behind London's Lloyd's Building and Paris' Pompidou Centre), the Senedd is a striking waterfront structure of concrete, slate, glass and steel, with an undulating canopy roof lined with red cedar. Free tours are at

11am daily, with extra tours from Thursday to Monday at 2pm and 3pm.

 **Sleeping**

PARK PLAZA   Hotel ££
(☎029-2011 1111; www.parkplazacardiff.com; Greyfriars Rd; r from £99; ☀) Luxurious without being remotely stuffy, the Plaza has all the facilities you'd expect from an upmarket business-oriented hotel (including a gym, pool and sauna). The rear rooms have leafy views over the Civic Centre.

PARC HOTEL   Hotel ££
(☎0871 376 9011; www.thistle.com/theparchotel; Park Pl; s/d from £74/79; @ ☎) Parc Hotel is a smart contemporary hotel in an elegant French-chateau-style shell, situated right in the heart of the main shopping area. It has tastefully decorated rooms, good facilities and helpful staff; use of a neighbouring gym, spa and sauna is included in the rates.

JOLYONS BOUTIQUE HOTEL   Hotel ££
(☎029-2048 8775; www.jolyons.co.uk; 5 Bute Cres; r from £76; ☎) A touch of Georgian elegance in the heart of Cardiff Bay, Jolyons has six individually designed rooms combining antique furniture with contemporary colours and crisp cotton sheets.

 Eating

RIVERSIDE REAL FOODMARKET   Market £
(www.riversidemarket.org.uk; Fitzhamon Embankment; ⏱10am-2pm Sun) What it lacks in size, the Riverside market makes up for in sheer yumminess, its stalls heaving with cooked meals, cakes, cheese, organic meat, charcuterie, apple juice and real ale.

ZERODEGREES   Italian ££
(www.zerodegrees.co.uk; 27 Westgate St; mains £8-16) Housed within a big, factory-like space, this microbrewery and restaurant combines all-day food with lip-smacking artisan-crafted beers.

Central Cardiff

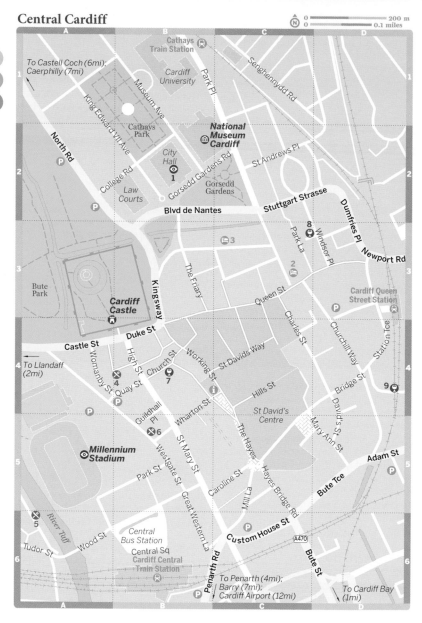

200 m
0.1 miles

To Castell Coch (6mi);
Caerphilly (7mi)

Cathays
Train Station

Cardiff
University

Cardiff
Cathays
Park

**National
Museum
Cardiff**

City
Hall
1

Law
Courts

Gorsedd
Gardens

Blvd de Nantes

Stuttgart Strasse

St Andrews Pl

Dumfries Pl

Newport Rd

8

Bute
Park

3

The Friary

2

Queen St

Cardiff Queen
Street Station

**Cardiff
Castle**

Kingsway

Duke St

Castle St

Charles St

Churchill Way

Station Tce

To Llandaff
(2mi)

High St

Womanby St

Quay St

Church St

Working St

St Davids Way

Hills St

Bridge St

9

4

7

Wharton St

St David's
Centre

Mary Ann St

David's St

Guildhall
Pl

6

Westgate St

St Mary St

The Hayes

Adam St

Bute Tce

**Millennium
Stadium**

Park St

Great Western La

Caroline St

Mill La

Hayes Bridge Rd

5

River Taff

Wood St

Central
Bus Station

Central Sq
Cardiff Central
Train Station

Custom House St

A470

Bute St

Tudor St

Penarth Rd

To Penarth (4mi);
Barry (7mi);
Cardiff Airport (12mi)

To Cardiff Bay
(1mi)

MADAME FROMAGE   Deli, Cafe £
(www.madamefromage.co.uk; 18 Castle Arcade;
mains £7-11; ⊙lunch) One of Cardiff's best
delis, with a range of charcuterie and
French and Welsh cheeses; there is also a
cafe with tables spilling into the arcade.

**WOODS BAR &
BRASSERIE**   Modern European ££
(☏029-2049 2400; www.knifeandforkfood.
co.uk; Stuart St; mains £11-16; ⊙lunch daily, dinner Mon-Sat) The historic Pilotage Building
has been given a modern makeover –

involving zany wallpaper, exposed stone walls and a floor-to-ceiling glass extension – to accommodate Cardiff Bay's best restaurant.

 **Drinking**

GWDIHW Bar
(www.gwdihw.co.uk; 6 Guildford Cres) The last word in Cardiff hipster-dom, this cute little bar has an eclectic line-up of entertainment (comedy nights, cake and craft markets, ukelele jams and lots of other live music, including micro-festivals that spill over into the car park), but it's a completely charming place to stop for a drink at any time.

BUFFALO BAR Bar
(www.myspace.com/wearebuffalobar; 11 Windsor Pl) A haven for cool kids about town, the laid-back

Buffalo features retro furniture, tasty daytime food, life-affirming cocktails and alternative tunes.

10 FEET TALL Bar
(www.10feettallcardiff.com; 12 Church St) The sister property to Buffalo Bar, this hip venue over three floors is a cafe, cocktail and tapas bar, and live-music venue.

ℹ Information

Cardiff Tourist Office (📞029-2087 3573; www.visitcardiff.com; The Hayes, Old Library; 🕑9.30am-5.30pm Mon-Sat, 10am-4pm Sun)

ℹ Getting There & Away

Arriva Trains Wales (www.arrivatrainswales.co.uk) operates all train services in Wales. Direct services from Cardiff include London Paddington (£39, 2¼ hours), Swansea (£7.70, 50 minutes), Fishguard Harbour (£22, three hours), Abergavenny (£12, 40 minutes) and Bangor (£75, 4¼ hours).

Millennium Stadium (p271)
SKYSCAN/CORBIS ©

ARCHITECT: JONATHON ADAMS; PHOTOGRAPHER: ARCAID/GETTY IMAGES ©

Don't Miss **Wales Millennium Centre**

The centrepiece and symbol of Cardiff Bay's regeneration is the superb Wales Millennium Centre, an architectural masterpiece of stacked Welsh slate in shades of purple, green and grey topped with an overarching bronzed steel shell. Designed by Welsh architect Jonathan Adams, it opened in 2004 as Wales' premier arts complex.

The roof above the main entrance is pierced by 2m-high, letter-shaped windows, spectacularly backlit at night, that spell out phrases from poet Gwyneth Lewis: 'Creu Gwir fel Gwydr o Ffwrnais Awen' (Creating truth like glass from inspiration's furnace) and 'In these stones horizons sing'.

The centre is home to several major cultural organisations, including the Welsh National Opera, National Dance Company, National Orchestra, Academi (Welsh National Literature Promotion Agency), HiJinx Theatre and Ty Cerdd (Music Centre of Wales). You can wander through the public areas at will, or go on an official guided tour that will take you behind the giant letters, onto the main stage and into the dressing rooms, depending on what shows are on.

NEED TO KNOW

📞029-2063 6464; www.wmc.org.uk; Bute Pl; guided tour adult/child £5.50/4.50; ⏰tours 11am & 2.30pm

Around Cardiff
Castell Coch

Cardiff Castle's little brother is perched atop a thickly wooded crag on the northern fringes of the city. Fanciful **Castell Coch** (CADW; 📞029-2081 0101; www.cadw. wales.gov.uk; adult/child £3.80/3.40;

⏰10am-4pm) was the summer retreat of the third marquess of Bute and, like Cardiff Castle, was designed by William Burges in gaudy Victorian Gothic style.

Lady Bute's huge, circular bedroom is pure fantasy: her bed, with crystal globes on the bedposts, sits beneath an extravagantly decorated and mirrored cupola, with 28 painted panels around the walls depicting monkeys (fashionable at the time, apparently, but just plain weird now).

Lord Bute's bedroom is small and plain by comparison, but the octagonal drawing room is another hallucinogenic tour de force. Its walls are painted with scenes from *Aesop's Fables*, the domed ceiling is a flurry of birds and stars, and the fireplace is topped with figures depicting the three ages of men and women.

Caerphilly (Caerffili)

You could be forgiven for thinking that **Caerphilly Castle** (CADW; ☎2088 3143; www.cadw.wales.gov.uk; adult/child £3.60/3.20; ⏰9am-5pm Apr-Oct, 9.30am-4pm Mon-Sat, 11am-4pm Sun Nov-Mar), with its profusion of towers and crenellations reflected in a duck-filled lake, was a film set rather than an ancient monument. While it often is used as a film set, it is also one of Britain's finest examples of a 13th-century fortress with water defences.

Most of the construction was completed between 1268 and 1271 by the powerful English baron Gilbert de Clare, Lord Marcher of Glamorgan (1243–95), in response to the threat of attack by Prince Llywelyn ap Gruffydd, prince of Gwynedd (and the last Welsh prince of Wales), who had already united most of the country under his control. In the 13th century Caerphilly was state of the art, one of the earliest castles to use lakes, bridges and a series of concentric fortifications for defence. To reach the inner court you had to overcome no fewer than three drawbridges, six portcullises and five sets of double gates. Much of what you see today is the result of restoration from 1928 to 1939 by the fourth marquess of Bute.

The easiest way to reach Caerphilly from Cardiff is by train (£3.80, 19 minutes), or you can catch Stagecoach buses A, B and 26 (45 minutes).

Detour:
Gower Peninsula (Y Gŵyr)

With its broad butterscotch beaches, pounding surf, precipitous clifftop walks and rugged, untamed uplands, the Gower Peninsula feels a million miles away from Swansea's urban bustle – yet it's just on the doorstep. This 15-mile-long thumb of land stretching west from Mumbles was designated the UK's first official Area of Outstanding Natural Beauty (AONB) in 1956. The National Trust (NT) owns about three-quarters of the coast, so access for walkers is good. The peninsula also has the best surfing in Wales outside Pembrokeshire.

The main family beaches, patrolled by lifeguards during the summer, are Langland Bay, Caswell Bay and Port Eynon.

SOUTH WALES
Tintern Abbey

The A466 road follows the snaking, steep-sided valley of the River Wye from Chepstow to Monmouth, passing through the straggling village of Tintern. It's a beautiful drive, rendered particularly mysterious when a twilight mist rises from the river and shrouds the illuminated ruins of **Tintern Abbey** (CADW; ☎01291-689251; www.cadw.wales.gov.uk; adult/child £3.60/3.20; ⏰9am-5pm Apr-Oct, 9.30am-4pm Mon-Sat & 11am-4pm Sun Nov-Mar; [P]). The huge abbey church was built between 1269 and 1301, stone shell and its remains surprisingly intact; the finest feature is tracery that once contained the magnificent west windows.

If you take the narrow country lane along the west bank of the Wye, a mile north of the turn-off where the A466 crosses the river into England, and 5 miles north of the abbey, you'll find the Michelin-starred **Crown at Whitebrook** (☎01600-860254; www.crownatwhitebrook.co.uk; Whitebrook; 2-/3-course lunch £25/28, 3-/6-/9-course dinner £48/55/70; ☺closed Sun dinner). The food is astonishingly good – inventive, intricately crafted and delicious. If you don't fancy driving afterwards, or the romantic ambience has worked its magic, get a room (single/double from £100/145).

Laugharne (Talacharn)

POP 2900

Sleepy little Laugharne (pronounced 'larn') sits above the tide-washed shores of the Taf Estuary, overlooked by a Norman castle. Dylan Thomas, one of Wales' greatest writers, spent the last four years of his life here, during which time he produced some of his most inspired work, including *Under Milk Wood;* the town is one of the inspirations for the play's fictional village of Llareggub (spell it backwards and you'll get the gist).

 Sights

DYLAN THOMAS
BOATHOUSE   Museum

(www.dylanthomasboathouse.com; Dylan's Walk; adult/child £4/1.95; ☺10am-5.30pm May-Oct, to 3.30pm Nov-Apr) Dylan Thomas lived here from 1949 to 1953 with his wife Caitlin and their three children. The parlour has been restored to its 1950s appearance, with the desk that once belonged to Thomas' schoolmaster father and recordings of the poet reading his own works. Upstairs are photographs, manuscripts, a short video about his life, and his death mask, which once belonged to Richard Burton. Downstairs is a cafe.

Along the lane from the Boathouse is the old shed where Thomas did most of his writing. It looks as if he has just

Left: Pembrokeshire Coast National Park;
Below: Puffin, Pembrokeshire Coast National Park
(LEFT) LATITUDESTOCK - TTL/GETTY IMAGES ©: (BELOW) PHOTONTRAPPIST/GETTY IMAGES ©

popped out, with screwed-up pieces of paper littered around.

Dylan and Caitlin Thomas are buried in a grave marked by a simple white, wooden cross in the grounds of **St Martin's Church**, on the northern edge of the town.

🛏 Sleeping & Eating

BOAT HOUSE   B&B **££**
(☎ 01994-427263; www.theboathousebnb.co.uk; 1 Gosport St; s/d from £40/70; @ 🛜) Friendly, homely and tastefully decorated, this is the smartest B&B in town. The building was formerly the Corporation Arms pub, where Dylan Thomas told stories in exchange for free drinks.

HURST HOUSE ON THE MARSH   Hotel **£££**
(☎ 01994-427417; www.hurst-house.co.uk; East Marsh; r £225; P 🛜 🏊) Having had a £5-million makeover, you would expect this converted Georgian farm on the salt-marsh flats south of Laugharne to be luxurious. Rooms have big beds, bold colours and roll-top baths, there's massage therapy on tap, and a convivial, clubbish lounge bar and restaurant.

PEMBROKESHIRE COAST NATIONAL PARK

Established in 1952, Pembrokeshire Coast National Park (Parc Cenedlaethol Arfordir Sir Benfro) takes in almost the entire coast and its offshore islands, as well as the Preseli Hills in the north and the inland waters of the Cleddau rivers near Milford Haven. Pembrokeshire's sea cliffs and islands support huge breeding populations of seabirds, while seals, dolphins, porpoises and whales are frequently spotted in coastal waters.

277

St Davids (Tyddewi)

POP 1800

Charismatic St Davids (yes, it has dropped the apostrophe from its name) is Britain's smallest city, its status ensured by the magnificent 12th-century cathedral that marks Wales' holiest site. The birth and burial site of the nation's patron saint, St Davids has been a place of pilgrimage for 1500 years.

◉ Sights & Activities

ST DAVIDS CATHEDRAL Church
(www.stdavidscathedral.org.uk; suggested donation £3) Hidden in a hollow and behind high walls, St Davids Cathedral is intentionally unassuming. The valley site was chosen in the vain hope that the church would be overlooked by Viking raiders, but it was ransacked at least seven times. Built on the site of a 6th-century chapel, the building dates mainly from the 12th to the 14th centuries.

BISHOP'S PALACE Ruin
(www.cadw.wales.gov.uk; adult/child £3.20/2.80; ◷10am-4pm) Across the river from the cathedral, this atmospheric ruined palace was begun at the same time as the cathedral, but its final, imposing form owes most to Henry de Gower, bishop from 1327 to 1347.

🖋 RAMSEY ISLAND Wildlife Reserve
Ramsey Island lies off the headland to the west of St Davids, ringed by dramatic sea cliffs and an offshore armada of rocky islets and reefs. The island is a Royal Society for the Protection of Birds (RSPB) reserve famous for its large breeding population of choughs – members of the crow family with glossy black feathers and distinctive red bills and legs – and for its grey seals.

Thousand Islands Expeditions
(☎01437-721721; www.thousandislands.co.uk; Cross Sq) is the only operator permitted to land day trippers on the island (adult/child £15/7.50). It has a range of other boat trips, including 2½-hour whale- and dolphin-spotting cruises (£60/30) and one-hour jet-boat trips (£25/10).

Voyages of Discovery (☎01437-721911; www.ramseyisland.co.uk; 1 High St) and **Aquaphobia** (☎01437-720471; www.aquaphobia-ramseyisland.co.uk; Grove Hotel, High St) offer a similar selection of cruises.

🛏 Sleeping

RAMSEY HOUSE B&B ££
(☎01437-720321; www.ramseyhouse.co.uk; Lower Moor; r £100; P🛜) The young owners have fashioned a fresh-looking B&B from their new house on the outskirts of town, which is still only a short stroll west from the centre.

St Davids Cathedral

ALANDALE
B&B ££

(📞01437-720404; www.stdavids.co.uk/guest house/alandale.htm; 43 Nun St; s/d £36/90; @🛜) A neat terraced house built in the 1880s for coastguard officers, Alandale has a bright, cheerful atmosphere – ask for one of the rooms at the back, which are quieter and have sweeping countryside views.

 Eating & Drinking

CWTCH
Modern Welsh £££

(📞01437-720491; www.cwtchrestaurant.co.uk; 22 High St; 2/3 courses £24/30; 🕐dinner Tue-Sat, daily high season) Stone walls and wooden beams mark this out as a sense-of-occasion place, as indeed does the price, yet there's a snugness that lives up to its name (*cwtch* means a cosy place or a cuddle).

SAMPLER
Teahouse £

(www.sampler-tearoom.co.uk; 17 Nun St; mains $5-7; 🕐lunch Mon-Thu, extended hours in high season) Named after the embroidery samples blanketing the walls, this may be the perfect exemplar of the traditional Welsh tearoom.

FARMER'S ARMS
Pub

(www.farmersstdavids.co.uk; 14 Goat St; mains £8-10) Even though St Davids is a bit of a tourist trap, you'd be hard-pressed finding a more authentic country pub. There's real ale and Guinness on tap, decent pub grub, and it's the place to be when the rugby's playing.

ℹ Information

National Trust Visitor Centre (📞01437-720385; High St; 🕐10am-5.30pm Mon-Sat, 10am-4pm Sun mid-Mar–Dec, 10am-4pm Mon-Sat Jan–mid-Mar)

Preseli Hills

The only upland area in the Pembrokeshire Coast National Park is the Preseli Hills (Mynydd Preseli), rising to 536m at Foel Cwmcerwyn. These hills are at the centre of a fascinating prehistoric landscape, scattered with hill forts, standing stones and burial chambers, and are famous as the source of the mysterious bluestones of Stonehenge. An ancient track called the **Golden Road**, once part of a 5000-year-old trade route between Wessex and Ireland, runs along the crest of the hills, passing prehistoric cairns and the stone circle of **Bedd Arthur**.

The largest dolmen in Wales, **Pentre Ifan** is a 4500-year-old neolithic burial chamber set on a remote hillside three miles southeast of Newport, signposted from the A487. The huge, 5m-long capstone, weighing more than 16 tonnes, is delicately poised on three upright bluestones.

MID-WALES
Brecon Beacons National Park

Rippling dramatically for 45 miles from Llandeilo in the west, all the way to the English border, Brecon Beacons National Park (Parc Cenedlaethol Bannau Brycheiniog) encompasses some of the finest scenery in Mid-Wales. High mountain plateaux of grass and heather, their northern rims scalloped with glacier-scoured hollows, rise above wooded, waterfall-splashed valleys and green, rural landscapes. It couldn't be more different than rock-strewn Snowdonia to the north, but it offers comparable thrills.

There are hundreds of walking routes in the park, ranging from gentle strolls to strenuous climbs. The park's staff organise guided walks and other active events throughout the summer. Maps and walk cards are available from the tourist offices of all the towns in and around the park, as well as the main park visitor centre (p279) near Libanus.

ℹ Information

National Park Visitor Centre (📞01874-623366; www.breconbeacons.org; Libanus; 🕐9.30am-5pm) The centre is off the A470 road, 5 miles southwest of Brecon and 15 miles north of Merthyr Tydfil.

Detour:
Centre for Alternative Technology

Founded in 1974, the **Centre for Alternative Technology** (CAT; ☎01654-705950; www.cat.org.uk; adult/child £8.50/4; ⏱10am-5.30pm) is a virtually self-sufficient workers' cooperative which acts as an ecologically driven laboratory and information source for alternative technologies. There are more than 3 hectares of displays dealing with topics such as composting, organic gardening, environmentally friendly construction, renewable energy sources, sewage treatment and recycling. It has about 130 on-site workers and 15 full-time residents. To explore the whole site takes about two hours – take rainwear as it's primarily outdoors. Kids love the interactive displays and adventure playground.

The site is about 3 miles from the village of Machynlleth.

Hay-on-Wye (Y Gelli Gandryll)
POP 1500

This pretty little town on the banks of the River Wye, just inside the Welsh border, has developed a reputation disproportionate to its size. Since the 1960s it's become the world's secondhand book capital, and now hosts the UK's largest and most prestigious **literary festival** in late May. The small town centre is made up of narrow sloping lanes, generously peppered with interesting shops, and peopled by the differing types that such individuality and so many books tend to attract.

 Sleeping & Eating

START   B&B ££
(☎01497-821391; www.the-start.net; Bridge St; r from £70; [P][☎]) Peacefully set on the fringes of town, this little three-bedroom place boasts an unbeatable riverside setting with beautiful gardens, homely rooms in a renovated 18th-century house and a flagstone-floored breakfast room.

BEAR   B&B ££
(☎01497-821302; www.thebearhay.co.uk; 2 Bear St; r £90, s/d without bathroom £50/70; [P][☎]) Beautifully renovated by its young owners, this 1590 coaching inn retains its historic ambience but combines it with interesting art, sisal floors, modern bathrooms and bright white walls.

THREE TUNS   Pub ££
(☎01497-821855; www.three-tuns.com; Broad St; mains £12-18) Hay's gastronomic heavyweight, this 16th-century pub has a large garden area for alfresco food and a fancier restaurant upstairs. The sophisticated international menu follows that dependable modern mantra: local, organic and sustainable.

SHEPHERDS ICE CREAM PARLOUR   Ice Cream £
(www.shepherdsicecream.co.uk; 9 High Town; single scoop £1.50; ⏱9.30am-5.30pm) Nobody should leave Hay without trying the homemade ice cream from Shepherds. It's made from sheep's milk, for a lighter, smoother taste.

🛍 Shopping

There are 23 secondhand and antiquarian bookshops in Hay, with hundreds of thousands of tomes stacked floor to ceiling across town.

RICHARD BOOTH'S BOOKSHOP   Books
(www.boothbooks.co.uk; 44 Lion St) The most well known, and still the best, with an excellent cafe.

ℹ️ Information

Tourist office (📞01497-820144; www.hay-on-wye.co.uk; Oxford Rd; 🕐10am-5pm Apr-Oct, 11am-1pm Nov-Mar)

SNOWDONIA NATIONAL PARK

Snowdonia National Park (Parc Cenedlaethol Eryri; www.eryri-npa.gov.uk) was founded in 1951 (making it Wales' first national park), primarily to keep the area from being loved to death. This is, after all, Wales' best known and most heavily used slice of nature, with the busiest part around Snowdon (1085m) itself. Around 350,000 people climb, walk or take the train to the summit each year, and all those sturdy shoes make trail maintenance a never-ending task for park staff.

The Welsh name for Snowdonia is Eryri (eh-*ruh*-ree) meaning 'highlands'. The Welsh call Snowdon itself Yr Wyddfa (uhr-*with*-vuh), meaning 'Great Tomb' – according to legend a giant called Rita Gawr was slain here by King Arthur and is buried at the summit.

Watkin Path (p284), Snowdon

The park authority publishes a free annual visitor newspaper, which includes information on getting around, park-organised walks and other activities.

Betws-y-Coed

POP 2030

If you're looking for a base with an Alpine feel from which to explore Snowdonia National Park, the bustling little stone village of Betws-y-Coed (*bet-us-ee-koyd*) stands out as a natural option.

◎ Sights & Activities

SWALLOW FALLS   Waterfall
(adult/child £1.50/0.50) Betws-y-Coed's main natural tourist trap is located 2 miles west of town alongside the A5. It's a beautiful spot, with the torrent weaving through the rocks into a green pool below.

GWYDYR FOREST   Walking, Cycling
The 28-sq-mile Gwydyr Forest, planted since the 1920s with oak, beech and larch, encircles Betws-y-Coed and is scattered with the crumbling remnants of lead

ALASDAIR THOMSON/GETTY IMAGES ©

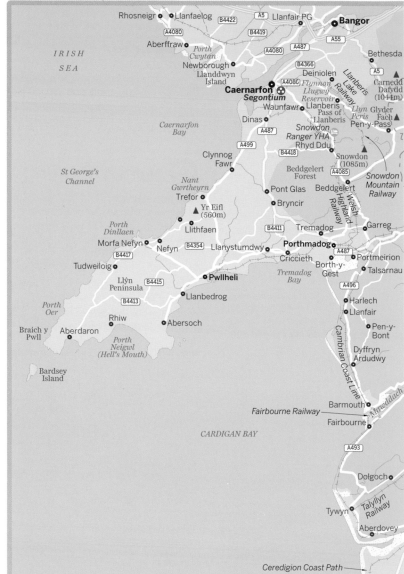

and zinc mine workings. It's ideal for a day's walking, though it gets very muddy in wet weather *Walks Around Betws-y-Coed* (£4.95), available from the National Park Information Centre, details several circular forest walks.

🛏 Sleeping & Eating

TY GWYN HOTEL Hotel ££
(📞01690-710383; www.tygwynhotel.co.uk;
r £56-130; P 🛜) This ex-coaching inn

AFON GWYN B&B ££

(☏01690-710442; www.guest-house-betws-y-coed.com; A470, Coed-y-Celyn; r £80-118; P)
This old stone house has been skilfully converted into a grand boutique guest house. The decor is faultlessly tasteful, with white-painted wooden panelling, hushed tones, glittering chandeliers and bathrooms bedecked in Italian tiles and marble.

BISTRO BETWS-Y-COED Restaurant ££

(☏01690-710328; www.bistrobetws-y-coed.com; Holyhead Rd; lunch £6-9, dinner £13-17; ⏱Wed-Sun, daily high season) This cottage-style eatery's statement of intent is 'modern and traditional Welsh'. It gets absolutely packed in summer: book ahead if you want to sample its locally made sausages, pheasant, and haddock and chips battered with Llandudno Orme real ale.

❶ Information

National Park Information Centre (☏01690-710426; www.betws-y-coed.co.uk; Royal Oak Stables; ⏱9.30am-5.30pm Easter-Oct, to 4.30pm rest of year)

❶ Getting There & Away

Betws-y-Coed is on the Conwy Valley Line (www.conwyvalleyrailway.co.uk), with six daily services (three on Sunday) to Llandudno (£5.60, 52 minutes) and Blaenau Ffestiniog (£4.50, 27 minutes).

Capel Curig
POP 200

Tiny Capel Curig, 5 miles west of Betws-y-Coed, is one of Snowdonia's oldest hill stations, and has long been a magnet for walkers, climbers and other outdoor junkies. The village spreads out along the A5, but the main clump of activity is at the intersection of the A4086. It's a heady setting, ringed by looming mountains.

The **Plas y Brenin** (☏01690-720214; www.pyb.co.uk), at the western edge of the village, is a multi-activity centre offering an array of residential courses including rock climbing, mountaineering, kayaking and canoeing. Taster days run throughout the school holidays with an introduction to two activities for £35.

has been welcoming guests since 1636, its venerable age borne out by misshapen rooms, low ceilings and exposed beams. Predictably, not all rooms have en suites.

Snowdon

No Snowdonia experience is complete without coming face-to-face with Snowdon (1085m), one of Britain's most awe-inspiring mountains and the highest in Wales. On a clear day the views stretch to Ireland and the Isle of Man over Snowdon's fine jagged ridges, which drop away in great swoops to sheltered cwms (valleys) and deep lakes. Even on a gloomy day you could find yourself above the clouds. Thanks to the Snowdon Mountain Railway it's extremely accessible – however, the summit and some of the walking trails can get frustratingly crowded.

 **Sights & Activities**

Climbing Snowdon

Six paths of varying length and difficulty lead to the summit, all taking around six hours return. Simplest (and dullest) is the **Llanberis Path** (9 miles return) running beside the railway line. The **Snowdon Ranger Path** (8 miles), starting at the Snowdon Ranger YHA, is also straightforward and tends to be less busy than Llanberis.

The two options which start from Pen-y-Pass require the least amount of ascent: the **Miner's Track** (7 miles) starts out gently but ends steeply; the **Pyg Track** (7 miles) is more interesting and meets the Miner's Track where it steepens.

The straightforward **Rhyd Ddu Path** (8 miles) is the least used route; the trailhead is on the Caernarfon–Beddgelert road (A4085).

Most challenging is the **Watkin Path** (8 miles), involving an ascent of more than 1000m on its southerly approach from Nantgwynant, and finishing with a scramble across a steep-sided scree-covered slope.

Make sure you're well prepared with warm, waterproof clothing and sturdy footwear. Check the weather forecast before setting out.

Snowdon by Rail

SNOWDON MOUNTAIN RAILWAY Railway
(☏ 0844 493 8120; www.snowdonrailway.co.uk; return adult/child £25/18; ☺ 9am-5pm mid-Mar–

Snowdon

ELI PASCALL-WILLIS/GETTY IMAGES ©

Oct) Those industrious, railway-obsessed Victorians have gifted today's visitors with an alternative to a three-hour mountain walk (six hours return): the UK's highest and only public rack-and-pinion railway, opened in 1896. Vintage steam and modern diesel locomotives haul carriages from Llanberis up to Snowdon's very summit in an hour. Return trips involve a scant half hour at the top before heading back down again. Single tickets can only be booked for the journey up (adult/child £18/15). Thousands of people take the train to the summit each season: make sure you book well in advance or you may miss out. Departures are also weather dependent and from March to May the trains can only head as far as Clogwyn Station (adult/child £19/15) – an altitude of 779m.

 ## Sleeping

PEN-Y-GWYRD — Hotel £
(📞01286-870211; www.pyg.co.uk; Nant Gwynant; r with/without bathroom 50/42) Eccentric but full of atmosphere, Pen-y-Gwryd was used as a training base by the 1953 Everest team, and memorabilia from their stay includes their signatures on the dining-room ceiling. At the time of writing the hotel was closed for renovations. You'll find it 5 miles southeast of Llanberis, at the junction of the A498 and A4086.

ℹ️ Information

Hafod Eryri Just below the cairn that marks Snowdon's summit, this striking piece of architecture opened in 2009 to replace the dilapidated 1930s visitor centre which Prince Charles famously labelled 'the highest slum in Europe'.

ℹ️ Getting There & Away

The Welsh Highland Railway stops at the trailhead of the Rhyd Ddu path, and there is a request stop (Snowdon Ranger Halt) where you can alight for the Snowdon Ranger path.

Dolgellau
POP 2400

Dolgellau is a charming little market town, steeped in history and boasting the highest concentration of listed buildings in Wales. It was a regional centre for Wales' prosperous wool industry in the 18th and early 19th centuries, and many of its finest buildings, sturdy and unornamented, were built at that time.

 ## Sleeping

FFYNNON — B&B £££
(📞01341-421774; www.ffynnontownhouse.com; Love Lane; s/d from £100/145; P 🛜) With a keen eye for contemporary design and a superfriendly welcome, this first-rate boutique guest house feels both homely and stylish.

BRYN MAIR HOUSE — B&B ££
(📞01341-422640; www.brynmairbedandbreakfast.co.uk; Love Lane; s/d from £75/95; P 🛜) On wistfully monikered Love Lane, this is an impressive stone house – a former Georgian rectory no less. Its three comfortable B&B rooms are all kitted out with DVDs and iPod docks; room 1 has sublime mountain views.

Eating

T. H. ROBERTS — Cafe £
(Glyndŵr St, Parliament House; mains £4-6; ⏰9.30am-5.30pm Mon-Sat; 🛜) It's easy to walk past this atmospheric Grade II–listed coffee shop, as it still looks exactly like the ironmonger's shop that it once was, with its original counter, glass cabinets, wooden drawers and other fittings.

MAWDDACH RESTAURANT & BAR — Modern Welsh ££
(📞01341-424020; www.mawddach.com; Llanelltyd; mains £11-17; ⏰lunch Wed-Sun, dinner Wed-Sat) Located 2 miles west of Dolgellau on the A496, Mawddach brings a touch of urban style to what was once a barn. The food is equally impressive: meat straight from nearby

If You Like...
Welsh Castles

After visiting Caerphilly (p275) and Caernarfon, there are plenty more fantastic fortresses to explore around Wales.

1 CONWY CASTLE
(CADW; adult/child £4.80/4.30; ⏰9.30am-6pm Jul & Aug, 9.30am-5pm Mar-Jun, Sep & Oct, 10am-4pm Mon-Sat, 11am-4pm Sun Nov-Feb) The most stunning of Edward I's Welsh fortresses, built between 1277 and 1307, Conwy Castle rises from a rocky outcrop with commanding views across the estuary and Snowdonia National Park.

2 HARLECH CASTLE
(CADW; adult/child £3.80/3.40; ⏰9.30am-6pm Jul & Aug, 9.30am-5pm Mar-Jun & Sep-Oct, 10am-4pm Mon-Sat, 11am-4pm Sun Nov-Feb) Edward I finished this intimidating building in 1289, the southernmost of his 'iron ring' of fortresses. Despite its might, the story book fortress has been called the 'Castle of Lost Causes' because it has been lucklessly defended so many times.

3 CARREG CENNEN
(www.carregcennencastle.com; adult/child £4/3.50; ⏰9.30am-6.30pm Apr-Oct, to 4pm Nov-Mar) Perched atop a steep limestone crag high above the River Cennen is Wales' ultimate romantic ruined castle, visible for miles in every direction. It's signposted from the A483, heading south from Llandeilo.

4 BEAUMARIS CASTLE
(CADW; adult/child £3.80/3.40; ⏰9.30am-6pm Jul & Aug, 9.30am-5pm Apr-Jun, Sep & Oct, 10am-4pm Mon-Sat, 11am-4pm Sun Nov-Mar) Sited on the island of Anglesey, and a World Heritage Site, Beaumaris Castle is another of Edward I's coastal fortresses, and with its stout walls and arrow slits it definitely has the 'wow' factor. Anglesey is easily reached from nearby Bangor.

farms, fresh local fish specials and traditional Sunday roasts (two/three courses £14.50/18.50).

ⓘ Information

Tourist Office & National Park Information Centre (☎01341-422888; Eldon Sq; ⏰9.30am-12.30pm & 1-5.30pm)

NORTH WALES
Caernarfon
POP 9700

Wedged between the gleaming Menai Strait and the deep purple mountains of Snowdonia, Caernarfon is home to a fantastical castle, its main claim to fame.

 Sights & Activities

CAERNARFON CASTLE Castle, Museum
(CADW; adult/child/family £5.25/4.85/15.35; ⏰9.30am-6pm Jul & Aug, 9.30am-5pm Apr-Jun, Sep & Oct, 10am-4pm Mon-Sat & 11am-4pm Sun Nov-Mar) Majestic Caernarfon Castle was built between 1283 and 1330 as a military stronghold, a seat of government and a royal palace. Inspired by the dream of Macsen Wledig recounted in the *Mabinogion*, Caernarfon echoes the 5th-century walls of Constantinople, with colour-banded masonry and polygonal towers, instead of the traditional round towers and turrets.

Despite its fairy tale aspect, it is thoroughly fortified. It repelled Owain Glyndŵr's army in 1404 with a garrison of only 28 men, and resisted three sieges during the Civil War before surrendering to Cromwell's army in 1646.

There is an exhibition on the investiture of today's Prince of Wales, HRH Prince Charles, in the **North East Tower**. In the **Queen's Tower** (named after Edward I's wife Eleanor) is the **Regimental Museum of the Royal Welsh Fusiliers**.

Don't Miss **Portmeirion Village**

Portmeirion is a uniquely oddball, gingerbread collection of buildings with a heavy Italian influence, masterminded by the Welsh architect Sir Clough Williams-Ellis. Starting in 1926, Clough collected bits and pieces from disintegrating stately mansions to create this weird and wonderful seaside utopia, designing and building many of the structures himself. Fifty years later, and at the ripe old age of 90, Clough deemed the village to be complete. Today the buildings are all listed and the site is a conservation area.

It's more like a stage set than an actual village; and, indeed, it formed the ideally surreal background for cult TV series *The Prisoner*, which was filmed here from 1966 to 1967.

Portmeirion is 2 miles east of Porthmadog – it's a straightforward walk. Buses aren't great: 98 (five services per day Monday to Saturday) runs nearest, but it's probably easiest to take a **taxi** (☎01766-514799).

NEED TO KNOW
www.portmeirion-village.com; adult/child £10/6; ⏱9.30am-7.30pm

---

FREE **SEGONTIUM ROMAN FORT** Ruin
(www.segontium.org.uk; Ffordd Cwstenin; ⏱12.30-4.30pm Tue-Sun) These stony foundations, dating back to AD 77, represent the westernmost Roman legionary fort of the Roman Empire, which had a crucial strategic position overlooking the Menai Strait. Sadly the museum is closed for the foreseeable future. The site is located about half a mile along the A4085 (to Beddgelert).

Sleeping & Eating

VICTORIA HOUSE B&B ££
(☎01286-678263; www.thevictoriahouse.co.uk; Church St; d £65-80; 📶) Victoria House is an exceptional four-bedroom guest

house with a homely feel, spacious modern rooms and some nice touches, such as an impressive selection of free toiletries and a DVD on the town's history in each room.

BLACK BOY INN B&B ££
(01286-673604; www.black-boy-inn.com; Northgate St; s/d from £65/95; P) Dating from 1522, the creaky but atmospheric rooms at this traditional inn have original wooden beams and panelling but a modern sensibility.

CAER MENAI B&B £
(01286-672612; www.caermenai.co.uk; 15 Church St; s/d from £45/57; @) A former county school (1894), this elegant building is on a quiet street nestling against the western wall. The seven en suite rooms were updated recently, and are fresh, clean and snug; number seven has sunset sea views.

ℹ Information

Tourist office (01286-672232; Castle Ditch; 9.30am-4.30pm Apr-Oct, 10am-3.30pm Mon-Sat Nov-Mar)

ℹ Getting There & Away

Caernarfon is the northern terminus of the Welsh Highland Railway tourist train, which runs to Porthmadog (£33 return, 2½ hours) via Dinas, Waunfawr, Snowdon Ranger, Rhyd Ddu and Beddgelert.

Porthmadog & Around
POP 3000

Despite a few rough edges, busy little Porthmadog (port-*mad*-uk) has charm and a conspicuously friendly populace. It straddles both the Llŷn Peninsula and Snowdonia National Park, and is handy for visits to the fantastical village of Portmeirion.

Left: Parterre Garden, Erddig (p290);
Below: Welsh Highland Railway

(LEFT) JOHN WARBURTON-LEE/GETTY IMAGES ©; (BELOW) GRAHAM BELL/GETTY IMAGES ©

Sights & Activities

FFESTINIOG & WELSH HIGHLAND RAILWAYS
Heritage Railway

(☎ 01766-516024; www.festrail.co.uk) There are 'little trains' all over Wales, a legacy of Victorian industry, but Porthmadog is exceptionally blessed.

The **Ffestiniog Railway (Porthmadog; adult/child return £19.60/17.65)** is a fantastic, twisting and precipitous line that was built between 1832 and 1836 to haul slate down to Porthmadog from the mines at Blaenau Ffestiniog, 13.5 miles away. Saved after years of neglect, it is one of Wales' most spectacular and beautiful narrow-gauge journeys. Nearly all services are steam-hauled.

Its sibling, the **Welsh Highland Railway (Porthmadog; adult/child return £33/29.70)**, is an amalgamation of several late-19th-century slate railways, and runs through equally lovely Snowdonian landscapes.

Sleeping & Eating

HOTEL PORTMEIRION & CASTELL DEUDRAETH
Hotel, Cottage £££

(☎ 01766-770000; www.portmeirion-village. com; Portmeirion; hotel s/d £225/289, castle s/d £199/239, cottage s/d £159/199) You can live the fantasy and stay within the famous fairy-tale village itself. Hotel Portmeirion (1926), overlooking the estuary, has classic, elegant rooms and a dining room designed by Sir Terence Conran.

GOLDEN FLEECE INN
Pub ££

(☎ 01766-512421; www.goldenfleeceinn.com; Market Sq, Tremadog; s/d from £45/65; 🛜) An inviting and friendly old inn with hop flowers hanging from the ceilings, real ales, decent pub grub (mains £4 to £12), and an open fire for cold nights. The rooms are comfortable and atmospheric; however, be prepared for noise until closing, or just join the party.

289

Detour:
Erddig

It might be a little off the beaten track, but the stately home of **Erddig** (NT; ☏01978-355314; www.nationaltrust. org.uk; adult/child £9.90/4.95, grounds only £6.30/3.15; ⏱house 12.30-4.30pm Mar-Nov, 11am-3.30pm Dec-Feb, grounds 11am-5.30pm Mar-Nov, 11am-4pm Dec-Feb, last admission 1hr before closing) is absolutely worth seeking out. This splendid National Trust property offers an illuminating glimpse into 18th-century upper-class life: original artwork and furniture is on display in the fine staterooms, while a formal, walled garden has been restored in Victorian style, and informative tours run twice daily.

Erddig lies 12 miles northeast of Llangollen on the A483 in the village of Rhostyllen.

ⓘ Information

Tourist office (☏01766-512981; High St, Porthmadog; ⏱9.30am-5pm Easter-Oct, 10am-3.30pm Mon-Sat Nov-Easter)

ⓘ Getting There & Away

Porthmadog is on the Cambrian Coast line, with direct trains to Harlech (£3, 22 minutes), Barmouth (£6.50, 48 minutes), Fairbourne (£7.30, 58 minutes), Machynlleth (£12.50, 1¾ hours), and in the other direction to Pwllheli (£4.50, 26 minutes). See the Ffestiniog & Welsh Highland Railways (p289) for steam services to Blaenau Ffestiniog, the Snowdon trailheads and Caernarfon.

Llandudno

POP 14,900

Llandudno is a master of reinvention. Developed as an upmarket Victorian holiday town, it still retains much of its 19th-century grandeur, yet continues to find new fans with its booming boutique accommodation, big-name retail outlets, and Welsh art and performance. No wonder the American travel writer Bill Bryson was moved to describe Llandudno as his 'favourite seaside resort'.

◉ Sights & Activities

GREAT ORME COUNTRY PARK
Interpretation Centre
From sea level it's difficult to gauge the sheer scale of the Great Orme, designated a Site of Special Scientific Interest (SSSI). The peak is home to several Neolithic sites, a cornucopia of flowers, butterflies and seabirds, a gang of wild goats, three waymarked summit trails (of which the **Haulfre Gardens Trail** is the easiest stroll to negotiate) and its own **visitor centre** (www.conwy.gov.uk/greatorme; ⏱10am-5.30pm Easter-Oct).

You can walk to the summit; take a ride on the **Great Orme Tramway** (www. greatormetramway.co.uk; adult/child return £5.90/4.10; ⏱10am-6pm Apr-Sep, to 5pm Mar & Oct), a masterpiece of Victorian engineering which leaves every 20 minutes from Church Walks; or ride Britain's longest **cable car** from the Happy Valley Gardens above the pier – departures are weather dependent.

LLANDUDNO PROMENADE & PIER
Waterfront
(⏱pier 9am-6pm) A trip to Llandudno isn't complete until you've strolled along the majestic sweep of the promenade, eating ice cream and shooing away seagulls. Queen Victoria herself watched **Professor Codman's Punch & Judy Show** (⏱2pm & 4pm Easter–mid-Sep), performed by the same family since 1860 – we hope she was amused.

🛏 Sleeping

ESCAPE B&B
Boutique Hotel £££
(☏01492-877776; www.escapebandb.co.uk; 48 Church Walks; r £99-140; P🛜) Escape, Llandudno's first boutique B&B, has nine

five-star rooms decorated in designer style and including a host of energy-saving and trendsetting features.

OSBORNE HOUSE Hotel **£££**
(01492-860330; www.osbornehouse.com; 17 North Pde; ste £145-175; **P** **@**) All marble, antique furniture and fancy drapes, the lavish Osbourne House takes a classical approach to aesthetics, and the results are impressive.

 **Eating & Drinking**

FISH TRAM CHIPS Cafe **£**
(Old Rd; fish & chips £7; noon-3pm & 4.30-7.30pm daily high season, noon-2pm & 5-7.30pm Tue-Sat, noon-2.15pm Sun low season) One of the tastiest and best-value fish suppers in North Wales, Fish Tram Chips is a pretty low-frills place but big on tasty, fresh fish and homemade side dishes with views across to the Great Orme Tramway station.

HAM BONE FOOD HALL & BRASSERIE Deli, Cafe **££**
(Lloyd St; sandwiches £4-7, mains £8-12; 8am-8pm) The best deli-cafe in Llandudno, the Ham Bone has a huge range of freshly made sandwiches, perfect for a picnic on the promenade. At night it becomes a brasserie, with great food made from scratch: pork-and-apple burgers, haddock-and-smoked-ham fishcakes,

huge pizzas, and an ever-changing range of specials.

SEAHORSE Seafood **£££**
(01492-875315; www.the-seahorse.co.uk; 7 Church Walks; mains £19, 2-course menu from £25.50; 5pm-late Tue-Sat) Puzzlingly for a coastal resort, this is Llandudno's only proper seafood restaurant – thankfully it's a good 'un!

Information

Llandudno Tourist Office (01492-577577; www.visitllandudno.org.uk; Mostyn St; 9am-5.30pm Mon-Sat, 9.30am-4.30pm Sun Apr-Oct, 9am-5pm Mon-Sat Nov-Mar)

Getting There & Away

Train

Arriva Trains (www.arrivatrainswales.co.uk) runs services to Holyhead (£12.80, 1½ hours), with a change of train necessary at nearby Llandudno Junction station. It also runs direct services from Llandudno to Blaenau Ffestiniog (£7.70, 1¼ hours) via Betws-y-Coed (£5.60, 40 minutes) on the Conwy Valley line.

The West Coast rail franchise was under review at the time of writing. It was being held temporarily by Virgin Trains (www.virgintrains.co.uk), with several direct services from Llandudno Junction to London Euston (six Monday to Friday, four on weekends).

Edinburgh & Central Scotland

Every visit to Scotland simply has to begin in Edinburgh, the elegant capital. Packed with more history and heritage per square inch than any other Scottish city, it's a place that rewards leisurely wandering – a stroll along the famous Royal Mile, a shopping spree on Princes St, a wander around the smart streets and Georgian squares of the New Town, and a picnic on the grassy lawns of Holyrood Park. And every corner turned reveals unexpected vistas of the Scottish landscape beyond – green hills, a glimpse of crags, a flash of distant sea.

Then it's time to leave the city and venture out to central Scotland's other sights. The neighbouring city of Glasgow offers quirky museums and sublime art nouveau architecture. Stirling tempts with a castle to rival Edinburgh, while Loch Lomond and the Trossachs serve up lake and mountain scenery.

For a final flourish there's St Andrews, the home of golf; Balmoral Castle, the holiday retreat of British monarchs since Victorian times; and glorious Speyside, dotted with dozens of whisky distilleries.

Edinburgh (p306)

Robert the Bruce, Stirling Castle (p328)

Edinburgh & Central Scotland

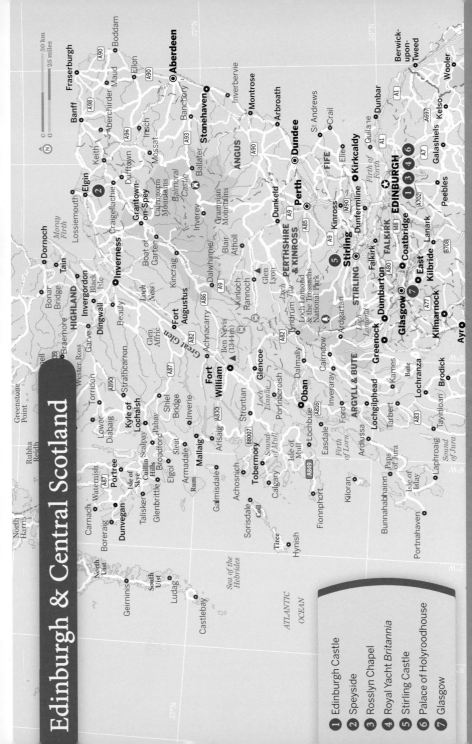

1 Edinburgh Castle
2 Speyside
3 Rosslyn Chapel
4 Royal Yacht *Britannia*
5 Stirling Castle
6 Palace of Holyroodhouse
7 Glasgow

Edinburgh & Central Scotland Highlights

DENNIS K. JOHNSON/GETTY IMAGES ©

①

Edinburgh Castle

The brooding, black crags of Castle Rock are the very reason for Edinburgh's existence – it was the most easily defended hilltop on the invasion route from England. Crowning the crag with a profusion of battlements, Edinburgh Castle is now Scotland's most popular pay-to-enter tourist attraction. Above: Edinburgh Castle; Top Right: Mons Meg Cannon; Bottom Right: St Margaret of Scotland, St Margaret's Chapel

Need to Know

BEST TIME TO VISIT Lunchtime (for the One O'Clock Gun) **SECRET SPOT** The cemetery for officers' dogs **For further coverage, see p306**

Edinburgh Castle Don't Miss List

PETER YEOMAN, HEAD OF CULTURAL HERITAGE AT HISTORIC SCOTLAND

1 HONOURS OF SCOTLAND

The crown, sceptre and sword of state are glittering symbols of our nationhood. They were first used at the coronation of Mary, Queen of Scots in 1543 when she was only nine months old. The centuries-old regalia are displayed in the Royal Palace alongside the Stone of Destiny.

2 ST MARGARET'S CHAPEL

The oldest building in the castle is a wee gem, possibly part of a tower keep built in the early 1100s to commemorate Scotland's royal saint, who died in the castle in 1093. The chapel is delightfully decorated inside with fine Romanesque architecture.

3 MONS MEG

Step outside the chapel and you are confronted by the great bombard Mons Meg, gifted to James II in 1457. This is a great vantage point for the firing of the One O'Clock Gun (fired daily except Sunday), causing many visitors to jump out of their skins! The views from here across the Georgian New Town to the Forth Estuary are truly magnificent.

4 DAVID'S TOWER

Deep beneath the Half Moon Battery lies David's Tower, built as a fancy residence for David II in 1371. Badly damaged in the siege of 1573, the tower became hidden in the foundations for the new battery, and was only rediscovered in 1912. The Honours of Scotland spent much of WWII here, hidden down a medieval loo!

5 CASTLE VAULTS

In 1720 21 pirates captured in Argyll were thrown into the castle dungeons. They had all sailed with one of the most infamous pirate-captains of the Caribbean, 'Black Bart' Roberts. The following decades saw a busy time for this state prison, stuffed full of prisoners from the wars with America and France. The reconstructed cells allow you to experience something of the squalor!

Speyside Whisky Trail

No trip to Scotland is complete without visiting a whisky distillery, and the Speyside region is the heartland of Scotch whisky, with no fewer than 50 distilleries. Dufftown lies at the middle of it all, within easy reach of seven distilleries, and sporting its own whisky museum.

Bottom: Taking a sample; Top Right: Corgarff Castle; Bottom Right: Soldier pushing a barrel of 70-year-old Speyside single malt whisky

Need to Know

BEST TIME TO VISIT May or September, for the Speyside festivals **BEST PHOTO OP** Casks at Speyside Cooperage **For further coverage, see p339**

②

WILL ROBB/GETTY IMAGES ©

Local Knowledge

Speyside Don't Miss List

IAN LOGAN, BRAND AMBASSADOR, CHIVAS BROTHERS

1 THE GLENLIVET DISTILLERY

The home of the most iconic single malt whisky in the world, the Glenlivet offers a great mix of old and new, and a chance to see how modern technology has been adapted to work alongside traditional techniques. If you are a whisky connoisseur, join me on my weekly tour and discover behind-the-scenes secrets. It's at Ballindalloch, 10 miles west of Dufftown.

2 SPEYSIDE COOPERAGE

The Speyside Cooperage gives you a chance to watch a craft that has changed little over the centuries – the quality of the cask is one of the biggest contributing factors to the flavour of a single malt. The team here supply barrels to distilleries all over the world and share with the distillers the passion of creating the finest whiskies in the world.

3 GORDON & MACPHAIL

The most famous whisky shop in the world, Gordon & MacPhail's in the town of Elgin, is home to some of the oldest whiskies in the world including a 70-year-old Mortlach. The owners have played an important part in making single malt whisky what it is today, bottling these whiskies long before the distillers ever did.

4 CORGARFF CASTLE

The impressive and remote Corgarff Castle was once home to the redcoats whose job it was to chase down illegal distillers in the early 19th century. The castle is near Cockbridge, 30 miles south of Dufftown on the road to Ballater.

5 GROUSE INN

Set deep in the heart of the old smuggling country, this remote pub at Cabrach, in the hills 10 miles south of Dufftown, has nearly 250 single malts on Optic with many more on display around the bar, a collection that is home to several rare and unique bottlings.

Rosslyn Chapel

The success of Dan Brown's novel *The Da Vinci Code* and the subsequent Hollywood movie has seen a flood of visitors descend on this beautiful and enigmatic 15th-century chapel (p315). Wreathed in ornate and mysterious stone carvings, it's been the subject of Knights Templar and Holy Grail conspiracy theories for decades, and provides the setting for both book and movie denouement.

3

MATTHEW MICAH WRIGHT/GETTY IMAGES ©

Royal Yacht Britannia

4

The *Britannia* (p315) served as the royal family's floating home during their foreign travels. Decommissioned in 1997 the ship is now permanently moored in Leith, and offers an intriguing insight into the Queen's private tastes. Don't expect a sumptuous royal residence – it's more like a comfortable country house with old-fashioned charm. The only double bed is in the honeymoon suite, once used by Bill and Hillary Clinton.

KARL BLACKWELL/GETTY IMAGES ©

Stirling Castle

While Edinburgh Castle tops the visitor stakes, in terms of history and heritage its sister fortress at Stirling (p328) is arguably more rewarding. This sturdy bastion has played a pivotal role in many key events of Scottish history, and was once a residence of the Stuart monarchs. Highlights include the Great Hall, the largest medieval banqueting hall ever built in Scotland.

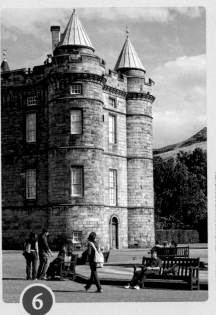

Palace of Holyroodhouse

This Edinburgh palace (p311) is Her Majesty the Queen's official residence in Scotland, but the building is better known for its association with Mary, Queen of Scots, who spent six eventful years (1561–67) living here. As well as Mary's private bedchamber, the palace brims with fascinating antiques and artworks, and after your visit you can wander around Holyrood Park (p311).

Glasgow

Scotland's second city (p321) is often eclipsed by the capital, but it's well worthy of a visit in its own right, with a wealth of wonderful museums, galleries and buildings – many of which were designed by Scotland's most gifted designer, Charles Rennie Mackintosh. Don't miss a visit to the Kelvingrove Art Gallery & Museum (p326), a treasure trove of quirky Victoriana.

Mackintosh-designed light

Edinburgh & Central Scotland's Best...

Cultural Experiences

◦ **Scottish National Gallery** (p314) Scotland's foremost repository of art

◦ **Royal Yacht Britannia** (p315) Wander the decks of the Queen's own holiday boat

◦ **Kelvingrove Art Gallery & Museum** (p326) Weird and wonderful exhibits at Glasgow's top museum

◦ **Mackintosh House** (p325) Marvel at the decorative detail in this reconstruction of Charles Rennie Mackintosh's Glasgow home

Castles & Palaces

◦ **Edinburgh Castle** (p306) Icon of the capital and home to the Stone of Destiny

◦ **Stirling Castle** (p328) Always in the shadow of Edinburgh, but can be a more rewarding visit

◦ **Culzean Castle** (p328) Stately castle surrounded by a landscaped park and wraparound views

◦ **Glamis Castle** (p338) Moody and marvellous, this is one of the region's most photogenic castles

Historic Sites

◦ **Palace of Holyroodhouse** (p311) The British monarch's official residence in Scotland, also a former home of Mary, Queen of Scots

◦ **Scott Monument** (p314) Lofty perch with stunning views of Edinburgh's Old Town skyline

◦ **Scone Palace** (p337) The site where countless generations of Scottish kings were crowned

◦ **Wallace Monument** (p332) Follow in the footsteps of the real-life Braveheart

Natural Beauty

○ **Holyrood Park, Edinburgh** (p311) Unexpected touch of the wilds and great viewpoint in the heart of the city

○ **Loch Lomond** (p333) Beautiful loch immortalised in song, easily reached from Edinburgh or Glasgow

○ **Speyside** (p339) Valley of the 'slivery Spey' and the heartland of Scotch whisky

○ **The Trossachs** (p333) Craggy hills and scenic lochs; often described as 'the Highlands in miniature'

Left: Highland cow, Loch Lomond;
Above: Speyside

Need to Know

ADVANCE PLANNING

○ **Six months before** Reserve a tee time for playing golf on St Andrews Old Course. Book accommodation if you plan to visit during festival time (August) or Hogmanay (New Year).

○ **One month before** Reserve accommodation for any other time of year.

○ **One week before** Book for Speyside distillery tours, Edinburgh Castle and other big sights.

RESOURCES

○ **Edinburgh Tourist Board** (www.edinburgh.org)

○ **Edinburgh Museums & Galleries** (www.edinburgh museums.org.uk)

○ **Edinburgh Festivals** (www.edinburghfestivals.co.uk)

○ **Glasgow** (www.seeglasgow. com)

○ **Speyside** (www. greaterspeyside.com; www. maltwhiskytrail.com)

○ **Loch Lomond & the Trossachs National Park** (www.lochlomond-trossachs. org)

○ **St Andrews** (www. visitfife.com)

GETTING AROUND

○ **Bus** Edinburgh and Glasgow have good bus networks.

○ **Car** The most time-efficient way to get around. Parking in Edinburgh city centre is difficult, so avoid bringing a car if you can.

○ **Train** Good for reaching major towns, but less useful for day-to-day getting around – the train lines skirt the region to the east and west.

BE FOREWARNED

○ **Crowds** Edinburgh is swamped by crowds during festival season in August.

○ **Weather** Scotland is notoriously wet, so come prepared with waterproofs and an umbrella.

○ **Golf** Accommodation is impossible to find when St Andrews hosts the Open Championships.

Edinburgh & Central Scotland Itineraries

Do a three-day loop and explore the best of the capital and surrounds. The five-day trip leads further north, into the central Scottish heartland.

3 DAYS

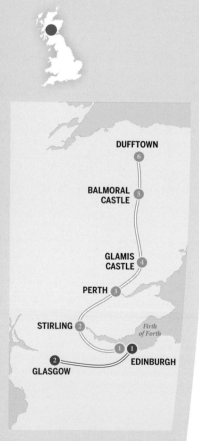

EDINBURGH TO GLASGOW

A Tale of Two Cities

Spend a couple of days getting to know **(1) Edinburgh**, beginning with the Royal Mile and the Old Town, a visit to the underground chambers of Real Mary King's Close, and an afternoon at Edinburgh Castle. On day two, focus on the New Town and Princes St, and spend the afternoon exploring the Palace of Holyroodhouse.

On day three, head west to **(2) Glasgow**, where the main highlights include the art nouveau work of Charles Rennie Mackintosh and the excellent Kelvingrove Art Gallery & Museum and Hunterian Museum.

Top Left: Riverside Museum (p324), Glasgow;
Top Right: Balmoral Castle (p338)

5 DAYS

EDINBURGH TO DUFFTOWN

Castle Country

Spend your first day or two in **(1) Edinburgh** then it's a short journey to **(2) Stirling**, where visiting the castle and the nearby Wallace Monument will take the best part of the day. Head east to **(3) Perth** for a visit to the Scone Palace, where Scottish kings were once crowned. If you have time, a detour to the notoriously haunted castle at **(4) Glamis** is well worth it.

The scenery gets wilder as you drive further north towards the Caingorm Mountains. Stop in for a visit to **(5) Balmoral Castle**, the royal family's holiday home (they usually visit in August). Then it's on into the Spey Valley, the spiritual home of Scottish whisky, centring on **(6) Dufftown**. There are lots of high-profile distilleries nearby where you can sample some of the good stuff.

Discover Edinburgh & Central Scotland

At a Glance

o **Edinburgh** (p306) Scotland's stately capital has museums and monuments aplenty.

o **Glasgow** (p321) The second city, with its own rough-and-ready character.

o **Stirling** (p328) Historic area awash with castles, battlefields and landmarks.

o **Northeast Scotland** (p338) Mountains, whisky distilleries and magical views.

St Giles Cathedral
CHRIS HEPBURN/GETTY IMAGES ©

EDINBURGH

POP 430,000

Edinburgh is a city that begs to be explored. From the vaults and wynds (narrow streets or alleys) that riddle the Old Town to the urban villages of Stockbridge and Cramond, it's filled with quirky comehither nooks that tempt you to walk just a little bit further. And every corner turned reveals sudden views and unexpected vistas – green sunlit hills, a glimpse of rust red crags, a blue flash of distant sea.

All these superlatives come together in August at festival time, when it seems as if half the world descends on Edinburgh for one enormous party.

◉ Sights

Edinburgh's main attractions are concentrated in the city centre – on and around the Old Town's Royal Mile between the castle and Holyrood, and in New Town. A major exception is the Royal Yacht *Britannia,* which is in the redeveloped docklands district of Leith, 2 miles northeast of the centre.

Old Town

THE ROYAL MILE

EDINBURGH CASTLE   Castle
(www.edinburghcastle.gov.uk; adult/child incl audioguide £16/9.60; ⊙9.30am-6pm Apr-Sep, to 5pm Oct-Mar, last admission 45min before closing) Edinburgh Castle has played a pivotal role in Scottish history, both as a royal residence – King Malcolm Canmore (r 1058–93) and Queen Margaret first made their home here in the 11th century – and as a military stronghold. The castle last saw military action in 1745;

from then until the 1920s it served as the British army's main base in Scotland.

The **Entrance Gateway**, flanked by statues of Robert the Bruce and William Wallace, opens to a cobbled lane that leads up beneath the 16th-century **Portcullis Gate** to the cannons ranged along the Argyle and Mills Mount batteries. The battlements here have **great views** over New Town to the Firth of Forth.

At the far end of Mills Mount Battery is the famous **One O'Clock Gun**, where crowds gather to watch a gleaming WWII 25-pounder fire an ear-splitting time signal at exactly 1pm (every day except Sundays, Christmas Day and Good Friday).

South of Mills Mount, the road curls up leftwards through **Foog's Gate** to the highest part of Castle Rock, crowned by the tiny, Romanesque **St Margaret's Chapel**, the oldest surviving building in Edinburgh.

The main group of buildings on the summit of Castle Rock are ranged around Crown Sq, dominated by the shrine of the **Scottish National War Memorial**. Opposite is the **Great Hall**, built for James IV (r 1488–1513) as a ceremonial hall and used as a meeting place for the Scottish parliament until 1639. Its most remarkable feature is the original, 16th-century hammer-beam roof.

The **Castle Vaults** beneath the Great Hall (entered from Crown Sq via the Prisons of War exhibit) were used variously as storerooms, bakeries and a prison. The vaults have been renovated to resemble 18th- and early-19th-century **prisons**, where graffiti carved by French and American prisoners can be seen on the ancient wooden doors.

On the eastern side of the square is the **Royal Palace**, built during the 15th and 16th centuries, where a series of historical tableaux leads to the highlight of the castle – a strongroom housing the **Honours of Scotland** (the Scottish crown jewels), the oldest surviving crown jewels in Europe. Locked away in a chest following the Act of Union in 1707, the crown (made in 1540 from the gold of Robert the Bruce's 14th-century coronet), sword and sceptre lay forgotten until they were unearthed at the instigation of the novelist Sir Walter Scott in 1818. Also on display here is the **Stone of Destiny**.

Among the neighbouring **Royal Apartments** is the bedchamber where Mary, Queen of Scots gave birth to her son James VI, who was to unite the crowns of Scotland and England in 1603.

SCOTCH WHISKY EXPERIENCE Exhibition
(www.scotchwhiskyexperience.co.uk; 354 Castlehill; adult/child incl tour & tasting £12.50/6.50; ⏰10am-6.30pm Jun-Aug, to 6pm Sep-May) A former school houses this multimedia centre explaining the making of whisky from barley to bottle in a series of exhibits, demonstrations and tours that combine sight, sound and smell, including the world's largest collection of malt whiskies; look out for Peat, the distillery cat! There's also a restaurant that serves traditional Scottish dishes with, where possible, a dash of whisky thrown in.

CAMERA OBSCURA Camera Obscura
(www.camera-obscura.co.uk; Castlehill; adult/child £10.95/7.95; ⏰9.30am-9pm Jul & Aug, 9.30am-7pm Apr-Jun & Sep-Oct, 10am-6pm Nov-Mar) Edinburgh's 'camera obscura' is a curious 19th-century device – in constant use since 1853 – that uses lenses and mirrors to throw a live image of the city onto a large horizontal screen. Stairs lead up through various displays to the **Outlook Tower**, which offers great views over the city.

ST GILES CATHEDRAL Church
(www.stgilescathedral.org.uk; High St; suggested donation £3; ⏰9am-7pm Mon-Fri, to 5pm Sat, 1-5pm Sun May-Sep, 9am-5pm Mon-Sat, 1-5pm Sun Oct-Apr) Properly called the High Kirk of Edinburgh (it was only a true cathedral – the seat of a bishop – from 1633 to 1638 and from 1661 to 1689), St Giles Cathedral was named after the patron saint of cripples and beggars. The present church dates largely from the 15th century – the beautiful **crown spire** was completed in 1495 – but much of it was restored in the 19th century.

Edinburgh

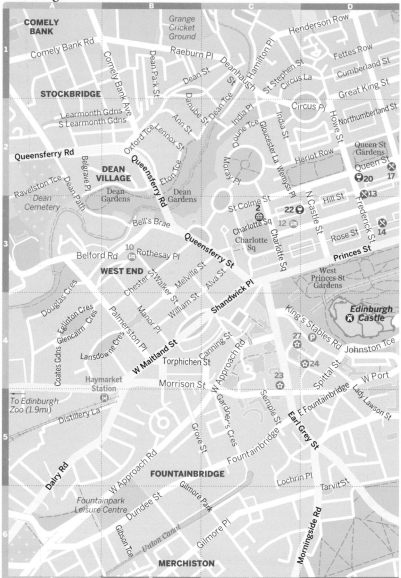

REAL MARY KING'S CLOSE   Historic Building
(☎ 0845 070 6244; www.realmarykingsclose.com; 2 Warriston's Close, High St; adult/child £12.95/7.45; ⏰ 10am-9pm Apr-Oct, to 11pm Aug, 10am-5pm Sun-Thu, to 9pm Fri & Sat Nov-Mar)

Part of the Royal Exchange was built over the sealed-off remains of Mary King's Close, and the lower levels of this medieval Old Town alley have survived almost unchanged in the foundations of the City Chambers for 250 years. Now

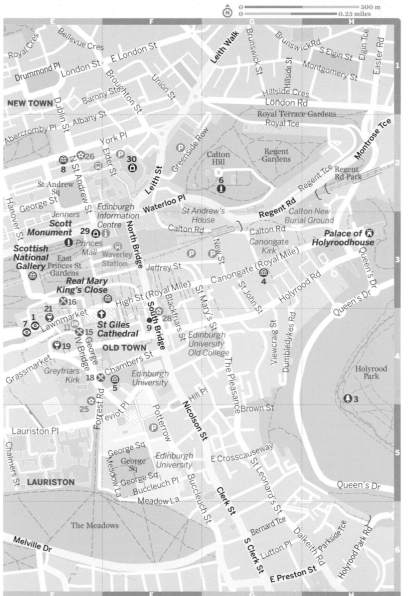

open to the public as the Real Mary King's Close, this spooky, subterranean labyrinth gives a fascinating insight into the daily life of 16th- and 17th-century Edinburgh. Costumed characters give tours through a 16th-century town house and the plague-stricken home of a 17th-century gravedigger. Advance booking recommended.

Edinburgh

FREE **MUSEUM OF
EDINBURGH** Museum
(www.edinburghmuseums.org.uk; 142 Canongate;
◷10am-5pm Mon-Sat year-round, 2-5pm Sun
Aug) You can't miss the colourful facade
of Huntly House, newly renovated in
bright red and yellow ochre, opposite the
Tolbooth clock. Built in 1570, it houses
a museum covering Edinburgh from its
prehistory to the present. Exhibits of
national importance include an original
copy of the National Covenant of 1638,
but the big crowd-pleaser is the dog collar
and feeding bowl that once belonged to
Greyfriars Bobby, the city's most famous
canine citizen.

FREE **NATIONAL MUSEUM OF
SCOTLAND** Museum
(www.nms.ac.uk; Chambers St; fee for special
exhibitions; ◷10am-5pm) Broad, elegant
Chambers St is dominated by the long
facade of the National Museum of
Scotland. Its extensive collections are
spread between two buildings, one
modern, one Victorian. The five floors of
the museum trace the history of Scotland
from geological beginnings to the 1990s,
with many imaginative and stimulating exhibits; audioguides are available in several
languages.

New Town

Edinburgh's New Town lies north of the
Old Town, on a ridge running parallel to
the Royal Mile and separated from it by
the valley of Princes Street Gardens. Its
regular grid of elegant, neoclassical terraces is the world's most complete and
unspoilt example of Georgian architecture and town planning. Along with the
Old Town, it was declared a Unesco World
Heritage Site in 1995.

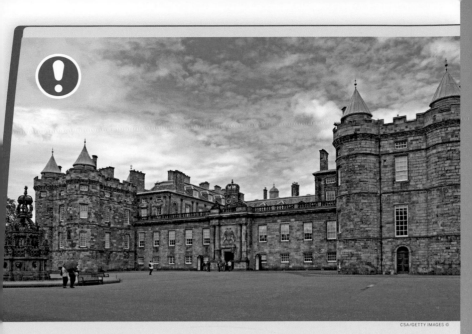

CSA/GETTY IMAGES ©

Don't Miss **Palace of Holyroodhouse**

This palace is the royal family's official residence in Scotland, but is more famous as the 16th-century home of the ill-fated Mary, Queen of Scots. The oldest surviving part of the building, the northwestern tower, was built in 1529 as a royal apartment for James V and his wife, Mary of Guise. Mary, Queen of Scots spent six turbulent years here, during which time she debated with John Knox, married both her first and second husbands, and witnessed the murder of her secretary David Rizzio. The palace is closed to the public when the royal family is visiting and during state functions (usually in mid-May, and mid-June to early July; check the website for exact dates).

The self-guided audio tour leads you through a series of impressive royal apartments, ending in the **Great Gallery**. The 89 portraits of Scottish kings were commissioned by Charles II and supposedly record his unbroken lineage from Scota, the Egyptian pharaoh's daughter who discovered the infant Moses in a reed basket on the banks of the Nile.

But the highlight of the tour is **Mary, Queen of Scots' Bed Chamber**, home to the unfortunate Mary from 1561 to 1567, and connected by a secret stairway to her husband's bedchamber. It was here that her jealous first husband, Lord Darnley, restrained the pregnant queen while his henchmen murdered her secretary – and favourite – Rizzio. A plaque in the neighbouring room marks the spot where he bled to death.

Outside the palace, **Holyrood Park** is a 263-hectare wilderness in the heart of the city. The former hunting ground of Scottish monarchs has varied landscape, including crags, moorland and loch. The highest point is the 251m summit of **Arthur's Seat**, the deeply eroded remnant of a long-extinct volcano.

NEED TO KNOW

www.royalcollection.org.uk; adult/child £10.75/6.50; ⏱9.30am-6pm Apr-Oct, to 4.30pm Nov-Mar

Royal Mile

A Grand Day Out

Planning your own procession along the Royal Mile involves some tough decisions – it would be impossible to see everything in a single day, so it's wise to decide in advance what you don't want to miss and shape your visit around that. Remember to leave time for lunch, for exploring some of the Mile's countless side

alleys and, during festival time, for enjoying the street theatre that is bound to be happening in High St.

The most pleasant way to reach the Castle Esplanade at the start of the Royal Mile is to hike up the zigzag path from the footbridge behind the Ross Bandstand in Princes Street Gardens (in springtime you'll be knee-deep in daffodils). Starting at **Edinburgh Castle ❶** means that the rest of your walk is downhill. For a superb view up and down the length of the Mile, climb the **Camera Obscura's Outlook Tower ❷** before visiting **Gladstone's Land ❸** and **St Giles Cathedral ❹**. If history's your

LONELY PLANET / GETTY IMAGES ©

Royal Visits to the Royal Mile

1561: Mary, Queen of Scots arrives from France and holds an audience with John Knox.
1745: Bonnie Prince Charlie fails to capture Edinburgh Castle, and instead sets up court in Holyroodhouse.
2004: Queen Elizabeth II officially opens the Scottish Parliament building.

Edinburgh Castle
If you're pushed for time, visit the Great Hall, the Honours of Scotland and the Prisons of War exhibit. Head for the Half Moon Battery for a photo looking down the length of the Royal Mile.

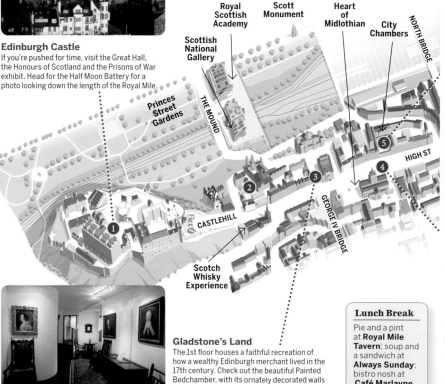

Royal Scottish Academy

Scott Monument

Heart of Midlothian

City Chambers

NORTH BRIDGE

Scottish National Gallery

Princes Street Gardens

THE MOUND

CASTLEHILL

GEORGE IV BRIDGE

HIGH ST

Scotch Whisky Experience

KARL BLACKWELL / GETTY IMAGES ©

Gladstone's Land
The 1st floor houses a faithful recreation of how a wealthy Edinburgh merchant lived in the 17th century. Check out the beautiful Painted Bedchamber, with its ornately decorated walls and wooden ceilings.

Lunch Break
Pie and a pint at **Royal Mile Tavern**; soup and a sandwich at **Always Sunday**; bistro nosh at **Café Marlayne**.

thing, you'll want to add **Real Mary King's Close** ⑤, **John Knox House** ⑥ and the **Museum of Edinburgh** ⑦ to your must-see list.

At the foot of the mile, choose between modern and ancient seats of power – the **Scottish Parliament** ⑧ or the **Palace of Holyroodhouse** ⑨ Round off the day with an evening ascent of Arthur's Seat or, slightly less strenuously, Calton Hill. Both make great sunset viewpoints.

TAKING YOUR TIME

Minimum time needed for each attraction:

Edinburgh Castle: two hours

Gladstone's Land: 45 minutes

St Giles Cathedral: 30 minutes

Real Mary King's Close: one hour (tour)

Scottish Parliament: one hour (tour)

Palace of Holyroodhouse: one hour

Real Mary King's Close

The guided tour is heavy on ghost stories, but a highlight is standing in an original 17th-century room with tufts of horsehair poking from the crumbling plaster, and breathing in the ancient scent of stone, dust and history.

Canongate Kirk

CANONGATE

ST MARY'S ST

SOUTH BRIDGE

Tron Kirk

⑥

⑦

⑧

⑨

Our Dynamic Earth

Scottish Parliament

Don't have time for the guided tour? Pick up a 'Discover the Scottish Parliament Building' leaflet from reception and take a self-guided tour of the exterior, then hike up to Salisbury Crags for a great view of the complex.

Palace of Holyroodhouse

Find the secret staircase joining Mary, Queen of Scots' bedchamber with that of her husband, Lord Darnley, who restrained the queen while his henchmen stabbed to death her secretary (and possible lover), David Rizzio.

St Giles Cathedral

Look out for the Burne-Jones stained-glass window (1873) at the west end, showing the crossing of the River Jordan, and the bronze memorial to Robert Louis Stevenson in the Moray Aisle.

EUROPHOTOS/ALAMY ©

COLIN PALMER PHOTOGRAPHY/ALAMY ©

JEAN-CHRISTOPHE GODET/ALAMY ©

PRINCES STREET

SCOTT MONUMENT   Monument

(www.edinburghmuseums.org.uk; East Princes Street Gardens; admission £3; ⊙10am-7pm Mon-Sat Apr-Sep, 9am-4pm Mon-Sat Oct-Mar, 10am-6pm Sun year-round) The eastern half of Princes Street Gardens is dominated by the Gothic spire of the Scott Monument, built by public subscription in memory of the novelist Sir Walter Scott after his death in 1832. The exterior is decorated with carvings of characters from his novels; inside you can see an exhibition on Scott, and climb the 287 steps to the top for a view of the city.

FREE SCOTTISH NATIONAL GALLERY   Gallery

(www.nationalgalleries.org; The Mound; fee for special exhibitions; ⊙10am-5pm Fri-Wed, to 7pm Thu) Designed by William Playfair, this imposing classical building with its Ionic porticoes dates from the 1850s.

The gallery houses an important collection of **European art** from the Renaissance to post-Impressionism, with works by Verrocchio (Leonardo da Vinci's teacher), Tintoretto, Titian, Holbein, Rubens, Van Dyck, Vermeer, El Greco, Poussin, Rembrandt, Gainsborough, Turner, Constable, Monet, Pissarro, Gauguin and Cézanne; each year in January the gallery exhibits its collection of **Turner watercolours**, bequeathed by Henry Vaughan in 1900.

The basement galleries dedicated to **Scottish art** include glowing portraits by Allan Ramsay and Sir Henry Raeburn, rural scenes by Sir David Wilkie and impressionistic landscapes by William MacTaggart.

GEORGE STREET & AROUND

Until the 1990s George St – the major axis of New Town – was the centre of Edinburgh's financial industry and Scotland's equivalent of Wall St. Today the big financial firms have moved to premises in the Exchange office district west of Lothian Rd, and George St's former banks and offices house upmarket shops, pubs and restaurants.

GEORGIAN HOUSE   Historic Building

(NTS; 7 Charlotte Sq; adult/child £6/5; ⊙10am-6pm Jul & Aug, to 5pm Apr-Jun & Sep-Oct, 11am-4pm Mar, to 3pm Nov) The National Trust for Scotland's Georgian House has been beautifully restored and furnished to show how Edinburgh's wealthy elite lived at the end of the 18th century.

FREE SCOTTISH NATIONAL PORTRAIT GALLERY   Gallery

(www.nationalgalleries.org; 1 Queen St; ⊙10am-5pm Fri-Wed, to 7pm Thu) The Venetian Gothic palace of the Scottish National Portrait Gallery reopened its doors in 2011 after a two-year renovation, emerging as one of the city's top attractions. Its galleries illustrate Scottish history through paintings, photographs

The view from Calton Hill

and sculptures, putting faces to famous names from Scotland's past and present, from Robert Burns, Mary, Queen of Scots and Bonnie Prince Charlie to Sean Connery, Billy Connolly and poet Jackie Kay.

CALTON HILL

Calton Hill (100m), rising dramatically above the eastern end of Princes St, is Edinburgh's acropolis, its summit scattered with grandiose memorials mostly dating from the first half of the 19th century. It is also one of the best viewpoints in Edinburgh, with a panorama that takes in the castle, Holyrood, Arthur's Seat, the Firth of Forth, New Town and Princes St.

Nelson Monument   Monument
(admission £3; 10am-7pm Mon-Sat & noon-5pm Sun Apr-Sep, 10am-3pm Mon-Sat Oct-Mar) Looking a bit like an upturned telescope – the similarity is intentional – and offering even better views, the was built to commemorate Admiral Lord Nelson's victory at Trafalgar in 1805. Take any Leith St bus.

Leith

ROYAL YACHT BRITANNIA   Historic Vessel
(www.royalyachtbritannia.co.uk; Ocean Terminal; adult/child £11.75/7.50; 9.30am-4.30pm Jul-Sep, to 4pm Apr-Jun & Oct, 10am-3.30pm Nov-Mar, last admission 90min before closing) One of Scotland's biggest tourist attractions is the former Royal Yacht *Britannia*. She was the British royal family's floating home during their foreign travels from the time of her launch in 1953 until her decommissioning in 1997, and is now moored in front of Ocean Terminal. The entire ship is a monument to 1950s decor and technology, and the accommodation reveals Her Majesty's preference for simple, unfussy surroundings – the Queen's own bed is surprisingly tiny and plain. There was nothing simple or unfussy, however, about the running of the ship. When the Queen travelled, along with her went 45 members of the royal household, 5 tons of luggage and a Rolls-Royce that was squeezed into a specially built garage.

Britannia was joined in 2010 by the 1930s racing yacht **Bloodhound**, which was owned by the Queen in the 1960s.

The Majestic Tour bus runs from Waverley Bridge to *Britannia* during opening times. Alternatively, take Lothian Bus 11, 22, or 35 to Ocean Terminal.

Greater Edinburgh

EDINBURGH ZOO   Zoo
(www.edinburghzoo.org.uk; 134 Corstorphine Rd; adult/child £15.50/11; 9am-6pm Apr-Sep, to 5pm Oct & Mar, to 4.30pm Nov-Feb) Opened in 1913, Edinburgh Zoo is one of the world's leading conservation zoos. Edinburgh's captive breeding program has saved many endangered species, including Siberian tigers, pygmy hippos and red pandas. The main attractions are the **penguin parade** (the zoo's penguins go for a walk every day at 2.15pm), the **sea lion** training session (daily at 11.15am), and the two **giant pandas**, Tian Tian and Yang Guang, who arrived in December 2011.

The zoo is 2.5 miles west of the city centre; take Lothian Bus 12, 26 or 31, First Bus 16, 18, 80 or 86, or the Airlink Bus 100 westbound from Princes St.

ROSSLYN CHAPEL   Church
(Collegiate Church of St Matthew; www.rosslynchapel.org.uk; adult/child £9/free; 9.30am-5pm Mon-Sat, noon-4.45pm Sun) The success of Dan Brown's novel *The Da Vinci Code* and the subsequent Hollywood film has seen a flood of visitors descend on Scotland's most beautiful and enigmatic church – **Rosslyn Chapel**. The chapel was built in the mid-15th century for William St Clair, third earl of Orkney, and the ornately carved interior – at odds with the architectural fashion of its time – is a monument to the mason's art, rich in symbolic imagery. As well as flowers, vines, angels and biblical figures, the carved stones include many examples of the pagan 'Green Man'; other figures are associated with Freemasonry and the Knights Templar. The symbolism of these images has led some researchers to conclude that Rosslyn is some kind of secret Templar repository, and it has been claimed that hidden vaults beneath the chapel could conceal anything from the Holy Grail or the head of John the Baptist to the body of Christ himself.

Rosslyn Chapel

Deciphering Rosslyn

Rosslyn Chapel is a small building, but the density of decoration inside can be overwhelming. It's well worth buying the official guidebook by the Earl of Rosslyn first; find a bench in the gardens and have a skim through before going into the chapel – the background information will make your visit all the more interesting. The book also offers a useful self-guided tour of the chapel, and explains the legend of the Master Mason and the Apprentice.

Entrance is through the **north door** ❶. Take a pew and sit for a while to allow your eyes to adjust to the dim interior; then look up at the ceiling vault, decorated with engraved roses, lilies and stars (can you spot the sun and the moon?). Walk left along the north aisle to reach the Lady Chapel, separated from the rest of the church by the **Mason's Pillar** ❷ and the **Apprentice Pillar** ❸. Here you'll find carvings of **Lucifer** ❹, the Fallen Angel, and the **Green Man** ❺. Nearby are **carvings** ❻ that appear to resemble Indian corn (maize). Finally, go to the western end and look up at the wall – in the left corner is the head of the **Apprentice** ❼; to the right is the (rather worn) head of the **Master Mason** ❽.

ROSSLYN CHAPEL & THE DA VINCI CODE

Dan Brown was referencing Rosslyn Chapel's alleged links to the Knights Templar and the Freemasons – unusual symbols found among the carvings, and the fact that a descendant of its founder, William St Clair, was a Grand Master Mason – when he chose it as the setting for his novel's denouement. Rosslyn is indeed a coded work, written in stone, but its meaning depends on your point of view. See *The Rosslyn Hoax?* by Robert LD Cooper (www.rosslynhoax.com) for an alternative interpretation of the chapel's symbolism.

Explore Some More

After visiting the chapel, head downhill to see the spectacularly sited ruins of Roslin Castle, then take a walk along leafy Roslin Glen.

Lucifer, the Fallen Angel
At head height, to the left of the second window from the left, is an upside-down angel bound with rope, a symbol often associated with Freemasonry. The arch above is decorated with the Dance of Death.

The Apprentice
High in the corner, beneath an empty statue niche, is the head of the murdered Apprentice, with a deep wound in his forehead above the right eye. Legend says the Apprentice was murdered in a jealous rage by the Master Mason. The worn head on the side wall to the left of the Apprentice is that of his mother.

North Door

The Master Mason
❽

Baptistery

Practical Tips

Buy your tickets in advance through the chapel's website (except in August, when no bookings are taken). No photography is allowed inside the chapel.

Green Man

On a boss at the base of the arch between the second and third windows from the left is the finest example of more than a hundred 'green man' carvings in the chapel, pagan symbols of spring, fertility and rebirth.

④
② Mason's Pillar
⑤ Lady Chapel
③

Sacristy

① North Aisle

Altar

Choir

South Aisle

⑥

⑦

The Apprentice Pillar

This is perhaps the chapel's most beautiful carving. Four vines spiral up the pillar, issuing from the mouths of eight dragons at its base. At the top is Isaac, son of Abraham, lying bound upon the altar.

Indian Corn

The frieze around the second window on the south wall is said to represent Indian corn (maize), but it predates Columbus' discovery of the New World in 1492. Other carvings seem to resemble aloe vera.

Tours

Walking Tours

**BLACK HART
STORYTELLERS** Walking Tours
(www.blackhart.uk.com; adult/concession £10/5)
Not suitable for young children. The 'City
of the Dead' tour of Greyfriars Kirkyard
is probably the scariest of Edinburgh's
'ghost' tours.

**EDINBURGH LITERARY
PUB TOUR** Walking Tours
(www.edinburghliterarypubtour.co.uk; adult/student £10/8) An enlightening two-hour trawl
through Edinburgh's literary history –
and its associated howffs (pubs) – in the
entertaining company of Messrs Clart
and McBrain.

MERCAT TOURS Walking Tours
(www.mercattours.com; adult/child £10/5)
Mercat offers a wide range of fascinating tours including history walks in the
Old Town and Leith, 'Ghosts & Ghouls'
tours and visits to haunted underground
vaults.

REBUS TOURS Walking Tours
(www.rebustours.com; adult/student £10/9)
Tours of the 'hidden Edinburgh' frequented by novelist Ian Rankin's fictional
detective John Rebus. Not recommended
for children under 10.

Bus Tours

CITY SIGHTSEEING Bus Tours
(www.edinburghtour.com; adult/child £12/5)
Bright-red open-top buses depart every
20 minutes from Waverley Bridge.

MAJESTIC TOUR Bus Tours
(www.edinburghtour.com; adult/child £12/5)
Runs every 30 minutes (every 20 minutes in July and August) from Waverley
Bridge to the Royal Yacht *Britannia* at
Ocean Terminal via the New Town, Royal
Botanic Garden and Newhaven, returning via Leith Walk, Holyrood and the
Royal Mile.

 **Sleeping**

Edinburgh is not short of accommodation, but you can guarantee the city will
be packed to the gills during the festival
period (August) and over Hogmanay
(New Year).

Old Town

HOTEL MISSONI Boutique Hotel £££
(☏0131-220 6666; www.hotelmissoni.com; 1
George IV Bridge; r £90-225; ☎) The Italian
fashion house has established a style
icon in the heart of the medieval Old
Town with this bold statement of a hotel:
modernistic architecture, black-and-white
decor with well-judged splashes of colour,
impeccably mannered staff and – most
importantly – very comfortable bedrooms and bathrooms with lots of nice
touches, from fresh milk in the minibar to
plush bathrobes.

New Town & Around

B+B EDINBURGH Hotel ££
(☏0131-225 5084; www.bb-edinburgh.com; 3
Rothesay Tce; s/d £99/140; ☎) Built in 1883
as a grand home for the proprietor of the
Scotsman newspaper, this Victorian extravaganza of carved oak, parquet floors,
stained glass and elaborate fireplaces
was given a designer makeover in 2011 to
create a striking contemporary hotel.

TIGERLILY Boutique Hotel £££
(☏0131-225 5005; www.tigerlilyedinburgh.
co.uk; 125 George St; r from £175; ☎) Georgian
meets gorgeous at this glamorous, glittering boutique hotel (complete with its own
nightclub) decked out in mirror mosaics, beaded curtains, swirling Timorous
Beasties textiles and wall coverings, and
atmospheric pink uplighting.

South Edinburgh

SOUTHSIDE GUEST HOUSE B&B ££
(☏0131-668 4422; www.southsideguesthouse.
co.uk; 8 Newington Rd; s/d £70/90; ☎) Though
set in a typical Victorian terrace, the
Southside transcends the traditional
guest house category and feels more like
a modern boutique hotel.

KARL BLACKWELL/GETTY IMAGES ©

45 GILMOUR RD
B&B ££

(☎ 0131-667 3536; www.edinburghbedbreakfast.com; 45 Gilmour Rd; s/d £70/140) A peaceful setting, large garden and friendly owners contribute to the appeal of this Victorian terraced house, which overlooks the local bowling green. Located 1 mile southeast of the city centre.

 Eating

Old Town

ONDINE
Seafood £££

(☎ 0131-226 1888; www.ondinerestaurant.co.uk; 2 George IV Bridge; mains £15-25; ⊗ lunch & dinner) One of Edinburgh's finest seafood restaurants, with a menu based on sustainably sourced fish. Take an octopus-inspired seat at the Crustacean Bar and tuck into oysters Kilpatrick, a roast shellfish platter, or just haddock and chips (with minted pea purée, just to keep things posh).

PORTO & FI
Cafe £

(www.portofi.com; 9 North Bank St; mains £4-8; ⊗ 10am-11pm Mon-Sat, to 9pm Sun) With its designer decor, a prime location overlooking the Mound, and a surprisingly sophisti-cated menu built around quality Scottish produce, this cafe is hard to beat for a breakfast of eggs Benedict or Stornoway black pudding (served till noon, all day Sunday) or lunch of smoked salmon cannelloni or roast fig and asparagus salad.

TOWER
Scottish £££

(☎ 0131-225 3003; www.tower-restaurant.com; National Museum of Scotland, Chambers St; mains £16-30; ⊗ noon-11pm) Chic and sleek, with a great view of the castle, Tower is perched in a turret atop the National Museum of Scotland building. A two-/three-course pretheatre menu (£16/22) is available from 5pm to 6.30pm, and afternoon tea (£16) is served from 3pm to 5pm.

New Town

THE DOGS
British ££

(☎ 0131-220 1208; www.thedogsonline.co.uk; 110 Hanover St; mains £9-13; ⊗ noon-4pm & 5-10pm) One of the coolest tables in town, this bistro-style place uses cheaper cuts of meat and less well known, more sustainable species of fish to create hearty, no-nonsense dishes such as lamb sweetbreads on toast, baked coley (a type of fish) with *skirlie* (fried oatmeal and onion), and devilled liver with bacon and onions.

CAFÉ MARLAYNE
French ££

(📞0131-226 2230; www.cafemarlayne.com; 76 Thistle St; mains £12-15; 🕐noon-10pm) All weathered wood and candlelit tables, Café Marlayne is a cosy nook offering French farmhouse cooking – *brandade de morue* (salt cod) with green salad, slow roast rack of lamb, *boudin noir* (black pudding) with scallops and sautéed potato – at very reasonable prices.

🗒MUSSEL INN
Seafood ££

(www.mussel-inn.com; 61-65 Rose St; mains £9-23; 🕐noon-10pm; 🪑) Owned by west-coast shellfish farmers, the Mussel Inn provides a direct outlet for fresh Scottish seafood. A kilogram pot of mussels with a choice of sauces – try leek, Dijon mustard and cream – costs £12.20.

🍷 Drinking

Old Town
BOW BAR
Pub

(80 West Bow) One of the city's best traditional-style pubs (it's not as old as it looks) serving a range of excellent real ales and a vast selection of malt whiskies, the Bow Bar often has standing-room only on Friday and Saturday evenings.

JOLLY JUDGE
Pub

(www.jollyjudge.co.uk; 7a James Ct; 🛜) A snug little howff tucked away down a close, the Judge exudes a cosy 17th-century atmosphere (low, timber-beamed, painted ceilings) and has the added attraction of a cheering open fire in cold weather.

New Town
OXFORD BAR
Pub

(www.oxfordbar.co.uk; 8 Young St) 'The Ox' has been immortalised by Ian Rankin, author of the Inspector Rebus novels, whose fictional detective is a regular here.

BRAMBLE
Cocktail Bar

(www.bramblebar.co.uk; 16a Queen St) One of those places that easily earns the sobriquet 'best-kept secret', Bramble is an unmarked cellar bar where a maze of stone and brick hideaways conceals what is arguably the city's best cocktail bar.

★ Entertainment

The comprehensive source for what's-on info is the *List* (www.list.co.uk), an excellent listings magazine covering both Edinburgh and Glasgow. It's available from most newsagents, and is published fortnightly on a Thursday.

Live Music

HENRY'S CELLAR
Live Music

(www.musicglue.com/theraft; 8a Morrison St) One of Edinburgh's most eclectic live-music venues, Henry's has something going on most nights of the week, from rock and indie to 'Balkan-inspired folk', funk to hip hop to hardcore, staging both local bands and acts from around the world.

WHISTLE BINKIE'S
Live Music

(www.whistlebinkies.com; 4-6 South Bridge) This crowded cellar-bar just off the Royal Mile has live music every night till 3am, from rock and blues to folk and jazz. Open-mic night on Monday and breaking bands on Tuesday are showcases for new talent.

SANDY BELL'S
Traditional Music

(25 Forrest Rd) This unassuming pub is a stalwart of the traditional music scene (the founder's wife sang with The Corries). There's music almost every evening at 9pm, and from 3pm Saturday and Sunday, plus lots of impromptu sessions.

Theatre, Musicals & Comedy

ROYAL LYCEUM THEATRE
Drama, Musicals

(www.lyceum.org.uk; 30b Grindlay St; 🕐box office 10am-6pm Mon-Sat, to 8pm show nights; 🪑) A grand Victorian theatre located beside the Usher Hall, the Lyceum stages drama, concerts, musicals and ballet.

TRAVERSE THEATRE
Drama, Dance

(www.traverse.co.uk; 10 Cambridge St; 🕐box office 10am-6pm Mon-Sat, to 8pm show nights) The Traverse is the main focus for new Scottish writing and stages an adventurous program of contemporary drama and dance.

STAND COMEDY CLUB Comedy
(www.thestand.co.uk; 5 York Pl) The Stand, founded in 1995, is Edinburgh's main independent comedy venue.

 **Shopping**

Princes St is Edinburgh's principal shopping street, lined with all the big high-street stores, with many smaller shops along pedestrianised Rose St and more expensive designer boutiques on George St. There are also two big shopping centres in the New Town – Princes Mall, at the eastern end of Princes St, and the nearby St James Shopping Centre at the top of Leith St, plus Multrees Walk, a designer shopping complex with a flagship Harvey Nichols store on the eastern side of St Andrew Sq.

For more offbeat shopping – including fashion, music, crafts, gifts and jewellery – head for the cobbled lanes of Cockburn, Victoria and St Mary's Sts, all near the Royal Mile in the Old Town; William St in the western part of New Town; and the Stockbridge district, immediately north of the New Town.

Information

Edinburgh Information Centre (📞0131-473 3868; www.edinburgh.org; Princes Mall, 3 Princes St; 🕓9am-9pm Mon-Sat, 10am-8pm Sun Jul & Aug, 9am-7pm Mon-Sat, 10am-7pm Sun May-Jun & Sep, 9am-5pm Mon-Wed, to 6pm Thu-Sun Oct-Apr)

Getting There & Away

Air

Edinburgh Airport (📞0131-333 1000; www.edinburghairport.com) Eight miles west of the city, has numerous flights to other parts of Scotland and the UK, Ireland and mainland Europe.

Train

The main terminus in Edinburgh is Waverley train station, located in the heart of the city.

You can buy tickets, make reservations and get travel information at the Edinburgh Rail Travel Centre (🕓4.45am-12.30am Mon-Sat, 7am-12.30am Sun) in Waverley station.

First ScotRail operates a regular shuttle service between Edinburgh and Glasgow (£12.90, 50 minutes, every 15 minutes), and frequent daily services to all Scottish cities including Aberdeen (£45, 2½ hours), Dundee (£23, 1¼ hours) and Inverness (£40, 3½ hours).

GLASGOW
POP 634,700

Displaying a disarming blend of sophistication and earthiness, Scotland's biggest city has regenerated and evolved over the last couple of decades to become one of Britain's most intriguing metropolises.

Top-drawer museums and galleries abound, and the city's proud industrial and artistic heritage is innovatively displayed. Charles Rennie Mackintosh's

Willow Tearooms (p324)
VISITBRITAIN/BRITAIN ON VIEW/GETTY IMAGES ©

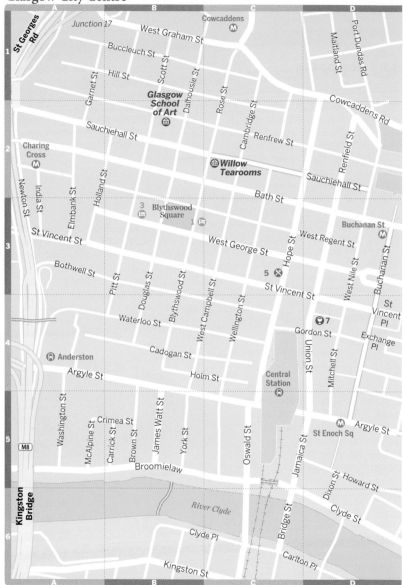

sublime works dot the town, while the River Clyde, traditionally associated with Glasgow's earthier side, is now a symbol of the city's renaissance.

Sights

In late July and early August of 2014, Glasgow hosts the 20th **Commonwealth Games** (www.glasgow2014.com), a 17-event

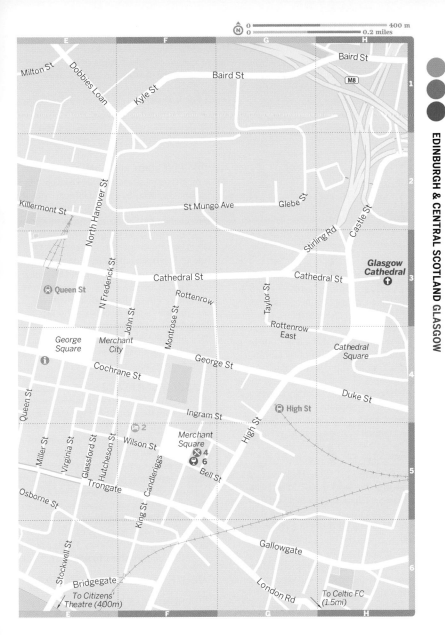

jamboree that will involve athletes from some 70 countries. Expect some improvements to the public-transport system; equally, expect some disruptions to services in the lead-up to the event.

City Centre
GLASGOW SCHOOL OF ART
Historic Building

(✆ 0141-353 4526; www.gsa.ac.uk/tours; 167 Renfrew St; adult/child/family £8.75/7/24;

Glasgow City Centre

🕐 9.30am-6.30pm Apr-Sep, 10.30am-5pm Oct-Mar) Mackintosh's greatest building, the Glasgow School of Art, still fulfils its original function, so just follow the steady stream of eclectically dressed students up the hill to find it. Excellent hour-long guided tours (roughly hourly summer; 11am, 1pm and 3pm winter) run by architecture students leave from here; this is the only way (apart from enrolling) you can visit the building's interior. They're worth booking by phone at busy times. Multilingual translations are available.

FREE **WILLOW TEAROOMS** Historic Building
(www.willowtearooms.co.uk; 217 Sauchiehall St; 🕐 9am-5pm Mon-Sat, 11am-5pm Sun) Admirers of the great Mackintosh will love the Willow Tearooms, an authentic reconstruction of tearooms Mackintosh designed and furnished in the early 20th century for restaurateur Kate Cranston. He had a free rein and even the teaspoons were given his distinctive touch.

East End

GLASGOW CATHEDRAL Church
(HS; www.historic-scotland.gov.uk; Cathedral Sq; 🕐 9.30am-5.30pm Mon-Sat, 1-5pm Sun Apr-Sep, closes 4.30pm Oct-Mar) An attraction that shouldn't be missed, Glasgow Cathedral has a rare timelessness. It's a shining example of Gothic architecture, and, unlike nearly all of Scotland's cathedrals, survived the turmoil of the Reformation mobs almost intact. Most of the current building dates from the 15th century.

The Clyde

Once a thriving shipbuilding area, the Clyde sank into dereliction during the postwar era, but is being rejuvenated.

FREE **RIVERSIDE MUSEUM** Museum
(www.glasgowmuseums.com; 100 Pointhouse Pl; 🕐 10am-5pm Mon-Thu & Sat, 11am-5pm Fri & Sun) The latest development along the Clyde is the building of this visually impressive new museum, the striking curved facades of which are the work of Iraqi architect Zaha Hadid. The main part of the collection is a transport museum; an atmospherically re-created Glasgow shopping street from the early 20th century puts the vintage vehicles into a social context. The **Tall Ship Glenlee** (www.thetallship.com; adult/child £5/3; 🕐 10am-5pm Mar-Oct, to 4pm Nov-Feb), a beautiful three-master launched in 1896, is berthed alongside the museum.

GLASGOW SCIENCE CENTRE Museum
(📞 0141-420 5000; www.gsc.org.uk; 50 Pacific Quay; Science Mall adult/child £9.95/7.95, IMAX, tower or planetarium £2.50; 🕐 10am-5pm Wed-Sun) Scotland's flagship millennium project, this superb museum will keep the kids entertained for hours (that's middle-aged kids, too!). It consists of an egg-shaped titanium-covered **IMAX** theatre (phone for current screenings) and an interactive **Science Mall** with floor-to-ceiling windows – a bounty of discovery for young, inquisitive minds. There's also a rotating **observation tower**, 127m high.

West End

FREE **HUNTERIAN MUSEUM** Museum
(www.hunterian.gla.ac.uk; University Ave; 🕐 10am-5pm Tue-Sat, 11am-4pm Sun) Housed in the glorious sandstone main building of the university, which is in itself reason enough to pay a visit, this quirky museum contains the collection of William Hunter (1718–83) renowned one-time student of the university. Pickled organs in glass

jars take their place alongside geological phenomena, potsherds gleaned from ancient brochs (prehistoric circular stone towers), dinosaur skeletons and a creepy case of deformed animals.

FREE HUNTERIAN ART GALLERY
Gallery

(www.hunterian.gla.ac.uk; 82 Hillhead St; ⏰10am-5pm Tue-Sat, 11am-4pm Sun) Across the road from the Hunterian Museum, the bold tones of the Scottish Colourists (Samuel Peploe, Francis Cadell, JD Fergusson) are well represented in this gallery, which also forms part of Hunter's bequest to the university.

MACKINTOSH HOUSE
Historic Building

(www.hunterian.gla.ac.uk; 82 Hillhead St; adult/concession £5/3; ⏰10am-5pm Tue-Sat, 11am-4pm Sun) Attached to the Hunterian Art Gallery, this is a reconstruction of the first home that Charles Rennie Mackintosh bought with his wife, noted artist and designer Mary Macdonald. It's fair to say that interior decoration was one of their strong points; the Mackintosh House is startling even today.

 Sleeping

City Centre

BRUNSWICK HOTEL
Hotel ££

(☎0141-552 0001; www.brunswickhotel.co.uk; 106 Brunswick St; d £50-95; 🛜🐾) You couldn't ask for a more relaxed and friendly Merchant City base. The rooms are all stylish with a mixture of minimalism and rich, sexy colours. There's an excellent restaurant downstairs and occasional nightclub in the basement.

MALMAISON
Hotel £££

(☎0141-572 1000; www.malmaison.com; 278 West George St; r/ste £160/345; 🛜🐾) Heavenly Malmaison is the ultimate in seductive urban accommodation. Cutting-edge but decadent and plush living at its best, this sassy sister of hospitality is super slinky and a cornerstone of faith in Glaswegian accommodation.

The Genius of Charles Rennie Mackintosh

Great cities have great artists, designers and architects contributing to the cultural and historical roots of their urban environment while expressing its soul and individuality. Charles Rennie Mackintosh was all of these. His quirky, linear and geometric designs have had almost as much influence on the city as Gaudí's have had on Barcelona. Many of the buildings Mackintosh designed in Glasgow are open to the public, and you'll see his tall, thin, art nouveau typeface repeatedly reproduced.

If you're planning to go CRM crazy, the **Mackintosh Trail ticket (£16)**, available at the tourist office or any Mackintosh building, gives you a day's free admission to all his creations as well as unlimited bus and subway travel.

BLYTHSWOOD SQUARE
Hotel £££

(☎0141-248 8888; www.blythswoodsquare.com; 11 Blythswood Sq; r £150-290; @🛜🐾) In a gorgeous Georgian terrace, this elegant five-star hotel offers plenty of inner-city luxury, with grey and cerise tweeds providing casual soft-toned style throughout. There's an excellent bar and superb restaurant, as well as a very handsome floorboarded and colonnaded salon space on the 1st floor that functions as an evening spot for cocktails.

West End

HOTEL DU VIN
Hotel £££

(One Devonshire Gardens; ☎0141-339 2001; www.hotelduvin.com; 1 Devonshire Gardens; r/ste from £160/425; P@🛜🐾) This is traditionally Glasgow's favoured hotel of the rich and famous, and the patriarch of sophistication and comfort. A study in elegance, it's sumptuously decorated and occupies three classical sandstone terrace houses. Breakfast is extra.

Don't Miss **Kelvingrove Art Gallery & Museum**

In a magnificent stone building, this grand Victorian cathedral of culture has been revamped into a fascinating and unusual museum, with a bewildering variety of exhibits, but not so tightly packed as to overwhelm. Here you'll find fine art alongside stuffed animals, and Micronesian shark-tooth swords alongside a Spitfire plane, but it's not mix and match: rooms are carefully and thoughtfully themed, and the collection is a manageable size. There's an excellent room of Scottish art, a room of fine French Impressionist works, and quality Renaissance paintings from Italy and Flanders. Salvador Dalí's superb *Christ of St John of the Cross* is also here. Best of all, nearly everything – including the paintings – has an easy-reading paragraph of interpretation next to it: you can learn a lot about art and more here, and it's excellent for the children, with plenty for them to do and displays aimed at a variety of ages. There are free hour-long guided tours leaving at 11am and 2.30pm. Bus 17, among many others, runs here from Renfield St.

NEED TO KNOW

www.glasgowmuseums.com; Argyle St; admission free; ⊙10am-5pm Mon-Thu & Sat, 11am-5pm Fri & Sun; 👬

EMBASSY APARTMENTS Apartment ££
(☏0141-946 6698; www.glasgowhotelsand apartments.co.uk; 8 Kelvin Dr; 1-/2-/4-person flat per night £60/80/99; 📶) Situated in the leafy West End on a quiet, exclusive street right on the edge of the Botanical Gardens, Embassy sleeps one to seven in studio-style apartments that have fully equipped kitchens and are sparkling clean.

ALAMO GUEST HOUSE B&B ££
(☏0141-339 2395; www.alamoguesthouse.com; 46 Gray St; d/superior d £95/145, s/d without bathroom £55/74; @📶) The Alamo may not sound like a quiet, peaceful spot, but that's exactly what this great little place

is. The decor is an enchanting mix of antique furnishings and modern design, with excellent bathrooms, and the breezy owners will make you very welcome.

Eating

City Centre

CAFÉ GANDOLFI Cafe, Bistro ££

(☎0141-552 6813; 64 Albion St; mains £11-15; ⏲9am-11.30pm) In the fashionable Merchant City, this cafe was once part of the old cheese market. Book a Tim Stead–designed, medieval-looking table in advance for well-prepared Scottish and Continental food. There's an expansion, specialising in fish, next door.

BRUTTI MA BUONI Mediterranean £

(☎0141-552 0001; www.brunswickhotel.co.uk; 106 Brunswick St; mains £7-11; ⏲11am-10pm; 👪) With dishes such as 'ugly but good' pizza and 'angry or peaceful' prawns, Brutti's menu draws a smile for its quirkiness and its prices.

MUSSEL INN Seafood ££

(☎0141-572 1405; www.mussel-inn.com; 157 Hope St; mains £10-18) Airy and easygoing, this two-level eatery – a longtime Rose St favourite in Edinburgh – has recently opened in Scotland's largest city. It specialises in sustainable scallops, oysters and mussels at affordable prices, served with a smile in a comfortable atmosphere.

West End

UBIQUITOUS CHIP Scottish £££

(☎0141-334 5007; www.ubiquitouschip.co.uk; 12 Ashton Lane; 2-/3-course dinner £35/40, brasserie mains lunch £7-12, dinner £12-15) The original champion of Scottish produce, The Ubiquitous Chip has won lots of awards for its unparalleled Scottish cuisine, and for its lengthy wine list. Named to poke fun at Scotland's perceived lack of finer cuisine, it offers a French touch but resolutely Scottish ingredients, carefully selected and following sustainable principles. The cute 'Wee Pub' down the side alley offers plenty of drinking pleasure.

MOTHER INDIA Indian ££

(☎0141-221 1663; www.motherindia.co.uk; 28 Westminster Tce, Sauchiehall St; mains £8-14; ⏲lunch Fri-Sun, dinner daily; 🍷👪) Glasgow curry buffs are forever debating the merits of the city's numerous excellent south Asian restaurants, and Mother India features in every discussion. It may lack the trendiness of some of the up-and-comers but it's been a stalwart for years and the quality and innovation on show is superb.

HEART BUCHANAN Cafe, Deli £

(www.heartbuchanan.co.uk; 380 Byres Rd; light meals £6-10; ⏲9am-4pm Mon-Sat, 10am-6pm Sun) The famous West End deli – give your nose a treat and drop in – has a small cafe space next door.

Drinking

City Centre

ARTÀ Bar

(www.arta.co.uk; 62 Albion St; ⏲5pm-3am Thu-Sat) This extraordinary place is so baroque that when you hear a Mozart concerto over the sound system, it wouldn't surprise you to see the man himself at the other end of the bar.

HORSE SHOE Pub

(www.horseshoebar.co.uk; 17 Drury St) This legendary city pub and popular meeting place dates from the late 19th century and is largely unchanged. It's a picturesque spot, with the longest continuous bar in the UK, but its main attraction is what's served over it – real ale and good cheer.

Information

The **List** (www.list.co.uk), available from newsagents (£2.20), is Glasgow and Edinburgh's invaluable fortnightly guide to films, theatre, cabaret, music, clubs – the works.

Glasgow Information Centre (☎0141-204 4400; www.seeglasgow.com; 11 George Sq; ⏲9am-5pm Mon-Sat) Excellent tourist office; makes local and national accommodation bookings (£4).

🛈 Getting There & Away

Air

Ten miles west of the city, **Glasgow International Airport** (GLA; www.glasgowairport.com) handles domestic traffic and international flights. **Glasgow Prestwick Airport** (PIK; www.glasgowprestwick. com), 30 miles southwest of Glasgow, is used by **Ryanair** (www.ryanair.com) and some other budget airlines, with many connections to the rest of Britain and Europe.

Train

As a general rule, Glasgow Central station serves southern Scotland, England and Wales, and Queen St station serves the north and east. There are buses every 10 minutes between them.

Scotrail (📞08457 55 00 33; www.scotrail. co.uk) runs Scottish trains. Destinations include: Edinburgh (£12.90, 50 minutes, every 15 minutes), Oban (£21.60, three hours, three to four daily), Fort William (£26.30, 3¾ hours, four to five daily), Dundee (£25.30, 1½ hours, hourly), Aberdeen (£45.20, 2½ hours, hourly) and Inverness (£79, 3½ hours, 10 daily, four on Sunday).

Culzean Castle & Country Park

The Scottish National Trust's flagship property, magnificent **Culzean** (NTS; 📞01655-884400; www.culzeanexperience.org; adult/child/family £15/11/36, park only adult/child £9.50/7; ⏰castle 10.30am-5pm Apr-Oct, park 9.30am-sunset year-round) is one of the most impressive of Scotland's great stately homes. The entrance to Culzean (kull-ane) is a converted viaduct, and on approach the castle appears like a mirage, floating into view. Designed by Robert Adam, who was encouraged to exercise his romantic genius in its design, this 18th-century mansion is perched dramatically on the edge of the cliffs. Robert Adam was the most influential architect of his time, renowned for his meticulous attention to detail and the elegant classical embellishments with which he decorated his ceilings and fireplaces.

Culzean is 12 miles south of Ayr.

STIRLING

POP 32,673

With an utterly impregnable position atop a mighty wooded crag (the plug of an extinct volcano), Stirling's beautifully preserved Old Town is a treasure trove of noble buildings and cobbled streets winding up to the ramparts of its dominant castle, which offer views for miles around. Clearly visible is the brooding Wallace Monument, a strange Victorian Gothic creation honouring the legendary freedom fighter of *Braveheart* fame. Nearby is Bannockburn, scene of Robert the Bruce's major triumph over the English.

Sights

STIRLING CASTLE
Castle

(HS; www.historic-scotland.gov.uk; adult/child £13/6.50; ⏰9.30am-6pm Apr-Sep, to 5pm Oct-Mar) Hold Stirling and you control Scotland. This maxim has ensured that a fortress of some kind has existed here since prehistoric times.

The current castle dates from the late 14th to the 16th century, when it was a residence of the Stuart monarchs. The undisputed highlight of a visit is the fabulous recently restored **Royal Palace**. The suite of six rooms – three for the king, three for the queen – is a sumptuous riot of colour. Particularly notable are the fine fireplaces, the re-created painted oak discs in the ceiling of the king's audience chamber, and the fabulous series of **tapestries** that have been painstakingly woven over many years.

The other buildings surrounding the main castle courtyard are the vast **Great Hall**, built by James IV; the **Royal Chapel**, remodelled in the early 17th century by James VI and with the original mural painting intact; and the King's Old Building. This is now home to the **Museum of the Argyll & Sutherland Highlanders** (admission free, donations encouraged), which traces the history of this famous regiment from 1794, including their defensive action in the Battle of Balaclava in 1854. Make sure you read the moving letters from WWI and WWII.

Stirling

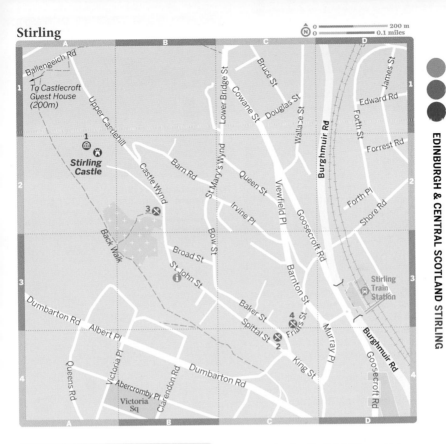

Stirling

◎ **Top Sights**

◎ **Sights**

✕ **Eating**

Until the last tapestry is completed, probably in late 2013, you can watch the weavers at work in the **Tapestry Studio** at the far end of the castle. Other displays include the **Great Kitchens**, bringing to life the bustle and scale of the enterprise of cooking for the king and, near the entrance, the **Castle Exhibition**, which gives good background information on the Stuart kings and updates on current archaeological investigations. The magnificent vistas from the **ramparts** are stirring.

Admission includes an audioguide, and free guided tours leave regularly from near the entrance.

OLD TOWN   Historic District
Stirling has the best surviving town wall in Scotland. It was built around 1547 when Henry VIII of England began the 'Rough Wooing' – attacking the town in order to force Mary, Queen of Scots to marry his son so that the two kingdoms could be united. The wall can be explored on the Back Walk, which follows the line of the wall from Dumbarton Rd to the castle.

Stirling Castle

Planning Your Attack

Stirling's a sizeable fortress, but not so huge that you'll have to decide what to leave out – there's time to see it all. Unless you've got a working knowledge of Scottish monarchs, head to the **Castle Exhibition** ❶ first: it'll help you sort one James from another. That done, take on the sights at leisure. First, stop and look around you from the **ramparts** ❷; the views high over this flat valley, a key strategic point in Scotland's history, are magnificent.

Next, head through to the back of the castle to the **Tapestry Studio** ❸, which is open for shorter hours; seeing these skilful weavers at work is a highlight. Track back towards the citadel's heart, stopping for a quick tour through the **Great Kitchens** ❹; looking at all that fake food might make you seriously hungry, though. Then enter the main courtyard. Around you are the principal castle buildings. During summer there are events (such as Renaissance dancing) in the **Great Hall** ❺ – get details at the entrance. **The Museum of the Argyll & Sutherland Highlanders** ❻ is a treasure trove if you're interested in regimental history, but missable if you're not. Leave the best for last – crowds thin in the afternoon – and enter the sumptuous **Royal Palace** ❼.

The Way Up & Down

If you have time, take the atmospheric Back Walk, a peaceful, shady stroll around the Old Town's fortifications and up to the castle's imposing crag-top position. Afterwards, wander down through the Old Town to admire its facades.

TOP TIPS

Admission Entrance is free for Historic Scotland members. If you'll be visiting several Scottish castles and ruins, a membership will save you plenty.

Vital Statistics First constructed: before AD1110. Number of sieges: at least 9. Last besieger: Bonnie Prince Charlie (unsuccessful). Cost of refurbishing the Royal Palace: £12 million.

DAVID ROBERTSON/ALAMY ©

Museum of the Argyll & Sutherland Highlanders
The history of one of Scotland's legendary regiments – now subsumed into the Royal Regiment of Scotland – is on display here, featuring memorabilia, weapons and uniforms.

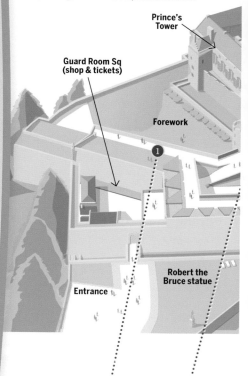

Prince's Tower

Guard Room Sq (shop & tickets)

Forework

Robert the Bruce statue

Entrance

Castle Exhibition
A great overview of the Stewart dynasty here will get your facts straight, and also offers the latest archaeological titbits from the ongoing excavations under the citadel. Analysis of skeletons has revealed surprising amounts of biographical data.

Royal Palace
The impressive new highlight of a visit to the castle is this recreation of the royal lodgings originally built by James V. The finely worked ceiling, ornate furniture and sumptuous unicorn tapestries dazzle.

Great Hall & Chapel Royal
Creations of James IV and VI, respectively, these elegant spaces around the central courtyard have been faithfully restored. The vast Great Hall, with its imposing beamed roof, was the largest medieval hall in Scotland.

King's Old Building

Nether Bailey

Grand Battery

Tapestry Studio (until late 2013)
An exquisite series of tapestries depicting a unicorn hunt, full of themes with Christian undertones, is being painstakingly reproduced here: each tapestry takes four years to make. It's fascinating to watch the weavers at work.

Ramparts
Perched on the walls you can appreciate the utter dominance of the castle's position atop this lofty volcanic crag. The view includes the site of Robert the Bruce's victory at Bannockburn and the monument to William Wallace.

Great Kitchens
Dive into this original display that brings home the massive enterprise of organising, preparing and cooking a feast fit for a Renaissance king. Your stomach may rumble at the lifelike haunches of meat, loaves of bread, fowl and fishes.

NATIONAL WALLACE MONUMENT
Monument

(www.nationalwallacemonument.com; adult/child £8.25/5.25; ⏱10am-5pm Apr-Jun, Sep & Oct, to 6pm Jul & Aug, 10.30am-4pm Nov-Mar) Towering over Scotland's narrow waist, this nationalist memorial is so Victorian Gothic it deserves circling bats and ravens. It commemorates the bid for Scottish independence depicted in the film *Braveheart*. Buses 62 and 63 run from Murray Pl in Stirling to the visitor centre, otherwise it's a half-hour walk from central Stirling.

😴 Sleeping

CASTLECROFT GUEST HOUSE
B&B ££

(☎01786-474933; www.castlecroft-uk.com; Ballengeich Rd; s/d £50/65; P @ 🛜) Nestling into the hillside under the back of the castle, this great hideaway feels like a rural retreat but is a short, spectacular walk from the heart of historic Stirling.

NEIDPATH
B&B £

(☎01786-469017; www.neidpath-stirling.co.uk; 24 Linden Ave; s/d £40/58; P 🛜) Offering excellent value and a genuine welcome, this is a fine choice and easily accessed by car. A particularly appealing front room is one of three excellent modernised chambers with fridges and good bathrooms.

Eating & Drinking

THE KITCHEN
Bistro ££

(☎01786-448833; www.thekitchenstirling.co.uk; 3 Friars St; mains £11-15) Likeable and laid-back on a central pedestrian street, this Stirling newcomer is doing things right. The small slate-floored dining area offers – in particular – excellent fish and seafood options with willing if slow service.

PORTCULLIS
Pub ££

(☎01786-472290; www.theportcullishotel.com; Castle Wynd; bar meals £8-12) Built in stone as solid as the castle that it stands below, this former school is just the spot for a pint and a pub lunch after your visit.

🌿 BREÁ
Cafe £

(www.breastirling.co.uk; 5 Baker St; mains £7-13; ⏱10am-9.30pm Tue-Sun; 🚼) Bringing a bohemian touch to central Stirling, this place has pared-back contemporary

Loch Arklet, The Trossachs

THOMAS DICKSON/GETTY IMAGES ©

decor and a short menu showcasing carefully sourced Scottish produce.

ⓘ Information

Stirling Information Centre (☎01786-475019; www.visitscottishheartlands.com; St John St; ⊙10am-5pm)

ⓘ Getting There & Away

First ScotRail (www.scotrail.co.uk) has services to/from a number of destinations, including the following:

Aberdeen £43.30, 2¼ hours, hourly weekdays, two-hourly Sunday

Dundee £17.70, one hour, hourly weekdays, two-hourly Sunday

Edinburgh £7.70, 55 minutes, twice hourly Monday to Saturday, hourly Sunday

Glasgow £8, 40 minutes, twice hourly Monday to Saturday, hourly Sunday

Perth £11.70, 30 minutes, hourly weekdays, two-hourly Sunday

THE TROSSACHS

The Trossachs region has long been a favourite weekend getaway, offering outstanding natural beauty and excellent walking and cycling routes within easy reach of the southern population centres. With thickly forested hills, romantic lochs and an increasingly interesting selection of places to stay and eat, its popularity is sure to continue, protected by its national-park status.

In summer the Trossachs can be overburdened with coach tours, but many of these are day trippers – peaceful, long evenings gazing at the reflections in the nearest loch are still possible. It's worth timing your visit not to coincide with a weekend.

Loch Katrine

This rugged area, 6 miles north of Aberfoyle and 10 miles west of Callander, is the heart of the Trossachs. From April to October two **boats** (☎01877-376315; www. lochkatrine.com; Trossachs Pier; 1hr cruise adult/

child £12/8) run cruises from Trossachs Pier at the eastern tip of Loch Katrine. One of these is the fabulous centenarian **steamship Sir Walter Scott**; check the website to see which boats depart when. From Stronachlachar (also accessible by car via Aberfoyle), you can reach the eastern shore of Loch Lomond at isolated Inversnaid. A tarmac path links Trossachs Pier with Stronachlachar, so you can also take the boat out and walk/cycle back (12.5 miles).

Loch Lomond & Around

The 'bonnie banks' and 'bonnie braes' of Loch Lomond have long been Glasgow's rural retreat – a scenic region of hills, lochs and healthy fresh air within easy reach of Scotland's largest city. The main tourist focus is along the A82 on the loch's western shore, and at the southern end, around Balloch, which can occasionally be a nightmare of jet skis and motorboats. The eastern shore, which is followed by the West Highland Way long-distance footpath, is a little quieter.

🏃 Activities

Boat Trips & Canoeing

The main centre for boat trips is Balloch, where **Sweeney's Cruises** (☎01389-752376; www.sweeneyscruises.com; Balloch Rd, Balloch) offers a range of trips including a one-hour cruise to Inchmurrin and back (adult/child £8.50/5, departs hourly).

Cruise Loch Lomond (www.cruise lochlomond.co.uk; Tarbet) is based in Tarbet and offers trips to Inversnaid and Rob Roy MacGregor's Cave. You can also be dropped off at Rowardennan and picked up at Inversnaid after a 9-mile hike along the West Highland Way (£14.50).

Lomond Adventure (☎01360-870218; www.lomondadventure.co.uk; Balmaha), in Balmaha, rents out Canadian canoes (£30 per day) and kayaks (£25).

Can You Experience (☎01389-756251; www.canyouexperience.com; Loch Lomond Shores, Balloch) hires out canoes (£12/17 per half-/full hour) and bicycles (£13/17 per three hours/full day), and offers a full-day guided canoe safari on the loch (adult/child £65/55).

🛏 Sleeping & Eating

OAK TREE INN Inn ££

(☎01360-870357; www.oak-tree-inn.co.uk; Balmaha; dm/s/d £30/60/75; P 🛜 👪) An attractive traditional inn built in slate and timber, the Oak Tree offers luxurious guest bedrooms for pampered hikers, and two four-bed bunkrooms for hardier souls. The rustic restaurant dishes up hearty lunches and dinners (mains £9 to £12), such as steak-and-mushroom pie, and roast Arctic char with lime and chive butter, and cooks an excellent bowl of Cullen skink (soup made with smoked haddock, potato, onion and milk).

DROVER'S INN Pub ££

(☎01301-704234; www.thedroversinn.co.uk; bar meals £7-12; ⏱lunch & dinner) This is one howff you shouldn't miss – a low-ceilinged place with smoke-blackened stone, bare wooden floors spotted with candle wax, barmen in kilts, and walls festooned with moth-eaten stags' heads and stuffed birds. There's even a stuffed bear and the desiccated husk of a basking shark. Ask to see your room before taking it.

ℹ Information

Balloch Tourist Office (☎0870 720 0607; Balloch Rd, Balloch; ⏱9.30am-6pm Jun-Aug, 10am-6pm Apr & Sep)

Balmaha National Park Centre (☎01389-722100; Balmaha; ⏱9.30am-4.15pm Apr-Sep)

National Park Gateway Centre (☎01389-751035; www.lochlomondshores.com; Loch Lomond Shores, Balloch; ⏱10am-6pm Apr-Sep, to 5pm Oct-Mar; 🛜)

ℹ Getting There & Away

Bus

First Glasgow (☎0141-423 6600; www.firstglasgow.com) buses 204 and 215 run from Argyle St in central Glasgow to Balloch and Loch Lomond Shores (1½ hours, at least two per hour).

Scottish Citylink (www.citylink.co.uk) coaches from Glasgow to Oban and Fort William stop at Luss (£8.20, 55 minutes, six daily), Tarbet (£8.20, 65 minutes) and Ardlui (£14.30, 1¼ hours).

Train

Train services include the following:

Glasgow to Balloch £4.70, 45 minutes, every 30 minutes

Glasgow to Arrochar & Tarbet £11, 1¼ hours, three or four daily

Glasgow to Ardlui £14, 1½ hours, three or four daily, continuing to Oban and Fort William

ST ANDREWS

POP 14,209

For a small place, St Andrews made a big name for itself, firstly as religious centre, then as Scotland's oldest university town. But its status as the home of golf has propelled it to even greater fame, and today's pilgrims arrive with a set of clubs.

The **Old Course**, the world's most famous, has a striking seaside location at the western end of town.

You'll need to book in advance to play via **St Andrews Links Trust** (☎01334-466666; www.standrews.org.uk). Reservations open on the first Wednesday in September the year before you wish to play. No bookings are taken for Saturdays or the month of September.

Unless you've booked months in advance, getting a tee-off time is literally a lottery; enter the ballot at the **caddie office** (☎01334-466666) before 2pm two days before you wish to play (there's no Sunday play). Be warned that applications by ballot are normally heavily oversubscribed, and green fees are £150 in summer.

👁 Sights

ST ANDREWS CATHEDRAL Ruin

(HS; www.historic-scotland.gov.uk; The Pends; adult/child £4.50/2.70, incl castle £7.60/4.60;

⏱9.30am-5.30pm Apr-Sep, to 4.30pm Oct-Mar)
The ruins of this cathedral are all that's left of one of Britain's most magnificent medieval buildings. Although founded in 1160, it was not consecrated until 1318, but stood as the focus of this important pilgrimage centre until 1559 when it was pillaged during the Reformation. St Andrew's supposed bones lie under the altar; until the cathedral was built, they had been enshrined in the nearby Church of St Regulus (Rule). All that remains of this church is **St Rule's Tower**, worth the climb for the view across St Andrews.

ST ANDREWS CASTLE   Castle
(HS; www.historic-scotland.gov.uk; The Scores; adult/child £5.50/3.30, incl cathedral £7.60/4.60; ⏱9.30am-5.30pm Apr-Sep, to 4.30pm Oct-Mar) With dramatic coastline views, the castle is mainly in ruins, but the site itself is evocative. It was founded around 1200 as the bishop's fortified home.

🛏 Sleeping

ABBEY COTTAGE   B&B ££
(☎01334-473727; coull@lineone.net; Abbey Walk; s £45, d £65-70; P 🛜) You know you've strayed from the B&B mainstream when your charming host's hobby is photographing tigers in the wild – don't leave without browsing her albums. There are three excellent rooms, all different, with patchwork quilts, sheepskins and antique furniture.

FAIRWAYS OF ST ANDREWS B&B ££
(☎01334-479513; www.fairwaysofstandrews.co.uk; 8a Golf Pl; s £80-120, d £90-150; 🛜) Just around the corner from golf's most famous 18th green, this is more in the boutique hotel than B&B class.

There are just three superstylish rooms; the best on the top floor is huge and has its own balcony with views over the Old Course.

HAZELBANK HOTEL   Hotel ££
(☎01334-472466; www.hazelbank.com; 28 The Scores; s £69-89, d £99-151; @ 🛜) Offering a genuine welcome, the family-run Hazelbank is the most likeable of the pleasingly old-fashioned hotels along the Scores. The front rooms have marvellous views along the beach and out to sea; those at the back are cheaper.

🍴 Eating

VINE LEAF   Scottish £££
(☎01334-477497; www.vineleafstandrews.co.uk; 131 South St; 2-course dinner £26.50; ⏱dinner Tue-Sat; ⚐) Classy, comfortable and well-established, the friendly Vine Leaf offers a changing menu of sumptuous Scottish seafood, game and vegetarian dishes.

St Andrews Golf Course
ANDREA PISTOLESI/GETTY IMAGES ©

St Andrews

0   200 m
0   0.1 miles

St Andrews Bay

North Sea

Old Course

Golf Pl

The Links

Golf Pl

Pilmour Pl

Playfair Tce

The Scores

North St

Murray Park

Murray Pl

Greyfriars Gdn

Bell St

Butts Wynd

College St

Church St

Market St

St Mary's Pl

Hope St

City Rd

Station Rd

Louden's Cl

Doubledykes Rd

Argyle St

Kinburn Park

South St

West Burn La

Queen's Gdns

Church Sq

Abbey St

South Castle St   North Castle St

St Andrews Castle

St Andrews Cathedral

The Pends

To Abbey
Cottage (400m)

To Leuchars
Train Station
(5mi); Dundee
(13mi)

To New Hall
(250m)

1

2

3

4

5

6

SEAFOOD RESTAURANT Seafood £££
(☎01334-479475; www.theseafoodrestaurant. com; The Scores; lunch/dinner £22/45) The Seafood Restaurant occupies a stylish glass-walled room, built out over the sea, with plush navy carpet, crisp white linen, an open kitchen and panoramic views of St Andrews Bay.

❶ Information

St Andrews Information Centre (☎01334-472021; www.visit-standrews.co.uk; 70 Market St; ⏱9.15am-6pm Mon-Sat, 10am-5pm Sun Jul & Aug, 9.15am-5pm Mon-Sat Sep-Jun, plus 11am-4pm Sun Apr-Jun, Sep & Oct)

❶ Getting There & Away

There is no train station in St Andrews itself, but you can take a train from Edinburgh (grab a seat on the right-hand side of the carriage for great firth views) to Leuchars, 5 miles to the northwest (£12.60, one hour, hourly). From here, buses leave regularly for St Andrews.

PERTH
POP 43,450

Sedately arranged along the banks of the Tay, this former capital of Scotland is a most liveable place with large tracts of enticing parkland surrounding an easily managed town centre. On its outskirts lies Scone Palace, a country house of staggering luxury built alongside the mound that was the crowning place of Scotland's kings.

◉ Sights

SCONE PALACE Palace
(www.scone-palace.co.uk; adult/child/family £10/7/30; ⏱9.30am-5pm Apr-Oct, closes 4.30pm Sat) 'So thanks to all at once and to each one, whom we invite to see us crowned at Scone.' This line from *Macbeth* indicates the importance of this place (pronounced 'skoon'), 2 miles north of Perth. Here in 838, Kenneth MacAlpin became the first king of a united Scotland and brought the **Stone of Destiny**, on which Scottish kings were ceremonially invested, to Moot Hill. In 1296 Edward I of England carted the talisman off to Westminster Abbey, where it remained for 700 years before being returned to Scotland.

These days, however, Scone doesn't really conjure up ye olde days of bearded warrior-kings swearing oaths in the mist because the palace, rebuilt in the early 19th century, is a Georgian mansion of extreme elegance and luxury.

The visit takes you through a succession of sumptuous **rooms** filled with fine French furniture and noble artworks. Scone has belonged for centuries to the Murray family, earls of Mansfield, and many of the objects have fascinating history attached to them (friendly guides are on hand).

Ancient kings were crowned atop **Moot Hill**, topped by a chapel, next to the palace.

From Perth's centre, cross the bridge, turn left and keep bearing left until you reach the gates of the estate (15 to 20 minutes' walking). From here, it's a half-mile to the palace.

❶ Getting There & Away

From Perth there are trains to the following destinations:
Edinburgh £14.50, 1¼ hours, at least hourly Monday to Saturday, every two hours Sunday

If You Like...
Whisky Distilleries

Visiting a distillery can be memorable, but only hard-core malthounds will want to go to more than two or three. Some are great to visit; others are depressingly corporate. Here are some of our favourites.

1 ABERLOUR DISTILLERY
(☎01340-881249; www.aberlour.com; tours £12; ⏰tours 10am & 2pm daily Apr-Oct, by appointment Mon-Fri Nov-Mar) Has an excellent, detailed tour with a proper tasting session. It's on the main street in Aberlour.

2 GLENFARCLAS DISTILLERY
(☎01807-500257; www.glenfarclas.co.uk; admission £5; ⏰10am-4pm Mon-Fri Oct-Mar, to 5pm Mon-Fri Apr-Sep, plus to 4pm Sat Jul-Sep) Small, friendly and independent, Glenfarclas is 5 miles south of Aberlour on the Grantown road. The last tour leaves 1½ hours before closing. The in-depth Connoioseur's Tour (Friday only July to September) is £20.

3 GLENFIDDICH DISTILLERY VISITOR CENTRE
(☎01340-820373; www.glenfiddich.co.uk; admission free; ⏰9.30am-4.30pm Mon-Sat, from noon Sun Easter–mid-Oct, 9.30am-4.30pm Mon-Fri mid-Oct–Easter) It's big and busy, but handiest for Dufftown and foreign languages are available. The standard tour starts with an overblown video, but it's fun, informative and free. An in-depth Connoisseur's Tour (£20) must be prebooked.

4 MACALLAN DISTILLERY
(☎01340-872280; www.themacallan.com; ⏰9.30am-4.30pm Mon-Sat Easter-Oct, 11am-3pm Mon-Fri Nov-Mar) Excellent sherry-casked malt. Several small-group tours are available (last tour at 3.30pm), including an expert one (£20); all should be prebooked. Lovely location 2 miles northwest of Craigellachie.

Glasgow £14.50, one hour, at least hourly Monday to Saturday, every two hours Sunday

Stirling £11.70, 30 minutes, one or two per hour

NORTHEAST SCOTLAND
Glamis Castle

Looking every inch the archetypal Scottish Baronial castle, with its roofline sprouting a forest of pointed turrets and battlements, **Glamis Castle** (www.glamis-castle.co.uk; adult/child £9.75/7.25; ⏰10am-6pm Mar-Oct, 10.30am-4.30pm Nov & Dec, closed Jan-Feb) claims to be the legendary setting for Shakespeare's *Macbeth* (his character is the Thane of Glamis at the start of the play). A royal residence since 1372, it is the family home of the earls of Strathmore and Kinghorne: the Queen Mother (born Elizabeth Bowes-Lyon; 1900–2002) spent her childhood at Glamis (pronounced 'glams') and Princess Margaret (the Queen's sister; 1930–2002) was born here. The one-hour guided tours depart every 15 minutes (last tour at 4.30pm, or 3.30pm in winter).

Glamis Castle is 12 miles north of Dundee.

Balmoral Castle

Eight miles west of Ballater lies **Balmoral Castle** (☎01339-742334; www.balmoralcastle.com; adult/child £9/5; ⏰10am-5pm Apr-Jul, last admission 4pm), the Queen's Highland holiday home, screened from the road by a thick curtain of trees. Built for Queen Victoria in 1855 as a private residence for the royal family, it kicked off the revival of the Scottish Baronial style of architecture that characterises so many of Scotland's 19th-century country houses.

The admission fee includes an interesting and well-thought-out audioguide, but the tour is very much an outdoor one through garden and grounds; as for the castle itself, only the ballroom, which displays a collection of Landseer paintings and royal silver, is open to the public. Don't expect to see the Queen's private quarters!

Balmoral is beside the A93 at Crathie and can be reached on the Aberdeen to Braemar bus.

The Cairngorms

The **Cairngorms National Park** (www.cairngorms.co.uk) encompasses the highest landmass in Britain – a broad mountain plateau with an average altitude of over 1000m and five of the six highest summits in the UK. Lower down, the high plateau gives way to scenic glens softened by forests of native Scots pine.

The Cairngorms are prime hill-walking territory, but even couch potatoes can enjoy a taste of the high life by taking the **Cairngorm Mountain Railway** (☎ 01479-861261; www.cairngormmountain.org; adult/child return £9.95/6.50; ☺10.20am-4pm May-Nov, 9am-4.30pm Dec-Apr), near Aviemore.

The most useful base for exploring is Aviemore, 30 miles southeast of Inverness. The town of Braemar is about 40 miles further southeast, and hosts Scotland's most famous **Highland Games** (www.braemargathering.org) in September.

For general information, consult the **Cairngorms National Park Authority** (www.cairngorms.co.uk).

SPEYSIDE

Dufftown

Rome may be built on seven hills, but Dufftown's built on seven stills, say the locals. Founded in 1817 by James Duff, fourth earl of Fife, Dufftown is 17 miles south of Elgin and lies at the heart of the Speyside whisky-distilling region.

◎ Sights

With seven working distilleries nearby, Dufftown has been dubbed Scotland's malt-whisky capital. Ask at the tourist office for a **Malt Whisky Trail** (www.maltwhiskytrail.com) booklet, a self-guided tour around the seven stills plus the Speyside Cooperage.

WHISKY MUSEUM Museum
(☎ 01340-821097; www.dufftown.co.uk; 12 Conval St; ☺1-4pm Mon-Fri May-Sep) As well as housing a selection of distillery memorabilia (try saying that after a few drams), the Whisky Museum holds 'nosing and tasting evenings' where you can learn what to look for in a fine single malt (£10 per person; 8pm Wednesday in July and August).

You can then test your new-found skills at the nearby **Whisky Shop** (☎ 01340-821097; www.whiskyshopdufftown.co.uk; 1 Fife St), which stocks hundreds of single malts.

SPEYSIDE COOPERAGE Historic Building
(☎ 01340-871108; www.speysidecooperage.co.uk; adult/child £3.50/2; ☺9am-4pm Mon-Fri) Here you can see the fascinating art of barrel-making in action. It's a mile from Craigellachie on the Dufftown road.

Sleeping & Eating

DAVAAR B&B B&B ££
(☎ 01340-820464; www.davaardufftown.co.uk; 17 Church St; s/d from £40/60) Just along the street opposite the tourist office, Davaar is a sturdy Victorian villa with three smallish but comfy rooms; the breakfast menu is superb, offering the option of Portsoy kippers instead of the traditional fry-up (which uses eggs from the owners' own chickens).

🍃 **A TASTE OF SPEYSIDE** Scottish ££
(☎ 01340-820860; 10 Balvenie St; 2-/3-course dinner £19.50/22; ☺noon-9pm Tue-Sun Easter-Sep, noon-2pm & 6-9pm Tue-Sun Oct-Easter) This upmarket restaurant prepares traditional Scottish dishes using fresh local produce, including a challenging platter of smoked salmon, smoked venison, brandied chicken liver pâté, cured herring, a selection of Scottish cheeses and homemade bread (phew!). A two-course lunch costs £11.

Scotland's Highlands & Islands

The Highlands are clear testimony to the sculpting power of ice and weather. From the subarctic plateau of the Cairngorms to the rocky summit of Ben Nevis, here the Scottish landscape is at its grandest, with high peaks bounded by wooded glens, deep lochs and rushing waterfalls.

Glencoe and Fort William draw hordes of hill walkers in summer and skiers in winter, while Inverness, the Highland capital, provides urban rest and relaxation. Not far away, Loch Ness and its elusive monster add a hint of mystery.

To the west are Scotland's many off-shore islands, including major highlights such as Skye and Mull. Even further off the track, beyond the mainland to the north sits another island group, the Orkneys, where intrepid travellers can admire some of the finest prehistoric sites in the whole of Britain.

Eilean Donan Castle (p359)

Scotland's Highlands & Islands

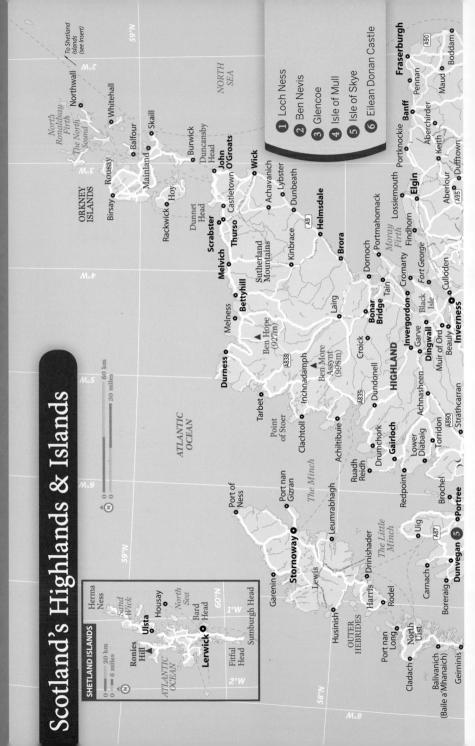

1 Loch Ness
2 Ben Nevis
3 Glencoe
4 Isle of Mull
5 Isle of Skye
6 Eilean Donan Castle

South Uist
Ludag
Castlebay
57°N
Isle of Skye
Talisker
Glenbrittle
Cullin Hills
Toscaig
Sconser
Kyle of Lochalsh
Eilean Donan Castle
6
Cannich
Drumnadrochit
Urquhart Castle
Loch Ness
Foyers
1
Grantown-on-Spey
Mossat
Insch
A96
Ellon
Kemnay
Aberdeen
Broadford
Kylerhea
Shiel Bridge
Elgol
Sleat
Isleornsay
A87
Kinloch Hourn
Fort Augustus
A9
Kincraig
Cairngorm Mountains
Balmoral Castle
Ballater
A93
Banchory
Armadale
Inverie
Glen Harris
Rum
Mallaig
Eigg
Galmisdale
Arisaig
Strathan
A82
Achnacarry
A86
Dalwhinnie
Inverey
Stonehaven
57°N
Glenfinnan
2
Grampian Mountains
Tarfside
Inverbervie
Sea of the Hebrides
Achosnich
Acharacle
Fort William
Ben Nevis (1343m)
ANGUS
Sorisdale
Coll
Crossapol
A861
Strontian
Kinlochleven
Kinloch Rannoch
Blair Atholl
Glamis Castle
A90
Montrose
Tobermory
Loch Linnhe
3
Glencoe
B846
Great Lyon
Calgary
Tiree
Sound of Mull
Great Coe
Kinlochetive
Kenmore
Alyth
Hynish
Portnacroish
A82
Loch Tay
Dunkeld
Arbroath
Lochdon
Isle of Mull
Dalmally
Tyndrum
PERTH & KINROSS
Perth
Dundee
Isle of Iona
A849
4
Lochbuie
Oban
Fionnphort
Comrie
ATLANTIC OCEAN
Easdale
A816
Cairndow
A9
FIFE
Inveraray
Firth of Lorn
Falkland
Crail
Ford
Ardgartan
Kinross
Isle of Colonsay
Kiloran
Stirling
M90
Elie
56°N
Ardlussa
ARGYLL & BUTE
Loch Lomond
STIRLING
Kirkcaldy
Dunfermline
Isle of Jura
Lochgilphead
Fintry
Firth of Forth
Gullane
Dunbar
56°N
Falkirk
Greenock
Dumbarton
FALKIRK
A1
Bunnahabhainn
A846
Edinburgh
Isle of Islay
Tarbert
A80
M8
Kilberry
Glasgow
Coatbridge
Bute
Berwick-upon-Tweed
Portnahaven
A83
East Kilbride
A702
Lochranza
Tayinloan
Lanark
Peebles
A697
A1
Laphroaig
Sound of Jura
Kilmarnock
Kelso
Isle of Arran
Brodick
B708
Galashiels
Wooler
6°W
Kilbrannan Sound
Ballyhillin
7°W
Campbeltown
Ayr
A7
Lagg
Hawick
North Channel
Kintyre
A77
A76
Gare Loch
NORTHERN IRELAND
Mull of Kintyre
5°W
Moffat
Rothbury

Scotland's Highlands & Islands Highlights

RICCARDO SPILA/CORBIS ©

① Loch Ness

Stretching along the glacier-gouged trench of the Great Glen, 23-mile-long Loch Ness contains more water than all the lakes in England and Wales combined. Its peaty depths conceal the mystery of its legendary monster, and thousands flock here each year in hope of catching a glimpse. Above: Fort Augustus; Top Right: Loch Ness Centre & Exhibition, Drumnadrochit; Bottom Right: Urquhart Castle

Need to Know

TOP TIP Drive the minor road on the loch's east side to avoid crowds
BEST PHOTO OP View from Urquhart Castle **For further coverage, see p354**

Local Knowledge

Loch Ness Don't Miss List

ADRIAN SHINE, LEADER OF THE LOCH NESS PROJECT

1 LOCH NESS CENTRE & EXHIBITION

I designed this exhibition myself, presenting the results of eight decades of research. The collection has everything from one-man submarines to the ROSETTA apparatus that opened the 10,000-year-old time capsule concealed within the loch's sediment layers. The exhibition does not have all the answers and it will certainly not try to sell you a monster. Instead, it places the mystery in its proper context, which is the environment of Loch Ness.

2 URQUHART CASTLE

If, having learned some of the inner secrets of the loch, you want to see it through new eyes, you cannot do better than visit Urquhart Castle. Perched on a rocky promontory jutting into Loch Ness, its exhibits recount the castle's history from a vitrified Pictish fort to its role in the Scottish Wars of Independence. The view from the Grant Tower is truly breathtaking.

3 FORT AUGUSTUS LOCKS

At the southern end of the loch there is a flight of locks on the Caledonian Canal, built by the great engineer Thomas Telford. It is always interesting to watch vessels being worked up this 'staircase' of water. British Waterways have a fascinating exhibition halfway up.

4 CRUISING THE LOCH

Venturing onto the water puts the seemingly tiny trunk road and Urquhart Castle into a new perspective. The Deepscan cruise boat runs from the Loch Ness Centre; I use this boat for my research and the skipper will tell you about his experiences. There are other cruise boats operating from Drumnadrochit, and the larger Jacobite vessels depart from Inverness.

5 WATERFALL WALKS

Starting from the car park at Invermoriston, cross the road to find the magnificent waterfall, then go back to take the path down the river through a mature beech wood to the shores of the loch. There is another famous waterfall at Foyers on the southeastern shore of Loch Ness, and Divach Falls up Balmacaan Rd at Drumnadrochit.

Ben Nevis

There's nowhere higher in Britain than the summit of Ben Nevis (p356), and that alone makes this mighty mountain an irresistible draw for hikers. Most people content themselves with looking at the view from nearby Fort William, but if you decide to tackle it, you'll need to be properly equipped – and wait for a favourable weather forecast.

TOM MARTIN/GETTY IMAGES ©

Glencoe

If you only have time to visit one Highland glen, make it this one (p354). It sums up the lonely grandeur and windswept majesty of the Scottish landscape. Catch it on a clear summer's day and you'll be treated to nonstop mountain views; come in midwinter and you'll likely be stuck in a wraparound white-out. Either way, be sure to keep your camera handy.

DAVID AUGUSTIN/GETTY IMAGES ©

Isle of Mull

4

Even without being immortalised in legend and song, Mull (p358) would still be a must-see for any visit to the Highlands. Ringed by miles of white sand and dotted with rugged hills, it's known for its stirring views and fantastic wildlife-watching – if you're lucky, you'll have the chance to spot seabirds, sea eagles or even a pod of dolphins. Dolphin in the Sound of Mull

5

6

Isle of Skye

Taking its name from the old Norse *sky-a*, meaning 'cloud island' (a Viking reference to the often mist-shrouded Cuillin Hills), this is the largest of Scotland's islands (p361), a 50-mile-long smorgasbord of velvet moors, jagged mountains, sparkling lochs and towering sea cliffs. The stunning scenery is the main attraction, but when the mist closes in there are plenty of castles and cosy pubs to retire to.

Eilean Donan Castle

Perched on a tiny island linked to the shore by an elegant arched bridge, Eilean Donan (p359) is perhaps the most picturesque of Scottish castles. Its image has graced everything from postcards to shortbread tins, and has appeared in many movies including *Highlander* and *The World Is Not Enough*. Despite its venerable appearance, it is actually a relatively modern restoration, dating from the early 20th century.

Scotland's Highlands & Islands' Best…

Drives

○ **Loch Ness** (p354) Classic loch views from Fort Augustus and Urquhart Castle

○ **Glencoe** (p354) Brooding mountain scenery looms over a narrow glen

○ **The Road to the Isles** (p357) From Fort William to Mallaig

○ **Glen Etive** (p363) This beautiful glen makes an ideal detour from Glencoe

Historic Sites

○ **Urquhart Castle** (p354) Impressive medieval castle overlooking the shores of Loch Ness

○ **Eilean Donan Castle** (p359) This archetypal Scottish fortress is scenically backed by sea and mountains

○ **Glencoe** (p354) Site of one of Scotland's most notorious massacres

○ **Skara Brae** (p365) Wander through Britain's best-preserved ancient settlement

Outdoor Experiences

○ **Conquering Ben Nevis** (p356) The Scottish hike to top them all

○ **Watching wildlife on Mull** (p359) Spot Mull's wildlife, either onshore or by boat

○ **Cruising Loch Ness** (p354) Keep your eyes peeled for Nessie

○ **Walking on Skye** (p361) Strap on your boots and explore Skye's hilly scenery

Islands

- **Mull** (p358) This large island boasts mountains, beaches, castles and even a railway

- **Skye** (p361) Sail over the sea to the best known of all Scottish islands

- **Iona** (p365) Tiny sacred island with a spiritual atmosphere

- **Orkney Islands** (p364) Rocky archipelago off Scotland's north coast, with many prehistoric remains

Need to Know

ADVANCE PLANNING

- **One month before** Book accommodation if visiting in summer, especially for popular spots such as Mull and Skye.

- **Two weeks before** If travelling by car, make reservations for any ferry crossings – as early as possible in summer.

- **One week before** Make bookings for wildlife-spotting boat trips.

RESOURCES

- **Highlands** (www.visithighlands.com)

- **Loch Ness** (www.visitlochness.com)

- **Cairngorms National Park** (www.visitcairngorms.com)

- **Fort William** (www.visit-fortwilliam.co.uk)

- **Skye** (www.skye.co.uk)

- **Caledonian Macbrayne** (www.calmac.co.uk)

GETTING AROUND

- **Bus** Run between major towns, but travel times can be long. Most islands have a limited bus network.

- **Car** The best way to explore the more remote glens and islands – but car ferry services to the more popular islands need to be reserved well ahead of time.

- **Ferry** Frequent services from Oban to Mull year-round; for Skye there's a ferry from Mallaig and a bridge at Kyle of Lochalsh.

- **Train** Scenic lines from Edinburgh or Glasgow to Inverness, Fort William, Oban, Mallaig or Kyle of Lochalsh.

BE FOREWARNED

- **Midges** These tiny biting flies are a pest from June to September, especially in still weather around dawn and dusk; bring insect repellent and wear long-sleeved clothing.

- **Weather** Always unpredictable on the west coast; be prepared for wet and windy days, even in the middle of summer.

Left: Ring of Brodgar (p365);
Above: Grazing sheep, Isle of Skye (p361)
(LEFT) BILL HEINSOHN/GETTY IMAGES ©;
(ABOVE) JAMES P. BLAIR/GETTY IMAGES ©

349

Scotland's Highlands & Islands Itineraries

The three-day trip takes in some big-name locations, while the five-day trip combines highlands with islands. The routes intersect at Fort William.

INVERNESS TO BEN NEVIS

Scottish Icons

Start your tour in **(1) Inverness**, capital of the Highlands, then head south on the A82 along the west bank of legendary Loch Ness. Stop at **(2) Drumnadrochit** to visit the monster exhibitions and Urquhart Castle, and perhaps take a cruise on the loch.

On day two, continue south via **(3) Fort William**, the self-proclaimed 'Outdoor Capital of the UK'. If the weather is good, get your boots on and go for a hike; if not, hop in the car and explore a few of the nearby glens, such as **(4) Glen Nevis** or **(5) Glencoe** a bit further afield.

On day three, hopefully the weather will be good enough for you to tackle Scotland's highest mountain, **(6) Ben Nevis**; if not, you could get an early start and head down the scenic coast road to Oban, the pretty coastal village which marks the departure point for ferries to the Isle of Mull.

5 DAYS

OBAN TO SKYE
Highland & Island Hopping

Our longer tour begins in **(1) Oban**, the 'gateway to the isles'. Take a day trip out to the smaller islands of Lismore or Kerrera, and in the evening walk up to McCaig's Tower.

The second day begins with the ferry ride across to the **(2) Isle of Mull**. Spend a day or two here, touring the island; options include the holy islet of Iona and the colourful island capital of Tobermory. The roads are narrow and the scenery stunning at every turn – two good reasons for allowing plenty of time.

Return to Oban and travel up the A828 towards **(3) Fort William**. Turn west

along the A830, the famous 'Road to the Isles'. Leave the main road at **(4) Arisaig**, signposted 'Alternative Coastal Route' for the best views. From the fishing harbour of **(5) Mallaig** take the ferry across to Armadale on the **(6) Isle of Skye**.

Spend the final day or two exploring Skye. Follow the scenic roads to Portree, the capital, via a stop at Sligachan for views of the Cuillin ridge. Return to the mainland via the Skye Bridge.

Cuillin Hills (p362), Isle of Skye
CHRIS HEPBURN/GETTY IMAGES ©

Discover Scotland's Highlands & Islands

Old Man of Storr (p364), Isle of Skye
DAVID C TOMLINSON/GETTY IMAGES ©

THE HIGHLANDS

Inverness

POP 55,000

Inverness, one of the fastest growing towns in Britain, is the capital of the Highlands. It's a transport hub and jumping-off point for the central, western and northern Highlands, the Moray Firth coast and the Great Glen.

 Sights

NESS ISLANDS   Park

The main attraction in Inverness is a leisurely stroll along the river to the Ness Islands.

They're a 20-minute walk south of the **castle (Castle St)** – head upstream on either side of the river (the start of the Great Glen Way), and return on the opposite bank.

 Tours

JACOBITE CRUISES   Boat Tours

(☎ 01463-233999; www.jacobite. co.uk; Glenurquhart Rd; adult/child £29/22; ⊕ twice daily Jun-Sep, once daily Apr-May) Boats depart from Tomnahurich Bridge for a 1½-hour cruise along Loch Ness, followed by a visit to Urquhart Castle (admission fee included in tour price) and a return to Inverness by coach. You can buy tickets at the tourist office and catch a free minibus to the boat.

JOHN O'GROATS FERRIES   Bus Tours

(☎ 01955-611353; www.jogferry.co.uk; ⊕ departs 7.30am) From May to September, daily tours (lasting 13½ hours; adult/child

£57/28.50) are run by bus and passenger ferry from Inverness bus station to Orkney.

 Sleeping

**ROCPOOL
RESERVE** Boutique Hotel **£££**
(☏01463-240089; www.rocpool.com; Culduthel Rd; s/d from £175/210; P ⊗) Boutique chic meets the Highlands in this slick and sophisticated little hotel, where an elegant Georgian exterior conceals an oasis of contemporary cool. A restaurant by Albert Roux completes the luxury package.

TRAFFORD BANK B&B **££**
(☏01463-241414; www.traffordbankguesthouse.co.uk; 96 Fairfield Rd; d £110-125; P ⊗) Lots of word-of-mouth rave reviews for this elegant Victorian villa that was once home to a bishop, just a mitre-toss from the Caledonian Canal and 10 minutes' walk west from the city centre.

 Eating

CONTRAST BRASSERIE Brasserie **££**
(☏01463-227889; www.glenmoristontownhouse.com/contrast.html; 22 Ness Bank; mains £13-20) Book early for what we think is the best restaurant in Inverness – a dining room that drips designer style, smiling professional staff, and truly delicious food.

CAFÉ 1 Bistro **££**
(☏01463-226200; www.cafe1.net; 75 Castle St; mains £10-23; ◷noon-9.30pm Mon-Fri, noon-2.30pm & 6-9.30pm Sat) Café 1 is a friendly and appealing bistro with candlelit tables amid elegant blonde-wood and wrought-iron decor.

ⓘ **Information**

Inverness Tourist Office (☏01463-252401; www.visithighlands.com; Castle Wynd; internet access per 20min £1; ◷9am-6pm Mon-Sat, 9.30am-5pm Sun Jul & Aug, 9am-5pm Mon-Sat, 10am-4pm Sun Jun, Sep & Oct, 9am-5pm Mon-Sat Apr & May)

Detour:
Cawdor Castle

Built in the 14th century, **Cawdor Castle** (☏01667-404615; www.cawdorcastle.com; adult/child £9.50/6; ◷10am-5.30pm May-Sep) was the home of the Thanes of Cawdor, one of the titles prophesied by the three witches for the eponymous character of Shakespeare's *Macbeth*. Macbeth couldn't have moved in, though, since the central tower dates from the 14th century (the wings were 17th-century additions), and he died in 1057.

ⓘ **Getting There & Away**

Air

Inverness Airport (INV; ☏01667-464000; www.hial.co.uk) There are scheduled flights to Amsterdam, Düsseldorf, London, Bristol, Manchester, Belfast, Stornoway, Benbecula, Orkney, Shetland and several other British airports.

Stagecoach Jet (www.stagecoachbus.com) Buses run from the airport to Inverness bus station (£3.30, 20 minutes, every 30 minutes).

Train

Services include:
- **Edinburgh** (£40, 3½ hours, eight daily)
- **Glasgow** (£40, 3½ hours, eight daily)
- **Kyle of Lochalsh** (£13, 2½ hours, four daily Monday to Saturday, two Sunday) One of Britain's great scenic train journeys.
- **London** (£100, eight hours, one daily) One daily direct; other services require a change at Edinburgh.

Loch Ness

Deep, dark and narrow, Loch Ness stretches for 23 miles between Inverness and Fort Augustus. Its bitterly cold waters have been extensively explored in search of Nessie, the elusive Loch Ness monster, but most visitors see her only in cardboard cut-out form at the monster exhibitions. A complete circuit of the loch is about 70 miles – travel anticlockwise for the best views.

Drumnadrochit

POP 800

Seized by monster madness, its gift shops bulging with Nessie cuddly toys, Drumnadrochit is a hotbed of beastie fever, with two monster exhibitions battling it out for the tourist dollar.

Sights & Activities

URQUHART CASTLE   Castle
(HS; ☏01456-450551; adult/child £7.40/4.50; ⏲9.30am-6pm Apr-Sep, to 5pm Oct, to 4.30pm Nov-Mar) Commanding a brilliant location 1.5 miles east of Drumnadrochit, with outstanding views (on a clear day), Urquhart Castle is a popular Nessie-watching hotspot. A huge visitor centre includes a video theatre and displays of medieval items discovered in the castle.

LOCH NESS CENTRE & EXHIBITION   Exhibition Centre
(☏01456-450573; www.lochness.com; adult/child £6.95/4.95; ⏲9am-6pm Jul & Aug, to 5.30pm Jun, 9.30am-5pm Easter-May & Sep-Oct, 10am-3.30pm Nov-Easter) The better of the two Nessie-themed exhibitions in Drumnadrochit, this one adopts a scientific approach that allows you to weigh the evidence for yourself. You'll find out about hoaxes and optical illusions, as well as learning a lot about the ecology of Loch Ness – is there enough food in the loch to support even one 'monster', let alone a breeding population?

NESSIE HUNTER   Boat Trips
(☏01456-450395; www.lochness-cruises.com; adult/child £15/10; ⏲Easter-Oct) One-hour monster-hunting cruises, complete with sonar and underwater cameras. Cruises depart from Drumnadrochit hourly (except 1pm) from 9am to 6pm daily.

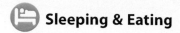 **Sleeping & Eating**

LOCH NESS INN   Inn ££
(☏01456-450991; www.staylochness.co.uk; Lewiston; s/d/f £89/102/145; P🛜) The Loch Ness Inn ticks all the weary traveller's boxes, with comfortable bedrooms (the family suite sleeps two adults and two children), a cosy bar pouring real ales from the Cairngorm and Isle of Skye breweries, and a rustic restaurant (mains £9 to £18) serving hearty, wholesome fare such as whisky-flambéed haggis, and roast rump of Scottish lamb.

DRUMBUIE FARM   B&B ££
(☏01456-450634; www.loch-ness-farm.co.uk; Drumnadrochit; per person from £30; ⏲Mar-Oct; P) Drumbuie is a B&B in a modern house on a working farm – the surrounding fields are full of sheep and highland cattle – with views over Urquhart Castle and Loch Ness.

ℹ Getting There & Away

Scottish Citylink and Stagecoach buses from Inverness to Fort William run along the shores of Loch Ness (six to eight daily, five on Sunday); those headed for Skye turn off at Invermoriston. There are bus stops at Drumnadrochit (£6.20, 30 minutes) and Urquhart Castle (£6.60, 35 minutes).

Glencoe

Scotland's most famous glen is also one of the grandest and, in bad weather, the grimmest. The southern side is dominated by three massive, brooding spurs, known as the **Three Sisters**, while the northern side is enclosed by the continuous steep wall of the knife-edged Aonach Eagach ridge. The main road threads its lonely way through the middle of all this mountain grandeur.

The Legend of Nessie

Highland folklore is filled with tales of strange creatures living in lochs and rivers, notably the kelpie (water horse) that lures unwary travellers to their doom. The use of the term 'monster', however, is a relatively recent phenomenon whose origins lie in an article published in the *Inverness Courier* on 2 May 1933, entitled 'Strange Spectacle on Loch Ness'.

The article recounted the sighting of a disturbance in the loch by Mrs Aldie Mackay and her husband: 'There the creature disported itself, rolling and plunging for fully a minute, its body resembling that of a whale, and the water cascading and churning like a simmering cauldron'.

In December 1933 the *Daily Mail* sent Marmaduke Wetherall, a film director and big-game hunter, to Loch Ness to track down the beast. Within days he found 'reptilian' footprints in the shoreline mud (soon revealed to have been made with a stuffed hippopotamus foot, possibly an umbrella stand). Then in April 1934 came the famous 'long-necked monster' photograph taken by the seemingly reputable Harley St surgeon Colonel Kenneth Wilson. The press went mad and the rest, as they say, is history.

In 1994, however, Christian Spurling – Wetherall's stepson, by then 90 years old – revealed that the most famous photo of Nessie ever taken was in fact a hoax, perpetrated by his stepfather with Wilson's help.

◉ Sights

GLENCOE FOLK MUSEUM Museum
(☏01855-811664; www.glencoemuseum.com; adult/child £3/free; ☺10am-4.30pm Mon-Sat Easter-Oct) This small, thatched-roof museum houses a varied collection of military memorabilia, farm equipment, and tools of the woodworking, blacksmithing and slate-quarrying trades.

GLENCOE VISITOR CENTRE Visitor Centre
(NTS; ☏01855-811307; www.glencoe-nts.org.uk; adult/child £6/5; ☺9.30am-5.30pm Easter-Oct, 10am-4pm Thu-Sun Nov-Easter) About 1.5 miles east of Glencoe village is this modern facility with an ecotourism angle.

 Sleeping & Eating

CLACHAIG INN Hotel ££
(☏01855-811252; www.clachaig.com; s/d from £70/92; P ☎ ☻) The Clachaig has long been a favourite haunt of hill walkers and climbers. As well as comfortable en suite accommodation, there's a smart, wood-panelled lounge bar with lots of sofas and armchairs, mountaineering photos, and climbing magazines to leaf through.

❶ Getting There & Away

Scottish Citylink buses run between Fort William and Glencoe (£7.50, 30 minutes, eight daily) and from Glencoe to Glasgow (£20, 2½ hours, eight daily). Buses stop at Glencoe village, Glencoe Visitor Centre, and Glencoe Mountain Resort.

Stagecoach bus 44 links Glencoe village with Fort William (35 minutes, hourly Monday to Saturday, three on Sunday) and Kinlochleven (25 minutes).

Fort William
POP 9900

Basking on the shores of Loch Linnhe amid magnificent mountain scenery, Fort William has one of the most enviable settings in the whole of Scotland. If it wasn't for the busy dual carriageway crammed between the town centre and the loch, and one of the highest rainfall records in the country, it would be almost idyllic.

Climbing Ben Nevis

As the highest peak in the British Isles, Ben Nevis (1344m) attracts many would-be ascensionists who would not normally think of climbing a Scottish mountain – a staggering (often literally) 100,000 people reach the summit each year.

Although anyone who is reasonably fit should have no problem hiking to the summit of Ben Nevis on a fine summer's day, an ascent should not be undertaken lightly. You will need proper walking boots (the path is rough and stony, and there may be soft, wet snowfields on the summit), warm clothing, waterproofs, a map and compass, and plenty of food and water. And don't forget to check the weather forecast (see www.bennevisweather.co.uk).

There are three possible starting points for the tourist track (the walkers' route) ascent – Achintee Farm; the footbridge at Glen Nevis Youth Hostel; and the car park at Glen Nevis Visitor Centre. The total distance to the summit and back is 8 miles; allow at least four or five hours to reach the top, and another 2½ to three hours for the descent.

Sights

WEST HIGHLAND MUSEUM Museum
(☎01397-702169; www.westhighlandmuseum. org.uk; Cameron Sq; ⏰10am-5pm Mon-Sat Apr-Oct, to 4pm Mar & Oct-Dec, closed Jan & Feb) This small but fascinating museum is packed with all manner of Highland memorabilia. Look out for the secret portrait of Bonnie Prince Charlie – after the Jacobite rebellions all things Highland were banned, including pictures of the exiled leader, and this tiny painting looks like nothing more than a smear of paint until viewed in a cylindrical mirror, which reflects a credible likeness of the prince.

Sleeping

LIME TREE Hotel ££
(☎01397-701806; www.limetreefortwilliam. co.uk; Achintore Rd; s/d from £80/110; P) Much more interesting than your average guesthouse, this former Victorian manse overlooking Loch Linnhe is an 'art gallery with rooms', decorated throughout with the artist-owner's atmospheric Highland landscapes.

GRANGE B&B ££
(☎01397-705516; www.grangefortwilliam. com; Grange Rd; r per person £58-63; P) An exceptional 19th-century villa set in its own landscaped grounds, the Grange is crammed with antiques and fitted with log fires, chaise longues and Victorian roll-top baths. It's located 500m southwest of the town centre.

 ## Eating & Drinking

LIME TREE Scottish £££
(☎01397-701806; www.limetreefortwilliam. co.uk; Achintore Rd; 2-/3-course dinner £28/30; ⏰dinner daily, lunch Sun) Fort William is not over-endowed with great places to eat, but the restaurant at this small hotel and art gallery has put the UK's Outdoor Capital on the gastronomic map. The chef won a Michelin star in his previous restaurant, and turns out delicious dishes built around fresh Scottish produce, such as seared saddle of Glenfinnan venison with red wine and rosemary jus.

**CRANNOG SEAFOOD
RESTAURANT** Seafood ££
(☎01397-705589; www.crannog.net; Town Pier; mains £16-20) The Crannog wins the prize for best location in town – perched on the

Town Pier, giving window-table diners an uninterrupted view down Loch Linnhe. Informal and unfussy, it specialises in fresh local seafood – there are three or four daily fish specials plus the main menu – though there are beef, poultry and vegetarian dishes, too.

Information

Fort William Tourist Office (☎01397-703781; www.visithighlands.com; 15 High St; internet per 20min £1; ⏰9am-6pm Mon-Sat, 10am-5pm Sun Apr-Sep, limited hours Oct-Mar)

Getting There & Away

Train

The spectacular **West Highland line** runs from Glasgow to Mallaig via Fort William. The overnight **Caledonian Sleeper** service connects Fort William and London Euston (£103 sharing a twin-berth cabin, 13 hours).

There's no direct rail connection between Oban and Fort William – you have to change at Crianlarich, so it's faster to use the bus.

- **Edinburgh** (£44, five hours, three daily) Change at Glasgow's Queen St station.
- **Glasgow** (£26.30, 3¾ hours, three daily, two on Sunday)
- **Mallaig** (£11, 1½ hours, four daily, three on Sunday)

THE ROAD TO THE ISLES

The 46-mile A830 road from Fort William to Mallaig is traditionally known as the Road to the Isles, as it leads to the jumping-off point for ferries to the Small Isles and Skye, itself a stepping stone to the Outer Hebrides. This is a region steeped in Jacobite history, having witnessed both the beginning and the end of Bonnie Prince Charlie's doomed attempt to regain the British throne in 1745–46.

The final section of this scenic route, between Arisaig and Mallaig, has been upgraded to a fast straight road. Unless you're in a hurry, opt instead for the more scenic old road (signposted Alternative Coastal Route).

Oban

Oban is a peaceful town on a delightful bay, with sweeping views to Kerrera and Mull. OK, that bit about peaceful is true only in winter; in summer the town centre is a heaving mass of humanity, its streets jammed with traffic and crowded with holidaymakers and day trippers headed for the islands. But the setting is still lovely.

There's not a huge amount to see in the town itself, but it's an appealingly busy place with some excellent restaurants and lively pubs, and it's the main gateway to the islands of Mull, Iona, Colonsay, Barra, Coll and Tiree.

Ben Nevis

BRIAN LAWRENCE/GETTY IMAGES ©

Oban

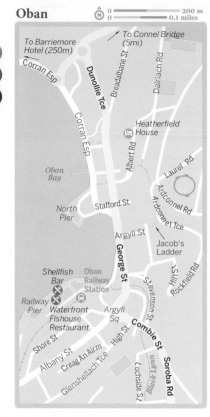

To Barriemore Hotel (250m)

To Connel Bridge (5mi)

WATERFRONT FISHOUSE
RESTAURANT Seafood ££

(☎01631-563110; www.waterfrontoban.co.uk; Railway Pier; mains £11-20; ☺lunch & dinner; ♿) Housed on the top floor of a converted seamen's mission, the Waterfront's stylish, unfussy decor in burgundy and brown, with dark wooden furniture, does little to distract from the superb seafood freshly landed at the quay just a few metres away.

SHELLFISH BAR Seafood £

(Railway Pier; mains £3-13; ☺9am-6pm) Here you can buy fresh and cooked seafood to take away – excellent prawn sandwiches (£2.95), dressed crab (£4.95), and fresh oysters for only 75p each.

🛈 Getting There & Away

Boat

CalMac (www.calmac.co.uk) ferries link Oban with the islands of **Mull**, **Coll**, **Tiree**, **Lismore**, **Colonsay**, **Barra** and **Lochboisdale** (South Uist).

Bus

Scottish Citylink (www.citylink.co.uk) operates intercity coaches to Oban, while **West Coast Motors** (www.westcoastmotors.co.uk) runs local and regional services. The bus terminal is outside the train station.

Glasgow (via Inveraray and Arrochar) £18, three hours, four daily.

Perth (via Tyndrum and Killin) £16, three hours, twice daily.

Fort William (via Appin and Ballachulish) £9.40, 1½ hours, three daily Monday to Saturday.

ISLE OF MULL

POP 2600

From the rugged ridges of Ben More and the black basalt crags of Burg to the blinding white sand, rose-pink granite and emerald waters that fringe the Ross, Mull can lay claim to some of the finest and most varied scenery in the Inner Hebrides, while the waters to the west of the

 **Sleeping**

BARRIEMORE HOTEL B&B ££

(☎01631-566356; www.barriemore-hotel.co.uk; Corran Esplanade; s/d from £70/99; [P] ?) The Barriemore enjoys a grand location, overlooking the entrance to Oban Bay. There are 13 spacious rooms here (ask for one with a sea view), plus a guest lounge with magazines and newspapers, and plump Loch Fyne kippers on the breakfast menu.

HEATHERFIELD HOUSE B&B ££

(☎01631-562806; www.heatherfieldhouse.co.uk; Albert Rd; s/d from £38/88; [P] [@] ?) The welcoming Heatherfield House occupies a converted 1870s rectory set in extensive grounds and has six spacious rooms.

BORIS BUSCHARDT/GETTY IMAGES ©

Don't Miss Eilean Donan Castle

Photogenically sited at the entrance to Loch Duich, near Dornie village, **Eilean Donan Castle** (01599-555202; www.eileandonancastle.com; adult/child £6/5; 9.30am-6pm Mar-Oct) is one of Scotland's most evocative castles, and must be represented in millions of photo albums. It's on an offshore islet, magically linked to the mainland by an elegant, stone-arched bridge. Keep an eye out for the photos of castle scenes from the movie *Highlander*. There's also a sword used at the battle of Culloden in 1746. The castle was ruined in 1719 after Spanish Jacobite forces were defeated at the Battle of Glenshiel, and it was rebuilt between 1912 and 1932.

Citylink buses from Fort William and Inverness to Portree will stop at the castle.

island provide some of the best whale-spotting opportunities in Scotland.

About two-thirds of Mull's population lives in and around Tobermory, the island's capital, in the north. Craignure, at the southeastern corner, has the main ferry terminal and is where most people arrive.

 Tours

BOWMAN'S TOURS Bus
(01680-812313; www.bowmanstours.co.uk)
Day trips from Oban to Mull, Staffa and Iona by ferry and bus.

MULL WILDLIFE EXPEDITIONS Wildlife Watching
(01688-500121; www.torrbuan.com) Offers full-day Land Rover tours of the island with the chance of spotting red deer, golden eagles, peregrine falcons, white-tailed sea eagles, hen harriers, otters and perhaps dolphins and porpoises. The cost (adult/child £43/40) includes pick-up from your accommodation or from any of the ferry terminals, a picnic lunch and use of binoculars. The timing of this tour makes it possible as a day-trip from Oban, with pick-up and drop-off at the Craignure ferry.

SEA LIFE SURVEYS Wildlife Watching
(☎01688-302916; www.sealifesurveys.com;
Ledaig) Runs whale-watching trips from
Tobermory harbour to the waters north
and west of Mull. An all-day whale-watch
(per person £80) gives up to seven hours
at sea (not recommended for kids under
14), and has a 95% success rate for sight-
ings. The four-hour Wildlife Adventure
cruise is geared more towards children
(£50/40 per adult/child).

🛏 Sleeping & Eating

Tobermory has the best choice of
accommodation.

HIGHLAND COTTAGE
HOTEL Boutique Hotel £££
(☎01688-302030; www.highlandcottage.co.uk;
Breadalbane St; d £150-165; ⏰mid-Mar–Oct;
P🛜) Antique furniture, four-poster beds,
embroidered bedspreads, fresh flowers
and candlelight lend this small hotel (only
six rooms) an appealingly old-fashioned
cottage atmosphere, but with all mod
cons including cable TV, full-size baths and
room service. There's also an excellent
fine-dining restaurant here.

SONAS HOUSE B&B ££
(☎01688-302304; www.sonashouse.co.uk;
The Fairways, Erray Rd; s/d £110/125, apt from
£90; P🛜🏊) Here's a first – a B&B with
a heated, indoor 10m swimming pool!
Sonas is a large, modern house that offers
luxury B&B in a beautiful setting with
superb views over Tobermory Bay; ask for
the 'Blue Poppy' bedroom, which has its
own balcony.

CAFÉ FISH Seafood ££
(☎01688-301253; www.thecafefish.com; The
Pier; mains £10-22; ⏰lunch & dinner) Seafood
doesn't come much fresher than the stuff
served at this warm and welcoming little
restaurant overlooking Tobermory harbour – as its motto says, 'The only thing
frozen here is the fisherman'!

Left: Elgol Beach, Isle of Skye;
Below: White-tailed eagle, Portree (p362)
(LEFT) CHRIS HEPBURN/.GETTY IMAGES ©; (BELOW) BLACKPOOL COLLEGE/GETTY IMAGES ©

ℹ Getting There & Away

There are three **CalMac** (www.calmac.co.uk) car ferries linking Mull with the mainland.

Oban to Craignure (passenger/car £5.25/46.50, 40 minutes, every two hours) The shortest and busiest route – booking advised for cars.

Lochaline to Fishnish (£3.10/13.65, 15 minutes, at least hourly) On the east coast of Mull.

Tobermory to Kilchoan (£5/25.50, 35 minutes, seven daily Monday to Saturday) Links to the Ardnamurchan peninsula; from May to August there are also five sailings on Sunday.

ISLE OF SKYE
POP 9900

The Isle of Skye (an t-Eilean Sgiatha-nach in Gaelic) takes its name from the old Norse *sky-a*, meaning 'cloud island', a Viking reference to the often mist-enshrouded Cuillin Hills. It's the biggest of Scotland's islands, a 50-mile-long smorgasbord of velvet moors, jagged mountains, sparkling lochs and towering sea cliffs.

ℹ Information

Portree Information Centre (☏01478-612137; Bayfield Rd, Portree; internet per 20min £1; ⏱9am-6pm Mon-Sat, 10am-4pm Sun Jun-Aug, 9am-5pm Mon-Fri, 10am-4pm Sat Apr, May & Sep, limited opening hours Oct-Mar)

Broadford Information Centre (☏01471-822361; car park, Broadford; ⏱9.30am-5pm Mon-Sat, 10am-4pm Sun Apr-Oct)

ℹ Getting There & Away

Boat

Despite there being a bridge, there are still a couple of ferry links between Skye and the mainland.

Isle of Skye

Mallaig–Armadale CalMac operates the Mallaig to Armadale ferry (www.calmac.co.uk; per person/car £4.35/22.60). It's very popular in July and August, so book ahead if you're travelling by car.

Glenelg–Kylerhea Skye Ferry (www.skyeferry.com; foot passenger/car with passengers £3/14; ⏰10am-6pm Easter–mid-Oct) runs a tiny vessel (six cars only) on the very worthwhile Glenelg to Kylerhea crossing.

Bus

○ **Glasgow to Portree** (£40, seven hours, four daily)

○ **Glasgow to Uig** (£40, 7½ hours, two daily) Via Crianlarich, Fort William and Kyle of Lochalsh.

○ **Inverness to Portree** (£23, 3½ hours, three daily)

Car & Motorcycle

The Isle of Skye became permanently tethered to the Scottish mainland when the Skye Bridge opened in 1995.

There are **petrol stations** at Broadford (open 24 hours), Armadale, Portree, Dunvegan and Uig.

Cuillin Hills

The Cuillin Hills are Britain's most spectacular mountain range. Though small in stature (**Sgurr Alasdair**, the highest summit, is only 993m), the peaks are near-alpine in character, with knife-edge ridges, jagged pinnacles, scree-filled gullies and acres of naked rock. While they are a paradise for experienced mountaineers, the higher reaches of the Cuillin are off limits to the majority of walkers.

The good news is that there are also plenty of good, low-level hikes within the ability of most. One of the best (on a fine day) is the steep climb from Glenbrittle camping ground to **Coire Lagan** (6 miles round trip; allow at least three hours).

 **Sleeping**

SLIGACHAN HOTEL Hotel ££
(📞01478-650204; www.sligachan.co.uk; per person £65-75; 🅿@🛜) The Slig, as it has been known to generations of climbers, is a near village in itself, encompassing a luxurious hotel, a microbrewery, self-catering cottages, a **bunkhouse** (📞01478-650458; www.sligachanselfcatering.co.uk; dm £16), a **campsite** (sites per person £5.50; ⏰Apr-Oct), a big barn of a pub (all-day bar meals £8 to £10) and an adventure playground.

❶ Getting There & Away

Bus 53 runs five times a day Monday to Friday (once on Saturday) from Portree to Carbost via Sligachan (50 minutes); for Glenbrittle, you'll have to hitch or walk the remaining 8 miles.

Portree (Port Righ)

POP 1900

Portree is Skye's largest and liveliest town. It has a pretty harbour lined with brightly painted houses, and there are great views of the surrounding hills.

 **Sleeping**

BEN TIANAVAIG B&B B&B ££
(📞01478-612152; www.ben-tianavaig.co.uk; 5 Bosville Tce; r £70-80; 🅿🛜) A warm welcome awaits from the Irish-Welsh couple who run

this B&B bang in the centre of town. All four bedrooms have a view across the harbour to the hill that gives the house its name and breakfasts include free-range eggs and vegetables grown in the garden.

BOSVILLE HOTEL Hotel ££
(☏ 01478-612846; www.bosvillehotel.co.uk; 9-11 Bosville Tce; s/d from £130/138; 📶) The Bosville brings a little bit of metropolitan style to Portree with its designer fabrics and furniture, flatscreen TVs, fluffy bathrobes and bright bathrooms.

Eating

HARBOUR VIEW SEAFOOD RESTAURANT Seafood ££
(☏ 01478-612069; www.harbourviewskye.co.uk; 7 Bosville Tce; mains £14-19; ⊙noon-3pm & 5.30-11pm Tue-Sun) The Harbour View is Portree's most congenial place to eat. It has a homely dining room with a log fire in winter, books on the mantelpiece and bric-a-brac on the shelves. And on the table, superb Scottish seafood, such as fresh Skye oysters, seafood chowder, succulent king scallops, langoustines and lobster.

CAFÉ ARRIBA Cafe £
(☏ 01478-611830; www.cafearriba.co.uk; Quay Brae; mains £4-8; ⊙7am-10pm May-Sep, 8am-5.30pm Oct-Apr; 🖉) Arriba is a funky little cafe, brightly decked out in primary colours and offering delicious flatbread melts (bacon, leek and cheese is our favourite) as well as the best choice of vegetarian grub on the island, ranging from a veggie breakfast fry-up to Indian-spiced bean cakes with mint yoghurt.

ⓘ Getting There & Around

Bus

The main bus stop is in Somerled Sq. There are seven Scottish Citylink buses a day, including Sundays, from Kyle of Lochalsh to Portree (£6, one hour) and on to Uig.

Local buses (Monday to Saturday only) run from Portree to Broadford (40 minutes, at least hourly)

♥ If You Like...
Scenic Glens

It's hard to beat Glencoe in the scenery stakes, but the Highlands are riven with many other glorious glens.

1 GLEN NEVIS
Magical Glen Nevis begins near Fort William and wraps itself around the southern flanks of Ben Nevis (1344m). Its amazing scenery makes it popular with movie makers – parts of Braveheart, Rob Roy and the Harry Potter movies were filmed there.

2 GLEN AFFRIC
Glen Affric is one of the most beautiful glens in Scotland, extends deep into the hills beyond Cannich, 13 miles west of Drumnadrochit. It's a wonderland of lochs, mountains and rare native wildlife.

3 GLEN ETIVE
At the eastern end of Glencoe, a minor road leads south along this peaceful and beautiful glen On a warm summer's day, there are many tempting pools to swim in and plentiful picnic sites.

4 GLEN TORRIDON
The drive along Glen Torridon is one of the most breathtaking in Scotland, overlooked by mighty, brooding mountains that tower over a winding, single-track road. The glen runs southwest from Kinlochewe and Loch Maree, about 50 miles west of Inverness.

via Sligachan (15 minutes); to Armadale (1¼ hours, connecting with the ferries to Mallaig); to Carbost (40 minutes, four daily); to Uig (30 minutes, six daily) and to Dunvegan Castle (40 minutes, five daily Monday to Friday, three on Saturday).

Dunvegan (Dun Bheagain) & Around

Skye's most famous historic building, and one of its most popular tourist attractions, is **Dunvegan Castle** (☏ 01470-521206; www.dunvegancastle.com; adult/child £9.50/5; ⊙10am-5pm Apr–mid-Oct), seat of the chief of Clan MacLeod. The oldest parts are the 14th-century keep and dungeon but most of it dates from the 17th to 19th centuries.

🛌 Sleeping & Eating

🍃 THREE CHIMNEYS
Modern Scottish £££
(☎01470-511258; www.threechimneys.co.uk; Colbost; 3-course lunch/dinner £37/60; ⏰lunch Mon-Sat mid-Mar–Oct, dinner daily year-round) Halfway between Dunvegan and Waterstein, the Three Chimneys is a superb romantic retreat combining a gourmet restaurant in a candlelit crofter's cottage with sumptuous five-star rooms (double £295, dinner/B&B per couple £415) in the modern house next door. Book well in advance, and note that children are not welcome in the restaurant in the evenings.

Trotternish

The Trotternish Peninsula to the north of Portree has some of Skye's most beautiful – and bizarre – scenery. On the eastern coast, the 50m-high, potbellied pinnacle of crumbling basalt known as the **Old Man of Storr**, is prominent above the road 6 miles north of Portree. North again is spectacular **Kilt Rock**, a stupendous cliff of columnar basalt whose vertical ribbing is fancifully compared to the pleats of a kilt, and the Quiraing, an impressive land-slipped escarpment bristling with crags and pinnacles.

On the western side of the peninsula, the peat-reek of crofting life in the 18th and 19th centuries is preserved in thatched cottages at **Skye Museum of Island Life** (☎01470-552206; www.skyemuseum.co.uk; adult/child £2.50/50p; ⏰9.30am-5pm Mon-Sat Easter-Oct). Behind the museum is Kilmuir Cemetery, where a tall Celtic cross marks the grave of Flora MacDonald.

Whichever way you arrive at **Uig** (oo-ig), the picture-perfect bay, ringed by steep hills, rarely fails to impress.

John O'Groats

Though it's not the northernmost point of the British mainland (that's Dunnet Head), John O'Groats still serves as the end-point of the mammoth cross-country trek from Land's End in Cornwall, a popular if arduous route for cyclists and walkers, many of whom raise money for charitable causes.

Two miles east, **Duncansby Head** provides a more solemn end-of-Britain moment with a small lighthouse and 60m cliffs sheltering nesting fulmars. From here a 15-minute walk through a sheep paddock yields spectacular views of the sea-surrounded monoliths known as **Duncansby Stacks**.

From May to September, a passenger ferry (p365) shuttles across to Burwick in Orkney. Ninety-minute wildlife cruises to the island of Stroma or Duncansby Head cost £17 (late June to August).

ORKNEY ISLANDS

There's a magic to the Orkney Islands that you'll begin to feel as soon as the Scottish mainland slips away astern. Consisting of 70 flat, green-topped islands stripped bare of trees by the wind, it's a place of ancient standing stones and prehistoric villages, an archipelago of old-style hospitality and Viking heritage narrated in the *Orkneyinga Saga* and still strong today. This is a region whose ports tell of lives led with the blessings and rough moods of the sea, and a destination where seekers can find melancholy wrecks of warships and the salty clamour of remote seabird colonies.

👉 Tours

JOHN O'GROATS FERRIES   Bus Tours
(☎01955-611353; www.jogferry.co.uk; ⏰May-Sep) If you're in a hurry, this operator runs a one-day tour of the main sites for £52, including the ferry from John O'Groats. You can do the whole thing as a long day-trip from Inverness.

Maes Howe

Egypt has the pyramids, Scotland has **Maes Howe** (HS; ☎01856-761606; www.historic-scotland.gov.uk; adult/child £5.50/3.30; ⏰tours hourly 10am-4pm). Constructed about 5000 years ago, it's an extraordinary place, a Stone Age tomb built from enormous sandstone blocks, some of which weighed many tons and were brought from several miles away. Entry is by 45-minute guided tours that leave on the hour. Be sure to reserve your tour-slot ahead by phone.

Ring of Brodgar

A mile north of Stenness is this wide circle of **standing stones** (HS; www. historic-scotland.gov.uk; admission free; ⊙24hr), some over 5m tall. The last of the three Stenness monuments to be built (2500–2000 BC). Free guided tours leave from the carpark at 1pm from June to August (Thursdays only during the rest of the year).

Skara Brae & Skaill House

A visit to extraordinary **Skara Brae** (HS; www.historic-scotland.gov.uk; joint ticket with Skaill House adult/child £6.90/4.10; ⊙9.30am-5.30pm Apr-Sep, to 4.30pm Oct-Mar), one of the world's most evocative prehistoric sites, offers the best opportunity in Scotland for a glimpse of Stone Age life. Idyllically situated by a sandy bay 8 miles north of Stromness, and predating Stonehenge and the pyramids of Giza, Skara Brae is northern Europe's best-preserved prehistoric village.

❶ Getting There & Away

Boat

Northlink Ferries (📞0845 6000 449; www. northlinkferries.co.uk) operates ferries from Scrabster to Stromness (passenger £16 to £19, car £50 to £55, 1½ hours, two to three daily), from Aberdeen to Kirkwall (passenger £20 to £30, car £75 to £104, six hours, three or four weekly) and from Kirkwall to Lerwick (passenger one way £16 to £23, car one way £58 to £96, six to eight hours, three or four a week) on the Shetland Islands. From May to September, John O'Groats Ferries (📞01955-611353; www.jogferry.co.uk) operates a passenger-only service from John O'Groats to Burwick, on the southern tip of South Ronaldsay (one way/return £20/30).

If You Like...
Scottish Islands

Mull and Skye are perhaps the best-known of Scotland's numerous islands, but there are many more to discover.

1 ISLAY
The most southerly of the Inner Hebrides, Islay (*eye*-lah) is best known for its single malt whiskies. There are eight working distilleries here, all of which offer guided tours. The quickest route to the island is with **Loganair/FlyBe** (www.loganair.co.uk), which flies from Glasgow to Islay (£62 one way, 45 minutes, two or three flights daily Monday to Friday, one or two Saturday and Sunday).

2 JURA
Just off the coast of Argyll, Jura is a wild and lonely island, where the population of red deer outnumber people by about 35 to one. A **car ferry** runs from Islay (passenger/car/bicycle £1.35/7.60/free, five minutes, hourly Monday to Saturday, every two hours Sunday), but there's no direct connection to the mainland.

3 TIREE
Low-lying Tiree is lush, green and windswept, known for its excellent beaches and birdwatching. A **CalMac** (www.calmac.co.uk) car ferry runs from Oban to Tiree (passenger/car £18.50/95 return, four hours, one daily), or you can catch a flight from Glasgow with **Loganair/Flybe** (www.loganair.co.uk).

4 IONA
An island set in a turquoise sea, Iona was the site of one of Scotland's first Christian communities, founded by St Columba in 563. Frequent ferries run from Fionnphort (£4.30 return, five minutes, hourly), or there are day-trips from Oban.

Bus

John O'Groats Ferries operates the summer-only Orkney bus service from Inverness to Kirkwall. Tickets (one way/return £38/52, five hours) include bus-ferry-bus travel from Inverness to Kirkwall. There are two buses daily from June to early September.

Great Britain
In Focus

Westminster Abbey (p63)
CHRISTOPHER HOPE-FITCH/GETTY IMAGES ©

Great Britain Today

Fireworks, London Olympics 2012

> *it is the impact of the global financial crisis that remains the biggest issue for most people in Britain today*

belief systems
(% of population)

87	2	1	10
Christian	Muslim	Hindu	Other

if Britain were 100 people

85 would be Caucasian
4 would be South Asian
2 would be African & Afro Caribbean
9 would be other

population per sq km

= 30 people

BRITAIN　　USA　　FRANCE

Change at the Top

For Britain and the British, the first dozen years of the 21st century have been a time of change, conflict, controversy and national soul-searching. And it doesn't look like settling down any time soon...

After 13 years in power, the Labour government was ousted in the May 2010 general election, and an unexpected agreement between the Conservative and Liberal-Democrat parties created the first coalition government in modern British history.

Under the helm of Prime Minister David Cameron (the Conservative leader) and Deputy PM Nick Clegg (the Liberal-Democrat leader), the new government got down to work. Plans included major reforms of hospital and health funding, and new laws allowing parents to set up their own schools. As both education and the National Health Service are perennial political hotspots, changes in these areas are heavily scrutinised and fiercely debated.

RICHARD BRYANT/ARCAID/CORBIS ©

The Olympian Glow

The nation's spirits were lifted in the summer of 2012 thanks to two big-ticket events: the celebrations to mark the Queen's Diamond Jubilee, followed by London's hosting of the 2012 Olympics and Paralympics. Despite plenty of British pessimism prior to the event, the Olympics were deemed a great success, kicking off with a gloriously odd opening ceremony by director Danny Boyle, and culminating in a record medal haul for Britain's athletes. Whether the Olympics will result in a long-lasting legacy for British sport remains to be seen – but it was certainly fun while it lasted.

Whither Great Britain?

But while the Olympics briefly brought the nation together, another major announcement showed deeper schisms at work. Scotland's decision to hold a referendum on independence in 2014 is a long-held dream for the Scottish National Party (SNP) and its ebullient leader, Alex Salmond – although controversially, only Scots will have the right to vote in an election. While opinion polls show the majority of Scots are against independence, as the campaigns on both sides begin in earnest, we may well see the end of a political union that has lasted since 1707.

Some cracks in the coalition appeared in late 2011, further strained in 2012, when Conservative 'rebels' blocked Lib-Dem moves to reform the House of Lords, which would have transformed the British parliament's second chamber into a fully elected body.

The Economies of Austerity

Beyond home politics, it is the impact of the global financial crisis, and Britain's own levels of debt, that remain the biggest issue for most people in Britain today. This has been addressed by the coalition government with an austerity package including tax increases and public spending cuts, while the Labour opposition espouses increased public spending, and points to slow economic growth as a failure of government policies. Which side is correct remains to be seen.

History

Hadrian's Wall (p255)

ALAN HEWITT/GETTY IMAGES ©

It may be a small island on the edge of Europe, but Britain has never been on the sidelines of history. For centuries, invaders and incomers have made their mark – Celts, Romans, Vikings, Anglo-Saxons, Normans – and the result is a fascinating mix of culture and language, a dynamic pattern that has shaped the nation and continues to evolve today.

First Arrivals

Stone tools discovered in eastern England show that human habitation in Britain stretches back at least 700,000 years, but the first structural signs of settlements emerge around 4000 BC, when early peoples constructed massive burial mounds and stone circles, most famously at Stonehenge.

3500 BC
First period of construction at Stonehenge begins.

Celts & Romans

By around 500 BC, the Celts had settled across much of the island of Britain, and a Celtic-British population – sometimes known as the 'ancient Britons' – developed. The next arrivals were the Romans, colonising the island they called Britannia from around AD 43.

Early England, Wales & Scotland

When the power of the Romans faded around AD 410, the province of Britannia went into decline, and a new wave of invaders – Angles and Saxons – crossed from the European mainland, setting the foundation for the English language and culture. Meanwhile the Celts were pushed to the island's fringes (especially present-day Wales and Scotland), in the process creating their own distinct cultures.

The Viking Era

Just as the new territories of England, Wales and Scotland were becoming established, Britain was again invaded – this time by Scandinavian Vikings, who conquered northeast England and made York their capital. Their advance south was halted by Alfred the Great, who brought the disparate Anglo-Saxon armies under one leader for the first time in history. His grandson, Athelstan, became the first King of England in 925.

1066 & All That

The next major landmark in Britain's history was the 1066 Battle of Hastings, when the Norman king William led an invading army into southern England. The Saxons were defeated, and William became king of England, earning himself the prestigious epithet of Conqueror.

Royal & Holy Squabbling

The early 12th century was marked by tension between church and state, culminating in Henry II's murder of 'turbulent priest' Thomas Becket at Canterbury Cathedral in 1170.

The next king, Richard I (aka the Lionheart), headed off to the Middle East on a series of Crusades, leaving his brother John to rule in his stead. According to legend,

The Best... Ancient Sites

1 Stonehenge (p184)

2 Avebury (p185)

3 Skara Brae (p365)

4 Hadrian's Wall (p255)

5 Bath's Roman Baths (p189)

AD 43
Emperor Claudius orders the Roman invasion of Britannia.

5th–7th centuries
Anglo-Saxons migrate to England and expand across the country.

1066
Norman French armies defeat the English at the Battle of Hastings.

it was during this time that Robert of Loxley, better known as Robin Hood, hid in Sherwood Forest and engaged in a spot of wealth redistribution.

Edward I in Wales & Scotland

By 1272 England was ruled by Edward I, an ambitious leader and skilled general. First he invaded Wales, building massive castles at places like Caernarfon and Conwy, that are still impressive today. Then Edward I was invited to choose a new Scottish king. Disputes arose from this decision and Edward I seized the opportunity to invade the country, forcing clan leaders to swear allegiance. In a final blow to Scottish pride, Edward removed the Stone of Scone, on which the kings of Scotland had been crowned for centuries. Edward's bloody suppression of the Scots inspired not obedience, but rebellion, and in 1297 at the Battle of Stirling Bridge, the English were defeated by a Scottish army under William Wallace (an episode which inspired the film *Braveheart*).

Robert the Bruce

The English soon reasserted themselves in Scotland. Edward II came to the throne, but lacked the military success of his forebear. Meanwhile, Robert the Bruce had crowned himself King of Scotland, and after a series of setbacks, decisively defeated the English at the Battle of Bannockburn in 1314, another milestone in Scotland's long struggle to remain independent.

The House of Lancaster

The year 1399 was another major milestone in Britain's history: King Richard II of England was ousted by a powerful baron called Henry Bolingbroke, who became King Henry IV – the first monarch of the House of Lancaster. His son Henry V led his forces to a famous defeat of France at the Battle of Agincourt, while his grandson Henry VI oversaw the building of several great houses of worship, including King's College Chapel in Cambridge and Eton Chapel near Windsor.

Henry VIII vs the Church

Of all the Henrys, the last is undoubtedly the most notorious. Henry VIII's main problem was fathering a male heir – hence the famous six wives. The pope's disapproval of Henry's divorce from his first wife, Catherine of Aragon, lead Henry to split from the Catholic Church and found the Church of England. The so-called Reformation sowed the seeds of division between Protestants and Catholics that still endures in some corners of Britain. In 1536 Henry 'dissolved' nearly all of the monasteries in England and Wales, and now only their ruins remain.

1459–87
The Wars of the Roses between the Houses of Lancaster and York.

1536 & 1543
Henry VIII signs the Acts of Union, formally uniting England and Wales. Henry VIII, by Hans Holbein the Younger

As if that wasn't enough, Henry VIII's other great contribution to British history was signing the Acts of Union (1536 and 1543), formally uniting England and Wales for the first time.

The Elizabethan Age

Henry VIII died in 1547 and, shortly after, his daughter became Elizabeth I (sometimes known as the 'Virgin Queen', since she never married). Her 45-year reign heralded a golden period for England: explorer Francis Drake circumnavigated the globe, Walter Raleigh led expeditions to the New World, and William Shakespeare penned some of the greatest plays ever written. But perhaps Elizabeth's greatest achievement was her defeat of the mighty Spanish Armada, allowing England to retain her independence and build on her growing global power.

The Best...
Historic
Cities

1 London

2 York

3 Edinburgh

4 Oxford

5 Bath

Mary, Queen of Scots

Meanwhile, things were afoot up north. Elizabeth's cousin Mary had become Queen of the Scots aged just six years old, following the death of her father James V in 1542. Having married the Dauphin of France, Mary later returned to claim the English throne on the grounds that Elizabeth was illegitimate.

Mary's plans failed. She was forced to abdicate from the Scottish throne and was held under house arrest for 19 years, before involving herself in a plot to overthrow Elizabeth, for which she was executed in 1587.

United Britain

The Virgin Queen never provided an heir, so in 1603 she was succeeded by her closest relative, the Scottish King James VI, son of the executed Mary. He became James I of England, the first king of the House of Stuart – but more importantly, he united England, Wales and Scotland under one monarch for the first time in history.

The War of Three Kingdoms

During the reign of Charles I (1625-49), a power struggle between king and parliament eventually degenerated into the War of the Three Kingdoms. The antiroyalist forces were led by Oliver Cromwell, a Puritan who preached against the excesses of the monarch and established church. After a long and bloody struggle, his parliamentarian (or Roundhead) army eventually defeated the king's forces (the

1642–49
English Civil War results in the execution of Charles I, and exile of Charles II.

1666
Great Fire of London burns much of the city to the ground.

1707
The Act of Union links England, Wales and Scotland under one parliament.

What's in a Name?

Visitors are often confused about the difference between England and Britain. But it's actually simple – England is just one of the three countries (along with Wales and Scotland) which collectively make up Great Britain. To complicate things official documents often refer to the United Kingdom which is a political state that also includes Northern Ireland. Clear enough? Don't worry – many British people aren't 100% sure of the difference either.

Cavaliers). The king was executed and England was declared a republic – with Cromwell hailed as 'Lord Protector', allowing him to enforce a raft of dictatorial (and hugely unpopular) laws.

Two years after Cromwell's death in 1658, parliament decided to re-establish the monarchy. Charles II, the exiled son of Charles I, returned to the throne, marking the beginning of the period known as the Restoration.

Age of Empire

In 1707, the Act of Union was passed, bringing an end to the independent Scottish Parliament, and finally linking the countries of England, Wales and Scotland under one parliament.

Stronger control over the British Isles was mirrored by even greater expansion abroad. The British Empire continued to grow in America, Canada and India, and laid claim to the newly discovered country of Australia following James Cook's epic voyage in 1768.

The empire's first major reverse came when the American colonies won the War of Independence (1776–83). Another challenge arose some time later, when French forces under Napoleon threatened to invade Britain and its territories, but were ultimately defeated by the heroic duo of Viscount Horatio Nelson and the Duke of Wellington, who won landmark victories at the Battles of Trafalgar (1805) and Waterloo (1815).

The Industrial Age

While the empire expanded, at home Britain had become the crucible of the Industrial Revolution. Steam power (patented by James Watt in 1781) and steam trains (launched by George Stephenson in 1825) transformed methods of production and transport, and the towns of the English Midlands became the world's first industrial cities. Huge numbers of people migrated from the countryside to work in the rapidly-expanding cities – a mass migration that was mirrored north of the Scottish border, when landowners expelled whole communities to make way for more profitable sheep farms, an event now known as the Highland Clearances.

1799–1815
Napoleon threatens invasion but is defeated at Trafalgar and Waterloo.

1837–1901
Under the reign of Queen Victoria, the British Empire expands its influence across the globe.

1914
The assassination of Archduke Franz Ferdinand of Austria leads to the outbreak of WWI.

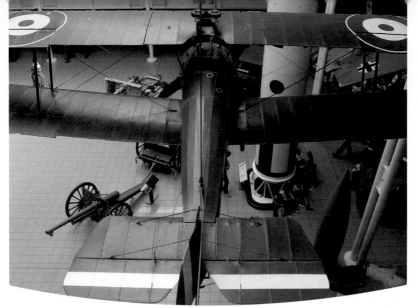

By the time Queen Victoria took the throne in 1837, Britain's colonies covered almost a quarter of the world's surface, and her factories and fleets dominated world trade. But her reign also marked an era of new social conscience: education became universal, trade unions were legalised, environmental laws were enacted, and the right to vote was extended to all classes (well, all males – women didn't get the vote until the efforts of the Suffragettes were successful a few decades later).

WWI

When Queen Victoria died in 1901, it seemed that Britain's energy fizzled out. In Continental Europe, other states were more active: the military powers of Russia, Austro-Hungary, Turkey and Germany were sabre-rattling in the Balkan states, a dispute that eventually culminated in WWI. When German forces entered Belgium on their way to invade France, Britain was drawn into the conflict. The next four years witnessed the emergence of 'trench warfare' and slaughter on a truly horrific scale; by the war's end in 1918, over a million Britons had died, not to mention millions more from the Commonwealth.

Biplane, Imperial War Museum (p75)

1939–45
WWII: Britain and its allies from America and the Commonwealth defeat Germany.

1953
The coronation of Queen Elizabeth II takes place in Westminster Abbey.

1979
Margaret Thatcher's Conservative Party wins the general election.

Disillusion & Depression

For soldiers who did return from WWI, disillusion led to questioning of the social order. Many supported the ideals of a new political force – the Labour Party, representing the working class – upsetting the balance long enjoyed by the Liberal and Conservative Parties.

The Labour Party was elected to government for the first time in 1923, in coalition with the Liberals, with James Ramsay MacDonald as prime minister. In the 1930s the world economy slumped and the Great Depression took hold. Even the royal family took a knock when Edward VIII abdicated in 1936 so he could marry a woman who was twice divorced and – horror of horrors – American.

The throne was taken by Edward's less-than-charismatic brother George VI and Britain dithered through the rest of the decade, with mediocre government failing to confront the country's deep-set social and economic problems.

WWII

Meanwhile, on mainland Europe, Germany saw the rise of Adolf Hitler, leader of the Nazi party. Many feared another war, but Prime Minister Neville Chamberlain met the German leader in 1938 and promised Britain 'peace for our time'. He was wrong. The following year Hitler invaded Poland, and two days later Britain was once again at war with Germany.

Chamberlain, reviled for his policy of 'appeasement', stood aside for a new prime minister, Winston Churchill. The war exacted a heavy toll on Britain – most notably during the Blitz, when much of London was levelled by the Luftwaffe, a phenomenon mirrored in many other British cities. By the time the war came to a close in 1945, Britain was utterly broke and facing a bleak future.

Swinging & Sliding

Seeking a new direction, the postwar years saw the rise of the socialist Labour Party, and the dawn of the 'welfare state'. The National Health Service was founded, providing free health care for all, and key industries (such as steel, coal and railways) were nationalised. In 1952, Elizabeth II came to the throne, and stayed there for six decades and counting.

During the Swinging Sixties, Britain became the centre of a new explosion in youth culture, but by the 1970s economic decline had set in once again, and the rest of the decade was marked by strikes, disputes and a general sense of discontent. Into the fray stepped an Iron Lady by the name of Margaret Thatcher, whose election in 1979 heralded a new but equally turbulent era.

1997
The Labour Party wins the general election with a record-breaking majority.

1999
Devolution leads to the formation of the Scottish Parliament and Welsh Assembly.

2007
Tony Blair resigns, and Gordon Brown takes over as Britain's prime minister.

The Thatcher Years

Love her or loathe her, no one could argue that Thatcher feared a fight. The nationalised industries were sold off, leading to widespread strikes and industrial disputes; the banks were deregulated, leading to a huge boom in London's financial district; and in 1982 the faraway Falkland Islands were regained by force following their invasion by Argentina. But ultimately Thatcher became a victim of her own conviction: her refusal to scrap the hugely unpopular 'poll tax' sparked nationwide riots, and ultimately led to her being booted from power in 1990.

New Labour, New Millennium

In the elections of 1997, the now rebranded 'New' Labour swept to power under fresh-faced leader Tony Blair. Among a host of other reforms, Mr Blair's government established devolved parliaments in Scotland and Wales, granting both countries limited control over their own taxation and public policy – something they hadn't enjoyed since the Act of Union in 1707.

Tony Blair and New Labour enjoyed an extended honeymoon period, and the next election (in 2001) was another walkover. Despite his controversial decision to participate in the wars in Afghanistan and Iraq, Labour won a historic third term in 2005, and Blair became the longest-serving Labour prime minister in British history. He finally resigned in June 2007, allowing Gordon Brown, the Chancellor of the Exchequer (the British term for Minister of Finance), to get the top job.

Unfortunately Brown's long-awaited leadership descended into disaster following the worldwide financial crisis in 2008. In the general election of 2010, a record 13 years of Labour rule came to an end, and a coalition between the Conservatives and the Liberal Democrats formed a new government, with David Cameron as prime minister.

The Best... History Museums

1 Ironbridge Gorge (p157)

2 SS Great Britain (p185)

3 Imperial War Museum (p75)

4 Greenwich Observatory (p85)

5 Jorvik (p225)

IN FOCUS HISTORY

2010

A coalition between Conservatives and Liberal-Democrats wins the election.

2012

London hosts the Olympic Games and the Queen celebrates her Diamond Jubilee.
Olympic Stadium (p84)

MARK CHIVERS/GETTY IMAGES ©

Family Travel

Jorvik Viking Centre (p225), York

MANOR PHOTOGRAPHY/ALAMY ©

Britain is great for travel with children because it's compact, with a lot of attractions in a small area. So when the kids in the back of the car say 'are we nearly there yet?', your answer can often be 'yes'. With a bit of planning ahead, and some online research to get the best bargains, having the kids on board can make a trip around Britain even more enjoyable.

Attractions

Many places of interest in Britain cater for kids as much as adults. At the country's historic castles, for example, mum and dad can admire the medieval architecture, while the kids can stomp off round the battlements. In the same way, many national parks and holiday resorts organise specific activities for children. It goes without saying that everything ramps up (both in prices and visitor congestion) during the school holidays.

Most visitor attractions offer family tickets (usually two adults plus two children) which offer a discount on individual entrance charges. Most offer cheaper rates for solo parents and kids too. Be sure to ask, as these are not always clearly displayed.

On the Road

If you're going by public transport, trains are great for families: intercity services have plenty of room for luggage and extra stuff like buggies (pushers), and the kids can move about a bit when bored. In contrast, they need to stay in their seats on long-distance coaches.

If you're hiring a car, most (but not all) rental firms can provide child seats – but you'll need to check this in advance. Most will not actually fit the child seats; you need to do that yourself, for insurance reasons. There are usually hefty child discounts available on most forms of public transport, too.

Accommodation

It's worth checking in advance that the place you're planning on staying at is happy to accept children. Some places are thoroughly child-friendly and will be able to provide cots, toys and babysitting services. Others (especially at the boutique end) prefer to maintain an adult atmosphere and consequently don't accept kids.

Many places also quote prices per person, so you might find yourself having to pay extra (albeit at a reduced rate) even if the kids share your room. Some B&Bs and hotels offer 'family suites' of two adjoining bedrooms with a shared bathroom.

Renting a self-catering cottage can be a good way to economise for family travellers, although obviously it means you'll be rooted to one particular area. Popular spots such as the Lake District, Devon, Cornwall and the Cotswolds have a particularly good selection to choose from.

The Best... Children's Attractions

1 Warwick Castle (p151)

2 Science Museum, London (p79)

3 Enginuity, Ironbridge (p157)

4 Eden Project, Cornwall (p206)

5 Jorvik Viking Centre, York (p225)

6 Natural History Museum, London (p79)

IN FOCUS FAMILY TRAVEL

Dining Out

Most cafes and teashops are child friendly. Restaurants are mixed: some offer highchairs and kiddy portions; others firmly say 'no children after 6pm'.

Children under 18 are usually not allowed in pubs serving just alcohol. Pubs serving meals usually allow children of any age (with their parents) in England and Wales, but in Scotland they must be over 14 and must leave by 8pm. If in doubt, ask the bar staff.

Breastfeeding in public remains mildly controversial, but if done discretely, will rarely attract comment.

All Change

On the sticky topic of dealing with nappies (diapers), most museums and other attractions in Britain usually have good baby-changing facilities.

Elsewhere, some city-centre public toilets have baby-changing areas, although these can be a bit grimy; your best bet for clean facilities is an upmarket department store.

On the road, baby-changing facilities are usually bearable at motorway service stations and OK at out-of-town supermarkets.

Need to Know

- **Changing facilities** In most large shopping centres, museums and attractions
- **Cots** Usually available at hotels, less common in B&Bs – ask in advance
- **Health** Just do as you'd do back home
- **Highchairs** Common in specific family-friendly restaurants
- **Nappies (diapers)** Sold in every supermarket
- **Transport** Look out for kids' discounts on trains and long-distance buses. Children under five usually travel free (but must give up the seat to paying passengers if transport is full).

Holiday Times

The best time for families to visit Britain is pretty much the best time for everyone else – from April/May to the end of September. It's worth avoiding August – the heart of school summer holidays – when prices go up and roads are busy, especially near the coast. Other school holidays are two weeks around Easter Sunday, and mid-December to early January, plus three week-long 'half-term' breaks – usually late February (or early March), late May and late October.

Information

Tourist offices are a great source of information for kids' activities – the shelves are usually loaded with leaflets advertising kid-friendly attractions in the local area. Ask at national park information centres too about activities for children. Many holiday resort towns also organise activities for children, especially during school-holiday periods.

Some handy websites:

- **Baby Goes 2** (www.babygoes2.com) Advice, tips and encouragement (and a stack of advertisements).

- **Mums Net** (www.mumsnet.com) No-nonsense advice on travel and more from a gang of UK mothers.

- **Travel for Kids** (www.travelforkids.com) Straightforward advice on kid-friendly places to visit.

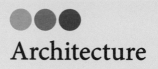

Architecture

Chatsworth House (p164)

DAVE PORTER PETERBOROUGH UK/GETTY IMAGES ©

One of the highlights of visiting Britain is the chance to explore its architectural heritage – encompassing everything from 5000-year-old stone circles to medieval cathedrals, thatched cottages and stunning stately homes. But don't make the mistake of thinking Britain is just one big museum piece. Landmark new buildings have sprung up in many major cities in recent years, demonstrating that Britain is still capable of mustering up a spirit of architectural adventure.

Early Foundations

The oldest 'buildings' in Britain are the grass-covered earth-mounds called 'barrows' (or 'tumuli') used as burial sites by Britain's prehistoric residents, but it's the country's many menhirs (standing stones) and stone circles which are the most obvious architectural legacy of the prehistoric past. No-one's quite sure what purpose they served, although they seem to have served some kind of sacred function. Famous examples include Stonehenge and Avebury in Wiltshire, and the Ring of Brodgar in the Orkney Islands.

Bronze Age & Iron Age

During these periods the architecture is on a more domestic scale. Hut circles can still be seen in several parts of Britain, most notably on Dartmoor in Devon and the stone village of Skara Brae on the Orkney Islands.

Chalk Figures

As you travel around Britain, look out for the chalk figures gracing many of the country's hilltops. They're made by cutting through the turf to reveal the white chalk soil below, so obviously are found in chalk areas – most notably in southwest England, especially the counties of Dorset and Wiltshire. Some figures, such as the Uffington White Horse, date from the Bronze Age, but most are more recent; the formidably endowed Cerne Abbas Giant is often thought to be an ancient pagan figure, although recent research suggests it was etched sometime in the 17th century.

During this era, people began to organise themselves into clans and tribes, and constructed hill forts for protection such as the ones at Maiden Castle in Dorset and Barbury Castle in Wiltshire.

The Roman Era

Roman remains are found in many towns and cities, mostly in England and Wales, as the Romans never colonised Scotland. There are impressive remains in Chester, Exeter and St Albans, and some in York, as well as the lavish Roman spa and bathing complex in Bath. But Britain's largest and most impressive Roman relic is the 73-mile sweep of Hadrian's Wall, built in the 2nd century AD as a defensive line stretching coast-to-coast across the country, for over 300 years marking the northern limit of the Roman Empire.

Medieval Cathedrals & Castles

In the centuries following the Norman invasion of 1066, Britain saw an explosion of architecture inspired by the two most pressing concerns of the day: worship and defence. Many landmark cathedrals were constructed during the early Middle Ages, including Salisbury, Winchester, Wells, Glasgow, St David's and Canterbury, plus York Minster, one of the finest cathedrals in all of Europe.

Alongside the churches and cathedrals, many abbeys and monasteries were built in Britain during the medieval period – nearly all of which were destroyed under the orders of Henry VIII between 1536 and 1540 as part of his dispute with the Catholic Church, or, in the case of Scotland, by Protestants during the Reformation that took place there. The period is now known as the 'dissolution of the monasteries' and the legacy today is picturesque ruins such as Melrose, Tintern, Fountains, Glastonbury, St Andrews and Rievaulx.

As for castles in Britain, you're spoilt for choice, ranging from atmospheric ruins like Tintagel to well-preserved structures like Warwick, Conwy, Stirling and Edinburgh. And then there's the most impressive of them all – the Tower of London, guardian of the capital for around 950 years.

Stately Homes

By the 17th century life had became more settled, and the nobility increasingly began to convert their draughty castles into lavish homes: Hardwick Hall and Burghley House are good examples of this fortress-to-finery process. Other nobles simply started from scratch on brand new stately homes, many of which were designed by the most famous architects of the day. Among the most extravagant are Chatsworth House, Stourhead and Blenheim Palace.

Sometimes, these improvements took place on a citywide scale: many of Britain's cities were heavily redeveloped during the Georgian era, including London, Edinburgh, Glasgow and the famous crescents and terraces of Bath.

Victoriana

The Victorian era – mainly the 19th century – was a time of great national confidence in Britain, reflected in a period of great building. A style called Victorian-Gothic developed, echoing the towers and spires that were such a feature of the original Gothic cathedrals. The best-known example of this style is the Palace of Westminster, better known as the Houses of Parliament and the tower of Big Ben, in London. Other highlights in the capital include London's Natural History Museum and St Pancras Train Station. The style was copied around the country, especially for civic buildings – the finest examples including Manchester Town Hall and Glasgow City Chambers.

The Industrial Era

Through the late 19th and early 20th century, as Britain's cities grew in size and stature, the newly moneyed middle classes built streets and squares of smart town houses.

During the Industrial Revolution, town planners oversaw the construction of endless terraces of 'back-to-back' and 'two-up-two-down' houses to accommodate the massive influx of workers needed to run the country's factories. In South Wales, similar houses – though often single storey – were built for the burgeoning numbers of coal miners, while the industrial areas of Scotland saw the rise of tenements, usually three or four storeys high, with a central communal staircase and two dwellings on each floor.

Postwar

During WWII many of Britain's cities were damaged by bombing, and the rebuilding that followed showed scant regard for the overall aesthetic of the cities, or for the lives of the people who lived in them. The rows of terraces were swept away in favour of high-rise tower blocks, while the 'brutalist' architects of the 1950s and '60s employed the modern and efficient materials of steel and concrete, leaving legacies such as London's South Bank Centre.

Perhaps this is why, on the whole, the British people are conservative in their architectural tastes, and often unhappy with experimental designs, especially when they're applied to public buildings. But a familiar pattern often unfolds: after a few years of resentment, first comes a nickname, then grudging acceptance, and finally – once the locals have become used to it – comes pride and affection for the new building. The Brits just don't like to be rushed, that's all.

21st Century

Over the last couple of decades, British architecture has started to redeem itself, and many big cities now have contemporary buildings their residents can rightly be proud of. Others, such as the much-criticised Scottish Parliament in Edinburgh, are still dividing opinion.

A new fashion for skyscrapers has recently taken hold in many cities, a trend perhaps started by London's cone-shaped Swiss Re building (now forever known as 'The Gherkin'). Leeds, Manchester, Brighton and Birmingham have all announced plans for new buildings over 200m high, while several more are currently being built on the London skyline, each with their own inevitable nickname (the Walkie Talkie, the Cheese Grater and so on). Tallest of all is 'The Shard', which opened in 2013 and at 309m is now one of Europe's tallest structures.

Writers & Artists

Dove Cottage (p252), Grasmere

The roots of Britain's literary heritage stretch back to Early English epics such as Beowulf. As the English language spread around the world, so too did English literature, such that writers like Shakespeare and Austen are well known far from their homeland. Britain's visual art scene is equally rich, and as you travel around the region you'll see vistas you may recognise from classic paintings.

Literature

First Stars

Modern English literature starts around 1387 with Geoffrey Chaucer's bawdy, allegorical *Canterbury Tales*, a mammoth poem based around fables, stories and morality tales, each told by one of the travelling pilgrims.

The next big name came two centuries later, when William Shakespeare entered the stage and penned his pantheon of histories, comedies and tragedies. It's still possible to visit various sites linked to Shakespeare in his birthplace of Stratford-upon-Avon, where you can also catch a play courtesy of the Royal Shakespeare Company – but for the authentic Elizabethan experience, you'll need to head for the reconstructed Globe Theatre on London's South Bank.

17th & 18th Centuries

The early 17th century saw the rise of the metaphysical poets, including John Donne and Andrew Marvell. Their vivid imagery and far-fetched 'conceits', or comparisons, daringly pushed the boundaries. In 'A Valediction: Forbidding Mourning', for instance, Donne compares the points of a compass with a pair of conjoined lovers. Racy stuff in its day.

The 18th century saw the birth of Scotland's best-loved lyricist and poet Robert Burns, whose work is still celebrated across the nation on Burns' Night, held on 25 January every year.

The Romantics

As the Industrial Revolution gathered steam in the late 18th and early 19th century, many writers increasingly turned towards the natural world and the power of imagination (in many cases helped along by a healthy dose of laudanum). Leading lights of the Romantic movement, as it became known, were William Blake, John Keats, Percy Bysshe Shelley, Lord Byron, Samuel Taylor Coleridge and William Wordsworth, whose most famous lines from *Daffodils*, 'I wandered lonely as a cloud', were inspired by a hike in the Lake District.

At around the same time, Sir Walter Scott produced his well-known novels such as *Waverley* and *Rob Roy*, both partly set in the Scottish Highlands.

Jane Austen

Almost two centuries after her death, Jane Austen is still one of Britain's best-known novelists, thanks to her exquisite observations of English class, society, love, friendship and buttoned-up passion – helped along by an endless stream of film and TV adaptations of her work. The city most associated with Austen is Bath; although she only lived there from 1801 to 1806, the city's Georgian streets and squares conjure an inescapably Austenesque atmosphere, and an intriguing museum commemorates her life and work.

Victoriana

Next came the reign of Queen Victoria and the era of industrial expansion. Novels increasingly began to explore social and political themes, epitomised by the work of Charles Dickens: in *Oliver Twist*, he captures the lives of young thieves in the London slums, while *Bleak House* critiqued the English legal system and *Hard Times* decried the excesses of capitalism.

Meanwhile, Thomas Hardy's works often dealt with the changing face of rural England; all his novels are based in the fictionalised county of Wessex, based on Dorset and the surrounding counties. Also popular during this period were two Scottish novelists: Robert Louis Stevenson, best known for his children's book *Treasure Island*, and Sir Arthur Conan Doyle, creator of detective Sherlock Holmes.

20th Century

The ideological chaos and social disruption of the postwar period fed into the fractured narratives of modernism. Perhaps the greatest British novelist of the interwar period is DH Lawrence, particularly known for his multi-generational family saga *Sons and Lovers*, and his controversial exploration of sexuality in *Lady Chatterley's Lover*.

Other landmark novels of the modern period include EM Forster's *A Passage to India*, about the hopelessness of British colonial rule, and the politically charged works of George Orwell such as *1984* and *Animal Farm*. Evelyn Waugh often dealt with the changing nature of British society – particularly the decline of the aristocracy, as

Children's Literature

British writers have produced some of the great works of children's fiction of the last century, from Charles Dodgson's mind-bending *Alice in Wonderland* through to Roald Dahl's mischievous tales and J.K. Rowling's mega-selling *Harry Potter* novels. A few classics that are particularly worth seeking out are *The Railway Children* by the children's writer E. Nesbit; Beatrix Potter's anthropomorphic *Tales* and Arthur Ransome's *Swallows and Amazons*, both of which were largely inspired by the scenery of the Lake District; and *The Wind in the Willows* by Kenneth Grahame, set on a stretch of the River Thames.

Oxford has particularly strong links with children's fiction: CS Lewis and JRR Tolkien both lived and worked here, while a fantastical version of the city features heavily in Philip Pullman's *His Dark Materials*.

examined in *Brideshead Revisited*. The Cold War era spawned many great novels by writers such as Graham Greene and John Le Carré, and also inspired Ian Fleming to create the archetypal British hero, James Bond.

The 20th century was also a great time for poets. Major names such as WH Auden, Stephen Spender and TS Eliot (an American by birth but a lifelong Anglophile) broke new poetic ground during the first half of the century, followed by modern poets including Ted Hughes and Philip Larkin. Wales also produced an iconic poet in Dylan Thomas, whose most famous work is *Under Milk Wood* (1954), examining the tensions and peculiarities of Welsh village life.

New Millennium

As the 20th century came to a close, the nature of multicultural Britain proved a rich inspiration for contemporary novelists. Hanif Kurieshi sowed the seeds with his ground-breaking 1990 novel *The Buddha of Suburbia,* examining the hopes and fears of a group of suburban Anglo-Asians in London, while the magical realist novels of Salman Rushdie attracted huge sales (and worldwide notoriety in the wake of his most controversial novel, *The Satanic Verses*).

Other big beasts of the British literary establishment include names such as Martin Amis, Ian McEwan, Iain Banks, Kazuo Ishiguro and David Mitchell, whose century-spanning work *Cloud Atlas* has had a Hollywood blockbuster treatment. Don't overlook Britain's 'popular' writers, who specialise in crime fiction or fantasy: the *Inspector Rebus* novels of Ian Rankin and the *Discworld* novels of Terry Pratchett attract huge sales.

The biggest event of the literary world is the Man Booker Prize (www.theman bookerprize.com), awarded to the year's best new novel written in English. Hilary Mantel, author of *Wolf Hall*, recently made history by winning the prize for the second time for her latest tale of Tudor intrigue, *Bring Up the Bodies*.

Painting & Sculpture

Early Days

For many centuries, Continental Europe – especially Holland, Spain, France and Italy – set the artistic agenda. The first artist with a truly British style and sensibility was arguably William Hogarth, whose riotous canvases exposed the vice and corruption of 18th-century London. His most celebrated work is *A Rake's Progress*.

While Hogarth was busy satirising society, other artists were hard at work showing it in its best light. The leading figures of 18th-century British portraiture were Sir Joshua Reynolds, Thomas Gainsborough and George Stubbs, the latter known for his intricate studies of animals (particularly horses). Most of these artists are represented at Tate Britain or the National Gallery in London.

19th Century

In the 19th century leading painters favoured images of the landscape. John Constable's idyllic depictions of the Suffolk countryside are summed up in *The Haywain* (National Gallery), while JMW Turner was fascinated by the effects of light and colour, with his works becoming almost entirely abstract by the 1840s.

The Pre-Raphaelite movement of the mid- to late 19th century explored the Victorian taste for myths and fairy tales. Key members of the movement included John Everett Millais; his *Ophelia* is an excellent example of their style, and can be seen at the Tate Britain gallery.

A good friend of the Pre-Raphaelites was William Morris; he saw late 19th-century furniture and interior design as increasingly vulgar, and with Dante Gabriel Rossetti and Edward Burne-Jones founded the Arts and Crafts movement to encourage the revival of a decorative approach to design. A close contemporary was Charles Rennie Mackintosh, who became one of the stars of the art-nouveau movement; his designs still grace many of Glasgow's buildings.

Early 20th Century

In the tumultuous 20th century, British art became increasingly experimental. Its place on the international stage was ensured by the monumental sculptures of Henry Moore and Barbara Hepworth (whose work can be seen at St Ives in Cornwall); the contorted paintings of Francis Bacon and the works of the Scottish Colourists – Francis Cadell, SJ Peploe, Leslie Hunter and JD Ferguson – have turned into the type of prints and postcards favoured by souvenir shops.

Postwar

The mid-1950s and early '60s saw an explosion of British artists plundering television, music, advertising and popular culture for inspiration. Leaders of this new 'pop-art' movement included David Hockney, who used bold colours and simple lines to depict his dachshunds and swimming pools; and Peter Blake, who designed the collage cover for The Beatles' landmark *Sgt. Pepper's* album.

The 1990s

The next big explosion in British art came in the 1990s; it was called 'Britart', and key figures included Damien Hirst and Tracy Emin. Another key artist of the period – and still going strong today – is the sculptor Antony Gormley, whose *Angel of the North*, a massive steel human figure with outstretched wings, was initially derided by the locals but is now an instantly recognised symbol of northeast England.

New Millennium

In 2008 a contest was announced to create a huge outdoor sculpture in Kent to counterbalance the *Angel of the North*. The final selection went to Mark Wallinger, winner of the 2007 Turner Prize, for his *White Horse of Ebbsfleet*. Due for completion in 2012, the project has stalled due to lack of funding. When (and if?) it is completed, the 50m-high work should be clearly seen from the nearby A2 main road and the train line between London and Paris – a 'Welcome to Britain' sign for the 21st century.

Music

The Proms (p390), Royal Albert Hall

If there's one thing Britain has given the world, it's great music. Ever since the days of the Fab Four and the Swinging Sixties this musical island has been producing world-beating bands, and it's a process that continues to this day. The Brits love their music.

Pop & Rock

Pioneers & Punks

Britain's brought pop to the world ever since The Beatles, The Rolling Stones, The Who, Cream, and The Kinks spearheaded the 'British Invasion' of the 1960s.

Glam rock swaggered in to replace peace and love in the early 1970s, with Marc Bolan and David Bowie donning spandex in a variety of chameleonic guises, succeeded by art-rockers Roxy Music and anthemic popsters Queen and Elton John. Meanwhile Led Zeppelin laid down the blueprint for heavy metal and hard rock, and 1960s psychedelia morphed into the spacey noodlings of prog rock, epitomised by Pink Floyd, Genesis and Yes.

By the late '70s the prog bands were looking out of touch and punk exploded onto the scene, with nihilistic lyrics and short, sharp, three-chord tunes. The Sex Pistols produced one landmark album (*Never Mind the Bollocks: Here's the Sex Pistols*), a clutch of (mostly banned) singles and a storm of controversy, ably assisted by The Clash, The Damned, The Buzzcocks and The Stranglers.

While punk burned itself out in a blaze of squealing guitars, New Wave musicians including The Jam and Elvis Costello took up the torch, blending spiky tunes and sharp lyrics into a poppier, more radio-friendly sound.

Ravers & New Romantics

The 1980s was mostly dominated by big pop bands with big egos and equally big hair, including acts such as Duran Duran, Wham and Culture Club, known for their flamboyant costumes and synthesised sounds. Meanwhile the Smiths took an entirely different direction based around Johnny Marr's guitars and Morrissey's arch (and often existentially bleak) lyrics.

The beats and bleeps of 1980s electronica fuelled the burgeoning dance-music scene of the early '90s. Pioneering artists such as New Order (risen from the ashes of Joy Division) used synthesised sounds to inspire the soundtrack for the ecstasy-fuelled rave culture, centred on famous clubs like Manchester's Haçienda and London's Ministry of Sound.

By the mid-1990s, Manchester was a focus for the burgeoning British indie scene, driven by guitar-based bands such as the Charlatans, the Stone Roses, James, Happy Mondays and Manchester's most famous musical export, Oasis. Such was the atmosphere and energy that the city was dubbed 'Madchester', and the whole world, it seemed, was 'up for it'. In the late 1990s indie segued into Britpop, a catch-all term covering bands Pulp and Blur (much to their distain, Oasis came under the banner too), all part of the short-lived phenomenon of 'Cool Britannia'.

New Millennium

The new millennium saw no let up in the British music scene's continual shifting and reinventing. Jazz, soul, R&B and hip-hop beats fused into a new 'urban' sound epitomised by artists like Jamelia, The Streets and Dizzee Rascal.

On the pop side, singer-songwriters are enjoying a renaissance thanks to multi-Grammy-winning Adele and contemporaries such as Ed Sheeran, Emeli Sandé and the late Amy Winehouse. The spirit of British indie has been kept alive by new bands (especially the all-conquering Coldplay), while traces of punk and postpunk live on in the music of artists such as Franz Ferdinand, The Arctic Monkeys, Muse and others.

Pop Today, Gone Tomorrow

Today's music scene is as fast-moving and varied as ever – trying to keep up with the latest acts is the main challenge. By the time you read this, half of the 'great new bands' of last year will have sunk without trace, and a fresh batch of unknowns will have risen to dominate the airwaves and download sites. This is true of the latest stars of reality TV

Live Music

Most cities have at least one concert hall regularly hosting big acts, as well as smaller venues where lesser-known acts strut their stuff. Bands large and small are pretty much guaranteed to play in London, but often tour extensively to major cities (Cardiff, Liverpool, Manchester and Glasgow usually feature).

For tickets and listings, agencies include **See** (www.seetickets.com) and **Ticketmaster** (www.ticketmaster.co.uk), or **Gigs in Scotland** (www.gigsinscotland.com) for info north of the border.

The Best...
Music
Venues

shows such as *The X-Factor*, who tend to produce a single or two and then disappear into obscurity.

A good place to check out who's hot are the UK's wealth of outdoor summer festivals. The original (and still the biggest) is held near Glastonbury in Somerset, but there are many more: Reading, Leeds and Hyde Park host their own major festivals, while other big names such as Latitude, Truck, Green Man and Bestival follow the Glastonbury tradition and are held out in the great British countryside.

Another good guide is the annual Mercury Music Prize (www.mercuryprize.com), awarded to the best British album of the last year.

Traditional & Folk Music

Scotland, England and Wales all have long histories of traditional folk music, each with its own distinctive styles and melodies. Well-known native instruments include the bagpipes in Scotland and the harp in Wales, while Wales also has a strong tradition of poetry and song (although perhaps the best-known genre – male voice choirs – is a relatively recent phenomenon). These days, the term 'folk music' generally refers to singers and musicians performing traditional (or traditional-style) songs accompanied by instruments such as guitar, fiddle and penny whistle.

British folk music mines a rich seam of regional culture, from the rhythmic 'waulking songs' of the tweed weavers of the Outer Hebrides to the jaunty melodies that accompany England's morris dancers. Local history plays its part too – many Welsh folk songs recall Owain Glyndŵr's battles against English domination, while English folk lyrics range from memories of the Tolpuddle Martyrs to sea shanties sung by Liverpool sailors. In Scotland, the Jacobite rebellion of 1745 was a rich source of traditional songs, while *Flower of Scotland* – written in 1967 by popular folk duo the Corries, and today the unofficial Scottish national anthem – harks back to the Battle of Bannockburn in 1314.

In the last decade or so, thanks largely to the rise in interest in world music, the folk music of Britain has enjoyed its biggest revival since the 1960s. Leading exponents include Eliza Carthy, Kate Rusby and Bellowhead, as well as Mumford & Sons, whose latest album became one of the fastest selling in history when it was released in 2012.

You can see traditional and folk music at informal gigs or jam sessions in pubs (notably in Edinburgh), or at events such as the annual folk festivals in Sidmouth and Cambridge, and cultural festivals such as the National Eisteddfod in Wales and the Mòd in Scotland.

Classical Music

Britain has 13 symphony orchestras, as well as dozens of amateur and youth orchestras, who stage concerts throughout the year. The biggest classical event of all is The Proms, one of the world's greatest music festivals, which takes place from July to September at London's Royal Albert Hall.

Well-known British composers include Edward Elgar, famous for his *Enigma Variations*; Gustav Holtz, who wrote *The Planets*; Benjamin Britten, particularly known for his two operas *Peter Grimes* and *The Turn of the Screw*; and Vaughan Williams whose well-known *A London Symphony* ends with chimes of Big Ben.

Sport

Old Trafford football stadium (p238)

PETER RICHARDSON/GETTY IMAGES ©

If you want a short cut into the heart of British culture, watch the British at play. They're passionate about their sport – as participants or spectators. Every weekend thousands of people turn out to cheer their favourite team, and sporting highlights such as Wimbledon keep the entire nation enthralled. The biggest sporting event of all – the Olympic Games – came to London in 2012, focusing the world's attention on this sports-mad nation.

Football (Soccer)

Despite what the fans may say in Madrid or Milan, the English football league has some of the finest – and richest – teams and players in the world. The Premier League is for the country's top 20 clubs, including internationally famous Arsenal, Liverpool and Manchester United, while 72 other teams from England and Wales play in the three divisions called the Championship, League One and League Two. In addition to the various leagues, there are also several cup competitions – the most famous of which is the knock-out FA Cup, which culminates in May at Wembley Stadium.

Many cities have a couple of major teams – Manchester United and Manchester City, or Liverpool and Everton, for example. When they play each other (usually twice a season) these games are known as 'local derbies', and the rivalry is especially intense.

London's Olympic Legacy

London's stint as host for the 2012 Olympics brought the city to the world's attention, and despite plenty of the inevitable British cynicism prior to the event, it was generally deemed a great success. Most of the major events took place around Stratford in London's East End; since the Olympics, the site has been renamed the Queen Elizabeth Olympic Park (p84), and you'll be able to enjoy a variety of parks, walks and landscaped areas alongside the sporting venues, as well as Anish Kapoor's helter-skelter style tower, the **ArcelorMittal Orbit**, which provides great views over the park.

The football season lasts from August to May, but tickets for the big games in the upper division are like gold dust, and cost £20 to £50, even if you're lucky enough to find one.

Rugby

A popular witticism holds that football is a gentlemen's game played by hooligans, while rugby is the other way around. There are two variants of the game: rugby union is played in southern England, Wales and Scotland; rugby league is the main sport in northern England, although there is crossover. Many rules and tactics of both codes are similar, but in league there are 13 players in each team (ostensibly making the game faster), while rugby union sides have 15 players each. Wales has a particularly special relationship with rugby – it's considered the national game, and for many Welsh people, football pales into insignificance in comparison.

The main season for club matches is roughly September to Easter, while the international rugby union calendar is dominated by the annual Six Nations Championship (England, Scotland, Wales, Ireland, France and Italy) between January and April. It's usual for the Scots to support Wales, or vice versa, when either team is playing the 'old enemy', England.

Cricket

Cricket has its origins in southeast England, with the earliest written record dating to 1598. It became an international game during Britain's colonial era, when it was exported to the countries of the Commonwealth. There are a number of different formats: one-day and Twenty20 matches last one day, while test matches usually stretch out over five days. Cricket's rules and terminology are infamously arcane, but for aficionados, it isn't just a sport – it's a way of life.

County cricket is the mainstay of the domestic game, while international one-day games and five-day test matches are played against sides such as Australia and the West Indies at landmark grounds like Lords in London and Headingley in Leeds. Test match tickets cost £25 to £100 and tend to sell fast. County championships usually charge £10 to £15, and rarely sell out. Twenty20 cricket is a TV-friendly short form of the game encouraging big scores; it's more interesting to watch, but decried by purists.

To catch a game, the easiest option of all – and often the most enjoyable – is stumbling across a local match on a village green as you travel around the country. There's no charge for spectators, and no one will mind if you nip to the pub during a quiet period. If you're lucky, the locals might even try and explain the rules.

Golf

Golf is a very popular sport in Britain, with millions taking to the fairways every week. The main golfing tournament for spectators is the Open Championship, often referred to simply as The Open (or the 'British Open' outside the UK). It's the oldest of professional golf's major championships (dating back to 1860) and the only one held outside the USA. It is usually played over the third weekend in July and the location changes each year, using nine courses around the country.

Perhaps the UK's most famous golfing destination is the Old Course at St Andrews, often dubbed the 'home of golf' as it was one of the first places the sport was played, all the way back in the early 1400s. Playing here is almost a spiritual experience for golf enthusiasts, but you'll need to plan well ahead to get a game.

If you fancy a round as part of your visit to Britain, there are around 2000 private and public golf courses to choose from, with 500 in Scotland alone. (There are more golf courses per capita in Scotland than in any other country in the world.) Some private clubs admit only members or golfers with a handicap certificate, but most welcome visitors. Public golf courses are open to anyone. A round costs around £10 to £20 on a public course, and up to £50 on private courses.

The Best... Sporting Locations

1 St Andrews (p334)

2 Millennium Stadium, Cardiff (p271)

3 Old Trafford, Manchester (p238)

4 Wimbledon, London (p43)

5 Queen Elizabeth Olympic Park, London (p84)

Tennis

Tennis is widely played in Britain, but the most famous tournament is the All England Lawn Tennis Championships – more commonly known as Wimbledon – when tennis fever sweeps through the country for the last week of June and the first week of July. In between matches, the crowds traditionally feast on strawberries and cream – that's 28 tonnes of strawberries and 7000L of cream annually, to be precise.

Demand for seats at Wimbledon (www.wimbledon.org) always outstrips supply, but to give everyone an equal chance the tickets are sold through a public ballot. You can also take your chance on the spot: about 6000 tickets are sold each day (but not on the last four days) and queuing at dawn should get you into the ground.

Food & Drink

Britain once had a reputation for bad food, but the nation has enjoyed something of a culinary revolution over the last few years. London is recognised as having one of the best collections of restaurants in the world, while all across the country stylish eateries and gourmet gastropubs are springing up practically everywhere you look.

British Classics

One foodie phenomenon you'll definitely encounter is the 'full English breakfast' (just 'full breakfast' in Wales and Scotland), more colloquially known as a 'fry-up', consisting of bacon, sausage, egg, mushrooms, fried tomatoes, baked beans and a choice of white or brown toast. Sometimes you'll also be offered black pudding – known in other countries as 'blood sausage' – and fried bread. It's fine to ask for just the bits you want (just bacon and egg, for example).

Some B&Bs offer other alternatives, such as kippers (smoked fish) – especially in Scotland – or a 'continental breakfast', which omits the cooked stuff and may even add something exotic like croissants.

Moving on to lunch, one of the many great inventions that Britain gave the world is the sandwich, supposedly invented in the 18th century by the aristocratic Earl of

Sandwich. Another classic – especially in pubs – is the ploughman's lunch. Basically it's bread and cheese, usually accompanied by a spicy pickle, salad and some onions, although you'll also find other variations, such as farmer's lunch (bread and chicken), stockman's lunch (bread and ham) and so on.

When it comes to main meals, a classic British dinner is roast beef. The most famous beef comes from Scotland's Aberdeen Angus cattle, while the best-known food from Wales is lamb. Venison – usually from red deer – is readily available in Scotland, as well as in parts of Wales and England, most notably in the New Forest.

The traditional accompaniment for British beef is Yorkshire pudding. It's simply roasted batter, but very tasty when properly cooked. Bring sausages and Yorkshire 'pud' together and you have another favourite dish: toad-in-the-hole.

But perhaps the best-known classic British staple is fish and chips, often bought as a takeaway. Sometimes the fish can be tasteless (especially when eaten far from the sea), but in towns with salt in the air this deep-fried delight is always worth trying.

Thanks to its colonial past, Britain has also become a nation of curry-lovers: a recent poll suggested that the Brits' favourite dish was actually chicken tikka masala. You'll find at least one curry house in most British towns – ask around for a local recommendation, as standards vary.

The Best... Local Classics

1 Fish and chips

2 Yorkshire pudding

3 Welsh rarebit

4 Cullen skink

5 A pint of bitter

6 A dram of whisky

Regional Specialities

Seafood is a highlight in this island nation, especially in Scotland, West Wales and southwest England. Scottish salmon is also well known, and available everywhere in Britain smoked or poached, but there's a big difference between the fatty version from fish farms and the tastier wild variety. Other British seafood includes herring, trout and haddock; in Scotland the latter is best enjoyed with potato and cream in the old-style soup called cullen skink.

Treats in northern England include Cumberland sausage, a tasty mix of minced pork and herbs so large it has to be spiralled to fit on your plate. In Scotland, the most famous meaty speciality is haggis, a large sausage made from a sheep's stomach filled with minced meat and oatmeal.

For a snack in central England, try Melton Mowbray pork pies, cooked ham compressed in a casing of pastry. A legal victory in 2005 ensured that only pies made in the eponymous Midlands town could carry the Melton Mowbray moniker – in the same way that fizzy wine from regions outside Champagne can't claim that name.

Another British speciality that enjoys the same protection is Stilton – a strong white cheese, either plain or in a blue-vein variety. Only five dairies in the country are allowed to produce cheese with this name.

A couple of other regional classics to look out for are Welsh rarebit – really just a sophisticated variation of cheese on toast, seasoned and flavoured with butter, milk and sometimes beer – and Scotch broth, a thick soup of barley, lentils and mutton stock.

British Beer

Among alcoholic drinks, Britain is best known for its beer. Typically ranging from dark brown to bright orange in colour, technically it is called 'ale', and is more commonly called 'bitter' in England and Wales. Traditionally made and stored beer is called 'real ale' and, for the unwary, the first sip may come as a shock – a warm, flat shock. It's an acquired taste, but the trick is to focus on the flavour: this beer doesn't need to be chilled or fizzed to make it palatable.

Whisky

The spirit most visitors associate with Britain – and especially Scotland – is whisky. (Note the spelling – it's *Irish* whiskey that has an 'e'.) More than 2000 brands are produced, but the two main kinds are single malt, made from malted barley, and blended whisky, made from unmalted grain blended with malts. Single malts are rarer and more expensive. When ordering a 'dram' in Scotland remember to ask for whisky – only the English and other foreigners say 'Scotch'.

Testing whisky in a distillery
LEON HARRIS/GETTY IMAGES ©

Survival Guide

Leeds Castle (p108)

VISITBRITAIN/BRITAIN ON VIEW/GETTY IMAGES ©

A-Z

Directory

●●●

Accommodation

Accommodation in Britain is as varied as the sights you visit. From hip hotels to basic barns, the wide choice is all part of the attraction.

B&BS

The B&B (bed and breakfast) is a great British institution. At smaller places it's pretty much a room in somebody's house; larger places may be called a 'guesthouse' (halfway between a B&B and a full hotel).

B&B prices are usually quoted per person, based on two people sharing a room. Some B&Bs simply won't take single people (unless you pay the full double-room price), especially in summer.

Advance reservations are preferred at B&Bs, and are essential during popular periods.

Many B&Bs require a minimum two-night stay at weekends. Some places reduce rates for longer stays (two or three nights) mid-week.

Most B&Bs serve enormous breakfasts; some offer packed lunches (around £5) and evening meals (around £12 to £15).

When booking, check where your B&B actually is. In country areas, postal addresses include the nearest town, which may be 20 miles away – important if you're walking!

HOTELS

There's a massive choice of hotels in Britain, from small town houses to grand country mansions, from no-frills locations to boutique hideaways. At the bargain end, single/double rooms cost from £30/40. Move up the scale and you'll pay £100/150 or beyond.

If all you want is a place to put your head down, budget chain hotels can be a good option. Options include:

o **Etap Hotels** (www. etaphotel.com)

o **Hotel Formule 1** (www. hotelformule1.com)

o **Premier Inn** (www. premierinn.com)

o **Travelodge** (www. travelodge.co.uk)

PUBS & INNS

As well as selling drinks, many pubs and inns offer lodging, particularly in country areas. For bed and breakfast, you'll pay around £20 per person for a basic room, around £35 for something better. An advantage for solo tourists: pubs often have single rooms.

SOMETHING COMPLETELY DIFFERENT

For some more unusual accommodation options, the **Landmark Trust** (01628-825925; www.landmarktrust. org.uk) rents historic buildings; your options include ancient cottages, medieval castles, Napoleonic forts and 18th-century follies. Or try **Distinctly Different** (www.distinctlydifferent.co.uk), specialising in unusual and bizarre places to stay.

●●●

Business Hours

BANKS

Monday to Friday, 9.30am to 4pm or 5pm; Saturday, main branches 9.30am to 1pm.

BARS, PUBS & CLUBS

o Standard hours for pubs: 11am to 11pm Monday to Sunday. Some pubs shut from 3pm to 6pm; some stay open to midnight or 1am Friday and Saturday.

o Standard hours for bars: 11am until midnight, often later, especially at weekends.

o Clubs open any time from 8pm to 10pm, until 2am or beyond.

Book Your Stay Online

For more reviews by Lonely Planet authors, check out http://hotels.lonelyplanet.com. You'll find independent reviews, as well as recommendations on the best places to stay. Best of all, you can book online.

CAFES & RESTAURANTS

o Standard hours for cafes: 9am to 5pm.

o Standard hours for restaurants: lunch noon to 3pm, dinner 6pm to 11pm (to midnight or later in cities). Most restaurants open daily; some close Sunday evening or all day Monday.

MUSEUMS & SIGHTS

o Large museums and sights usually open daily.

o Smaller places open daily in high season but operate weekends only or completely close during low season.

Price Ranges

Reviews of places to stay use the following price ranges, all based on double room with private bathroom in high season. Hotels in London are more expensive than the rest of the country, so have different price ranges.

	London	Elsewhere
£	<£90	<£60
££	£90–180	£60–130
£££	>£180	>£130

POST OFFICES

o Monday to Friday, 9am to 5pm (5.30pm or 6pm in cities).

o Saturday, 9am to 12.30pm; main branches to 5pm.

SHOPS

o Monday to Friday, 9am to 5pm (5.30pm or 6pm in cities).

o Saturday, 9am to 5pm.

o Sunday, larger shops open 10am to 4pm. London and other cities have convenience stores open 24/7.

Climate

London

Edinburgh

Cardiff

Customs Regulations

Britain has a two-tier customs system: one for goods bought duty-free outside the EU; the other for goods bought in another EU country where tax and duty is paid. For details go to www.hmce.gov.uk and search for 'Customs Allowances'.

DUTY-FREE

The duty-free limits for goods from outside the EU include 200 cigarettes or equivalent in cigars, 4L of wine, 1L of spirits, 60cc of perfume, and other goods worth up to £390.

TAX & DUTY PAID

There is no limit on goods from within the EU (if taxes have been paid), but customs officials use the following guidelines to distinguish personal use from commercial imports: 800 cigarettes, 200 cigars, 10L of spirits, 90L of wine and 110L of beer.

●●● Discount Cards

There's no specific discount card for visitors to Britain, although travel cards are discounted for younger and older people.

●●● Electricity

230V/50Hz

●●● Gay & Lesbian Travellers

Britain is a generally tolerant place for gays and lesbians. London, Manchester and Brighton have flourishing gay scenes, and in other sizeable cities (even some small towns) you'll find communities not entirely in the closet. That said, you'll still find pockets of homophobic hostility in some areas. Resources include the following:

○ **Diva** (www.divamag.co.uk)

○ **Gay Times** (www.gaytimes.co.uk)

○ **London Lesbian & Gay Switchboard** (☎0300 330 0630; www.llgs.org.uk)

○ **Pink Paper** (www.pinkpaper.com)

●●● Health

No immunisations are mandatory for visiting Britain. For more information, check with your health or medical provider in your own country before you travel.

Regardless of nationality, everyone receives free emergency treatment at accident and emergency (A&E) departments of state-run National Health Service (NHS) hospitals. European Economic Area (EEA) nationals get free nonemergency treatment (ie the same service British citizens receive) with a European Health Insurance Card (EHIC) validated in their home country. Reciprocal arrangements between Britain and some other countries (including Australia) allow free medical treatment at hospitals and surgeries, and subsidised dental care.

If you don't need hospital treatment, chemists (pharmacies) can advise on minor ailments such as sore throats and earaches. In large cities, there's always at least one 24-hour chemist.

●●● Heritage Organisations

A highlight of a journey through Britain is visiting the numerous castles and historic sites that pepper the country. Membership of a heritage organisation gets you free admission (usually a good saving) as well as information handbooks and so on.

The **National Trust** (NT; www.nationaltrust.org.uk) is a charity protecting historic buildings and land with scenic importance across England and Wales. Annual membership costs £53 (with discounts for people under-26 and families). A Touring Pass allows free entry to NT properties for one/two weeks (£23/28 per person); families and couples get cheaper rates. The **National Trust for Scotland** (NTS; www.nts.org.uk) is similar.

English Heritage (EH; www.english-heritage.org.uk) is a state-funded organisation responsible for numerous historic sites. Annual membership costs £47 (couples and seniors get discounts). An Overseas Visitors Pass allows free entry to most sites for 9/16 days for £23/27 (with cheaper rates for couples and families). In Wales and Scotland the equivalent organisations are **Cadw** (www.cadw.wales.gov.uk) and **Historic Scotland** (HS; www.historic-scotland.gov.uk).

You can join at the first site you visit. If you join an English heritage organisation, it covers you for Wales and Scotland, and vice versa.

Insurance

Although everyone receives free emergency treatment, regardless of nationality, travel insurance is still highly recommended It will usually cover medical and dental consultation and treatment at private clinics, which can be quicker than NHS places – as well as the cost of any emergency flights – plus all the usual stuff like loss of baggage. Worldwide travel insurance is available at www.lonelyplanet.com/travel_services.

Internet Access

Internet cafes are surprisingly rare in Britain, especially away from big cities and tourist spots. Most charge from £1 per hour, but out in the sticks you can pay up to £5 per hour.

Public libraries often have computers with free internet access, but only for 30-minute slots, and demand is high. All the usual warnings apply about keystroke-capturing software and other security risks.

If you'll be using your laptop to get online, an increasing number of hotels, hostels, stations and coffee shops (even some trains) have wi-fi access, charging anything from nothing to £5 per hour.

Legal Matters

o You must be over 18 to buy alcohol and cigarettes. You usually have to be 18 to enter a pub or bar, although rules

are different for under-18s if eating. Some bars and clubs are over-21 only.

o Illegal drugs are widely available, especially in clubs. Cannabis possession is a criminal offence; punishment for carrying a small amount may be a warning, a fine or imprisonment. Dealers face stiffer penalties, as do people caught with other drugs.

o On buses and trains (including the London Underground), people without a valid ticket are fined on the spot – usually around £20.

Money

The currency of Britain is the pound sterling (£). Paper money ('notes') comes in £5, £10, £20 and £50 denominations. Some shops don't

accept £50 notes because fakes circulate.

ATMS

ATMs (usually called 'cash machines' in Britain) are common in cities and even small towns. Watch out for tampered ATMs; a common ruse is to attach a card-reader or mini-camera.

CHANGING MONEY

Cities and larger towns have banks and exchange bureaux for changing your money into pounds. Check rates first; some bureaux offer poor rates or levy outrageous commissions. You can also change money at some post offices – very handy in country areas, and exchange rates are fair.

CREDIT & DEBIT CARDS

Visa and MasterCard credit and debit cards are widely accepted in Britain. Most

Scottish Pounds

Scotland issues its own currency (including a £1 note) that's interchangeable with the money used in the rest of Britain. Although in reality you'll find shops more readily accept them in the north of England than in the south. Banks will always change them.

businesses will assume your card is 'Chip and PIN' enabled (using a PIN instead of signing). Some smaller country B&Bs don't take cards, so you'll need to pay with cash.

TIPPING

In Britain you're not obliged to tip if the service or food was unsatisfactory (even if it's been automatically added to your bill as a 'service charge').

o **Restaurants** Around 10%. Also at teashops and smarter cafes with full table service. At smarter restaurants waiters expect tips nearer 12% or 15%.

o **Taxis** 10%, or rounded up to the nearest pound, especially in London. It's less usual to tip minicab drivers.

o **Toilet attendants** Around 50p.

o **Pubs** Around 10% if you order food at the table and your meal is brought to you. If you order and pay at the bar (food or drinks), tips are not expected.

Public Holidays

Holidays for the whole of Britain:

New Year's Day 1 January

Easter March/April (Good Friday to Easter Monday inclusive)

May Day First Monday in May

Spring Bank Holiday Last Monday in May

Summer Bank Holiday Last Monday in August

Christmas Day 25 December

Boxing Day 26 December

In England and Wales most businesses and banks close on official public holidays (hence the quaint term 'bank holiday'). In Scotland, bank holidays are just for the banks, and many businesses stay open.

On public holidays, some small museums and places of interest close, but larger attractions have their busiest times.

Safe Travel

Britain is a remarkably safe country, but crime is not unknown in London and other cities. Watch out for pickpockets and hustlers in crowded areas popular with tourists such as around Westminster Bridge in London. When travelling by tube, tram or urban train services at night, choose a carriage containing other people.

Unlicensed minicabs – a bloke with a car earning money on the side – operate in large cities, and are worth avoiding unless you know what you're doing. Some have been known to drive round in circles, then charge an enormous fare. There have also been cases of robbery or rape. To avoid this, use a metered taxi or phone a reputable minicab company and get an up-front quote for the ride.

School Holidays

Roads get busy and hotel prices go up during school holidays. Exact dates vary from year to year and region to region, but are roughly as follows:

o **Easter Holiday** Week before and week after Easter

o **Summer Holiday** Third week of July to first week of September

o **Christmas Holiday** Mid-December to first week of January

There are also three week-long 'half-term' school holidays – usually late February (or early March), late May and late October. These vary between Scotland, England and Wales.

Telephone

AREA CODES

Area codes in Britain do not have a standard format or length, eg ✆020 for London, ✆0161 for Manchester, ✆01225 for Bath, ✆029 for Cardiff, ✆0131 for Edinburgh, ✆015394 for Ambleside. Area codes are followed as usual by the individual number.

NATIONAL CODES

○ ✆**0500** or ✆**0800** Free calls

○ ✆**0845** Calls at local rate, wherever you're dialling from within the UK

○ ✆**087** Calls at national rate

○ ✆**089** or ✆**09** Premium rate

○ ✆**07** Mobile phones, more expensive than calling a landline

INTERNATIONAL CODES

○ To call outside the UK dial ✆00, then the country code (1 for USA, 61 for Australia etc), the area code (you usually drop the initial zero) and the number.

○ The international code for Britain (and the rest of the UK) is 44.

OPERATOR

For help and reverse-charge (collect) calls:

○ National operator ✆100

○ International operator ✆155

DIRECTORY

For directory enquiries, a host of agencies compete for your business and charge from 10p to 40p; numbers include ✆118 ✆192, ✆118 118, ✆118 500 and ✆118 811.

Time

○ In winter (late October to late March) Britain is on GMT/UTC 0.

○ In summer (late March to late October) Britain uses daylight saving so the time is GMT/UTC +1. In summer, if it's noon in London, it's 9pm in Melbourne (Australia) and 7am in New York (USA).

Tourist Information

All British cities and towns, and some villages, have a tourist information centre or visitor information centres – for ease we've called all these places 'tourist offices'. Such places have helpful staff, books and maps for sale, leaflets to give away, and advice on things to see or do. Some can also assist with booking accommodation.

Before leaving home, check the comprehensive website of Britain's official tourist board, **Visit Britain** (www.visitbritain.com), covering all the angles of national tourism, with links to numerous other sites.

Travellers with Disabilities

All new buildings have wheelchair access, and even hotels in grand old country houses often have lifts, ramps and other facilities. Smaller B&Bs are often harder to adapt, so you'll have less choice here.

Getting around in cities, new buses have low floors for easy access, but few have conductors who can lend a hand when you're getting on or off. Many taxis take wheelchairs, or just have more room in the back.

For long-distance travel, coaches may present problems if you can't walk, but the main operator, **National Express** (www.nationalexpress.com) has wheelchair-friendly coaches on many routes. For details, see the website or ring their dedicated Disabled Passenger Travel Helpline on ✆0121-423 8479.

On most intercity trains there's more room and better facilities, compared with travel by coach, and usually station staff around; just have a word and they'll be happy to help. A **Disabled Person's Railcard** (www.disabledpersons-railcard.co.uk) costs £20 and gets you 33% off most train fares.

Useful organisations:

○ **Disability Rights UK** (www.disabilityrightsuk.org) Published titles include *Holiday Guide*. Other services include a key for 7000 public disabled toilets across the UK.

- **Good Access Guide** (www.goodaccessguide.co.uk)
- **Tourism for All** (www.tourismforall.org.uk)

Visas

If you are a European Economic Area (EEA) national, you don't need a visa to visit (or work in) Britain. Citizens of Australia, Canada, New Zealand, South Africa and the USA are given leave to enter the UK at their point of arrival for up to six months (three months for some nationalities), but are prohibited from working without a visa. For more info see www.ukba.homeoffice.gov.uk.

Transport

Getting There & Away

As London is a global transport hub, it's easy to fly to Britain from just about anywhere. In recent years, the massive growth of budget ('no-frills') airlines has increased the number of routes – and reduced the fares – between Britain and other countries in Europe.

The other main option for travel between Britain and mainland Europe is ferry, either port-to-port or combined with a long-distance bus trip, although journeys can be long and financial savings not huge compared with budget airfares.

International trains are a much more comfortable and 'green' option; the Channel Tunnel allows direct rail services between Britain, France and Belgium, with onward connections to many other European destinations.

Flights, cars and rail tickets can be booked online at lonelyplanet.com/bookings.

✈ AIR

LONDON AIRPORTS

For details of getting from the airports into the city, see p103.

Heathrow (LHR; www.heathrowairport.com) Britain's main airport for international flights; often chaotic and crowded. About 15 miles west of central London.

Gatwick (LGW; www.gatwickairport.com) Britain's number-two airport, mainly for international flights, 30 miles south of central London.

Stansted (STN; www.stanstedairport.com) About 35 miles northeast of central London, mainly handling charter and budget European flights.

Luton (LTN; www.london-luton.co.uk) Some 35 miles north of central London, well known as a holiday-flight airport.

Passport Check

Travelling between Britain's three nations of England, Scotland and Wales is easy. The bus and train systems are fully integrated and in most cases you won't even know you've crossed the border. Passports are not required – although some Scots and Welsh may think they should be!

London City (LCY; www.londoncityairport.com) A few miles east of central London, specialising in flights to/from European and other UK airports.

REGIONAL AIRPORTS

Some planes on European and long-haul routes avoid London and use major regional airports including Manchester and Glasgow. Smaller regional airports such as Southampton, Cardiff and Birmingham are served by flights to and from continental Europe and Ireland.

LAND

CHANNEL TUNNEL PASSENGER SERVICE

High-speed **Eurostar** (www.eurostar.com) train passenger services shuttle at least 10 times daily between London and Paris (2½ hours) or Brussels (two hours). Buy tickets from travel agencies, major train stations or the Eurostar website.

The normal one-way fare between London and Paris/Brussels costs £150 to £180; advance booking and off-peak travel gets cheaper fares as low as £40 one-way.

CHANNEL TUNNEL CAR SERVICE

Drivers use **Eurotunnel** (www.eurotunnel.com). At Folkestone in England or Calais in France, you drive onto a train, get carried through the tunnel and drive off at the other end.

Trains run about four times an hour from 6am to 10pm, then hourly through the night. Loading and unloading takes an hour; the journey lasts 35 minutes.

The one-way cost for a car and passengers is between £70 and £150 depending on the time of day; promotional fares often bring it nearer £50.

SEA

FERRY ROUTES

The main ferry routes between Britain and other European countries include the following:

o Dover–Calais (France)

o Dover–Boulogne (France)

o Newhaven–Dieppe (France)

o Harwich–Hook of Holland (Netherlands)

o Hull–Zeebrugge (Belgium)

o Hull–Rotterdam (Netherlands)

o Portsmouth–Santander (Spain)

o Portsmouth–Bilbao (Spain)

o Holyhead–Dun Laoghaire (Ireland)

o Fishguard–Rosslare (Ireland)

FERRY BOOKINGS

Book direct with operators or use the very handy www.ferrybooker.com – a single site covering all sea-ferry routes, plus Eurotunnel.

Brittany Ferries (www.brittany-ferries.com)

DFDS Seaways (www.dfdsseaways.co.uk)

Irish Ferries (www.irishferries.com)

P&O Ferries (www.poferries.com)

Stena Line (www.stenaline.com)

Transmanche (www.transmancheferries.com)

Getting Around

For getting around Britain your first main choice is going by car or public transport.

Having your own car makes the best use of time, and helps reach remote places, but rental and fuel costs can be expensive for budget travellers (while traffic jams in major cities hit everyone) – public transport is often the better way to go. As long as you have time, using a mix of train, bus, taxi, walking and occasionally hiring a bike, you can get almost anywhere in Britain without having to drive.

The main public transport options are train and long-distance bus (called coach in Britain). Services between major towns and cities are

generally good, although at peak times you must book in advance to be sure of getting a ticket. If you book ahead early or travel at off-peak periods – ideally both – train and coach tickets can be very cheap.

AIR

Britain's domestic air companies include British Airways, easyJet and Ryanair. If you're really pushed for time, flights on longer routes across Britain (eg Exeter or Southampton to Newcastle, Edinburgh or Inverness) are handy, although you miss the glorious scenery in between. On some shorter routes (eg

Information Service

Traveline (☎ 0871 200 2233; www.traveline.org.uk) is a very useful information service covering bus, coach, taxi and train services nationwide, with numerous links to help plan your journey. By phone, you get transferred automatically to an adviser in the region you're phoning *from;* for details on another part of the country, you need to key in a code number (☎ 81 for London, ☎ 874 for Cumbria etc) – for a full list of codes, go to the Traveline website.

London to Newcastle, or Manchester to Newquay) trains compare favourably with planes on time, once airport downtime is factored in. On costs, you might get a bargain airfare, but trains can be cheaper if you buy tickets in advance.

०७० BICYCLE

Britain is a compact country, and hiring a bike – for an hour or two, or a week or longer – is a great way to really see the country if you've got time to spare.

RENTAL IN LONDON

London is famous for its Barclays Cycle Hire Scheme (known as 'Boris bikes' after the mayor that introduced them to the city). Bikes can be hired on the spot from automatic docking stations. For more information visit the **Transport for London** (www.tfl.gov.uk) website. Other rental options in the capital are listed at www.lcc.org.uk.

RENTAL ELSEWHERE

Tourist towns such as Oxford and Cambridge have plentiful bike rental options, and bikes can also be hired in national parks or forestry sites now primarily used for leisure

activities, such as Kielder Water in Northumberland, Grizedale Forest in the Lake District and the Elan Valley in Mid-Wales. In some areas, disused railway lines are now bike routes, notably in the Peak District in Derbyshire. Rental rates start at about £10 per day, or £20 for something half decent.

🚌 BUS & COACH

If you're on a tight budget, long-distance buses are nearly always the cheapest way to get around, although they're also the slowest – sometimes by a considerable margin. Many towns have separate stations for local buses and long-distance coaches; make sure you go to the right one!

National Express (www.nationalexpress.com) is the main coach operator, with a wide network and frequent services between main centres. North of the border, services tie in with those of **Scottish Citylink** (☎ 0871 266 3333; www.citylink.co.uk), Scotland's leading coach company. Fares vary: they're cheaper if you book in advance and travel at quieter times, and more expensive if you buy your ticket on the spot and it's Friday afternoon.

As a guide, a 200-mile trip (eg London to York) will cost £15 to £20 if you book a few days in advance.

🚗 CAR & MOTORCYCLE

Travelling by car or motorbike around Britain means you can be independent and flexible, and reach remote places. Downsides for drivers include traffic jams and high parking costs in cities.

CAR RENTAL

Compared with many countries (especially the USA), hire rates are expensive in Britain; the smallest cars start from about £120 per week, and it's around £250 per week for a medium car. All rates include insurance and unlimited mileage, and can rise at busy times (or drop at quiet times).

Some main players:

o **Avis** (www.avis.co.uk)

o **Budget** (www.budget.co.uk)

o **Europcar** (www.europcar.co.uk)

o **Sixt** (www.sixt.co.uk)

o **Thrifty** (www.thrifty.co.uk)

Another option is to look online for small local car-hire companies that can undercut the international franchises. Generally those in cities are cheaper than in rural areas. Using a rental-broker site such as **UK Car Hire** (www.ukcarhire.net) can also help find bargains.

INSURANCE

It's illegal to drive a car or motorbike in Britain without (at least) third-party insurance. This will be included with all rental cars. If you're bringing a car from Europe you'll need to arrange it.

PARKING

Many cities have short-stay and long-stay car parks; the latter are cheaper though may be less convenient. 'Park & Ride' systems allow you to park on the edge of the city then ride to the centre on frequent nonstop buses for an all-in-one price.

Yellow lines (single or double) along the edge of the road indicate restrictions. Nearby signs spell out when you can and can't park. In London and other big cities, traffic wardens operate with efficiency; if you park on the yellow lines at the wrong time, your car will be clamped or towed away, and it'll cost you £100 or more to get driving again. In some cities there are also red lines, which mean no stopping at all. Ever.

ROADS

Motorways and main A-roads deliver you quickly from one end of the country to another. Lesser A-roads, B-roads and minor roads are much more scenic – ideal for car or motorcycle touring. You can't travel fast, but you won't care.

Speed limits are usually 30mph (48km/h) in built-up areas, 60mph (96km/h) on main roads and 70mph (112km/h) on motorways and most (but not all) dual carriageways.

ROAD RULES

A foreign driving licence is valid in Britain for up to 12 months.

Drink driving is taken very seriously; you're allowed a maximum blood-alcohol level of 80mg/100mL (0.08%) – campaigners want it reduced to 50mg/100mL.

Some other important rules:

o drive on the left

o wear fitted seat belts in cars

o wear helmets on motorcycles

o give way to your right at junctions and roundabouts

o always use the left lane on motorways and dual carriageways unless overtaking (although so many people ignore this rule, you'd think it didn't exist)

o don't use a mobile phone while driving unless it's fully hands-free (another rule frequently flouted)

LOCAL TRANSPORT

LOCAL BUS

There are good local bus networks year-round in cities and towns. Buses also run in some rural areas year-round, although timetables are designed to serve schools and businesses, so there aren't many midday and weekend services (and they may stop running during school holidays), or buses may link local villages to a market town on only one day each week.

In tourist areas (especially national parks) there are frequent services from Easter to September. However, it's always worth double-checking at a tourist office before planning your day's activities around a bus that may not actually be running.

In this book, along with the local bus route number, frequency and duration, we have provided indicative prices if the fare is over £5. If it's less than this, we have generally omitted the fare.

LOCAL BUS PASSES

If you're taking a few local bus rides in one area, day passes (with names like Day Rover, Wayfarer or Explorer) are cheaper than buying several single tickets. Often they can be bought on your first bus, and may include local rail services. It's always worth asking ticket clerks or bus drivers about your options.

How Much To…?

When travelling by long-distance bus, coach or train in Britain, it's important to realise that there's no such thing as a standard fare. Prices vary according to demand and when you buy your ticket. Book well in advance and travel on Tuesday mid-morning and it's cheap. Buy your ticket on the spot late Friday afternoon and it'll be a lot more expensive. Ferries use similar systems. We have generally quoted sample fares somewhere in between the very cheapest and most expensive options. The price you pay will almost certainly be different.

🚕 TAXI

There are two sorts of taxi in England: those with meters that can be hailed in the street; and minicabs, which are cheaper but can only be called by phone. Unlicensed minicabs operate in some cities (see p402).

In London, most taxis are the famous 'black cabs' (some with advertising livery in other colours) which charge by distance and time. Depending on the time of day, a 1-mile journey takes five to 10 minutes and cost £5 to £9.

In rural areas, taxis need to be called by phone; the best place to find the local taxi's phone number is the local pub. Fares are £2 to £3 per mile. Handy resources:

○ **National Cabline** (☎0800 123444) Call from a landline phone; the service pinpoints your location and transfers you to an approved local taxi company.

○ **Train-Taxi** (www.traintaxi. co.uk) Portal site to help 'bridge the final gap' between the train station and your hotel or other final destination.

🚃 TRAIN

For long-distance travel around Britain, trains are generally faster and more comfortable than coaches but can be more expensive, although with discount tickets they're competitive – and often take you through beautiful countryside. The British like to moan about their trains, but around 85% run on time. The other 15% that get delayed or cancelled mostly impact commuter services rather than long-distance journeys.

INFORMATION

Your first stop should be **National Rail Enquiries** (☎ 08457 48 49 50; www.nationalrail.co.uk), the nationwide timetable and fare information service. Its website advertises special offers and has real-time links to station departure boards and downloadable maps of the rail network.

OPERATORS

About 20 different companies operate train services in Britain, while Network Rail operates track and stations. For some passengers this system can be confusing at first, but information and ticket-buying services are mostly centralised. If you have to change trains, or use two or more train operators, you still buy one ticket – valid for the whole journey. The main railcards and passes are also accepted by all train operators.

TICKETS & RESERVATIONS

Once you've found the journey you need on the National Rail Enquiries website, links take you to the relevant train operator to buy the ticket. This can be posted (UK addresses only) or collected at the station on the day of travel from automatic machines.

You can also use a centralised ticketing service to buy your train ticket. These cover all train services in a single site, and make a small booking fee on top of every ticket price. The main players include:

○ **QJump** (www.qjump.co.uk)

○ **Rail Easy** (www.raileasy. co.uk)

○ **Train Line** (www. thetrainline.com)

To use operator or centralised ticketing websites you always have to state a preferred time and day of travel, even if you don't mind when you go, but you can change it as you go through the process, and with a little delving around you can find some real bargains.

You can also buy train tickets on the spot at stations, which is fine for short journeys (under about 50 miles), but discount tickets for longer trips are usually not available and must be bought in advance by phone or online.

COSTS

For longer journeys, on-the-spot fares are always available, but tickets are much cheaper if bought in advance. The earlier you book, the cheaper it gets. You can also save if you travel off-peak. Advance purchase usually gets a reserved seat, too.

Whichever operator you travel with and wherever you buy tickets, these are the three main fare types:

○ **Anytime** Buy anytime, travel anytime – usually the most expensive option.

○ **Off-peak** Buy ticket any time, travel off-peak.

○ **Advance** Buy ticket in advance, travel only on specific trains – usually the cheapest option.

For an idea of the price difference, an Anytime single ticket from London to York will cost £100 or more, an Off-peak around £80, with an Advance around £20, and even less if you book early enough or don't mind arriving at midnight.

The cheapest fares are nonrefundable, so if you miss your train you'll have to buy a new ticket.

TRAIN CLASSES

There are two classes of rail travel: first and standard. First class costs around 50% more than standard fare (up to double at busy periods) and gets you bigger seats, more leg-room, and usually a more peaceful business-like atmosphere, plus extras like complimentary drinks and newspapers. At weekends some train operators offer 'upgrades' to first class for an extra £10 to £15 on top of your standard class fare, payable on the spot.

DISCOUNT PASSES

If you're staying in Britain for a while, passes known as **Railcards** (www.railcard. co.uk) are available:

o **16-25 Railcard** For those aged 16 to 25, or a full-time UK student.

o **Senior Railcard** For anyone over 60.

o **Family & Friends Railcard** Covers up to four adults and four children travelling together.

Railcards cost around £28 (valid for one year, available from major stations or online) and get 33% discount on most train fares, except those already heavily discounted. With the Family card, adults get 33% and children get 60% discounts, so the fee is easily repaid in a couple of journeys.

LOCAL & REGIONAL PASSES

Local train passes usually cover rail networks around a city (many include bus travel too) and are detailed in the relevant sections throughout this guide.

If you're concentrating your travels on southeast England (eg London to Dover, Weymouth, Cambridge or Oxford) a **Network Railcard** (www.railcard.co.uk/network; per year £28) covers up to four adults and up to four children travelling together outside peak times.

NATIONAL PASSES

For country-wide travel, **BritRail** (www.britrail. com) passes are available for visitors from overseas. They must be bought in your country of origin (not in Britain) from a specialist travel agency. Available in three different versions (England only; all Britain; UK and Ireland) for periods from four to 30 days.

Behind the Scenes

Author Thanks
OLIVER BERRY

Thanks to Cliff Wilkinson for the *Discover Great Britain* gig and all of the authors whose research and words contributed to this book. David Carroll, Dan Corbett and the rest of the SPP team for being there whenever we needed you! Special thanks to Susie, Molly and Gracie Berry, and to all the people I met out on the road.

Acknowledgments

Climate map data adapted from Peel MC, Finlayson BL & McMahon TA (2007) 'Updated World Map of the Köppen-Geiger Climate Classification', *Hydrology and Earth System Sciences*, 11, 163344.

Illustrations pp70–1, pp76–7, pp256–7, pp312–3, pp316–17 and pp330–1 by Javier Zarracina.

Cover photographs: Front: Seven Sisters, Sussex, Olimpio Fantuz/4Corners ©; Back: Caernarfon Castle, Wales, Granville Harris/Loop Images Ltd/Alamy©.

This Book

This 3rd edition of Lonely Planet's *Discover Great Britain* guidebook was researched and written by Oliver Berry, Fionn Davenport, Marc Di Duca, Belinda Dixon, Peter Dragicevich, David Else, Damian Harper, Anna Kaminski, Catherine Le Nevez, Fran Parnell, Andy Symington and Neil Wilson. This guidebook was commissioned in Lonely Planet's London office, and produced by the following:

Commissioning Editors Clifton Wilkinson, Katie O'Connell

Coordinating Editors Lauren Hunt, Jeanette Wall

Coordinating Cartographer Valeska Cañas

Coordinating Layout Designer Lauren Egan

Managing Editor Angela Tinson

Senior Editors Andi Jones, Martine Power

Managing Cartographers Adrian Persoglia, Anthony Phelan

Managing Layout Designers Chris Girdler, Mazzy Prinsep

Assisting Editors Anne Mason, Charlotte Orr

Assisting Cartographers Alex Leung, Andrew Smith

Assisting Layout Designers Nicholas Colicchia, Carlos Solarte, Wendy Wright

Cover Research Naomi Parker

Internal Image Research Aude Vauconsant, Kylie McLaughlin

Thanks to Anita Banh, Ryan Evans, Larissa Frost, Jane Hart, Genesys India, Jouve India, Trent Paton, Raphael Richards, Dianne Schallmeiner, John Taufa, Gerard Walker, Juan Winata

SEND US YOUR FEEDBACK

We love to hear from travellers – your comments keep us on our toes and help make our books better. Our well-travelled team reads every word on what you loved or loathed about this book. Although we cannot reply individually to postal submissions, we always guarantee that your feedback goes straight to the appropriate authors, in time for the next edition. Each person who sends us information is thanked in the next edition, the most useful submissions are rewarded with a selection of digital PDF chapters.

Visit **lonelyplanet.com/contact** to submit your updates and suggestions or to ask for help. Our award-winning website also features inspirational travel stories, news and discussions.

Note: We may edit, reproduce and incorporate your comments in Lonely Planet products such as guidebooks, websites and digital products, so let us know if you don't want your comments reproduced or your name acknowledged. For a copy of our privacy policy visit lonelyplanet.com/privacy.

Index

D

E

000 Map pages

T

Talacharn 276-7
Tate Boat 75
Tate Britain 78-9
Tate Liverpool 245
Tate Modern 56, 73-4
Tate St Ives 206
taxis 408
telephone services 403
tennis 393
Thames, the 76-7
theatre 15
theatres
 Donmar Warehouse 97
 Globe Theatre 57, 74
 National Theatre 97
 Old Vic 97
 Royal Court Theatre 97
 Royal Shakespeare
  Company 155
theft 402
Thermae Bath Spa 192
Thomas, Dylan 276
time 403
Tintagel Castle 195
Tintern Abbey 275-6
tipping 402
Tiree 365
toilets 101
tourist information 403
tours
 Bath 192
 Cambridge 120
 Canterbury 107
 Edinburgh 318
 London 60-1, 86
 Oxford 141-3
 Stonehenge 185
 York 227
Tower Bridge 68
Tower of London 19, 54-5,
 68, 70-1

Trafalgar Square 66
train travel 408-9
travel to/from Great Britain
 404-5
travel within Great Britain 49,
 405-9
trekking, see hiking & walking
Trinity College (Cambridge)
 117
Trinity College (Oxford)
 139-40
Trooping the Colour 43
Trossachs, the 333
Trotternish 364
TV 401

U

University Church of St Mary
 the Virgin 129
Urquhart Castle 345, 354

V

vacations 402
Victoria & Albert Museum
 78-9
Vikings 225, 371
Vindolanda Roman Fort &
 Museum 254
visas 404

W

Wales 259-91, **261**
 highlights 262-7
 itineraries 268-9
 planning 267
 travel within 267
 websites 267
Wales Millennium Centre 274
walking, see hiking & walking
walking tour 60-1

Warwick 151-2
Warwick Castle 133, 151
weather 48, 399
websites 47, see also individual
 locations
weights 401
Wells 174, 194-6
Welsh Castles 280
Westminster Abbey 63
Westminster Catheral 65
whale-watching 358
whisky 25, 338, 339, 396
White Cliffs 108-9
wi-fi 48
wildlife-watching 18
Wiltshire 180-5
Wimbledon 43
Winchcombe 147-8
Winchester 180-2
Winchester Cathedral 180
Windermere 250-1
Windsor 114-16, **115**
Windsor Castle 114-15
Woburn Abbey & Safari Park
 150
Wordsworth, William 252, 253
WWI 375
WWII 376

Y

Y Gelli Gandryll 280-1
Y Gŵyr 275
Yeoman Warders 54-5, 68, 70
York 13, 211-15, 224-30, **228**
York Minster 226
Yorkshire Dales 219
Yorkshire Dales National Park
 233-5

Z

zoos 81, 315

NOTES

NOTES

420

421

How to Use This Book

These symbols will help you find the listings you want:

◉	Sights	⊙	Tours	⊙	Drinking
🏖	Beaches	⊛	Festivals & Events	⊙	Entertainment
⊕	Activities	🛏	Sleeping	⊙	Shopping
⊜	Courses	⊗	Eating	⊙	Information/Transport

These symbols give you the vital information for each listing:

☏	Telephone Numbers	🛜	Wi-Fi Access	🚍	Bus
⊙	Opening Hours	⊠	Swimming Pool	⊛	Ferry
P	Parking	✔	Vegetarian Selection	Ⓜ	Metro
⊝	Nonsmoking	📄	English-Language Menu	Ⓢ	Subway
❄	Air-Conditioning	👪	Family-Friendly	⊖	London Tube
@	Internet Access	🐾	Pet-Friendly	🚋	Tram
				🚆	Train

Reviews are organised by author preference.

Map Legend

Sights

- ◐ Beach
- ⊜ Buddhist
- ⊙ Castle
- ⊙ Christian
- ⊙ Hindu
- ⊙ Islamic
- ⊙ Jewish
- ⊙ Monument
- ⊜ Museum/Gallery
- ⊙ Ruin
- ⊙ Winery/Vineyard
- ⊙ Zoo
- ◎ Other Sight

Activities, Courses & Tours

- ⊜ Diving/Snorkelling
- ⊜ Canoeing/Kayaking
- ⊙ Skiing
- ⊙ Surfing
- ⊜ Swimming/Pool
- ⊙ Walking
- ⊙ Windsurfing
- ⊙ Other Activity/Course/Tour

Sleeping

- 🛏 Sleeping
- ⊙ Camping

Eating

- ⊗ Eating

Drinking

- ⊙ Drinking
- ⊜ Cafe

Entertainment

- ⊙ Entertainment

Shopping

- ⊙ Shopping

Information

- ⊜ Post Office
- ⊙ Tourist Information

Transport

- ⊕ Airport
- ⊗ Border Crossing
- 🚍 Bus
- ⊕ Cable Car/Funicular
- ⊛ Cycling
- ⊖ Ferry
- 🚈 Monorail
- P Parking
- Ⓢ S-Bahn
- ⊖ Taxi
- 🚆 Train/Railway
- 🚋 Tram
- ⊖ Tube Station
- Ⓤ U-Bahn
- Ⓜ Underground Train Station
- • Other Transport

Routes

- Tollway
- Freeway
- Primary
- Secondary
- Tertiary
- Lane
- Unsealed Road
- Plaza/Mall
- Steps
- Tunnel
- Pedestrian Overpass
- Walking Tour
- Walking Tour Detour
- Path

Boundaries

- International
- State/Province
- Disputed
- Regional/Suburb
- Marine Park
- Cliff
- Wall

Population

- ⊙ Capital (National)
- ⊙ Capital (State/Province)
- ⊙ City/Large Town
- ⊙ Town/Village

Geographic

- ⊙ Hut/Shelter
- ⊙ Lighthouse
- ⊙ Lookout
- ▲ Mountain/Volcano
- ⊙ Oasis
- ⊙ Park
-)(Pass
- ⊙ Picnic Area
- ⊙ Waterfall

Hydrography

- River/Creek
- Intermittent River
- Swamp/Mangrove
- Reef
- Canal
- Water
- Dry/Salt/Intermittent Lake
- Glacier

Areas

- Beach/Desert
- Cemetery (Christian)
- Cemetery (Other)
- Park/Forest
- Sportsground
- Sight (Building)
- Top Sight (Building)

PETER DRAGICEVICH

Wales Wales has held a fascination for Peter ever since he was sent to write about Welsh castles for one of his first ever newspaper travel features. Since then he's coauthored dozens of Lonely Planet titles, including the stand-alone *Wales* guidebook and *Walking in Britain*, where he got to trek around the entirety of the beautiful Pembrokeshire coast. And while his name may not be Welsh, it does have more than half a dragon in it.

DAVID ELSE

As a professional writer, David has authored more than 40 books, including several editions of Lonely Planet's *England* and *Great Britain* guides. His knowledge comes from a lifetime of travel around the country – often on foot – a passion dating from university years, when heading for the hills was always more attractive than visiting the library. Originally from London, David has lived in Yorkshire, Wales and Derbyshire, and is now a resident of the Cotswolds. For the 10th edition of *Great Britain*, David's research took him from the Isle of Wight in the south to the Isle of Skye in the north – via most of the bits in between.

DAMIAN HARPER

London & Around Born in London and growing up in Notting Hill, Damian went to school in Hampshire for a decade, cultivating a sense of affection for both city and country. Writing for Lonely Planet for more than 15 years, Damian recently turned his attention from far-flung cultures to his lush and well-watered homeland, revelling in England's diversity, good looks, insular charms, awe-inspiring sense of history and entirely intelligible local tongue (in the main).

ANNA KAMINSKI

London & Around; Oxford & Central England Anna's love affair with England began in 1991 once she got over the shock of moving from the Soviet Union to Cambridge – her home for the next 20 years. Since budget flights hadn't been invented at the time, her parents tirelessly tried to instil some culture in her by taking her to every museum, castle, church and stately home in a 250-mile radius, most of which she revisited with great pleasure during this research trip. Memorable moments from her most recent trip include slurping fresh oysters in Aldeburgh, driving along some impossibly narrow country lanes in the Cotswolds and getting acquainted with Oxford's ghosts.

CATHERINE LE NEVEZ

York & Northern England Catherine first roadtripped around Great Britain aged four and she's been roadtripping here at every opportunity since. She completed her Doctorate of Creative Arts in Writing, Masters in Professional Writing, and post-grad qualifications in Editing and Publishing along the way, as well as dozens of Lonely Planet guidebooks and newspaper, magazine and online articles covering the UK, Europe and beyond. Roaming castle ruins and corridors of stately homes were highlights of researching this book, as was discovering idyllic countryside pubs.

FRAN PARNELL

Wales Early family holidays in Wales ignited Fran's love of the country, undimmed even after being dismissed from a B&B for sneaking in fish and chips. Studying for a Masters degree in Anglo-Saxon, Norse and Celtic fanned the flames: the romance of the medieval Welsh stories and poems has never left her. A particular highlight of this research trip was watching the sun set from the lofty ruins of Castell Dinas Brân.

ANDY SYMINGTON

Edinburgh & Central Scotland; Scotland's Highlands & Islands Andy's Scottish forebears make their presence felt in a love of malt, a debatable ginger colour to his facial hair and a love of wild places. From childhood slogs up the M1 he graduated to making dubious road trips around the firths in a disintegrating Mini Metro and thence to peddling whisky in darkest Leith. While living there, he travelled widely around the country in search of the perfect dram, and, now resident in Spain, continues to visit very regularly.

NEIL WILSON

York & Northern England; Edinburgh & Central Scotland; Scotland's Highlands & Islands Neil has made many cross-border forays into 'God's own country' from his home in Edinburgh, as well as regular expeditions to every corner of Scotland. It's a toss-up whether the hiking, mountain-biking and beer is better in Yorkshire or north of the border. Neil is a full-time travel writer based in Edinburgh, and has written around 60 guidebooks for various publishers.

Our Story

A beat-up old car, a few dollars in the pocket and a sense of adventure. In 1972 that's all Tony and Maureen Wheeler needed for the trip of a lifetime – across Europe and Asia overland to Australia. It took several months, and at the end – broke but inspired – they sat at their kitchen table writing and stapling together their first travel guide, *Across Asia on the Cheap*. Within a week they'd sold 1500 copies. Lonely Planet was born.

Today, Lonely Planet has offices in Melbourne, London and Oakland, with more than 600 staff and writers. We share Tony's belief that 'a great guidebook should do three things: inform, educate and amuse'.

Our Writers

OLIVER BERRY

Coordinating Author; Bath & Southwest England; York & Northern England Oliver is a writer and photographer based in Cornwall. Among many other projects for Lonely Planet, Oliver has written the first editions of *Devon, Cornwall & Southwest England* and *The Lake District*, and worked on several editions of the *England* and *Great Britain* guides. You can see some of his latest work at www.oliverberry.com and follow him at www.twitter.com/olivertomberry.

Read more about Oliver at:
lonelyplanet.com/members/oliverberry

FIONN DAVENPORT

York & Northern England Fionn has been traipsing about Northern England's bigger burgs for over a decade and has found that the cities of the north are simply fantastic; a rich repository of culture, fine museums, terrific restaurants, bucolic landscapes and – most importantly – peopled by a few million lovable gruffs that exude a no-nonsense warmth. Fionn is a full-time travel writer and broadcaster based in Dublin, Ireland – you can catch him on Newstalk 106-108 (www.newstalk.ie).

MARC DI DUCA

London & Around Originally from Darlington, County Durham, Marc has been a northerner-gone-south since 2000 and covered his adopted corner of weald and down for the past two editions of Lonely Planet's *England* and *Great Britain*. A travel author for eight years, Marc has updated and written the Lonely Planet guides of *Ukraine, Russia, Trans-Siberian Railway, Poland* and *Germany*, though he can usually be found in Sandwich, Kent, where he lives with his Kievite wife, Tanya, and their two sons.

Read more about Marc at:
lonelyplanet.com/members/madidu

BELINDA DIXON

Bath & Southwest England Belinda made a gleeful bolt for the sunny southwest for her post-grad, having been drawn there by the palm trees on campus. Like the best Westcountry limpets, she's proved hard to shift since and now writes and broadcasts in the region. Research highlights for this book included kayaking up (and riding the tide down) the River Dart, hugging sarsen stones at Avebury, tasting freedom on the Isle of Wight, and oh-so-diligently testing the pick of Plymouth's newest eateries.

← More Writers ....

Published by Lonely Planet Publications Pty Ltd
ABN 36 005 607 983
3rd edition – July 2013
978 1 74220 565 6
© Lonely Planet 2013   Photographs © as indicated 2013
10 9 8 7 6 5 4 3 2 1
Printed in China